Love-Letters and Privacy in Modern China

Studies on Contemporary China

The Contemporary China Institute at the School of Oriental and African Studies (University of London) has, since its establishment in 1968, been an international centre for research and publications on twentieth-century China. *Studies on Contemporary China*, which is edited at the Institute, seeks to maintain and extend that tradition by making available the best work of scholars and China specialists throughout the world. It embraces a wide variety of subjects relating to Nationalist and Communist China, including social, political, and economic change, intellectual and cultural developments, foreign relations, and national security.

Love-Letters and Privacy in Modern China

The Intimate Lives of Lu Xun and Xu Guangping

BONNIE S. McDOUGALL

OXFORD
UNIVERSITY PRESS

This book has been printed digitally and produced in a standard specification in order to ensure its continuing availability

OXFORD
UNIVERSITY PRESS

Great Clarendon Street, Oxford OX2 6DP

Oxford University Press is a department of the University of Oxford.
It furthers the University's objective of excellence in research, scholarship,
and education by publishing worldwide in

Oxford New York

Auckland Cape Town Dar es Salaam Hong Kong Karachi
Kuala Lumpur Madrid Melbourne Mexico City Nairobi
New Delhi Shanghai Taipei Toronto

With offices in

Argentina Austria Brazil Chile Czech Republic France Greece
Guatemala Hungary Italy Japan South Korea Poland Portugal
Singapore Switzerland Thailand Turkey Ukraine Vietnam

Oxford is a registered trade mark of Oxford University Press
in the UK and in certain other countries

Published in the United States
by Oxford University Press Inc., New York

Reprinted 2007

ISBN 978-0-19-925679-2

For Anders and Torkel

It is an interesting question—what one tries to do, in writing a letter—partly of course to give back a reflection of the other person.

Virginia Woolf, *A Reflection of the Other Person*

Contents

Part IV: Conclusion

Acknowledgements

The idea for this book stems directly from the translation of *Letters between Two* into English, a task I was first commissioned to carry out by the Foreign Languages Press in 1980. While employed full-time by the FLP in Peking between 1980 and 1983 and freelance for another two years, I was able to complete a first rough draft with assistance from my FLP colleagues. I also had the great good fortune to meet the world's leading authority on *Letters between Two*, Wang Dehou, from whose works and counsel I have profited immensely. On hearing of my project, William Lyell very generously made available to me the partial translation he had been working on; although our translation styles are very different, I owe a great deal to his knowledge of Chinese language, literature, and society.

For the present study I am most grateful to the British Academy Research Leave Scheme and the Faculty of Arts at the University of Edinburgh for grants that enabled me to take a year's leave in 1998–9 as part of a wider project, 'Private Writing in Public Spaces', a comprehensive survey of modern Chinese letters, diaries and memoirs. For travel to Cambridge, MA, I am grateful for grants from the Faculty Research Travel Fund and to the Carnegie Foundation; for travel to Tokyo, I am grateful for the award of the British Academy Exchange with the Japan Society for the Promotion of Science; and for travel to Cambridge, England I am grateful to the British Academy. For my second year of leave, I must thank the Center for Chinese Studies at the National Central Library in Taipei for a three-month fellowship in autumn 1999 and to Soochow University for employment from February to July 2000. For my final year of leave, I am grateful for the award of a ten-month residential fellowship from the Netherlands Institute for Advanced Study. For advice and assistance I particularly wish to thank Hamish MacAndrew (The University of Edinburgh), Ezra F. Vogel (director, Fairbank Center for East Asian Research, Harvard University), Leo Ou-fan Lee (East Asian Languages and Civilisations, Harvard University), Fujii Shôzô (University of Tokyo), D. M. McMullen (St John's College, University of Cambridge), Kang Li-chun, Sun Hsiu-ling, and Francis Tu (Center for Chinese Studies, National Central Library, Taipei), Henk Wesseling (NIAS) and Yang Yi (Chinese Academy of Social Sciences). Among the many friends and colleagues who offered ideas, suggestions, and criticism, I am particularly grateful to the following: Anders Hansson, Tommy McClellan, Robert Hillenbrand, Kam Louie, Louise Edwards, Mabel Lee, Agnes Syrokomla-Stefanowska, Helen Dunston, Paul Clark, Lynn Jamieson, Kate Day, Frank Dikötter, Stefan Feuchtwang, Harriet Evans, Helmut Martin, Bridie Andrews, Ellen Widmer, Suzanne Ogden, Paul

Cohen, Patrick Hanan, Stuart Schram, Katherine Karlitz, Joseph P. McDermott, John Crook, Guy Deutscher, Margaret Pierson, Sally Church, John Moffett, Michael Loewe, Michel Hockx, Joseph R. Allen, Juha Tähkämaa, David Pattinson, Hilary Chung, Helen Parker, Tong Shenxiao, Eva Hung, David Pollard, Anne Simpson, Kathryn Lowry, Hsiung Ping-chen, and Chen Xiaoming.

Dramatis Personae

Lu Xun's family and close friends
Zhou Fuqing (1837–1904): his grandfather
Zhou Fengyi (aka Zhou Boyi) (1860–96): his father
Lu Rui (1857–1943): his mother

Zhu An (1879–1947): his wife
Zhou Haiying (1929–): his son by Xu Guangping

Zhou Zuoren (1885–1967): his younger brother
Hata Nobuko (1888–1962): Zuoren's wife

Zhou Jianren (1888–1984): his youngest brother
Hata Yoshiko (1897-1964): Jianren's wife
Wang Yunru (1900–1990): Jianren's common-law wife

Xu Xiansu (1901–86): personal friend
Xu Qinwen (1897–1984): writer; Xiansu's brother
Yu Fen, Yu Fang, and Yu Zao: personal friends

Xu Guangping's family and close friends
Xu Bingyao: her father
Mme Song: her mother
Xu Chongxi: her eldest brother
Xu Chonghuan: her elder brother
Xu Yueping: her younger sister

Xu Chongqing: an elder male cousin
Xu Leping: a younger female cousin

Li Xiaohui: a male cousin
Li Xueying: a female cousin
Chen Yanxin: Xueying's husband
Xu Bing'ao: her uncle in Shanghai (her father's younger brother)
Aunt Feng

Chang Ruilin: fellow-student in Tientsin (from Peking)
Xie Dunnan: Ruilin's husband (from Amoy)

Political figures in China, 1911–26
Yuan Shikai: the first president of the Republic of China

Cai Yuanpei: the first Minister of Education in the Republic of China
Duan Qirui: premier of China in the 1920s
Sun Yat-sen: leader of the Nationalist Party
Zhang Zuolin: northern warlord

Friends and colleagues at Peking Women's Normal College, 1925–6
Xu Shouchang: acting principal of WNC, 1923–4
Yang Yinyu: principal of WNC, 1924–5
Lin Yutang: writer and scholar
Xu Zuzheng: writer and scholar
Shen Yinmo: writer and scholar
Ma Yuzao: scholar
Qian Xuantong: scholar
Shen Jianshi: scholar
Lin Zhuofeng, Liu Hezhen, Lu Xiuzhen, Lü Yunzhang, and Wang Shunqing: students

Literary and academic figures in Peking and Shanghai, 1925–32
Yu Dafu: writer
Sun Quan: Yu Dafu's wife
Wang Yiugxia: Yu Dafu's mistress
Sun Fuyuan: personal friend and editor
Guo Moruo: writer and political activist
Cheng Fangwu: writer and political activist
Hu Shi: philosopher and educationalist
Gu Jiegang: historian
Chen Yuan: literary critic and scholar
Xu Zhimo: poet
Zhang Shizhao: writer and educationalist
Rou Shi (Zhao Pingfu): writer

Political figures in China, 1927–68
Mao Zedong, leader of the Chinese Communist Party
Jiang Qing: Mao Zedong's third wife
Zhou Enlai: premier of the PRC, 1949–66
Deng Yingchao: Zhou Enlai's wife

Abbreviations

LDS	*Liang di shu*
LXQJ	*Lu Xun quan ji*
LXSW	*Lu Xun Selected Works*
LDSYJ	*Wang Dehou, 'Liang di shu' yanjiu*
LDSZS: YX. SG	*'Liang di shu' zhenshu: Yuanxin. Shougao*
LXZPQB	*Lu Xun zuopin quan bian: 'Liang di shu'*
LBT	Lu Xun and Xu Guangping, *Letters between Two*
OC	the original correspondence between Lu Xun and Xu Guangping
XGPWJ	*Xu Guangping wen ji*
WNC	[Peking] Women's Normal College
XQN	*Xin qingnian*

All references to and quotations from the letters are from the original correspondence (OC) unless otherwise specified. Letters or parts of letters in the OC which are not included in or which differ from LDS are from LDSYJ, or, if not in LDSYJ, then from LXZPQB. References to LDS are from the versions in LXQJ; citations are by letter number and date, with further reference to the English translation in LBT. A finding list of the letters by number and date is given in Appendix I in LBT. Translations of the published and unpublished correspondence are my own unless otherwise identified.

1

Introduction

The correspondence between Lu Xun (1881–1936), modern China's greatest writer, and Xu Guangping (1897–1968), his former student and his partner from 1927 to the end of his life, gives a unique insight into their private lives: how they felt about current events, about life in general, about themselves, and about each other. This book is about their intimate lives and their search for privacy as revealed in their published and unpublished letters.

Letters as a Literary Genre

Letters are such familiar, everyday things, and letter-writing as a form of communication or self-expression seems such an obvious and natural act that we tend not to remark on its ancient and universal lineage. Despite manifest differences in language, sentiment, and style, there are some features of letter-writing which are found repeatedly down the centuries across the world, some obviously learned behaviour, some apparently spontaneous rediscoveries by letter-writers everywhere. Extended into metaphor, letter-writing becomes synonymous with writing itself: more narrowly defined, a letter is a form of written communication addressed specifically to one or more persons and signed by one or more persons. Whether intended by the sender to be read by a single person or to be publicly circulated, a letter is primarily a vehicle for the expression of personal emotions and thoughts, although narration of events, philosophical discussion, or scientific enquiry can form a part or even the whole. Letters can be written on business, social, and personal matters; they can be formal and informal, individual or collective, open or intimate. The correspondents can be literate or illiterate (employing professional scribes, friends, or family), of any age past infancy, male or female, of any social class, living far apart or nearby, and of any country where writing exists.[1]

As written texts, letters occupy an intermediate place between literature in its widest sense on the one hand and imaginative literature or *belles-lettres* on the other. Published letters by professional literary writers, sometimes circulated within the writer's lifetime and after having undergone a process of revision, have an even greater claim to be considered as a literary genre. It can be surmised that any written text by a famous writer, or any letter to a famous writer even by an unknown person, would be regarded more or less unconsciously by its author as destined for eventual publication. Personal letters also share a characteristic with creative literature as a vehicle for expressing an individual's thoughts and emotions. As a genre, letters are unique in being dialogic by nature: a response, usually in the form of another letter in reply, is expected and sometimes anticipated.

The correspondence published by Lu Xun and Xu Guangping during their lifetime, *Letters between Two* (1933), has a strong claim to be regarded as *belles-lettres*: although only one of the two authors was a professional writer, he was at the time and still is modern China's most famous literary intellectual; and the original correspondence (hereafter abbreviated as OC) was edited for style as well as for content before publication. The letters, both published and unpublished, also dwell on subjective thoughts and emotions. Nevertheless, Lu Xun's deletion of certain letters or parts of letters from the published correspondence shows that it was originally for restricted circulation.

Love-Letters

Love-letters are a special sub-genre of correspondence. They are not necessarily more personal, more intimate or more deeply felt than any other kind of letter, but it is a common presumption that they are, and to publish one's own love-letters, either from one side or from both, raises particularly complex questions in regard to assumptions on privacy. Although the correspondence between Lu Xun and Xu Guangping, both original and published, is more than love-letters, it is also the love-letters of two people who had their own characteristic ways of expressing affection. The restraint both writers exhibit may also have been influenced by the contemporary vogue for published love-letters, which Lu Xun's circle regarded with derision, as well as by Lu Xun's habitual caution and the lingering influence of traditional attitudes towards intimate revelations.

Privacy

Letters and letter-writing are so commonplace that there is rarely a need to define them. The terminology for and about letters shifts over time within cultures but is not itself controversial, being mostly related to writing materials or functions, while between different languages there is ready translation without much if any loss of meaning. The universality of letter-writing is hardly disputed, nor is its antiquity. About privacy there is no such agreement. The very existence of a sense of privacy in China of the past and present has been challenged (George Steiner once claimed that privacy began in Europe in the 18th century, when bourgeois man picked up a book he owned in his own room and read it silently[2]), and it is often asserted that the Chinese do not value privacy as it is understood in the contemporary English-speaking world.[3] While it is easy to locate instances of privacy in China, it is considerably more complicated to find evidence of the conceptualization of privacy (e.g. as a value).[4]

In modern English-speaking countries, on the other hand, there has been unprecedented interest in privacy in recent years, especially in the US: as in the case of letters, the phenomenon comes under closest scrutiny when it appears to be under threat.[5] There are two main schools of thought among writers on privacy in the second half of the twentieth century. One school, which could be called particularistic, sees privacy as a product of European civilization (or of Western capitalism), emerging in the eighteenth century, flourishing in the nineteenth century, becoming a dominant value in the twentieth century, yet under critical threat at the end of this century. The people writing in this vein are mostly historians, political scientists, and sociologists; they treat privacy as an issue; they tend to define privacy narrowly and negatively as a defence against intrusion; they quote Arendt, Habermas, and Steiner.[6] The other school is universalistic: these writers regard privacy as a human universal; they tend to be anthropologists, psychologists, and philosophers; they define privacy broadly to encompass variety and change; they treat privacy as a mental capacity, a value and a psychological need; and they tend to refer to Goffman and Malinowksi.[7] Many works in both categories have a crusading spirit.

In this study, it will be maintained that a sense of privacy is one of the most basic mental capacities of human beings all over the world.[8] The nature, mechanisms, functions, contents, and values of privacy will differ from country to country, culture to culture, and person to person, but a sense of privacy appears to be as universal as the capacity to speak and think. It is closely related to bodily activities, especially reproduction and excretion, but also to mental activities such as rights of choice, and to relationships between people, such as privacy in correspondence. This study focuses on privacy in modern Chinese society; modern Anglophone Western societies (the United Kingdom, Australia and New Zealand, the United States and Canada) will be referred to as comparators, and some reference will be made to premodern concepts of privacy in China. Privacy has been approached through many disciplines: law, sociology, psychology, economics, politics, history, and anthropology, to name a few. This study is the first to employ the methodology of literary criticism: it examines the genre, the form, the style, and the context of a particular text, in this case, a collection of letters edited for publication, *Letters between Two*, and its originals.

Letters and Privacy

Privacy of correspondence is a generally accepted norm that is protected in many countries by law, especially since the United Nations 1960 declaration on human rights specifying privacy and correspondence in Article 17.[9] Love-letters, along with diaries and intimate journals, are commonly regarded as indisputably belonging to a private realm (whether of the family or of the individual),[10] and their unauthorized publication, even if not subject to legal sanctions, is regarded as morally reprehensible. When letters are published by one or both authors themselves, they are almost inevitably first edited, and it is the comparison between the original and published versions that can give us the clearest idea of what is considered private by the authors. Not all deletions or recensions (substitutions of words or passages) are due to what an English-speaking reader might regard as personal privacy, however; other reasons are prudence (e.g. to avoid giving offence or causing embarrassment to people mentioned in the letter who are still living or whose relatives might take offence); prudery (to avoid being seen in a poor light); aesthetic taste (by improving the style or correcting the grammar); and hindsight (including political correctness). All of these kinds of deletions and recensions can be found in *Letters between Two*. Other changes take the form of additions, which can deflect readers' attention from what is considered private, while what is retained can in many cases clarify by comparison what is not considered private.

Structure

Part I relates the story of how Lu Xun and Xu Guangping became a couple: their lives before meeting, their courtship, and their partnership—not married but living together and raising a child. This story also includes their families and friends, their studies, and their work. The focus will be on their intimate lives, the detail of which will be taken chiefly from their correspondence. It does not elaborate on the well-known details of Lu Xun's political and literary life; Lu Xun's indigestion is given more attention than his preparations for launching a new magazine.

Part II begins with a general survey of letters, imagined letters, and love-letters in China and in the West. This is followed by a description of the correspondence itself in terms of its publication history, the frequency and physical appearance of the letters, the forms of address and style, and an analysis of common themes: the letters themselves, the separation, current events, literature, courtship, and love. Part III examines the 'personal space' created by the deletions, recensions, retentions, and additions to *Letters between Two* in regard to its vocabulary, and relates it to the functions and values of privacy as defined in English-language studies.

The Conclusion compares attitudes towards privacy among modern Chinese writers who published or withheld their love-letters from publication, in the context of modern Chinese history.

After I had completed the first rough draft of the translation of *Letters between Two*, it occurred to me that it would have been better to have had two translators working on the letters, one translating Lu Xun's letters and one taking Xu Guangping's. When I subsequently realized the extent of the revisions carried out by Lu Xun this ideal seemed less relevant: Lu Xun's rewriting made the two letter-writers appear more similar in regard to their language style, thinking, and conduct. Lu Xun's Preface to *Letters between Two* mentions some factors behind its publication; unspoken factors can be detected from the processes that led to the making of *Letters between Two*. The differences between the original and the published correspondence also show that readers wishing to understand the relationship between the couple as well as their views on themselves and their world at the time the letters were written must consult the originals; *Letters between Two*, on the other hand, is best seen as a semi-fictional work which represents Lu Xun's thinking in the early 1930s.

Sources

This study is deeply indebted to the painstaking work carried out by Wang Dehou in '*Liang di shu' yanjiu* [Research on *Letters between two*], first published in 1982, in which he analyses differences between the original correspondence and the published version. Lu Xun studies in China alone amount to a lifetime's reading. The most recent comprehensive bibliography of Chinese books and articles is *Lu Xun yanjiu shulu* [Bibliography of Lu Xun studies] (1987), edited by Ji Weizhou *et al.*; covering the period from 1926 to the end of 1983 (in the case of some periodicals including 1984), it gives summaries and outlines of hundreds of books and thousands of articles on Lu Xun, Xu Guangping, and members of the Zhou family. From this bibliography it is clear that far from being a discredited subject after his adulation during the Cultural Revolution, research on Lu Xun expanded greatly in the late 1970s and early 1980s. Limitations on the scope and depth of these studies were still in force, however: little attention was given to Lu Xun's private life, Zhu An, Lu Xun's wife, is rarely mentioned, and *Letters between Two* is not regarded as a primary text.[11] The breakthrough came in 1982 with Wang Dehou's research on *Letters between Two*. Attention to Lu Xun's relations with Zhu An and Xu Guangping increased in the late 1980s, and new revelations based on previously unpublished letters, essays, and reminiscences finally made possible a study of Lu Xun's private life in the 1990s. (Two other helpful bibliographic aids are the Kyoto University database on Lu Xun studies in Chinese and Japanese, and the special issue on Lu Xun in Taiwan of *Guowen tiandi* [The world of Chinese language and literature], no. 76, vol. 7 no. 4 (September 1990), pp. 11–53.)

The chief source of the present work is the correspondence between Lu Xun and Xu Guangping between 1925 and 1932, of which the greater part was published in 1933 under the title *Letters between Two*; the earliest edition I have seen is 1937, and the edition used here is that reprinted with annotations in *Lu Xun quan ji* [Lu Xun's complete works] (1981). A comparison between the original and published texts with an extensive commentary is in '*Liang di shu' yanjiu* by Wang Dehou, first published in 1982 and revised in 1995. The original letters sent by Lu Xun were first published in *Lu Xun zhi Xu Guangping shujian* [Lu Xun's letters to Xu Guangping] in 1979; this has extensive notes. The original letters of both Lu Xun and Xu Guangping were published in *Lu Xun Jing Song tongxin ji: 'Liang di shu' de yuanxin* [The correspondence between Lu Xun and Jing Song: the original letters in *Letters between Two*] (1984), which has a postface by Zhou Haiying but no notes. A facsimile edition of the original letters and of the original manuscript of *Letters between Two* was published as a boxed set of two volumes in 1996, with a foreword by Zhou Haiying, the son and only child of Lu Xun and Xu Guangping. (As indicated in recent research by Raoul D. Findeisen, facsimile publications are not necessarily fully authentic reproductions of original manuscripts, but this set is considered reliable.) A new annotated edition of the published correspondence with the unpublished letters in an appendix, compiled by Wang Dehou *et al.*, was published in 1998. There are some discrepancies in the readings of the original manuscripts and also in the notes; on the whole I have followed the readings and notes by Wang Dehou. (For a discussion on the copyright of these letters, see Chapter 9.)

Next most important as a source is Lu Xun's diary. Lu Xun kept a diary from 5 May 1912 to 17 October 1936; it does not record major events in his life and times but lists details such as letters received and sent, visits to and by friends and colleagues, book and magazine purchases, lectures and meetings given and attended, the cost of some purchases (including alcohol), the amount of salary or fee he receives, presents of books and other gifts made to or by him, visits to the hospital on his own behalf or to accompany his mother, sleepless nights, the weather, and similar events. The entries are brief and rarely express the author's thoughts or feelings. As with any autobiographical writing, however, it cannot be assumed that Lu Xun's diary is an accurate record of events. For example, it is known from the letters that he left out such things as the Dragon Boat Day visit by Xu Guangping and others in 1925, the occasion when Xu Guangping and Xu Xiansu stayed in his house in August 1925, and most of Xu Guangping's visits from September 1925 to the time they left Peking in August 1926; again, not all the letters in *Letters between Two* are recorded.[12] The diary was not published during his own lifetime, but Xu Guangping began transcribing it for publication in 1935. *Lu Xun riji* [Lu Xun's diary] was first published in 1951 by Shanghai chubanshe and reprinted by Renmin wenxue chubanshe in two volumes in 1959; a revised edition was published in 1976.

Lu Xun's main autobiographical essays are in *Zhao hua xi shi* [Dawn blossoms plucked at dusk], mostly reminiscences about his childhood which leave an impression of general doom and decay. *Lu Xun zishu* [Lu Xun in his own words] (1936) is a compilation from unidentified sources of other autobiographical writings, with a short essay by Zhou Zuoren on Lu Xun's life and work. Between 1946 and when he died in 1966, Zhou Zuoren wrote altogether eleven books about Lu Xun and it is said that six more were in the press when the Cultural Revolution broke out;[13] his works such as *Lu Xun xiaoshuo li de renwu* [The characters in Lu Xun's fiction] and *Lu Xun de gujia* [Lu Xun's old home] portray a comfortable, even prosperous and happy childhood in a large gentry family. There is an extensive bibliography of works by and about Zhou Zuoren himself. The indispensable guides are the two-volume *Zhou Zuoren yanjiu ziliao* [Zhou Zuoren research materials] (1986) edited by Zhang Juxiang and Zhang Tierong, and the same editors' *Zhou Zuoren nianpu* [Zhou Zuoren chronology] (rev. ed. 2000), plus the excellent survey in William Cheong-loong Chow's dissertation, 'Chou Tso-jen: a serene radical in the new culture movement'. More recent studies on Zhou Zuoren by Shu Wu and others are less censorious than their predecessors about his collaboration with the Japanese during the Second World War. Zhou Jianren, the third brother, wavers between the two: written much later in time, his dictated reminiscences in *Lu Xun gujia de bailuo* [Lu Xun's family in decline] (1984) make generous use of hindsight to glorify Lu Xun, denigrate Zuoren, and gloss over such things as their father's drinking.

Shortly after Lu Xun's death, Xu Shouchang began work on a chronology of his life, consulting Xu Guangping for details and also on sensitive matters such as

Lu Xun's marriage to Zhu An and his relationship with Xu Guangping.[14] This was never published in book form. Five chronologies covering Lu Xun's life and major works were published between 1970 and 1984, the last and most comprehensive being the four-volume *Lu Xun nianpu* [Lu Xun chronology] under the general editorship of Li Helin (1981–84).[15]

Xu Guangping wrote many essays, articles, and lectures about Lu Xun. Among the earliest and most intimate was the essay 'Lu Xun xiansheng de richang shenghuo', [Mr Lu Xun's daily life] (1939), in which she describes his sleeping habits, his fondness for certain kinds of food and drink, the care he took in preserving letters, magazines, and books, his health, and so on. Her first full-length collection of reminiscences was *Xinwei de jinian* [In grateful commemoration] (1951), a series of short essays written by Xu Guangping between Lu Xun's death in 1936 and 1949 with a preface by Feng Xuefeng on behalf of Xu Guangping, dated 1951 and a postface by the compiler, Wang Shiqing, dated 1950. These essays are still reasonably frank on such things as financial need being a motive in their leaving Peking in 1926. She does not mention her first love affair or attempted suicide—after all, it is not her biography. More significant omissions are on how their relationship changed from student–teacher to friends and colleagues to lovers, and her initial misgivings in regard to communist involvement in the student movement. Her other sketches about Lu Xun's daily life and habits, written in the late 1930s and the 1940s, were collected and published under the title *Guanyu Lu Xun de shenghuo* [On Lu Xun's life] in 1954. The third set was *Lu Xun huiyi lu* [Reminiscences of Lu Xun] (1961).

According to her preface to *Lu Xun huiyi lu*, dated November 1959, since 1954 Xu Guangping had many times been urged by others to write more about Lu Xun. Until then she had always refused, but the Great Leap Forward inspired her to make a new effort. Starting in July 1959, she prepared herself by reading Lu Xun's diary and his other works, along with materials about Lu Xun by other writers, and reminiscences about other world-famous figures. This took about a month, but after she started to write, from between mid-August to 20 September, she came to a halt. The tenth anniversary celebrations of the PRC in October 1959 gave her renewed inspiration, and she completed the first draft of the manuscript at the end of November. Failing health (high blood pressure) was a problem. The work was published in May 1961, the unexplained delay most likely due to the economic crisis of the early 1960s. As her biographer admits, there are some errors in this collection (e.g. about such things as their attitude towards the communist involvement in the college protest).[16] Confusingly, a new volume with the same title, *Lu Xun huiyi lu*, but with different contents was issued in 1976.

After the end of the Cultural Revolution, Lu Xun studies began to give more attention to Xu Guangping herself. This shift in focus can be seen in *Xu Guangping yi Lu Xun* [Xu Guangping reminisces about Lu Xun], compiled by Ma Tiji and published in 1979 to commemorate the tenth anniversary of her death. The preface by Tang Tao (dated 1978) comments on her life after 1936, when he saw her frequently. *Xu Guangping yi Lu Xun* consists of 115 articles and other writings by Xu Guangping from 1925 to 1965 (including those listed above), arranged in five sections: (1) articles and lectures commemorating anniversaries of Lu Xun's death; (2) prefaces and postfaces to new publications of Lu Xun's works and works about Lu Xun, such as Wang Shiqing's biography; (3) articles on specific aspects of Lu Xun's works; (4) articles generally on Lu Xun's thinking, works, daily life, conversations, and so on; (5) Xu's book commemorating Lu Xun. Although all of the above are about Lu Xun, there are also an appendix of articles about Xu Guangping and a bibliography of Xu Guangping's writings.

Next to appear was *Xu Guangping* (1995), a collection of reminiscences by others plus her unpublished essays and other works; the postface by Chen Shuyu and Liu Lihua acknowledges the assistance of Zhou Haiying and his wife Ma Xinyun. Expanding on this is *Xu Guangping wen ji* [Xu Guangping's collected works] (1998); the editor is said to be [Zhou] Haiying. In three volumes, it includes Xu Guangping's earliest reminiscence of her childhood, 'Wo de xiaoxue shidai' [My time at primary school], first published 25 November 1939, her essays on the women's movement, and the letters she wrote to Lu Rui, Zhu An, Hu Shi, and Zhou Zuoren after Lu Xun's death. More reminiscences and a selection of her published and unpublished essays are included in *Xu Guangping jinian ji* [Xu Guangping commemorative volume] (2000), edited by the Shanghai Lu Xun Memorial Museum in cooperation with the Shanghai branch of the Association for the Promotion of Democracy in China and the Women's Federation; the postface is by Wang Xirong who also contributes an article, and Zhou Haiying was also involved.

Reminiscences of Lu Xun by his friends, colleagues, and students are almost too plentiful. One of the earliest and most useful is Xu Shouchang's *Wo suo renshi de Lu Xun* [The Lu Xun I knew], but like most of those which followed, its hagiographic tone is pronounced. Yu Dafu is less reverential in *Huiyi Lu Xun* [Reminiscences of Lu Xun], written in 1938. Yu Fang, *Wo jiyi zhong de Lu Xun xiansheng* [The Mr Lu Xun of my memories] (1981), with a preface by Zhou Jianren, gives an account of Lu Xun's domestic life in Peking. Yu Fang was one of three sisters, Fen, Fang, and Zao; Lu Xun was closest to Yu Fen, but Yu Fang was Zhu An's confidant. Xu Qinwen's *Xuexi Lu Xun xiansheng* [Studying Mr Lu Xun] (1959) also gives insight into Lu Xun's home life in Peking. Feng Xuefeng's reminiscences are important for the later years. The main sources are now readily available in the two three-volume sets *Lu Xun huiyi lu (sanpian)* [Reminiscences of Lu Xun (articles)] and *Lu Xun huiyi lu (zhuanzhu)* [Reminiscences of Lu Xun (monographs)] jointly compiled by the Lu Xun Museum, the Lu Xun Research Room and *Lu Xun yanjiu yuekan* [Lu Xun studies monthly] in 1997.

Among the many biographies of Lu Xun, Wang Shiqing's 1959 *Lu Xun zhuan* [A biography of Lu Xun] was for many years the standard version, but it contains such obvious falsehoods as 'Lu Xun went immediately to Canton [on being invited to a chair in Zhongshan University in 1926], his heart brimming with confidence'. Wang Xiaoming's 1993 *Wufa zhimian de rensheng: Lu Xun zhuan* [Life that cannot be faced directly: a biography of Lu Xun] is an example of the new scholarship on

Lu Xun; Niu Daifeng's 1998 *Lu Xun zhuan* relates previously unpublishable detail on Lu Xun's private life.

The main biographies of Xu Guangping are *Xu Guangping yi sheng* [A life of Xu Guangping] (1981) by Chen Shuyu and *Lu Xun yu Xu Guangping* [Lu Xun and Xu Guangping] (1986) by Fan Zhiting. Chen Shuyu is the director of the Lu Xun Museum in Peking, and his biography is detailed and contains notes on sources. It has prefaces by Xu's son, Zhou Haiying, and Tang Tao, and can be regarded as authoritative and respectful. (An early version appeared in Ma Tiji, *Xu Guangping yi Lu Xun*.) Fan Zhiting is even more detailed but lacks all citations and it is difficult to tell how reliable it is. However, the manuscript was vetted by Xu Shouchang, and Fan also had help from Zhou Haiying. Both biographies rely heavily on imaginative reconstruction, and although their portraits of Lu Xun are more nuanced than Wang Shiqing's, they are still glamourized: Xu Guangping is idealized as an obedient student, devoted spouse, and loyal Party member, with only occasional reminders of her great spirit. This holds for sensationalist books like Ceng Zhizhong's *San ren xing* [A love triangle] (1990) and Li Yunjing's *Lu Xun de hunyin yu jiating* [Lu Xun's marriage and family] (1990). Most recent is *Lu Xun yu Xu Guangping*, by Ni Moyan and Chen Jiuying, published in January 2001.

There is still no full-length, reliable biography of Lu Xun in English. The main Western biographies of Lu Xun are William Schultz, 'Lu Hsun: The Creative Years' (1955), Harriet Mills, 'Lu Hsun, 1927–1936' (1963), and Leo Lee, *Voices from the Iron House* (1987). All of these refer to Lu Xun's letters and diaries but Xu Guangping's place in Lu Xun's life is given scant attention. The story of Lu Xun and Xu Guangping's as a couple in Part I is not intended to be a complete record but draws on their public activities for comparison and continuity.

Part I

Intimate Lives

Sir, more than kisses, letters mingle Soules;
For, thus friends absent speake. This ease controules
The tediousnesse of my life: But for these
I could ideate nothing which could please . . .
John Donne, 'To Sir Henry Wotton'

What dangerous machines letters are. Perhaps it is just as well that they are going out of fashion. A letter can be endlessly reread and reinterpreted, it stirs imagination and fantasy, it persists, it is red-hot evidence.

Iris Murdoch, *The Black Prince*

2

Xu Guangping 'in the Front Row': 1898–1925

Mr Lu Xun:

The person who grasps her pen to write this letter to you is someone who has studied under you for almost two years, who every week keenly looks forward to those rare classes on the history of fiction, just one hour in over thirty hours a week, a young student who sits in the front row at your lectures and who likes to speak out in class in words that are similarly firm, unselfconsciously and straightforwardly. Her many doubts and her indignation at injustice, long stored within, can perhaps no longer be suppressed, and therefore she sets forth her complaints to her teacher . . .

The youth of the present day really descend further day by day into the ninth circle of Hell! Maybe I am also one of them. Although one hour a week of your instruction can quicken my heart and strengthen my vigour, yet the danger is great! Teacher! I wonder if you have ever considered that 'to save one life is superior to building a seven-storey pagoda'? Teacher! Although you are usually so stern, I wish you would now relax your sternness, and if you can succour a single soul then succour this one! Teacher! In such extremity does this person 'anxiously await orders'![1]

With these impassioned words Xu Guangping opened and closed her first letter to Lu Xun, written in March 1925. So daring was her approach to her famous teacher that he pruned the opening paragraph and deleted the last one altogether when he revised their correspondence for publication. The evidence from her writing and conduct suggests that Xu Guangping had unusual strength of character. At the age of twenty-seven when she first wrote to Lu Xun, she qualified as an intellectually and sexually emancipated 'New Woman'.

Xu Guangping's family came from Panyu county in Kwangtung. During her childhood they occupied a large mansion in Gaodi Street, Canton, whose imposing entrance, flanked by two lions, enclosed over a hundred people.[2] Among the family's forebears was a former Governor General of Kwangtung and Kwangsi,[3] from whom Guangping was said to have inherited her stubbornness. The family's wealth and power had declined by the time of her birth. Her father, Xu Bingyao, was the son of a concubine and occupied a low position in the family hierarchy. He was physically frail and not good at business. His wife came from an overseas merchant family by the name of Song, based in Macao. She was educated and capable, but her feet were bound and she needed two servants to support her when she walked any distance.[4]

Born in 1898, Guangping was the twenty-third in her generation.[5] Apart from her parents, she spent most of her childhood with her eldest brother, Chongxi, her elder brother, Chonghuan, an elder cousin, Chongqing, an elder sister who died at the age of nine *sui*, a younger cousin, Leping, and a younger sister, Yueping.[6] Her childhood name was Xia. When it was time for her to start school, her father gave her the name Guangping, the first character indicating the name of the province and the second an abbreviation of the term Taiping [Great peace]; there was also an echo of the name of a famous prime minister, Song Guangping.[7]

Guangping attended the family's private school from the age of eight *sui*, along with Chongxi, Chonghuan, and Chongqing. Also at the school were three children of her father's sister: a boy called Li Xiaohui, a girl, Li Xueying, and another boy. When an elderly aunt objected that if girls studied alongside boys, they would rob the boys of their intelligence, her mother defended their decision to allow Guangping to study alongside the boys. After some fuss, she was even allowed to learn Mandarin.[8]

The older girls in her generation had bound feet, and one day shortly after she had begun to attend school, her mother set about binding her feet.[9] Although she had earlier submitted to having her ears pierced, Guangping fretted at the restriction to her freedom of movement, and appealed to her father the following morning. After arguing with her mother, her father insisted that the wrappings be discarded. Guangping's mother died not long after this incident, but as she was never very fond of her mother she was not greatly affected.[10] She was much closer to her father, despite his sometimes reckless behaviour. Three days after she was born, at a drunken party, he had promised to marry her into the Ma family. Around the age of twelve, as she became aware of the arranged match, she pleaded to be released, but he was adamant that he could not go back on his word. Instead, she conceived the idea that an independent career might provide a way out of her predicament.[11]

Xu Guangping's father took Chonghuan to attend school in Peking, leaving the family in the care of Chongxi, who was by now married with children. As anti-Qing sentiment grew in the lead-up to the 1911 revolution, Chongxi decided to seek temporary refuge for them at their maternal grandparents' home in Macao; her father and Chonghuan joined them soon afterwards. Xu Guangping's schooling come to a temporary halt. She had not yet learned to read newspapers, so Chongxi, who had studied in Nanking and was sympathetic to the revolutionaries' aims, read the papers to her and explained the republican cause.

The family moved back to Canton in 1912, and Guangping entered the school attached to the Canton Girls' Normal School. Around this time her father began to take in the newspaper *Pingmin bao* [The common man], and Xu Guangping was by now able to read it for herself. She and Yueping would walk into town to buy its Saturday supplement, *Funü zhoukan* [Women's weekly], which advocated women's rights, and other new books advertised in its pages.[12] In 1915, she secretly sent a letter to the woman revolutionary Zhuang Hanqiao; when her father heard about it, he put a stop to her correspondence but not to her enthusiasm for politics.[13]

The death of her brother Chongxi at the age of thirty *sui* was a terrible blow that affected Guangping for many years. It was followed in 1917 by another heavy blow, the death of her father at the age of sixty *sui*.[14] When the Ma family renewed their attempts to close the marriage, Guangping appealed to Chonghuan, who had returned to Canton for the funeral. Chonghuan devised a way to fend off the Ma family and agreed that she should go to live in the north, since her marriage prospects in Canton had been adversely affected by the broken betrothal and at the age of nineteen she was already losing her attraction in traditional matchmaking. However, as the new head of the family, he considered that they could not afford her further studies. Guangping then secured the aid of a paternal aunt who lived in Tientsin to take the entrance exams for the Chihli [Hopeh] First Girls' Normal School in Tientsin. Founded by Yuan Shikai in 1906, the school attracted students from all parts of the country.

Guangping left Canton in 1917 for Tientsin. When she passed the qualifying exams, Chonghuan sold some of the family's paintings and gave Guangping two hundred dollars for her school expenses. This was enough to take her through her first year, and in her second year she won a bursary.[15]

Guangping's best friend at school, and for many years after, was Chang Ruilin from Peking.[16] Their attachment led to trouble. As she wrote to Lu Xun in 1926, 'When I was in Tientsin, a classmate of mine from primary school came to visit, but finding that Miss Chang [Ruilin] and I were pretty thick gave me a proper dressing-down. I was so ashamed and embarrassed, I rushed away and swallowed some poison; the whole affair was a stupid business. Afterwards people urged me not to be so "earnest", and when I thought it over, my fault was really in being too earnest. Now that person is dead . . .'[17] The imputation is that Guangping had a lesbian relationship with Ruilin; the angry visitor may have been Li Xiaohui, who became a student at Peking University in 1919.

In December 1917 Xu Guangping contributed four short essays in classical Chinese to the school magazine.[18] Her first experience of practical politics came during the boycott against Japanese goods following the nationalist May Fourth movement of 1919. As she wrote in a 1925 letter to Lu Xun,

> Your mention of everfast glue brought to mind a ridiculous business. At that time in Tientsin we collected some ready-made vanishing-cream jars, and made great quantities of everfast glue. These we peddled everywhere on trays selling at a low price. Since we did not use any capital to buy the jars, it should not have been possible for us to make a loss, but in the end we still lost money with no reward to show for our efforts. The quality of our product did not come up to what was being sold on the market, so people were not willing to buy very enthusiastically. We also thought of a way to make small toys, using plaster moulds to cast hollow wax dolls, fancy dogs, lions and so on. We hoped to replace the thin rubber toys on the market, but we could never match them and in the end failed in the same way.[19]

Guangping also took part in giving propaganda speeches and helped to edit the student journal. Their group formed links with a nearby boys' school, flouting the rule that boys and girls should not mix, and both took part in a mass public demonstration in June. Deng Yingchao, a much younger student at her school, became a leading activist in the movement; Zhou Enlai, newly returned from Japan, became involved somewhat later.[20] At one noisy demonstration in October 1919 where the police were summoned to maintain order, Guangping had a personal confrontation with a policeman who snatched the banner she was carrying.

On graduation from the Girls' Normal School in 1921, Xu Guangping was kept on as a teacher. The following year, however, she decided to seek further education in Peking. One attraction may have been that Chang Ruilin was returning to Peking; another may have been Li Xiaohui. Guangping enrolled in the Chinese department of Women's Normal College in Peking in the autumn of 1922.[21] While not ideal, the college offered room and board, and tuition was free; even more importantly, the college was known to have hired a number of distinguished scholars from Peking University as part-time teachers as well as the foreign-trained full-time staff.[22] The famous writer and translator Zhou Zuoren, for example, had lectured there in May on male and female equality in literature, and began teaching part-time on a regular basis in September.[23]

After her move to Peking, Guangping spent much of her time with Li Xiaohui. Then in late December 1922, she contracted scarlet fever, probably from Chang Ruilin, and moved into Chang's home to be looked after. For lack of proper diagnosis and treatment, however, her illness brought her close to death. Li Xiaohui came to see her several times in the first days of the New Year while she was lying ill, but on 23 February, when she had recovered enough to inquire after him, she learnt that he had become infected himself and died on 7 January. Hearing the news, she tried to commit suicide by swallowing *teng huang*.[24]

Recovering from her illness and distress, Guangping showed characteristic resolution in becoming general secretary of the Student Council. Since the May Fourth Incident in 1919, students had become used to exerting power through protests and demonstrations, and the students at the Women's Normal College were as militant as any other in the capital. She also supplemented her funds by tutoring the sons of a department head in the Foreign Ministry, an onerous daily duty that she refers to as "man's calamity" (a term from Mencius).[25]

In autumn 1923 a new part-time teacher joined the staff: Zhou Zuoren's brother Zhou Shuren, whose identity as the even more famous writer Lu Xun was just then becoming known. Xu Guangping attended his course on the history of Chinese fiction. Although she was taller than average and did not have defective sight or hearing, she always sat in the first row of the classroom, perhaps anxious not to miss anything, perhaps wanting to make an impression. She was not shy either in delivering her opinions in class or outside; in September 1923 she wrote a short article on the difficulties that young women faced walking around in public places unescorted.[26]

The acting principal of the College, Xu Shouchang, came under pressure in August 1923 from a student faction opposed to the way he conducted school affairs, and he resigned in February 1924. His replacement, Yang Yinyu, then head of the English department, appeared to be well qualified for the position. After studying in Japan, she had taught mathematics, physics, and chemistry and had been dean of studies at the College. In 1918 she went to the United States, where it was said that she came under the influence of Dewey at Columbia University. Yang Yinyu's supporters also held that a woman principal should head a woman's college. Within a few months of her appointment, however, some students were already organizing protests against her.

During the 1924 summer vacation Xu Guangping made a trip to Lushan, staying with a paternal aunt. Her travel essay, written in vernacular Chinese, was published in the College's annual journal.[27] That autumn, Zhou Shuren presented a new course, blending modern literary criticism and psychology. Among its attractions to Xu Guangping were his lectures on 'physiology' (i.e. presumably on sexuality).[28] At one point (when exactly this happened is not clear) she was caught off guard by finding him staring at her, but she boldly returned his gaze.[29]

For the student body in general, the new school year got off to a bad start. Yang Yinyu expelled three students from the preparatory school who had returned late, and abused the student representatives who acted for the expelled students. By November 1924, one student faction began to agitate for her removal as principal, and by January 1925 the whole student body had come out in favour of her dismissal. At this stage it is difficult to sort out the rights and wrongs of the students' case.[30] Some of the complaints against Yang Yinyu were trivial, such as the exception some students took to the way she dressed, with a white ribbon in her hair, a black cheongsam, and a cape round her shoulders.[31] On the other hand, it was surely unwise of Yang Yinyu to forbid students from taking part in a capital-wide funeral procession for the Nationalist leader Sun Yat-sen following his death in March 1925, on the grounds that he did not set a good moral example for her students.[32]

Sun Yat-sen's death had occurred at a particularly delicate moment. The Chinese Communist Party, founded in 1921, had originally regarded the Nationalist Party led by Sun Yat-sen as their chief rival on the left. In June 1923, however, the Communist International (Comintern) decided that the defeat of the warlord government in Peking was to be its primary objective, and ordered the Communist Party to cooperate with the Nationalist Party. The Nationalist Party had its base in the south, at Canton. In 1923, Sun Yat-sen was invited to Peking to discuss the possibility of a truce with the Peking régime, then headed by Duan Qirui. Sun's unexpected death brought an end to negotiations, and preparations began in the south for a joint Nationalist–Communist challenge to the north. Yang Yinyu, who had good connections within Duan Qirui's government, objected to the left-wing tendencies of the student activists in her school.

Xu Guangping at first stood aside from the anti-Yang agitation; suspecting that it was being pushed by Communists for their own ends, she was reluctant to take sides.[33] Yang Yinyu was active on her own behalf, however, and it was rumoured that she had offered opportunities for overseas study or employment as teachers after graduation to students who agreed to abandon the protest. Seeing her classmates switch sides, Xu Guangping felt indignant but isolated, and she was not sure what her next move should be. In March 1925 she resolved to write to her teacher to ask for his guidance.

3

Lu Xun's 'Life without Love': 1881–1925

Brother Guangping:

I received your letter today. I'm afraid there are some questions I can't answer, but for the moment I'll scribble a few lines . . .

That is all I can say about my own way of dealing with life; it is more like a game than a steady march along the true path of life (there may be a true path in life, but I don't know). I believe that writing it down may not necessarily be of much use to you but it is all I can do.[1]

Answering Guangping's letter, Lu Xun was hesitant, even apologetic, reluctant to disappoint her but not able to offer easy solutions. In revising the letter for publication, he found no need to change more than a couple of phrases to make his meaning clearer. At the age of forty-four, prudence and restraint in personal matters had become second nature to him. His one daring touch was in his term of address: 'brother' Guangping. He signed himself as she addressed him, Lu Xun.

Lu Xun, first named Zhou Zhangshou, was the eldest of three brothers to survive childhood. The Zhou family was from Shaoxing, Chekiang, and although not as prosperous as the Xu family in Canton, they lived in a large compound and drew income from rents and official salaries.[2] His mother, Lu Rui, was also from a well-established family; her brothers had passed the first stage of the old examination system although she herself was not literate.[3] When Zhangshou was born in 1881, it was expected that like his forebears he would undergo a traditional education and take an official post. The disgrace and imprisonment of his grandfather, the early death of his father, and the family's shortage of funds made these plans more difficult to achieve.[4] After an early education in the family school, he went on to the Jiangnan [Central China] Naval Academy at Nanking, where he registered under the name Zhou Shuren, and then to the Jiangnan Army Academy's School of Railways and Mines. At school, Shuren wrote home regularly to his grandfather, his mother, and his younger brother; the third brother was still too young.[5]

A month after graduating in 1902, Shuren accepted a scholarship from the Jiangnan military training office to study in Japan.[6] In Tokyo he first enrolled at the newly established Kôbun Gakuin [Great culture college] to study Japanese;[7] he also found time for physical exercise, practising armed and unarmed martial arts, and emulating Spartan warriors. His chief confidant was Xu Shouchang, also from Shaoxing, who arrived at the college in September. In Shuren's absence, his mother Lu Rui arranged his betrothal to a distant relative, Zhu An,[8] and Shuren wrote home to register his dismay.[9] However, he did not defy his mother, stipulating only that Zhu An should be educated and unbind her feet.[10]

Shuren's first years in Japan coincided with a flurry of activity in new fiction and journalism. The most prominent of the Chinese activists in Japan was Liang Qichao, who had left China in October 1898 after the failure of the reform movement to effect changes in the Qing court; cut off from direct political power, he turned to fiction as a vehicle for promoting reform.[11] Very much under Liang Qichao's influence,[12] Shuren became a subscriber and contributor to a student magazine. By the time he completed his Japanese course, the range of his publications was balanced fairly evenly between science journalism and science fiction. Student journalism does not provide a living, and as the time came to leave Kôbun Gakuin in 1904, Shuren was obliged by the terms of his scholarship to choose a course of study leading towards a career within the armed forces.

Shuren originally planned to study mining at Tokyo University, but the entry requirements were high and he was advised to consider an alternative.[13] He decided on medicine, influenced by recollections of his father's and youngest brother's deaths following treatment by traditional Chinese medicine. As he was aware, medicine had been crucial to Japan's progress in modernization, and it offered a pathway into Western science and a promising career whether within the army or outside it. In September 1904, Shuren left Tokyo to enter the medical college at Tohoku University in northern Japan. But he found that medical studies did not appeal to him, and during a spring vacation trip to Tokyo in early 1906 he confided in Xu Shouchang that his decision to leave Tokyo and to abandon mining had led him along a false path.[14] (There is no explanation why he rejected other options in the military or engineering careers for which he had been trained.) He returned to Tokyo in March 1906 without a degree, but by enrolling in a German language school he was entitled to continue his student stipend.

Summoned by a telegram saying that his mother was ill, Shuren returned to Shaoxing in the summer of 1906 to find it a ruse. A rumour was circulating in Shaoxing that he had been seen with a Japanese woman and a small child, and Zhu An's family was pressing for the marriage to take place. Shuren finally yielded. In addition to his strong sense of obligation towards his mother, he thought that having contracted tuberculosis he might not have long to live anyway.[15] It is thought that he only found out that Zhu An was still uneducated and had bound feet after the ceremony, and that he refused to consummate the marriage.

Shuren returned to Tokyo a few days later, leaving his wife at home. With him was his younger brother and devoted follower, who had taken the name Zuoren when he entered the Jiangnan Naval Academy. Like Shuren, Zuoren had tried his hand at journalism, although his earliest efforts, writing for *Nüzi shijie* [Female World] under a female pseudonym,[16] were of a radically different nature from his brother's. After graduating from the Academy, Zuoren also received a scholarship from the Jiangnan military training office to study in Japan, and on leaving Shanghai, he cut off his queue. He did not enter Kôbun Gakuin, however, but took private classes in Japanese. The two brothers lived together in Tokyo, collaborating on translation and journalistic projects. In reminiscences written after his brother's death, Zuoren recalls that they lived simply, adopting a Japanese way of living. Shuren was severely critical of other Chinese students in Japan; some, in return, also found him cold and aloof.[17] Zuoren also notes that at this time, Shuren grew a moustache, started smoking cigarettes, and liked to eat peanuts, Western snacks and sweets, and to drink milkshakes.[18]

Shuren apparently had no romantic or sexual encounters in Japan, unlike many other Chinese students who formed relationships that led to marriage (as happened to Guo Moruo)[19] or visited brothels (like Yu Dafu).[20] The absence of references to sex, love, or marriage in Shuren's own writings of the period (excluding his letters) is not conclusive proof of asceticism. The prospect of a loveless future as a married man may, nevertheless, have been a spur in his ambition to achieve eminence in public life.

Away from Tokyo, Shuren had lost touch with student journalism, and on his return he set his mind on a career in letters. (Seventeen years later, having established his reputation as a fiction writer, Lu Xun wrote that he had decided to quit medicine in 1906 to devote himself to literature [*wenxue*] after watching slides showing his countrymen passively watching Japanese soldiers execute Chinese people who had spied for the Russians. Although the meaning of the word *wenxue* was unrestrictive at this time, there is no contemporary evidence that Lu Xun intended at the time to devote himself to creative literature.) But his first attempt to set up a journal ended in failure, and the articles he prepared for it ended up in another provincial student magazine. Even on publication, however, Shuren's journalism made no discernable impact. Apart from the blow to his self-esteem, this failure left Shuren at age twenty-six with few qualifications beyond literacy for earning a livelihood. In April 1908, he supplemented his income by proof-reading; he also spent a considerable time on freelance literary and journalistic translation in 1907 and 1908.

In April 1908, Shouchang rented a house near Ueno Park; Shuren and Zuoren joined him, and two other Chinese students made up the numbers. Their servant was a young Japanese woman, Hata Nobuko.[21] Shuren, Zuoren, and Shouchang moved out of the 'house of five' in January 1909 and took up lodgings nearby. In March, Zuoren and Nobuko registered their marriage with the Tokyo police. Their liaison added to Shuren's responsibilities as head of the family.

Xu Shouchang returned to China in April 1909 to take up a post as dean in the Zhejiang Normal College in Hangchow [Zhejiang shifan xuetang]. Under increasing financial pressure and his mother's urgings, Shuren also agreed to return in July 1909, putting an end to his dream of going to Germany for further studies. On his return to China in August 1909, Shuren first taught chemistry and physiology at Shouchang's college, but following Shouchang's departure, he became unhappy with the school's administration and left as well. Invited to teach at the Shaoxing Elementary Normal School, founded by the educational reformer Cai Yuanpei, he left Hangchow in July 1910 and returned to Shaoxing. Two months after he had begun teaching in the autumn, he accepted the position of academic supervisor at Shaoxing Prefectural Secondary School, a new-style school, with responsibility also for the curriculum in biology and museum studies. Among the students at the school were several who later became close friends and allies, including Sun Fuyuan and Song Zipei.[22]

In Shaoxing, Shuren lived at the school and returned to the family home on Sundays. At home he relaxed with friends, usually over rice wine, and it may have been at this time that his heavy drinking began.[23] He also passed the time compiling pre-Tang works on the geography and history of the Shaoxing region, and started to collect examples of early fiction. Financial problems were troubling, however, and in March 1911, Shuren wrote to Zuoren urging him to return home; when that had no effect, he went to Tokyo himself in May to apply more pressure.[24] Rather oddly under these circumstances, he resigned from his own job in July 1911 to start a new project, compiling foreign articles on science and technology. He hoped to get a job as a translator in a Shanghai bookshop but was turned down.

Zuoren returned to China at the end of summer, like his brother reluctantly and without having graduated. Nobuko came with him, and they were formally married in Shaoxing. Zuoren did not immediately find work but helped Shuren in compiling old texts. Unable to speak Chinese, Nobuko was lonely and fell ill.

The republican revolution of 1911 opened up new opportunities for Shuren, and he returned to Shaoxing Secondary School in October. The following month, in return for his support for the new military governor of Shaoxing, he was appointed principal of the Shaoxing Elementary Normal School. His first work of original fiction, 'Huai jiu' [Memories of the past], written in classical Chinese, was produced that winter.[25] He did not submit it for publication nor follow it up with other stories, and his compilations also remained unfinished; although he was unable to hold down any teaching post for more than a few months, he was also hesitant about pursuing a writing career.

In February 1912, no longer on good terms with the military governor, Shuren resigned. He tried again to get work as a translator with a Shanghai publisher, and while he was waiting for the response, another opportunity arose.[26] The Republic of China had been proclaimed in Nanking in January 1912, and Cai Yuanpei was appointed Minister of Education. Cai Yuanpei invited Xu Shouchang to join him, and Shouchang in turn persuaded him to appoint Shuren as well. Shuren had repeatedly expressed his dislike of the narrow provincial life in Shaoxing, and this appointment was an invitation to return to a wider stage. When Shuren left Shaoxing for Nanking in February 1912, the move took him further away than could have been expected. The ministries were relocated to Peking in March 1912, and Shuren and Shouchang followed in May.

Zuoren remained behind in Shaoxing to look after Lu Rui, Zhu An, and their third brother, Jianren, as well as his own growing family. His first child, a boy, was born in May 1912, and Nobuko's younger sister, Yoshiko, escorted by her brother, came over to help out.[27] Zuoren began to teach English in Shaoxing in March 1913; soon after, Jianren began to teach science.

Shuren's main responsibility at the Ministry of Education was to supervise libraries, museums, and galleries. Cai Yuanpei resigned in July 1913, giving way before the government's growing conservatism. Without Cai Yuanpei's patronage, Shuren's prospects for promotion were poor; on the other hand, the ministry provided him with an income (most of which was sent back to Shaoxing) and the leisure to follow his own interests. One of the first entries in the diary he began to keep in Peking records a visit to Liulichang to buy books and curios, a custom he followed throughout his fourteen years in Peking. Hobbies of this period also included compiling new editions of traditional fiction, the study of Buddhist sutras, and collecting rubbings of old inscriptions, especially illustrations and portraits. Although he claimed to have few visitors, his diary records that friends joined him at dinner and accompanied him to sites of historical or scenic interest in Peking.

Shuren corresponded regularly with his mother, Zuoren and Nobuko and made visits to Shaoxing in 1913 and 1916. He was consulted about the plan for Jianren to marry Yoshiko, although he did not attend their wedding in February 1914.[28] Nobuko gave birth to two daughters in 1914 and 1915.[29] In contrast to his brothers, Shuren lived as a bachelor at the Shaoxing hostel in Peking. Whether or not his celibacy was total, it was presumably a contributing factor to the melancholy ascribed to him at this time.

At Zuoren's urging, 'Memories of the Past' was sent to the journal *Xiaoshuo yuebao* [Short story monthly], where it was published in 1913; although prominently featured, it failed to make an impact.[30] When the magazine *Xin qingnian* [New youth] was established in 1915 to promote intellectual and cultural reforms, Shuren gave it only cursory attention.[31] The literary career he had hoped for in 1906 seemed beyond his reach. Zuoren, on the other hand, was writing essays and short fiction at a great rate and seemed to have no trouble in placing them for publication.

When Cai Yuanpei was appointed chancellor of Peking University in January 1917, Shuren suggested that Zuoren be engaged to teach foreign languages. Zuoren left Shaoxing in March and moved in with Shuren at the Shaoxing hostel. Zuoren recorded in his diaries that they often had visitors whom they entertained with drinks and dishes ordered from nearby restaurants.[32] From August 1917 one of their frequent visitors was Qian Xuantong, a fellow-student from Japan now lecturing at Peking University. Qian Xuantong urged them both to write for *New Youth*. Zuoren was the first to respond, and the first of his many contributions appeared in February 1918. When Zuoren's appointment as a professor of Western literature and languages at Peking University was finally approved in September 1917, Shuren worked on his lecture notes as well as on his translations and poems.[33] Zuoren soon became the more active of the two brothers, and his prestige as a professor was enhanced by his innovative poems, essays, and translations in *New Youth* and other crusading journals of the new literature movement.

Shuren finally chose to enter the new literary scene in spring 1918. His first vernacular short story, 'Kuangren riji' [Diary of a madman] was written on 2 April and published in the May issue of *New Youth* under the pen-name Lu Xun. The first syllable, Lu, is his mother's surname; the second syllable, Xun, meaning swift, is homophonous with the word meaning to die for a cause, or to be buried with one's master, as a slave or concubine might be.[34] In May, he sent three poems in the vernacular to *New Youth* under the pen-name Tang Si, which could mean waiting or serving in the Tang dynasty; but *tang* also has a wide range of meanings, while *si* is homophonous with many words, including 'private' and 'death'.[35] He also contributed to the 'random jottings' column in *New Youth* using both Lu Xun and Tang Si as pen-names.

Shuren's attacks on old customs in *New Youth* were in ironic contrast to his own submission to convention. He voiced his frustration in a short essay written and published in *New Youth* in January 1919, signed Tang Si: 'What thoughts can I have staying at home all day, where the most I can see is a sickly sky through a square window? . . . What is love? I do not know either.' The essay goes on to discuss 'the evil results of loveless marriages', and continues, 'We shall cry of the bitterness of life without love, the bitterness of having nothing to love'.[36] A few months later, in another short essay entitled 'Women xianzai zenyang zuo fuqin' [What is required of us as fathers today] and signed with the same pen-name, he condemned people who resorted to brothels and concubinage, but few of his readers were aware just how unlikely it was that the author himself would ever become a father.[37] Only a handful of close friends knew that the satirist Lu Xun, the loveless Tang Si, and the middle-aged ministry official Zhou Shuren were the same person.[38]

Shuren did not take part in the May Fourth demonstrations in 1919, relying on younger friends such as Sun Fuyuan to keep him informed. That year he was especially preoccupied with family matters, having decided to buy a large house in Peking where the whole family could live together. The two brothers, Nobuko, her three children, and her brother moved into a courtyard house at No. 11 Badaowan Lane in the western part of the city in November.[39] On 1 December Shuren travelled to Shaoxing to sell the old family home, and on 29 December he escorted Lu Rui, Zhu An, Jianren, Yoshiko, and his two nephews to their new home.

Altogether fourteen stories and a much larger number of short essays, written under the names Lu Xun, Ba Ren, or Tang Si were published between 1918 and 1922. Although Shuren stayed aloof from the literary societies that had begun to proliferate, his stories and essays made him a leading figure among the new writers.[40] On Zuoren's recommendation, the head of the Chinese department, Ma Yuzao, invited Shuren to give a series of lectures on the history of Chinese fiction at Peking University in 1920.[41] He started his lectures in December, and in January 1921 he was also engaged part-time at Peking Normal University. His lectures became so popular that they attracted many auditors who later became close friends.[42] These students were among the first to realize that their teacher was the famous writer Lu Xun.

At home, the atmosphere was sometimes tense: Lu Rui blamed Zhu An for not having children while Zhu An blamed Shuren for refusing even to speak to her.[43] Shuren lived alone in a small room near the gate to the second courtyard but joined his wife and mother in the main set of rooms for meals. Zuoren, Nobuko, their children, and Nobuko's brother shared the rear courtyard with Jianren, Yoshiko, and their children. Day-to-day finances were managed by Nobuko, to whom Shuren and Zuoren handed over the greater part of their salaries, keeping back a small sum for personal expenses and, in Shuren's case, rather more for books and rubbings.[44]

There were two or three maids who looked after the children and did the cleaning, as well as a doorkeeper, a cook, a rickshaw puller, and so on.[45]

The household arrangements were changed in 1920 when Xu Xiansu, a native of Shaoxing and former student of Jianren's, was invited to move into Badaowan for the summer.[46] She lived in the rear courtyard but had her meals in the second courtyard with Lu Rui and Zhu An. Shuren joined them occasionally but began to take most of his meals with his brothers and their families in the rear courtyard. Xu Xiansu's elder brother Qinwen became a frequent visitor, and although Xiansu moved out when she began attending college in 1921 she returned on Sundays and during vacations. Sometimes she came with her classmate Yu Fen, also a former student of Jianren's who shared a house with her sisters in Zhuanta [Brick Pagoda] Lane.[47]

Jianren had not been able to find work in Peking, and in September 1921, thanks to Zuoren and Hu Shi's efforts, he left for a job as translator at the Commercial Press in Shanghai and editor of its magazines *Dongfang zazhi* [Eastern miscellany] and *Funü zazhi* [Women's magazine].[48] Yoshiko and the children continued to live at Badaowan, and he sent money back from Shanghai for their support; Shuren became Xiansu's legal guarantor. Shuren moved into a room in the first courtyard but frequently visited the rear courtyard for meals and to discuss literary matters with Zuoren and household matters with Nobuko.[49]

Zuoren began teaching part-time at Peking Women's Normal College in September 1922. By now a prominent member of the literary world, he enlivened Badaowan by inviting his colleagues back home and welcoming young writers to come and visit. One regular visitor was Yu Dafu, a celebrated young author of new fiction on themes of sexual and patriotic frustration. He had already had some contact with Zuoren, whom he knew as the translator of his favourite Japanese novelist, Satô Haruo, and it was Zuoren who introduced him to Shuren.[50]

In July 1923 Shouchang invited Shuren, Ma Yuzao, Lin Yutang[51] and other teachers from Peking University to lecture at the College. Shuren's short stories appeared in book form as *Nahan* [Outcry] by Lu Xun in August 1923. The critical success of his stories, the stimulation of his teaching, and the improvement in his financial situation from his extra duties should have brought Shuren stability as well as satisfaction, but life at Badaowan was irretrievably disrupted by a dispute between Shuren and Zuoren.[52]

Neither brother liked to talk about their dispute; even Lu Rui professed not to know the cause, and Shuren never discussed it with Jianren.[53] Shuren told friends that Zuoren was too extravagant and that Nobuko was mainly to blame, but their quarrel was too serious to be merely about household expenses. As well as complaining that her housekeeping budget had been reduced, Nobuko accused Shuren on 14 July of having made sexual advances to her. That day, Shuren noted in his diary that from then on he would eat alone in his own room. Whether or not Shuren did take liberties with his sister-in-law, she complained to Zuoren the following day. Zuoren believed her. On 18 July he wrote to his brother breaking off relations with him and delivered the letter by hand the following day.

Shuren decided to move out: custom decreed that the elder brother give way to the younger. Xiansu mentioned to his mother that there were some vacant rooms in the courtyard where the Yu sisters lived, and with Sun Fuyuan and Xu Qinwen acting as middlemen, it was soon arranged that that Shuren would move to Brick Pagoda Lane.[54] Shuren offered Zhu An the choice of staying at Badaowan or returning to Shaoxing, but she was reluctant to be left behind with the two Japanese women, while to go back to Shaoxing as an abandoned wife was not an attractive alternative; she chose to follow Shuren.[55] Together with their servant, Wang Ma, they moved into their new accommodation on 2 August.[56] Lu Rui remained at Badaowan but often came to visit and sometimes stayed overnight.[57] There were three Yu sisters: Fen, Fang, and Zao. Within a short while they were all on very familiar terms: Shuren called the two elder sisters 'Wild pig' and 'Wild cow'; in return they called him 'Wild snake'. Qinwen, Xiansu, and Fuyuan contributed to the informal atmosphere.

The rupture between the brothers was awkward for their friends, who on the whole preferred not to take sides. When Zhou Zuoren resigned his teaching post at Women's Normal College, Xu Shouchang persuaded him to stay on, and the two continued to correspond until the outbreak of the war against Japan.[58] Sun Fuyuan acted as the brothers' intermediary for *Yu Si* [Thread of Talk], a new journal; Shuren continued to contribute but declined to take part in editorial meetings, where Zuoren was the dominant figure.

Yu Dafu arrived back in Peking to teach statistics at Peking University in October 1923. On his first visit to Brick Pagoda Lane, Zhu An opened the door but she was not introduced to him and he remembered having been told that Shuren and his wife were not on good terms.[59] Another visitor to Brick Pagoda Lane, the young writer Zhang Tingqian, told him that in order to repress his sexual feelings Shuren did not wear padded trousers in winter.[60] By way of contrast, Yu Dafu's wife, Sun Quan, was an educated woman, and they had exchanged poems during their betrothal; moreover, despite their frequent separations, Sun Quan gave birth to four children between 1922 and 1928.[61] Although Yu Dafu complained of his loneliness in Peking in letters to Guo Moruo and Cheng Fangwu[62] and gave a picture of an unhappy marriage in his fiction, he could have considered himself quite fortunate compared with Lu Xun in 1923.

Shuren started teaching at Women's Normal College in October 1923. His main course, as at Peking University and Peking Normal University, was 'An Outline History of Chinese Fiction'.[63] In December 1923 he was invited by the student association to give a guest lecture to introduce their performance of Ibsen's *A Doll's House*. Another talk on 26 December, published a year later under the title 'Nuola zou hou zen yang?' [What happens after Nora leaves home?], became one of his best-known essays.[64] It was followed in the New Year by another of his best-known essays, on genius, and in the early spring of 1924 he wrote two of his most famous stories, both based on his 1919 visit home: 'Zhufu' [A new-year's sacrifice] and 'Zai jiulou shang' [In the tavern].

Living in Brick Pagoda Lane and giving lectures at three universities seems to have increased rather than interfered with his creativity, but their rooms were too cramped for a long-term stay. Borrowing money from Xu Shouchang and his ministry colleague Qi Zongyi, Shuren bought a house at No. 21 West Third Lane inside Fuchengmen in October 1923, but it needed renovation and they remained at Brick Pagoda Lane until early summer the following year. Shuren noted in his diary the rising tide of student protest at Women's Normal College in May 1924.[65] He nevertheless continued with his teaching, recording in his diary the salary payments that helped pay for his new housing.

Shuren, Lu Rui, and Zhu An moved into West Third Lane on 25 May 1924. The new house was also in traditional style, with two courtyards. A set of rooms on the south in the front courtyard housed a library and was also used for receiving visitors, and the family rooms were to the north. Lu Rui had the room on the east and Zhu An had the room on the west; the connecting middle room was for meals. Behind the middle room Shuren had an extra room built as a study, where he also slept and received friends. This room, which overlooked the back courtyard, was nicknamed 'the Tiger's Tail' [*laohu weiba*]. In addition to their maid, Wang Ma, a rickshaw driver also came to live in the compound; he rented a rickshaw that stood outside, mainly for Shuren's use.[66]

Compared to life at Badaowan and Brick Pagoda Lane, West Third Lane was desolate at first.[67] Among the first visitors were Xiansu, the Yu sisters, and a student from Women's Normal College, Wang Shunqing: the whole family came out to welcome them to their new home, and Shuren then showed them around.[68] In June 1924, Shuren went back to Badaowan to pick up his books and bookcases, but an altercation broke out between him and his brother. Zhang Fengju and Xu Zuzheng, two young writers who were on friendly terms with both brothers, were summoned by telephone by Zuoren to come and hear his complaints against Shuren.[69] Around the same time, rumours reached Peking that Jianren had fallen in love with one of his students and was living with her in Shanghai. Shuren consistently supported Jianren, but Zuoren was less forgiving. When Shuren also fell in love with one of his students the following year, Zuoren regarded both brothers as having given way to a ridiculous middle-aged desire to renew their youth through liaisons with younger women, and criticized both as 'polygamous'.[70]

Yang Yinyu, the new principal, was keen to retain the special staff recruited by Xu Shouchang. In the summer of 1924 Zhou Shuren was asked to stay on at Women's Normal College for the next school year. He had felt uncomfortable under the new régime and tendered his resignation, but he withdrew it at the students' request and duly signed a new contract.[71] Yang Yinyu paid her respects to Shuren in person at his home in September. That autumn Shuren presented a new course at the College, 'Symbols of Anguish', adapted from his translation of a book by that name by the Japanese scholar Kuriyagawa Hakuson.

Shuren's creative vigour continued unabated, possibly encouraged by the favourable reception of *Outcry* in 1924. Between 1924 and 1925 he wrote eleven stories, published first in periodicals and then in the collection *Panghuang* [Hesitation] in 1925. He also wrote several of his best essays at this time; in one, he even mentioned his wife, for the first and only time in his writing.[72] Shuren and Zuoren were also among the founders of a new literary journal, *Thread of Talk*, launched in November 1924 by two former students of Lu Xun's, Sun Fuyuan, and Li Xiaofeng.[73] Lin Yutang was a contributor, although personally and philosophically he was also close to the group around *Xiandai pinglun* [Contemporary review], founded by Hu Shi, Chen Yuan, and Xu Zhimo in December 1924.

By the middle of the 1920s, Zhou Shuren had become transformed into Lu Xun: professional writer, charismatic teacher, and pioneering scholar, surrounded by a band of disciples for whom he acted as a moral and intellectual leader, more famous finally than his younger brother. His diary records a constant stream of visitors and correspondence with other well-known figures from literary and intellectual circles such as Hu Shi, Gu Jiegang, and Yu Dafu. Nor was Lu Xun short of female company. He corresponded with several young women including Xiansu, Yu Fen, and Hu Pingxia, and was also friendly with a certain Miss Xu Yijing, who came to visit him in December 1924 along with Miss Gao Xiuying.[74] On New Year's Day, 1925, Lu Xun was invited to lunch by Sun Fuyuan, along with Xiansu, Qinwen, and the three Yu sisters; afterwards they went to see a film. He returned home in the late afternoon and wrote the following prose poem, 'Xiwang' [Hope]:

My heart is extraordinarily lonely.

But my heart is very tranquil, void of love and hate, joy and sadness, colour and sound.

I am probably growing old. Is it not a fact that my hair is turning white? Is it not a fact that my hands are trembling? The hands of my spirit must also be trembling. The hair of my spirit must also be turning white . . .

I knew of course that my youth had departed . . .

So I have to grapple alone with the dark night in the emptiness. Even if I cannot find the youth outside me, I would at least have a last fling in my own old age. But where is the dark night? Now there are neither stars nor moonlight, no vagueness of laughter, no dance of love. The young people are very peaceful, and before me there is not even a real dark night.

Despair, like hope, is but vanity.

New Year's Day, 1925[75]

4

Courtship: March 1925–August 1926

Xu Guangping addressed her letter to Lu Xun the writer, rather than to Mr Zhou, her teacher. She would have known little about Shuren, the married celibate who endured years of frustrated ambition and depression before his rise to celebrity only a short time earlier. Lu Xun, who had not taken part in any political activity since 1911, might seem an unlikely advisor on College protests. As a famous writer, however, at the very least he might be able to publicize the students' cause.

It is unlikely that one of her motives in writing was the pursuit of a romantic relationship. As well as being some seventeen years her senior, Lu Xun was shorter than she was, he smelled of tobacco and alcohol, and his teeth were badly stained.[1] The letter was not particularly private: before sending it, Xu Guangping showed it to her classmate, Lin Zhuofeng.[2] It was slapdash in appearance (perhaps deliberately so), and its tone fluctuated between extreme formality and impassioned disclosures of her anguished state of mind. There is also a touch of flirtatiousness in her line that 'depression becomes more intimate than a lover', and in her postscript she jokes about whether or not she should describe herself as female. Showing herself characteristically judgemental towards her fellow-students as well as the principal, she asks for guidance on what kind of political action would also be morally upright, imagining her teacher as a kind of Buddha wreathed in clouds of smoke.[3]

Lu Xun received her letter the same day and replied to it at once.[4] His style is also formal and although he responds at considerable length his tone is cautious and his advice is to exercise caution. There is nothing personal in his letter about her and no indication that he has ever paid any particular attention to her in class. Even his eccentric form of address, a formula commonly used between males of about the same age and social standing, does not suggest any existing relationship between them: he might have used it to any student, male or female, who wrote to him for guidance.[5]

Ignoring Lu Xun's advice, Xu Guangping decided to go public with an article in *Funü zhoukan* [Women's weekly], a magazine edited by the College student society and issued as one of three supplements sponsored by *Jingbao* [Peking gazette].[6] Her article, which appeared on 18 March, argued that appointing a woman as principal was not in itself sufficient to obtain good governance. A letter by a 'A Female Reader' appeared in *Contemporary Review* on 20 March defending Yang Yinyu. Xu Guangping's rejoinder appeared in *Jing bao fukan* [Peking gazette supplement] on 24 March.

On 3 April, the Ministry of Education sent an official to inquire into the situation at the College. The dean of studies, Xue Xieyuan, who was showing him around, gave orders for the students' protest posters to be taken down. The students countered by putting up posters on his office door attacking him. Xue Xieyuan then summoned Xu Guangping to his office 'to interrogate and intimidate' her. Later the same day he issued a statement blaming five students, including Xu Guangping and Liu Hezhen, for the troubles and submitted his resignation. Wang Jiuling, the new Minister of Education,[7] who had attempted without success to find a new principal, resigned on 13 April.

Zhang Shizhao (1881–1973), who had been Minister of Justice since October 1924, was appointed Acting Minister of Education on 14 April, and his plans to reform education were announced in *Peking Gazette* on 25 April. Unlike some of his predecessors, Zhang Shizhao's literary, political, and educational qualifications for the position were considerable. Although the same age as Lu Xun, he had a longer history as an active supporter of the revolutionary movement and had been closely associated with Liang Qichao as a student in Japan in 1905–7. He then spent four years in Edinburgh, sending back reports on contemporary British politics, society, and intellectual debates. On returning to Shanghai in 1912, he worked for the republican journal *Min li bao* [People's independence daily]. His contributions to the monthly *Jiayin zazhi* (The tiger magazine; published in Japan by Zhang Shizhao with Chen Duxiu and others, 1914–16) and its successor *Jiayin rikan* (The tiger daily, published in China in 1917) were major influences in the development of Chinese journalism. At the same time, he also held posts as advisor or secretary to a succession of high-ranking political figures, and was briefly chancellor of Peking University in 1922.[8] A frequent visitor to Nankai Middle School in the late 1910s when Zhou Enlai was a student there, he was a mentor and benefactor to Zhou in his early career[9] and is also thought to have helped the young Mao Zedong. To Lu Xun at this time, however, he was a detested supporter of Duan Qirui's warlord government.

While these events were taking place, the relationship between Lu Xun and Xu Guangping entered a new stage. In her letter of 20 March she referred to herself as *xiao gui* [young devil]; Lu Xun took up the epithet in his letter of 8 April, and she used it as part of her signature in her reply.[10] From that point on, their correspondence took on a teasing note which became more pronounced over the following days.

Xu Guangping's first visit to Lu Xun's home was with Lin Zhuofeng on 12 April. It was apparently an impromptu call, and two young writers were also present, Li Xiaofeng and Zhang Yiping.[11] When Lu Xun next wrote, on 14 April, he explained that although there were opportunities for them to meet in person they would not usually be alone, so that it was still 'convenient' to exchange letters. In another sign of their growing intimacy, he insists on doing small tasks for her, such as sending her copies of magazines. He also comments on how protective he feels about his students, in what seems to be a disguised reference to her in particular.[12]

Xu Guangping wrote down her impressions of the visit in her next letter; like his, this letter broke through the customary formality between teacher and student.[13] She called his room a '*mimi wo*' [secret nest], and although she parodied a conventional romantic style in the description that follows, it seemed that she had begun to feel physically attracted to him.[14] She showed uneasiness again about the time he wastes on trivial matters like sending her copies of magazines.

On 20 April, Xu Guangping and her classmates persuaded Lu Xun to take them on an outing to the Historical Museum at Meridian Gate, followed by a walk in Central Park: his initial reluctance to do this, and their triumph when they succeed, are the subject of a good deal of teasing on both sides. That evening, Xu Guangping wrote to ask for his advice on her career; fed up with private teaching, she thought of responding to an advertisement in the press for an editor.[15] In his return letter, Lu Xun promised to make inquiries on her behalf but warned that the advertised appointment was probably already fixed.[16] He encouraged her instead to send him articles for publication in the new journal he was about to launch, *Mangyuan* [The Wilderness], to be published as a supplement to *Peking Gazette*.[17] Somewhat taken aback at her enthusiasm about her visit to his home, he prolonged the moment by testing her powers of observation. In this letter, he also hints that he is 'not at all "detached"' in regard to 'the young devils'.

On 23 April, Lu Xun wrote two very different prose poems. The first, 'Si huo' [Dead fire][18] plays on the theme of extinction and self-sacrifice, a subject that Lu Xun had raised in his first letters to Xu Guangping. In Leo Lee's words,

> The way to the future for the 'dead fire' is a choice between extinction and self-sacrifice. . . . the metaphor of the dead fire refers to Lu Xun's inner predicament: entrapped in the cold, barren recesses of his heart is a passion which does not want to lie dormant forever; it cries out for a life of action which, according to the workings of paradoxical logic in the poem, ultimately leads to death. It seems that these pieces mirror a contradictory state of mind: one side of the poet is darkly pensive and resigned, but the other side pulsates with a certain restlessness for action.[19]

The second piece, 'Gou de bojie' [The dog's retort],[20] is in Lu Xun's bleaker voice:

> . . . the poet confronts the protagonist—a dog—in a prolonged debate, at the end of which the dog emerges as the winner. Again the fable preaches a reverse moral: that animals, not being snobbish, are better than men . . .[21]

If these prose poems relate to Lu Xun's actual circumstances at the time, 'Dead Fire' may refer to the growing but dangerous attraction between him and Xu Guangping, while 'The Dog's Retort' is his reaction to the growing tension between the two parties (the student protesters v. the authorities) at the Women's Normal College.[22]

As she became more confident in their special relationship, Xu Guangping lost some of her awe for his authority. She heightened her teasing over the Meridian Gate excursion and her visit to his home in her letter of 25 April, and her exaggerated humility at the beginning of the letter implies mixed feelings in regard to their teacher–student status:

In 'The World in a Cotton-padded Gown', the author [whom Xu Guangping mistakenly believed to be Lu Xun] seizes hold of his friends to bring them to trial, believing that they have taken his 'thoughts', 'friendship' . . . and even 'want to make me a machine for their personal use'. I then felt very guilty and examined my conscience to see if I was also one of those who 'plunders from all sides'. Alas, although I dare not regard myself as a friend, nevertheless, for a student to 'plunder' her teacher, that is still terrible! And to 'plunder' her teacher flagrantly, that is . . . terrible! This is why public morality is not as of old. Why should an ambitious scholar not arise and defend himself?

Following her earlier remarks about the gender demarcation between them, she conjured up the possibility of gender transformation:

If you were really 'compelled' or 'defeated' that day, in short it was because you had not yet attained Mahayana in the technique of 'transubstantiation', otherwise you could have transformed yourself into a female teacher, and then what harm would there have been in 'leading troops' (what I have just said is also 'preposterous', what is there so outlandish about a male teacher 'leading troops'), or transformed yourself into a woman . . ., and then what harm would there have been in going on the attack and breaking out of the encirclement? But if in the end you were 'compelled', is it because the dividing line [between the male and the females] is drawn too clearly, or because old conventions and habits are not easy to eradicate?![23]

Lu Xun prolonged the exchange about the Meridian Gate and her visit to his home with the ungallant remark that 'I have heard that young ladies are given to dissolving into tears.'[24] On a different level of intimacy, he discussed his motives for starting *The Wilderness*:

The condition of literature in China at the present time is really quite poor, though there are indeed some people who can write poetry and fiction. What we lack most are 'critics of civilisation' and 'critics of society'. My getting people together in *The Wilderness* to raise a clamour is mostly to attract henceforth new critics of this kind; although my tongue may be cut out, there are still people who will speak out and continue to rip the mask from the old society. Unfortunately, most of the manuscripts we have received up to now are still fiction.

Lu Xun was still writing fiction himself at this point.

In submitting an article for *The Wilderness*, Xu Guangping had to cope with Lu Xun in yet another superior role as her editor as well as her teacher. Her response was to be become very arch as she rejected being referred to as 'the young gentleman' in his letters. She suggested her class nickname, Melon Peel (a pun on the sound of her name), be used as the pen-name for her article: 'it may arouse some amusement.'[25] Lu Xun rebuked her levity but encouraged her in exaggerated terms to continue to submit material to *The Wilderness*.[26]

It seemed impossible for them to write at this stage without facetiousness. Although their eyes and thoughts might stray, the barriers of age and status that stood between them were substantial. It was a new crisis in College affairs that broke down these barriers and brought a deeper level to their mutual understanding and support.

Students in Peking had planned to hold a demonstration in front of Tiananmen on 7 May, National Humiliation Day, commemorating Japanese demands to Yuan Shikai's government in 1915 for the surrender of national territory. Demonstrations had already taken place, despite a Ministry of Education ban, on 1 and 4 May. The ministry then issued a decree forbidding schools and colleges to allow students to take the day off, and posted guards at school gates. Some students managed to break through and gathered in front of Tiananmen, where they had a bloody clash with armed police and mounted troops. Many students were wounded and more than a dozen were arrested. At two o'clock that afternoon, the students besieged Zhang Shizhao's home to protest against his ban on National Humiliation Day observances; some damage was caused to Zhang's house during the fracas. Armed police charged the protesters; many more students were wounded and eighteen were arrested.

The same morning there was also an incident at the Women's Normal College. A National Humiliation Day commemoration had been organized for nine o'clock in the morning, and the students were waiting quietly in the assembly hall. When Yang Yinyu on her authority as principal attempted to take the podium as chairman, however, the students created an uproar. The Student Council asked her to withdraw, but she pounded the table and demanded that the police be summoned. The students refused to be intimidated and Yang Yinyu was in the end forced to leave the hall.

On Zhang Shizhao's orders, the director of the education department in the Ministry of Education, Liu Baizhao, gave public support to Yang Yinyu. That afternoon, Yang Yinyu invited seven members of the Student Council to a dinner at the Sian Restaurant on Western Changan Avenue. Early on the morning of 9 May, she posted a notice announcing the expulsion of six members of the Council, who included Liu Hezhen and Xu Guangping.

Caught up in these events, Lu Xun and Xu Guangping suspended their letters to each other for almost a week.[27] Xu Guangping's next letter was on 9 May, breaking the news of her expulsion from the College and expressing outraged innocence. Lu Xun's response was not to her but to the press. In an article dated 10 May 1925, which appeared in *Peking Gazette Supplement* on 12 May, he attacked 'a college president' who 'hires thugs . . . to intimidate helpless students of her own sex' and who 'seized the opportunity provided by another student movement outside to rally jackals and foxes to help her expel students who have displeased her'. In a familiar pun on Yang's surname, he excoriated 'sheep in the guise of wild beasts' and 'wild beasts in the guise of sheep'.[28] This was Lu Xun's first published reference to the student protest, and his first act of political protest since 1911.

Following a mass rally on 11 May, the student activists marched to the principal's office and sealed off her rooms. They also posted a notice at the gate forbidding her to enter the College grounds. A meeting of students and staff was held on 12 May at which Lu Xun was present. On the same day, following another student demonstration outside his home, Zhang Shizhao resigned from his posts as Acting Minister of Education and Minister of Justice and left Peking.

Xu Guangping's next letter was still very sombre and is the only letter in which no alterations were made for publication.[29] She had just read one of Lu Xun's articles in *The Wilderness*, and was inspired to write a response. For this article, entitled 'Huaiyi' [Doubt], she chose the pen-name Jing Song. She did not explain the origin of this pen-name but it could be interpreted as 'respect [my mother] Song',[30] her choice of her mother surname echoing Lu Xun's. Lu Xun wrote back the next day, praising her article in his customary teasing way but then confessing that he was no longer in the mood for the kind of banter that characterized their April letters. He expressed pessimism at the outcome of the College protest and of the world in general, and again hinted that he was thinking of giving up writing as a hopeless cause.[31]

On 21 May, the Student Council invited members of the teaching staff at Women's Normal College to attend a meeting at four o'clock. When Lu Xun turned up, he found in the staffroom a notice from Yang Yinyu inviting department heads, full-time teachers, and members of the Teachers' Union to attend an emergency meeting at the Pacific Lake Restaurant at seven o'clock that evening; as a part-time teacher, Lu Xun was not included in the invitation. The same evening he wrote an article published in *Thread of Talk* on 1 June in which he dropped his pretence at anonymity, named the college and its principal, defined Yang Yinyu's attitude towards her students as that of a traditional mother-in-law towards her daughters-in-law, and related a vision of 'educationalists murdering students between cups of wine under the bright candelabra . . .'.[32]

Lu Xun also drafted a public statement supporting the students, which appeared in *Peking Gazette* on 27 May signed by seven of the College teachers. Xu Guangping wrote to him that evening to express her gratitude for their stand.[33] This letter was the most serious and personal she had written since the correspondence began just over two months earlier. After relating her exclusion from class (her name had been inked out from the class role), she went on to disclose her early encounters with unhappiness: the deaths of her brother and father, then her own illness, and her attempted suicide in her first year at Women's Normal College. She concluded with a subdued kind of teasing, scolding Lu Xun about his heavy drinking and smoking. Earlier, on 28 May, Xu Guangping had paid her second visit to Lu Xun's home, accompanied by her classmate Lü Yunzhang; this time there were no other visitors present, although Lu Yan turned up later, but apparently Lu Xun had rather a lot to drink.

The teachers' public statement supporting the students prompted a response from Chen Yuan, head of the English department at Peking University and one of the editors of *Contemporary Review*. In the statement, presumably to verify their identity, each of the seven teachers had written down his university affiliation and place of origin; as it happened, all except one were from the Chinese department of Peking University and were originally from Chekiang. In his column 'Xianhua' [Idle chat], written under his pen-name Xiying,[34] Chen Yuan claimed that the statement confirmed the rumour that the unrest at Women's Normal College 'was incited by teachers in a certain university department from a certain locality, now occupying positions of power in Peking educational circles'. He claimed that 'the educational world . . . is like a stinking latrine, which it is everyone's duty to clean up'.

Lu Xun expressed surprise and anger at Chen Yuan's article in his next letter to Xu Guangping:

On the pretext of 'rumour', Xiying's article portrays this agitation as 'incited by teachers in a certain university department from a certain locality', which clearly refers to 'teachers in the Chinese department from Shaoxing'. I don't know about the others, but when it comes to my denunciation of Yang Yinyu, it was after this agitation had started, but the generals of the Yang clan have nevertheless falsely incriminated me, in what can only be called an exceedingly vile way. But whether I'm from Chekiang or anywhere else, once I have started on my denunciation it will continue. Yang Yinyu does not have the power to excise my tongue, so she will have to suffer my denunciations for a while yet.[35]

His response to Xu Guangping's revelations in her letter of 27 May expressed distress at her sufferings. He urged her not to be infected by his own dark outlook on life, and encouraged her to continue to write for *The Wilderness*: 'When the "troubles" are to some extent resolved, the "harmful mare" should send some more discussion articles.' The term 'harmful mare' [from *hai qun zhi ma*; the horse that harms (or leads astray) the herd; abbreviated to *hai ma*] was a reference to a phrase in Yang Yinyu's statement noting that the six students are being expelled in order to avoid 'harming the others'.[36]

News of the May Thirtieth Incident reached Peking on 31 May 1925. On 1 June, *Peking Gazette* reported that a crowd of more than ten thousand people, protesting at the arrest of more than a hundred demonstrators in the International Settlement in Shanghai, was fired on by Indian police under British command; ten people were killed and many more wounded. The incident inflamed the Peking students, who immediately organized a rally in the capital. Lu Xun, however, was just as inclined to blame the Chinese as the British,[37] and his writing continued to dwell on College affairs and Chen Yuan's defence of Yang Yinyu. His rebuttal to Chen Yuan's attack appeared on 1 June in *Peking Gazette Supplement*, under the title 'Bing fei xianhua' [Not idle chat].[38]

In Xu Guangping's next letter, she criticizes his 'indulgence in alcohol' but softens it by confessing that 'the young devil also frequently indulges.'[39] This is her second reference to Lu Xun's drinking problem, which becomes a persistent topic over the next few letters. In reply he wrote, 'In fact I don't drink much at all, I am well aware of the dangers of drink. There are many times now when I don't drink, as long as no-one is urging me. There is no reason why it would not be possible to live a little longer'. There is another hint of their closer relations in his signature, which appears simply as 'Xun'.[40] Lu Xun was less than frank about his drinking, as Xu Guangping was soon to find out. Around this time, Lu Xun was buying for his own consumption mainly Fen liquor (one of the most lethal of the famous grain-based spirits) and whisky. According to his friend and colleague, Shen Jianshi, he was addicted to tobacco, alcohol, and sweets.[41]

The Peking demonstration in protest at the May Thirtieth Incident was arranged for 3 June, starting out from Peking University and heading for Tiananmen. Several dozen universities and colleges and some 50,000 students took part, Xu Guangping among them. Although dismayed by the competition between Peking University and Peking Normal University activists, she was greatly cheered by the opportunity to stage a side-protest against Yang Yinyu, who had come out to watch, and happily adopted Yang's abuse of her as a compliment: 'Teacher, you see how this "harmful mare" is so unbridled that she is unmanageable. What can be done?'[42]

Lu Xun stayed at home, writing attacks on intellectuals like Chen Yuan and Xu Zhimo who were critical of the student movement against the Western powers and Japan. Lin Zhuofeng went to see him on 5 June to collect donations for the 30 May protesters. She may have brought back a report that he was drinking, because Xu Guangping returned to the subject on 5 June: 'There are always plenty of people to 'urge one to drink' and there are always plenty of dishes around to go with drinking; for my part, I only request that you put aside and pay no attention to outside elements.' But as if in compensation (and perhaps also in response to his change in signature), her opening and closing salutations revert to her early mock-respectful tone.

At the College, the students were on strike, the principal had left, and the dean of studies and the head of general administration had resigned. Among the students there was much activity: 'lecturing, collecting donations, propaganda, and so on'. But with the summer vacation coming soon, Xu Guangping foresaw how the strike would dissipate as the students returned home, and that as a boarder, she was in a particularly vulnerable position. Also troubling was Lu Xun's silence. After a week had passed with no reply to her last letter she wrote to him again, showing signs of strain. She makes a great fuss about her own drinking and dwells on their difference in status:

> This evening after getting 'slightly drunk' (?), I hastily dashed off a short article; taking my inspiration from the circumstances, I have given it the title 'Alcohol Addiction'. For a long time the Shanghai incident has left me so troubled that I 'cannot play a tune'! Hence I am acutely aware of its crudity, and hope in your distinguished positions as 'editor' and 'teacher' you will probe and prune it. If it manages to escape 'the white light' and scrape through the seventeenth examination, I ask you please to list it at the very bottom of the honour roll of X issue of *The Wilderness*, and I shall be 'immeasurably honoured and moved to tears of gratitude'!
>
> Respectfully awaiting denunciation!!!!
> The young devil, Xu Guangping[43]

Lu Xun received her letter on 13 June and responded the same evening with apologies for having been busy:

> To be bored is more terrible than anything else, because it is produced from inside oneself and there is usually no remedy for it. Drinking can help, but it can also make things worse. In the summer vacation when I have more leisure, I should like to rest for a few days, doing absolutely nothing and reading absolutely nothing. But I don't know if this would be possible . . .

Your earlier letter opposes drinking, how is it that you became 'slightly drunk' on this occasion? There are too many fine words in your masterpiece; I propose to delete some of them and then grant it a place in issue X of *The Wilderness*.[44]

After mailing the letter on 14 June, Lu Xun received a visit from Xu Guangping and Lü Yunzhang that afternoon. A few days later, he wrote two particularly bitter prose poems expressing disgust for mankind and condemning self-sacrifice as meaningless. They appear to match the pair described above. In 'Shidiao de hao diyue' [The lost good hell],[45] dated 16 June, Lu Xun describes man as worse than the devil (i.e. worse than being a dog); in 'Mujie wen' [Epitaph],[46] dated 17 June, the setting is even more desolate than hell:

. . . the ghost of a bizarre serpent-monster tells his story through the hollowed spaces of an eroded tombstone: . . . Inscribed in this imaginary epitaph, dedicated to that strange incarnation of the martyr spirit that takes revenge by inflicting pain upon himself, is the message of a final insoluble paradox: now that he is dead, how can he ever find out the meaning of his life and his sacrifice?[47]

The former resembles 'The Dog's Retort' as a response to the political manoeuvrings at the College; the second, like 'Dead Fire', expresses despair at his own ghost-like existence. Although he was attracted to the young women around him, Lu Xun dared not fall in love, having sacrificed sexual fulfilment for the sake of his mother and social respectability.

Xu Guangping's next letter is curious. She addressed him as 'Respected Teacher Mr Lu Xun' (as in Letter 2 and more recently in Letter 27) although there was no obvious reason for her to do so, and referred again to his home as 'a secret nest'. Although still depressed, contemplating the alternatives 'to throw myself into a river clasping a rock' (i.e. commit suicide as a political act, in the manner of Qu Yuan) or to go mad, she then assured him that 'the young devil is really an ordinary person who eats and sleeps well, who laughs and enjoys herself just like everyone else'. Her final words are for him 'to quaff another cup'.[48] Her mixed emotions seem to echo his as she veers between threats of suicide and reassurances of normality.

Zhang Shizhao returned to Peking on 18 June 1925, letting it be known that he had warlord backing in the form of money and force if needed. Anticipating his return to office, Yang Yinyu put a notice in several papers that she was enrolling students for the new academic session. Four heads of department from Women's Normal College petitioned the government on 17 June for the appointment of a new education minister to settle College affairs. Meanwhile, Peking students went ahead with plans for anti-British and anti-Japanese demonstrations in Peking on 25 June. Under ordinary circumstances, Xu Guangping would most likely have taken part in the demonstration, despite the danger; it was perhaps for that very reason that Lu Xun arranged a diversion.

Dragon Boat Festival, which that year fell on 25 June, was a public holiday, and Lu Xun had invited Xu Guangping to his place for a meal, after which they would visit the fair at the nearby White Dagoba Temple. Also invited were Xu Xiansu, Wang Shunqing, Yu Fen, and Yu Fang. But what should have been a pleasant occasion ended badly: egged on by the young women, Lu Xun got very drunk. At one point he pressed Xu Guangping's head down (to make her shut up?), and he also shook his fist at the Yu sisters, who burst into tears. The guests decided to go to the White Dagoba Temple by themselves. Lu Xun continued drinking alone, and when he went to the temple some time later he was unable to find them.[49]

Xu Xiansu blamed Xu Guangping for this incident, telling her that drinking was bad for Lu Xun's health and that his mother disapproved. That evening or the next day, Xu Guangping wrote to apologize.[50] Lu Xun received her letter on the morning of 27 June. His reply the next day, headed 'Instruction' without any opening salutation, is unusually defensive and wholly unconvincing:

> You young ladies can only think of ways to exaggerate after you have fled back to your own nests; in fact your courage is as small as a sesame seed (and a very small one at that) and your abilities only extend to joint flight. In order to gloss over your flight, you say 'I was about to hit people with something' . . . But after 2:00 p.m. that day I drank six more cups of Shaoxing wine and five bowls of grape wine. I then went to the White Dagoba Temple four times, but unfortunately you had all fled and I couldn't find you . . . To sum up again, I was by no means drunk on Dragon Boat Day and I was not 'about to' hit anyone. As for 'bursting into tears', it's a specialty of young ladies and has nothing to do with me . . .. But my plan was only to shake my fist at the two young ladies from 'a certain locality', no more; because these two young ladies have recently come under the influence of the Grand Tutoress . . .[51]

Xu Guangping wrote again on 28 June, still blaming herself for having encouraged him to drink too much and again apologizing at length.[52] Lu Xun replied on 29 June:

> Last night, or perhaps this morning, I remember having sent you a letter that should have reached you by now. I have just received your missive of the 28th and must write a few lines in answer, that is, to ask if the reason for the young devil's repeated and endless apologies, in fear and trepidation, is that she may have been listening to some rumour or other from a young lady from 'a certain locality' [i.e. Xu Xiansu]. (Refuting a rumour will not necessarily put an end to it.)
>
> Firstly, alcoholism is a possibility, but I am certainly no alcoholic. Even if I were, it would still be my own behaviour and nothing to do with anyone else. Now that I have reached my half-century and hold the position of lecturer, must I not even exercise my own judgment about how much alcohol I can consume, and even suffer irritation from babes in arms? This is surely impossible!
>
> Secondly, I will certainly not accept any 'prohibitions'. Even my mother does not forbid me to drink. Up to the present I have been truly drunk only one and a half times, and was by no means as moderate as I was this time.
>
> In order to gloss over her flight, however, the young lady from 'a certain locality' will certainly elaborate on this story, which was picked from I don't know where (it may have been obtained from the Grand Tutoress), so that the young devil couldn't help panicking and apologising endlessly. But, whether it is the Grand Tutoress or the Supreme Grand Tutoress her observation is still not necessarily correct. I know myself that I was not in the least drunk that day, even less to the point of being stupid, and I remember in full shaking my fist at my 'landladies' and pressing down the young devil's head, nor have I forgotten the wretched business of everyone taking flight.[53]

Xu Guangping replied to both letters on 30 June in a more playful mood, denying that they had 'fled' the 'secret nest'.[54]

The Dragon Boat Day incident was another turning point in their relationship.[55] On 2 July, Xu Guangping made her first visit alone to Lu Xun's home, followed by an evening visit with Xu Xiansu and Wang Shunqing on 6 July. The mutual teasing in their letters took the form of elaborate salutations or mock-abuse. Writing on 9 July, Lu Xun claimed that the reason that her 'masterpieces' were published so frequently in *The Wilderness* is because the magazine 'is in the grip of famine' but that if she allowed herself 'to grow lazy and perfunctory, I will have to attack you violently: so be careful!'[56]

Lu Xun's prose poems over these few days reflect his changing moods. 'Tuibaixing de chandong' [Tremors of degradation],[57] written on 29 June, is an especially pointed attack on the futility of life, sacrifice, and procreation; 'Li lun' [Expressing an opinion],[58] dated 8 July, is aggressively sarcastic; in 'Si hou' [After death],[59] dated 12 July, he sees himself as a battered sacrificial victim. This is followed by a long pause; the next prose poem appeared in December.

Between 13 and 17 July, five letters passed between Lu Xun and Xu Guangping, all of which were omitted from *Letters between Two*.[60] Although they do not contain exchanges of conventional endearments or other romantic language, they are more playful, relaxed, and happy than previously, and their exclusion from publication suggests that they were felt to be too personal. On 19 July, Xu Guangping visited again with Lü Yunzhang; on 21 July she came with Qi Zongyi, and Wang Shunqing turned up with all three of the Yu sisters; and on 27 July she came with Xiansu and Shunqing. When his health took a turn for the worse, Guangping, Xiansu, and Shunqing on a visit to his home on 28 July urged him to take better care of himself. Lu Xun wrote to her at the end of July to explain why he had decided against publishing her latest submission to *The Wilderness*.[61] Then the correspondence ceased. Their courtship had been launched, and they were meeting frequently and in private. Letters were no longer needed.

Over the summer of 1925, Lu Xun was occupied with several publishing ventures. *The Wilderness* was reorganized as a fortnightly, and a new group, *Weiming she* [Unnamed society] was set up to publish another fortnightly and also a series of book-length translations. Xu Guangping began to act as his amanuensis, copying his manuscripts and proof-reading.[62] Xu Guangping, and through her Lu Xun, were both still very much involved in the student protest. It was around this time that Lu Xun finally turned away from his antiquarian activities and began instead to collect books on the Russian Revolution and the Soviet Union.[63] Yu Dafu, returning to Peking from his new job in Wuchang to spend the summer with Sun Quan (who became pregnant with their second child), found Lu Xun enjoying the battle. He had not previously met Xu Guangping and was not aware of their intimate involvement.[64]

Zhang Shizhao was confirmed as full Minister of Education on 28 July and immediately took measures to close the College down completely. Yang Yinyu set up premises the next day for enrolling students for the new semester in the autumn, and on 30 July, posters appeared all over campus announcing the dissolution of the Student Council. About thirty students were still living on campus, including Xu Guangping, and they were joined by students from Peking University and Peking Normal University in a show of support. At the students' request, Lu Xun and other teachers went to the College to act as witnesses that the female students were not getting up to improper behaviour with the male students. Soldiers and police surrounded the grounds on 1 August and stormed the buildings. Liu Hezhen and several others were wounded in the attack but the students stayed put. The authorities then ordered the gates to be locked and the electricity was cut off.

On 5 August, Lu Xun wrote denouncing the rumours of sexual impropriety and the authorities' actions on 1 August;[65] the following day he wrote another attack on Yang Yinyu.[66] Public opinion ran strongly against the authorities. The government withdrew the forces surrounding the College, restored the water and electricity supplies, and announced Yang Yinyu's resignation.

On 7 August, the students rented a house in Zongmao Lane to continue their studies. Xu Shouchang agreed to resume his former post as principal, and Lu Xun was among the sympathisers who offered to give lectures. A College Affairs Committee, which included Lu Xun and Xu Guangping as members, was set up the same day. One of its first acts was to refuse to accept the authority of the Ministry of Education. Zhang Shizhao dispatched a messenger to Lu Xun, offering to appoint him as principal if he would stop making trouble, but Lu Xun declined. Zhang Shizhao then asked Duan Qirui to approve Lu Xun's dismissal from the ministry, and the order was announced on 14 August. Xu Shouchang and Qi Zongyi then resigned in protest. Remarkably, Lu Xun's mother accepted the close friendship between her eldest son and his student with equanimity, even after it led to his losing his job.[67]

On 17 August, Zhang Shizhao declared that the College would be reorganized as the National Peking Women's University, with himself as head of the preparatory committee. On 19, 20, and 22 August, Liu Baizhao led a series of armed raids on the College, and some students were injured as they were driven out. Xu Guangping managed to escape to seek help from other student groups. Reports that she had disappeared caused Lu Xun to fear the worst, and he sent out allies to find her. The Ministry then announced that the six ringleaders, including Xu Guangping, were to be sent back under armed guard to their home towns. Xu Guangping, now homeless, moved in to the south wing at West Third Lane with Xu Xiansu. Xiansu stayed until the end of the year; it is not clear how long Guangping was there.[68]

Lu Xun's decision to offer shelter to Xu Guangping at the height of the protest movement was an act of generosity and compassion. But as news of their intimacy spread in Lu Xun's circle, it provoked intense and unsympathetic gossip.[69] Lu Xun was naively taken aback at the hostility shown among his disciples to the master appropriating for himself a much younger woman from their own cohort. The scandal was threefold: the disparity of age, the violation of the student–teacher bond, and the installation of Xu Guangping like a concubine in the family residence. Lu Xun appeared to be reverting to habits not sanctioned by the new morality, and his previous rectitude, which had marked him off from scandalous figures like Xu Zhimo, made his behaviour all the more shocking. Angered at what seemed to him disloyalty and possibly also feeling somewhat guilty at his own conduct, Lu Xun began to include younger people among his enemies. It is clear from his fiction and essays written that autumn that his temper was if anything even more vindictive than before.

The daily meetings of the Committee, suspended on 19 August, were resumed on 25 August but became less frequent. On 31 August, Lu Xun formally lodged a complaint against Zhang Shizhao. Xu Guangping and Lu Xun spent the Mid-Autumn Festival together, eating moon-cakes and drinking wine.[70] In early September, new premises for the College were set up at Zongmao Lane, and Lu Xun became a frequent visitor to the site, either for meetings of the Committee or in preparation for the new school year. Lu Xun suffered a recurrence of his TB at this time, due to fatigue, smoking, and drinking, and paid several visits to a doctor.[71] Zhu An was also ill and spent several days in hospital.[72] Xu Guangping often visited Lu Xun at home, but her visits are not recorded in Lu Xun's diary.[73] The College formally reopened on 21 September, and Lu Xun gave his first lecture two weeks later, on 9 October.

At some time in the summer or early autumn, Xu Guangping and Lu Xun became lovers. The event is celebrated in a short narrative (or prose poem) written by Xu Guangping on 12 October and published in December under the title 'Tongxing-zhe' [Fellow-travellers] with the pen-name Ping Lin.[74] The two characters in the narrative are an unnamed 'she' and 'he', but in the kind of gender reversal which characterizes their writing to or about each other, the 'she' stands for Lu Xun and the 'he' is Xu Guangping. The defining event in the essay is 'his' discovery that despite 'his' admonitions and deteriorating health, 'she' was still drinking heavily. When 'he' returned home he burst into tears, and at that moment realized that 'he' was in love with 'her'. The lovers are faced with all kinds of difficulties, but 'regardless of advantage or disadvantage, right or wrong, good or evil, with one heart and one mind they run towards love'. Classed as 'autobiography' in Xu Guangping's collected works,[75] this narrative has also been described as their oath or declaration of love.[76]

An equally odd piece, written around the same time and also signed Ping Lin, is 'Fengzi shi wo de ai' [Aeolus is my love . . .].[77] The narrative explains that Aeolus (or Master Wind, i.e. Lu Xun) is female but is regarded by the narrator ('I', i.e. Xu Guangping) as male because of the narrator's homosexual inclinations. This narrative was not published during the author's lifetime. If, as has been suggested, it is an account of how their love was consummated, Xu Guangping was the one to make the first advance by seizing Lu Xun's hands; he then enfolded her in a gentle but warm embrace. Xu Guangping's ambivalence on her sexual identity may owe something to her coldness towards her mother and worship of her father; it may also be related to her intense relationship with Chang Ruilin at the age of nineteen.

Whether or not Lu Xun enjoyed a similar ambivalence, he accepted Xu Guangping's role-playing and her determined wooing with a mixture of pleasure and caution. On 17 October, he wrote 'Gudu-zhe' [The loner], his bleakest fiction on the theme of unlikely heroes; on 21 October, he wrote 'Shang shi' [Mourning the dead], where the young writer Juansheng who seduces his idealistic girlfriend remains to the end unconscious of his own hypocrisy.[78] Neither of these stories were published at the time, although two later stories were published before being collected in *Hesitation*. After Lu Xun's affair with Xu Guangping had become common gossip, it was said that Lu Xun portrayed himself in the person of Juansheng: 'he could not have written such a story had he not had this experience'; Lu Xun's reaction was to laugh, and lament the difficulty of being a man.[79] If we accept an autobiographical reading, 'Mourning the Dead' could stand as a warning to Xu Guangping about the dangers facing transgressive women, or as a warning about the unreliability of younger men; it might also suggest a conflict in Lu Xun's own mind between love and ambition.

Throughout October and November Lu Xun made frequent visits to the College but records only one visit by Xu Guangping in his diary (8 November, when she came with Lu Xiuzhen). On 30 November, the Committee accompanied the students in a triumphal procession from Zongmao Lane back to the original campus; its restoration was formally announced on 24 December. Zhang Shizhao had submitted his resignation in November, and his residence was attacked and demolished on 25 December during a student riot.[80] The Committee welcomed the new principal and dissolved itself on 13 January, declaring itself satisfied with the outcome. Lu Xun was reinstated in his ministry post that month, and the affair was at an end.

Over the next few years, Lu Xun launched savage verbal attacks on many named and unnamed targets,[81] being especially vindictive about anything connected with Xu Guangping. In 'Not Idle Chat (3)', dated 22 November, for example, he referred to people stirring up 'slander' about a girl student as 'beasts'.[82] Lu Xun's most unpleasant remarks were directed very personally at Yang Yinyu, culminating in 'Guafu zhuyi' [On widow-ism], dated 23 November, which suggested that as a spinster she was unnaturally celibate and therefore unfit to act as a school principal.[83] Eventually even those on the same side felt embarrassed. In November and December 1925, first Zhou Zuoren and then Lin Yutang (both of whom had backed the student protest) broached the subject of 'fair play' in *Thread of Talk*.[84] Lu Xun was not deterred but he gave way to self-pity. Two prose poems, dated 14 and 26 December, attack the pretensions of scholars. In another prose poem, 'La ye' [Blighted leaf], also dated 26 December, Lu Xun refers both to his recurrent TB and to the love and concern for him shown by Xu Guangping (whose 'Fellow-Travellers' he had just arranged to have published).[85] Whether it was because his health recovered slightly or because of Xu Guangping's support, Lu Xun regained his aggression in propounding his doctrine of 'beating the dog in the water' in *The Wilderness* on 29 December, drawing into the second paragraph a reference to Chen Yuan, then warming up to a direct attack on both Yang Yinyu and Chen Yuan.[86] Although he did not openly criticize Hu Shi in these essays, it was around this time that their friendly intercourse ceased, presumably since Chen Yuan and Hu Shi were close associates.[87]

Chen Yuan saw himself as impartial in this verbal clash: he claimed that he played straight and Lu Xun played crooked.[88] For Lu Xun, there was no room for compromise or gentlemanly restraint in an affair that touched him personally and involved the woman with whom he was in love. Honour was in the end satisfied. During the student protest, Lu Xun transformed himself from one of his vacillating protagonists into an heroic figure, fearless in the struggle, firmly on the side of young rebels against the new establishment, and publicly labelled as an enemy of the government. His liaison with Xu Guangping gave him the need to prove himself, and the renewed vigour that resulted from it.

Lu Xun continued his attacks on Zhang Shizhao and Chen Yuan in January 1926 in essays such as 'Xuejie de san hun' [Three spirits in the teaching profession].[89] In February he began to write recollections of his childhood, studies in Japan, and teaching in Shaoxing, first published in *The Wilderness* and later reprinted under the title *Zhao hua xi shi* [Dawn blossoms plucked at dusk] in 1927. The first of these, dated 21 February, is marred by petty barbs against Zhang Shizhao, Chen Yuan, and Xu Zhimo. By the second essay, dated 10 March, he had for the moment shaken off this irritation, but the March 18 Incident gave new force to his old grudge.

On 18 March 1926, forty-seven students were killed in a demonstration to petition the warlord government in Peking. Among the dead were two students from the College, Liu Hezhen and Yang Dequn. Xu Guangping had taken part in the demonstration earlier that day and had intended to return to it after a hasty visit to Lu Xun's home, but Lu Xun had detained her there to copy some manuscripts, claiming that petitions were useless. When Xu Xiansu and Xu Shouchang delivered the news, Xu Guangping rushed back to the College only to find her two classmates' dead bodies still bleeding from their wounds.[90] There were protest assemblies at the College on 22 and 26 March, which Lu Xun attended, as well as their funerals on 25 March. Lu Xun's prose poem and essays commemorating the deaths are among his most moving works.[91]

Lu Xun's defence of the students and communist organizers[92] also ensured his place on the list of fifty-four proscribed intellectuals, which also included Zuoren, Xu Shouchang, Shen Jianshi, Ma Yuzao, and Lin Yutang, issued by Duan Qirui on 9 April. Nonetheless, the last of his prose poems, 'Yi jiao' [The awakening][93] (10 April) praises the young people he knew who continued to publish their ideas, and in comparison with 'Hope', it seems that Lu Xun had after all found some hope during the course of the past fifteen months. On 15 April Lu Xun went into hiding, that is, continuing to give lectures, pick up his mail at home and visit his friends during the day but taking refuge in a series of foreign-owned hospitals by night. Clashes between warlords from the north and north-east exacerbated the danger. Lu Xun returned to West Third Lane in early May, deeply in debt and in poor health.[94]

Lu Xun's contempt for the Duan Qirui régime and its supporters was not allayed by the feeble defence offered by Chen Yuan, who observed that the students should not have been demonstrating at all, and that those who urged them on were ultimately responsible for their deaths.[95] Slighting references to Chen Yuan also turn up in the third and sixth essays in *Dawn Blossoms Plucked at Dusk*, dated 10 May and 23 June, as Peking became an increasingly unpleasant environment.

Unable to operate effectively in the north, the Nationalist Party had established a so-called 'national' government in the rich southern province of Kwangtung alongside a provincial government that it also controlled. (References to 'the Party' in the correspondence invariably refers to the Nationalist Party.) Attracted by the prospects of working with a reformist régime, left-wing writers from the Creation Society such as Guo Moruo and Cheng Fangwu left for Canton that summer for jobs in the university or administration. The new government had its own currency and set up its own military force, the National Revolutionary Army, in August 1925. By 1926, the country was divided into two armed camps: the National Revolutionary Army in the south, and the warlord armies of central and north China. Although greatly outnumbering the revolutionary forces, the warlords did not present a united front; the Nationalist and Communist forces, on the other hand, set up a joint task force to expel the warlords and unite China under a single national government. The 'Northern Expedition' set out on 9 July 1926.

Lin Yutang, one of Lu Xun's colleagues at Peking University and Women's Normal College, was a native of Amoy [Xiamen], and his father, a Presbyterian pastor, was a good friend of the chancellor of Amoy University, Lim Boon Keng. Whether through his father's intervention or by fortunate coincidence, Lin Yutang was invited in May 1926 to become dean of the arts faculty and secretary of the Institute of Chinese Studies; his elder brothers Lin Mengwen and Lin Yulin and his younger brother Lin You were also at Amoy University. Before taking up his position in June, Lin Yutang took the opportunity to invite several of his Peking associates to teach in Amoy as well: Gu Jiegang and Sun Fuyuan were among those who accepted. To Lu Xun, he offered a joint appointment as professor in the Chinese department and research professor at the Institute.

It seemed like a good idea to leave Peking, not only because of the threat of political persecution. Despite the bravado of Xu Guangping's prose poems, it was awkward to conduct their affair under the gaze of Lu Xun's mother, his wife, their friends, and their colleagues. Living together in Canton or Shanghai might be less of a problem but there was no offer on the table for Lu Xun from either place, and he was not prepared to risk living off royalties. For Lu Xun to go to Amoy inevitably spelled separation, but being apart would put their feelings to the test and also give them time to work out an arrangement by which they could be together. The choices open to them were limited. Divorce was apparently out of the question, although Zhu An's feelings were otherwise not a major source of concern (they were never mentioned in the correspondence), and neither of them ever mentioned any legal consequences arising from adultery.[96] It was also never specified by either of them what exactly the problem was, but it was clearly his problem: it was Lu Xun, not her, who feared damage to his reputation or to hers, or was unwilling to offend his mother's sense of propriety. After some hesitation, Lu Xun accepted a two-year contract in the Chinese department and at the Institute. On 28 July he received the first instalment of his salary and travelling expenses.

Lu Xun later described himself as having 'fled to Amoy to escape persecution by Premier Duan Qirui and his stooges'.[97] He also hoped to find some peace and quiet in which to recover his health. In her 1941 reminiscences, Xu Guangping claimed that they left Peking partly for the sake of society and partly for financial reasons.[98] (The expression 'for the sake of society' at this period often meant work that contributed to public well-being, such as education; biographers usually drop the reference to their financial needs.)

In any event, Xu Guangping also needed to find a job; having graduated from the Women's Normal College, and with Lu Xun going south, she had no reason to stay in Peking.[99] Returning to Canton to teach was an obvious move. Her cousin Li Xueying had married Chen Yanxin, a lecturer in geology at Kwangtung University, and through him Guangping obtained a temporary position for one semester at her old school, Girls' Normal School; it was an advantage also that by this time she had joined a left-wing Nationalist Party group in Peking.[100] The prospect of reunion with her family was a doubtful benefit. As she told Lu Xun, her eldest brother had died leaving his widow with four young sons. The widow lived with Guangping's youngest sister in the family home, and Guangping was aware that although her elder brother gave some support, they were still in difficult circumstances and would look to her also for some financial assistance for the boys' education. Guangping confessed that she had mixed feelings about taking on this responsibility.[101]

Canton was not so very far from Amoy, and they discussed the possibility of reuniting there.[102] Xu Guangping stated in 1941 that they had made a pact to work for two years before meeting again.[103] It is not clear whether the period of two years was suggested by Amoy University or by Lu Xun.[104] Xu Guangping seems to have thought at the time that they would meet again within a year,[105] and it seems likely that Lu Xun planned to make a short trip to Canton from Amoy over the summer vacation.[106]

On 13 August Lu Xun was given a farewell party at the College, followed by lunch with Xu Guangping, Lu Xiuzhen, and Lü Yunzhang; in return he invited them to lunch at his home on 16 August. Another farewell lunch at which Xu Guangping was present took place on 21 August at Central Park. On 22 August Lu Xun gave an address to the College at a meeting to commemorate the anniversary of the College's disbanding the previous year.[107] All seemed well. Then on 30 August, four days after Lu Xun and Xu Guangping left Peking, Women's Normal College was reorganized as the Normal Department of the Peking Women's College; the new Minister of Education, Ren Kecheng, was the principal, and the dean of the new department was Lin Suyuan.[108] The College premises were taken over by force, Ren and Lin heading some forty security officers and soldiers from garrison headquarters.[109] As Xu Guangping and Lu Xun were soon to find out, their triumph had been premature; their departure was timely.

5

Separation: September 1926–January 1927

Lu Xun and Xu Guangping left Peking together by train on the afternoon of 26 August 1926. Many of their friends came to see them off, including Qi Zongyi, Gao Ge (Gao Changhong's brother), and Xiang Peiliang; Sun Fuyuan had gone ahead. The train arrived in Tientsin that evening, where they stayed overnight. In the morning Lu Xun bought postcards for Xu Xiansu and Qi Zongyi, and they boarded the Shanghai express at noon. They arrived in Shanghai on the morning of the twenty-ninth and put up at Huning Hotel. For them the journey had been a rare chance to be alone together; among the people seeing them off and those who saw them in Shanghai, it raised intense speculation about their relationship.

The following morning, with Jianren's assistance, Lu Xun moved to Mengyuan Hotel; later in the afternoon, he helped Xu Guangping move to the house of her uncle, Xu Bing'ao,[1] whose children Xu Guangping regarded as her younger sisters and brothers. That evening, Lu Xun went to the Beixin Press and the Kaiming Bookstore to see friends. On 30 August, Xu Guangping paid a visit to Lu Xun with one of her cousins, after which the two young women spent some time shopping and calling on other relatives. That night Shanghai's literary and intellectual world held a big party for Lu Xun, but Guangping did not attend. The next day Guangping called by again, and while she was there Gao Changhong showed up with another friend.

At midnight on 1 September, with his brother to see him off, Lu Xun went on board the 'Xinning' for Amoy, travelling 'Chinese class' (i.e. second-class). The same night, accompanied by two of her young male cousins, Xu Guangping boarded the 'Guangda' for Canton.

Xu Guangping re-opened the correspondence, writing in sections on board her ship; marking a new stage in their relationship, she addressed him in English as 'My dear teacher' and signed herself 'Your H M' [harmful mare]. Typically, despite a show of reluctance, she took part in propaganda meetings held on her boat. Xu Guangping expressed misgivings about their separation, which she described as being for only a year, and already began to think about how Lu Xun might make his way from Amoy to Canton.[2] Lu Xun stayed mostly in his cabin and maintained his customary reserve with his cabin-mate; catching sight of another ship on the horizon he wondered if it was hers, and hoped that she would write as soon as she had arrived (as if she might not). He postponed writing until a few days after his arrival in Amoy, foolishly imagining that he should wait until she had arrived in Canton. He continued to address her as 'Brother Guangping' and signed himself 'Xun'.[3]

The single topic above all that occupied their attention in the letters that followed was whether and when Lu Xun would come to Canton. Both of them took it for granted that this would be for the purpose of resuming their affair. She was persistent about this from beginning to end, only seeming to waver in order to challenge him. Lu Xun, by contrast, found it difficult to make up his mind even when opportunities offered.

On arrival, Lu Xun moved directly into makeshift accommodation at the Institute of Chinese Studies; Xu Guangping put up at a hotel for one night, stayed with Li Xueying and Chen Yanxin the following night, and then moved into temporary accommodation at her school's old site on 8 September.[4] It took some time for the rhythm of their correspondence to be established, and on many occasions their letters crossed or appeared to go astray, causing great anxiety. Another cause for unease was Lu Xun's health, especially his indigestion and his heavy drinking and smoking. The tone of the letters at the beginning, however, was generally relaxed and intimate as they exchanged information about their new jobs and conditions.

There was much to relate, for their circumstances were very different. Xu Guangping was back in her home town. Soon after her arrival she went to the family home in Gaodi Street to observe the anniversary of her mother's death. Yueping still lived at the old family home with Chongxi's widow; Guangping described them to Lu Xun as being lonely and sad.[5] Rather rashly she agreed to pay the school fees for her four orphaned nephews, but when her own salary was not paid in full, she was unable to make good her promise. On her first salary payment, she received in cash only a fraction of her nominal $180 per month; the rest was in bonds or paid over as donations to various worthy causes, and throughout her employment at the school funds for salaries were always short. Other relatives were not persuaded that she was short of cash, however, and kept pestering her for money.[6] Her cousin Chongqing, on the other hand, was now director of the provincial Department of Education and quite prosperous.[7]

Xu Guangping's main problem was at her school. The Kwangtung Provincial First Girls' Normal School was set up in 1907, at the former site of a Qing imperial residence. In 1923 the school moved to a new address, the old site being used for dormitories and an attached primary school, and the programme was upgraded from four to six years. The principal was Liao Bingyun, whose brother Liao Zhongkai had been assassinated by order of a right-wing Nationalist faction in 1925 when he was governor of Kwangtung. Xu Guangping's main task was to teach Sun Yat-sen's 'Three People's Principles' to each of the upper four years, a total of eight hours a week.[8] As a Party member, she was also appointed moral tutor, which meant that she was responsible for dormitory supervision and for propagating Nationalist Party doctrine.[9] Unluckily for her, right-wing students had gained the upper-hand in Canton and their influence had spread to her school. Xu Guangping soon found herself on the receiving end of the students' demands, facing accusations of being a communist because of her friendship with the principal as well as for her record of student protest in Peking.

Lu Xun was followed to Amoy by three of his Peking students and rejoined several former colleagues on the staff. His relations with students were mostly good throughout his stay: he helped with student publications but refrained from playing a leading role or acting as their spokesman, complaining occasionally about their demands on his time. He also remained on good terms with Lin Yutang throughout his stay in Amoy, and expressed appreciation for the kindness he received from Lin's family. He was critical, however, of the chancellor Lim Boon Keng[10] and the university's founder Tan Kha Kee,[11] whose Confucian views he mocked openly as well as in letters to Guangping.

Apart from Xu Guangping, Lu Xun had many other correspondents, including Xiansu, who had moved into West Third Lane to help look after Lu Rui and Zhu An; Xiansu also wrote separately to Xu Guangping. He also wrote frequently to Jianren, whose life was complicated by his low salary, his heavy drinking, and his affair with one of his former students, Wang Yunru.[12] He resumed his autobiographical sketches for *Dawn Blossoms Plucked at Dusk*, the last five for the most part free of his continuing preoccupation with his *Contemporary Review* opponents. He also wrote two updated historical fables, to be published in *Gu shi xin bian* [Old tales retold] in 1936,[13] and worked on other projects such as a topical history of Chinese literature. Although he complained that writing and teaching were incompatible, he was very productive, if not especially creative, in Amoy. His salary was generous ($400 per month), he had no administrative duties, and since no one enrolled in one of his three courses, he enjoyed a lighter teaching load than he had expected: these things made his existence tolerable. The incomprehensibility of the local language, the laziness of the servants, and the blandness of the canteen food were relatively minor sources of irritation. Later during his stay, he remarked to Xu Guangping on the poor standard of sanitation in Amoy.[14]

Lu Xun found himself with time on his hands: 'I'm even a little bored, so that I wish classes would start soon, and also that the term of my contract would soon be up.'[15] Boredom turned into irritation at his colleagues, who passed the time playing Peking opera records, flirting, and eating sweets.[16] His main target was a former colleague from Peking University, Gu Jiegang, newly appointed professor of history at Amoy; Lu Xun described him slightingly as a disciple of Hu Shi and a member of Chen Yuan's faction.[17] Lu Xun had been on good terms with both Gu Jiegang and Hu Shi but their relationship had soured over the Women's Normal College affair. He detested Huang Jian, who had been on the administrative staff at Women's Normal College and was now the dean's secretary. His closest associates were Sun Fuyuan and Shen Jianshi, but Jianshi was anxious to return to Peking. A few days later, Lu Xun tried to resign his position in the Institute and wrote to Guangping that he might not be able to last a full year.[18]

Picking up his hint, Xu Guangping asked why he wished his contract would soon be up and wondered if she should come for a visit to Amoy.[19] Lu Xun failed to respond to this suggestion and dampened the prospect of his resignation: he'd only meant that he wanted the time to pass quickly until 1928.[20]

Xu Guangping next suggested that she leave her school at the end of the semester,[21] and then that Lu Xun should come to Kwangtung University,[22] where he had several friends and acquaintances including Yu Dafu.[23] Realizing belatedly that he had raised false hopes with his complaints, Lu Xun wrote back that 'on the whole, I would prefer to teach here for at least one year, otherwise I would already have fled to Canton or Shanghai'.[24] In his next letter he admitted, 'At the beginning I never stopped thinking about Canton, but after learning about the situation there, I haven't been thinking about it much at all lately . . . The main reason I am not too happy here is primarily because most of the people around me bore me with their dull conversation . . . [But] As long as I can find peace of mind there's no reason why I can't stay on here quietly for the time being'.[25] Yet the very next day he changed his mind again. Kwangtung University, which had been renamed Zhongshan University [Sun Yat-sen University] and was being restructured, had sent telegrams inviting him, Lin Yutang, and Shen Jianshi to go to Canton to supervise the reorganization. On 16 October Lu Xun wrote, 'So I am very much inclined to leave AU by the end of this semester at the latest'.[26]

This was the last exchange for several weeks where each answered the other's most recent letter. The crossing of letters in the mail was caused by several factors, including the inefficiency of the postal delivery at each end, delays to the mail boat as a consequence of the war, and Xu Guangping's resort to sending letters by express mail, which sometimes took longer to reach Lu Xun than ordinary mail. The main reason was that both of them were compulsive about writing almost every day, while the impulse to send a letter as soon as one arrived from the other was hard to resist. The confusion caused by crossed letters added greatly to Xu Guanpging's distress at Lu Xun's failure to make up his mind to come to Canton, either for a visit or for a longer stay. (The arrangement adopted by Lu Xun for *Letters between Two* makes the crossed letters hard to follow: his letters form the main chronological sequence, while some of her letters follow his even if they were written earlier.)

On 18 October, when Xu Guangping received his letter of 10 October, she expressed relief that he was 'fairly contented' but wondered if it was to deceive her into not worrying. However, she still urged him to come to Canton: 'If you are interested in coming to Kwangtung to work there are quite a few of your old acquaintances here, so now is the right time to try. But this naturally is only if it is quite impossible for you to continue in your present position.' This and the next letter she sent express.[27]

Within a few days Lu Xun had changed his mind yet again, deciding against an immediate visit to Canton and still ambivalent about fulfilling his contract in Amoy: 'I'm not making long-term plans . . . I'm really much lazier than before, and often relax and enjoy myself without doing anything at all.'[28] 'We can put off talking about another position for me elsewhere, because although I've no intention of staying here for any length of time, there is no immediate need for me to decide to leave, so I actually feel very much at ease.'[29] Sun Fuyuan left for Canton on 20 October alone.

Lu Xun was aware of his unpopularity with his colleagues, but even his discomfort at the wear and tear of academic life failed to stir him into action.[30] Of more immediate concern was Gao Changhong's quarrel with his protégé Wei Suyuan.[31] Lu Xun at first did not want to become directly involved, but when he learnt more about Changhong's attacks on him personally he became deeply disturbed. At the time he did not disclose the nature of Changhong's abuse to Xu Guangping, but it was around this time he wrote the first draft of his horribly surreal story of bloodthirsty revenge, 'Zhu jian' (Forging the swords).[32]

Xu Guangping's next letter sounded even more depressed, partly because of family problems but partly because of Lu Xun's reluctance to break his contract with Amoy. Her own contract had only a few months to run and she saw no prospects of staying on at Girls' Normal. A member of the provincial government offered her a job as head of the Swatow Municipal Women's Bureau and concurrently principal of the Swatow Girls' Secondary School, but her acceptance would in effect rule out their reunion for some time. Ever hopeful, she turned down the Swatow offer and turned up the pressure on Lu Xun: 'But supposing that someone were to invite you [here], I don't see why you shouldn't give it a try.'[33] It was not until 23 October that she received his letter (dated 16 October but posted on 19 October) announcing the telegram from Zhongshan University; she immediately wrote another express letter urging him to take up the invitation, then go back to Amoy, break his contract and finally return to Canton.[34]

Lu Xun received her letter of 22 October on 27 October, but when he answered the following day, her more urgent letter of 23 October had still not arrived. His letter expressed concern, offered sensible advice, and showed that he shared her feelings, but it did not respond to her need for a show of commitment on his part.[35] Even when he received her letter of 23 October on 29 October, he still did not understand, repeating that it was inconvenient to go to Canton right away but adding that 'As for where I'll go in the next half-year, that's not in question. I won't go to either Peking or Shanghai, and if there's nowhere else I can still hang around here for the rest of the year. It's solely up to me now whether I go or stay, and outsiders' machinations can't for the moment dislodge me.'[36] He put forward two reasons for his hesitation: he did not want to desert Lin Yutang, nor was he willing to be pushed out by Gu Jiegang's 'faction'.

On 27 October, having received his indecisive letter of 21 October, Xu Guangping returned to the subject of a post for him at Zhongshan University; this time she mentioned the lower salary and the high cost of living as possible disadvantages, although Lu Xun had not listed them as factors in his indecision.[37] Nevertheless, it was this letter that seemed to sway him: 'If ZU definitely wants me to come and if I can be of some value after I get there, then I'll go there before the beginning of the semester [i.e. in March]. Nothing here presents a problem apart from it not being very fair to Yutang.'[38] In his next letter, however, Lu Xun explained that he was by no means sure that he was wanted by the university and was reluctant to place too much hope in getting an offer from them. (In the published version, Lu Xun suppresses these doubts and makes the decision appear to be purely a matter of his own choice with the added line: 'Anyway, it's of no great consequence whether I go or not, it seems, so there's no need for me to rush down there.'[39]) In the same letter, he joked about how he refused to answer straightforwardly the administration's questions about Sun Fuyuan's movements (i.e. playing the same kind of game as they played with him).

Sun Fuyuan returned from Canton on 6 November with a verbal offer to Lu Xun of a professorship at Zhongshan University. The next day Lu Xun wrote to Wei Suyuan that he had decided to leave Amoy because it was so dull.[40] Nevertheless, in a long letter to Xu Guangping in three parts dated 6–8 November, Lu Xun continued to dither. First he offered a visit at the lunar New Year when he would have a three-week break; then he said that he may well accept after all unless the teaching load were too heavy (it didn't matter about the salary), which would interfere with his writing; and then he concluded 'we should still see how the situation looks later on.'[41] Unless it was his fear of scandal, revived by gossip from Canton relayed by Sun Fuyuan on his return, it is hard to imagine why Lu Xun was so reluctant to commit himself.

Xu Guangping replied to Lu Xun's affectionate but evasive letter of 28 October on 4 November. Her manner was detached, and she noted that she might be too busy to write over the next few days because of the school protest.[42] Lu Xun received it on 8 November and replied the following day. He also seemed distant: 'In the last few days I've now felt somewhat hesitant about going to Canton to teach, in case the situation there might be just as when I was in Peking. It would be hard to stay in Amoy for a long time, of course, and there's nowhere else to go; it really is a little worrying.'[43] It is not clear if he is worried about the political situation or by the prospect of scandal, but a few days later he expressed concern that 'lots of people' knew him in Canton so that 'in a matter of days I might be just as busy there as in Peking'.[44]

The student protest at Xu Guangping's school reached its height in early November: the militant faction threatened violence against the principal (sending her a letter with a drawing of a gun), and even the students who used to be friendly to Guangping ignored or even glared at her. Reading Lu Xun's half-hearted letters of 28 and 29 October, Guangping issued what for her came close to an ultimatum on 7 November:

> Until the day the semester finishes I will remain in charge, but as soon as it is over I shall leave immediately. If Swatow is still short of teachers then I will go to Swatow; otherwise I'll look for some other job . . . It is all right if you don't come to Kwangtung for the time being; I certainly won't insist on your coming. Nevertheless when I hear of the situation in Amoy, I'm afraid you won't be able to put up with other people's insults, alone and depressed with no-one at your side to comfort you.[45]

She even failed to rise to his attempt to provoke her about his foolhardy jump over a fence behind his building, which resulted in two small cuts to his leg:[46]

> When [I read how] you jumped over the barbed wire fence, I silently conjured up a vision of a small child jumping back and forth, and even though I was afraid he would stumble and injure himself, it was a pure delight to see. If this were 'a reprimand', then my educational

principles would be fundamentally in error. It is in the nature of children to be lively, and while we may guide them towards proper conduct it is not permissible to suppress them deliberately. This is what I advocate as an educationalist.[47]

(The edited version of this passage in *Letters between Two* is rather stiff, but the affectionate tone of the original softens the sense of strain in the rest of the letter.)

Xu Guangping next wrote on 11 November, responding to his letters posted on 2 and 5 November. Having calmed down a little, she assured him that she would not leave Canton until after the New Year vacation. She also resumed her wifely attitude towards him, knitting a vest for him now that the weather had turned cold.[48] A couple of days later, during a few days of relative quiet at the school, she bought him a present, a seal stick made of 'venus-glass' which she had intended to hand over to him but then decided to post along with the knitted vest.[49] He was evidently forgiven for his indecision, although it is hard to say why. When his letter of 8 November arrived on 15 November, and perhaps reassured by press reports that he had consented to come to Zhongshan University, she hedged a little: '[after January] I am willing to stay in Canton and look for work here if you are coming, but otherwise I'll go to Swatow.' Her next comments, on the cost of living in Canton, and that he will find it 'busier and more troublesome than in Amoy', were perhaps meant to test his resolve.[50]

Lu Xun's reply to her ultimatum of 7 November was conciliatory.[51] He told her that he had received a letter from Zhongshan University inviting him to come as the new professor of Chinese literature but that he still could not decide, because 'a friend of mine might go to Swatow, and in that case even if I go to Canton what difference will it make to being in Amoy?' Knowing that she had not yet received this letter, he continued to soothe her hurt feelings in his next: 'If you're not absolutely set on leaving [Canton], then Fuyuan is going to Canton in the middle of next month and I can ask him to see if they have a vacancy at ZU for some kind of advisor to female students.'[52] For himself, 'Although I had decided some time ago not to stay on at the university, I hadn't decided whether it should be at the end of this semester or in summer next year. But now I simply have to leave at the end of the semester . . .' Nevertheless, 'It is also hard to decide for the moment where to go, but anyway, no matter what, I should definitely go to Canton for a visit during the New Year vacation; even if I have nowhere to eat I can't stay on in Amoy'.[53]

Her next letter was on 16 November, after receiving his of 10 November. This time she responded to his hesitation and complaints not with a challenge but with warmth and tact:

. . . would you like me to take this opportunity to take a visit to Amoy, so I can see my teacher and talk to him again and find out what you have been doing over the last few days, since you seem to be extremely lonely.[54]

Receiving her letters of 15 and 16 November, Lu Xun was for once decisive: 'I have decided to leave here by the end of the semester (the end of January) at the latest and go to Zhongshan University.'[55] The following day, 21 November, Lu Xun wrote to Zhang Tingqian, who had been appointed to Amoy University, replying to Zhang's queries about a rumour that had been circulating in Peking about Lu Xun's imminent departure from Amoy. Lu Xun confirmed that he was planning to leave but urged Zhang to come anyway, the sooner the better.[56]

Xu Guangping's next letter was written on 21 and 22 November. The crisis at the school had become more acute. The principal had suddenly resigned on 17 November, and in the absence of anyone in authority at the school, she had no one to whom she could submit her resignation; at the same time, she felt unable to walk out. The only recourse was to appeal to the department of education asking for a new principal to be appointed. Although she had not heard from Lu Xun since 10 November, press reports that he had agreed to come to Zhongshan University were a comfort, and she dealt briskly with the list of reasons he had given for not coming. At the end of her letter, she referred more bluntly than before, but still indirectly, to her belief that Lu Xun's marriage was the chief obstacle delaying his visit to Canton.[57]

As the likelihood of their reunion became firmer, however, Lu Xun's resolve appeared to weaken. On 25 November he wrote, 'Today, I lodged a stiff protest [about the prospect of a reduced budget for the Institute] at a conference with the chancellor, and revealed my intention of resigning.'[58] Unexpectedly, the chancellor gave in, although Lu Xun was pretty sure that he would renege on his promises of support. But Lu Xun had more on his mind than the budget:

> Naturally I want to leave here quickly, but it is hard to predict what the outcome might be. For the next six months I think it would be best for H. M. not to take her direction from my direction but to go to whatever place she finds agreeable. Otherwise, perhaps because of this she might do work which is very irksome and not in line with her wishes, and the outcome is still not clear to see. My emotions have risen and fallen like waves, but for the past few days I've been a little calmer. I thought about it for some time without reaching a conclusion, but I am now of the opinion that this semester is already three-fifths over, and it's not long before the end of the year, I could go to Canton and take a look, and even if right now I can't leave AU, it seems I could manage another five months, and then Yutang can't use my contract as an excuse, and I will be free. Naturally, how it would be after that, I am naturally quite vague.[59]

Lu Xun received her letter of 21 and 22 November on 27 November and replied the following day. Responding to her implied reproach, he agreed in very guarded language that 'by doing as they'd talked about in Peking it could be fairly safe', and concluded,

> As the first step I will certainly leave here at the end of the year and take up the professorship at ZU. But I hope very much that someone will also be at the same place, so that she can at least talk to me often and encourage me to do something that will be of benefit to others.[60]

Before receiving this reassurance, however, Xu Guangping was confronted with the inexplicable irresolution in his letters of 15, 18, and 20 November. If her letter of 2 December is a true expression of her feelings, she must have felt close to despair about their future together:

> It makes it impossible for me to say anything if you 'become calmer' because you're afraid I'll be 'uneasy'. . . I don't have 'a direction' for myself, and there is nowhere 'I find agreeable,' or if there is, it cannot materialize at present . . . .

. . . My heart is in turmoil, I can't find the right words, and I am afraid that what I say will give you some new queer impressions, but if I don't write a few lines, I fear you will be waiting for a letter, I feel it's very unpleasant communicating through letters, it takes time and is totally inadequate in conveying anything.

KU is naturally not an ideal place for sacrificing yourself, so that when you speak of staying on at AU, I find it difficult to say more.

But I still think that writing cannot represent one's thoughts, and as for where exactly you will end up, if you were to ask me, I think it would be best if we could talk about this in person and go over it exhaustively.[61]

Believing the matter to be settled, Lu Xun for the first time in a long while reverted to his former role as teacher in his letter of 2 December, asserting his old authority in patronising and teasing her at the same time.[62] When he received a few days later her unhappy letter of 2 December, however, he responded immediately: 'What was in the letter of the twenty-sixth is already in the past, it will just be a subject for joking about at the end of the year.'[63] He expected that he would not be too busy at ZU because 'I might have someone to help me copying material and so on': that someone, of course, was her.

The correspondence finally resumed its previous tone: relaxed, familiar, and even cheerful in places. She looked forward to her new role as his translator and guide in Canton and teasingly referred to him as 'a real Ah Q';[64] he started a letter by scolding her for being 'silly' and finished with a joke about her 'order' that he should not use the outside postbox at night.[65] On 14 December, he acknowledged that his indecision (or caution) had led them to the brink of rupture:

Alas, after I'd posted the letter of the 23rd it almost provoked a disaster of major proportions and earned me a severe rebuke. Fortunately, being under the protection of the Supreme Emperor, shortly thereafter I sent the missive of the 29th, explaining that the previous epistle was a concoction of treachery and heresy and cancelling it accordingly. In consequence I was awarded praise for being 'a simpleton' and favoured by being granted an 'order'; how fortunate it is that 'he who does good a thousand blessings shall receive.'[66]

Xu Guangping returned to the question of whether or not she was being 'sacrificed' in her letter of 12 December,[67] and they argued in a friendly manner over the issue in the next few letters. On 19 December, to avoid being appointed as acting principal, Xu Guangping took sick leave from the school and moved into her sister-in-law's quarters at Gaodi Street.[68] This led to a great deal of anxiety about letters possibly going astray, and Lu Xun resorted to sending registered and duplicate letters just in case. The other main concern was the date of his departure from Amoy, which at one point seemed likely to be delayed until February.[69]

On 21 December, Lu Xun learnt from Yu Dafu that he was unhappy at Zhongshan University and had decided to return to Shanghai.[70] On 24 December, Zhang Tingqian and his wife Sun Peiqun arrived in Amoy, bearing news of the rumours sweeping Peking about his affair with Xu Guangping.[71] None of this affected his new-found resolve.[72] Li Yu'an, who had been employed as a teaching assistant, was also leaving Zhongshan, creating two vacancies in the Chinese department, and Lu Xun wrote to Sun Fuyuan, who was back briefly in Canton, to arrange for Xu Shouchang to replace Yu Dafu and Xu Guangping to replace Li Yu'an.[73] Xu Guangping was a little anxious lest people should talk[74] but was persuaded to accept.[75]

Lu Xun formally submitted his resignation on 31 December, effective immediately.[76] Once the students in Amoy found out that he was leaving, they immediately protested, linking his departure to their calls for reform; they appeared not to know of the personal reasons behind his decision.[77] Some eventually followed him to Canton, although not as many as he had expected.[78] On the eve of his departure from Amoy, Lu Xun wrote a long, emotional letter to Xu Guangping, revealing the full extent of the gossip about them and how it had affected him. For the first time, he admitted in so many words that he had fallen in love.[79]

The last letter in Part II of *Letters between Two* was written by Lu Xun on board the 'Soochow' from Amoy to Hong Kong, which departed 16 January. On board with him were a student whom he suspected of being a spy for the Amoy University authorities, and three Cantonese students intending to enrol at Zhongshan University (more students were to follow): 'I have already put all of them under martial law so that this person cannot find out anything on board.'[80] For the remainder of his life, Lu Xun would continue to see spies on all sides, whether checking on his private life or his political activities.

The letters from 1926 and early 1927, compared with those from 1925, contain much richer detail about the outside world as well as their own thoughts and emotions. They discussed the tense political and military situation as the Northern Expedition proceeded; the problems they encountered in their workplace; Lu Xun's difficulty in adjusting to academic life as a full-time member of staff; the climate; their need for privacy, living in a residential campus; and their daily habits, health, and clothing. Above all, they were preoccupied by the future of their own relationship. As in Peking, Xu Guangping was the one to push, Lu Xun the one to hedge.[81] (Claims that Lu Xun 'resolved without hesitation' to go to Canton when he received the offer from Zhongshan University, and that he set off with 'his heart brimming over with excitement and militancy' are ludicrously wide of the mark.[82]) In the end, their letters were the means by which they overcame external obstacles as well as their own doubts and hesitation to plan a future together.

6

Living Together: January 1927–June 1929

The 'Soochow' reached Canton, via Hong Kong, on 18 January 1927. Because the date of his departure was decided at the last moment Lu Xun had not been able to inform Xu Guangping, and he put up at an inn for the night. He went to Gaodi Street to see her that evening, and she and Sun Fuyuan helped him to move to Zhongshan University on the following day. He moved into the room vacated by Sun Fuyuan on the third floor of the Bell Tower in the centre of the campus.[1] From then on he saw Xu Guangping almost every day, although he does not necessarily record her visits in his diary unless it is a special event, such as when she came with some fresh fish on 30 January. She was generally there to serve tea to the never-ending stream of guests, and there were also frequent outings and visits to restaurants. Lu Xun introduced her as his student.[2]

It could be said that Lu Xun and Xu Guangping began to live together at this time. In 1935, he wrote in a letter to Xiao Jun that he didn't remember when they started to live together but that it was seven or eight years ago,[3] and their cohabitation could have been a gradual matter rather than starting on a fixed date. It was also not the sort of event that he was likely to record in his diary.

Lu Xun's arrival in Canton was greeted with a mixture of enthusiasm and doubt. By the doubters he was accused of being evasive ('neither blue nor red') and of coming to Canton to hide; Xu Guangping, meeting this charge with vigour, helped to create the myth that his main reason for coming was to contribute to the revolutionary struggle.[4] For his part, Lu Xun was disappointed by the conservative atmosphere, and he attacked the right-wing Nationalist government in several public lectures over the next few months. One of the most famous, 'Wu sheng de Zhongguo' [Silent China], was given in Hong Kong on 18 February; Xu Guangping travelled with him as his interpreter.[5]

Lu Xun was the only full professor at the university. Despite his instructions to Sun Fuyuan on wanting to avoid administrative work, he was concurrently head of the department of Chinese and in February he also became dean. One of his first acts was to appoint Xu Shouchang as a lecturer; shortly after, he appointed Xu Guangping as his assistant.[6] After their return from Hong Kong on 20 February, Xu Shouchang moved into Lu Xun's room in the Bell Tower, but it is said that he tactfully gave the couple time to be alone together.

The new semester started on 1 March. As in Amoy, Lu Xun soon found himself in dispute with the chancellor, Dai Jitao (1890–1949). Dai Jitao, who was several years younger than Lu Xun, had joined the Alliance Society when he was a student in Japan. He was one of the founders of the Chinese Communist Party but then joined the Nationalist Party and became a member of the executive in 1924. After Sun Yat-sen's death he moved further to the right. Under his influence, the right was gaining the upper hand in the conflict between left and right factions within the university. When Gu Jiegang was offered an appointment early in the new semester, Lu Xun at first demanded that the university choose between them but was obliged to give way.[7]

Lu Xun soon began to resent the demands on his time from colleagues and students on campus. After some false starts, Lu Xun, Xu Guangping, and Xu Shouchang went together to look at a house on White Cloud Road on 16 March; it suited their needs, and the three of them moved in on 29 March. As well as a kitchen, lavatory, maid's room, and a combined living and dining room, there were also three bedrooms. Xu Guangping had her own room, and acted as their housekeeper. Here Lu Xun was able to concentrate again on his writing and preparing lectures. Xu Guangping appeared in his diary only when they were invited out by friends as a couple, or when he sent her on an errand to buy books or an alarm clock. It is not known if Xu Guangping's family realized that they were living together, but they accepted Lu Xun as her companion. When he rented rooms to open a branch office of Beixin Press on 25 March, Xu Yueping was placed in charge.[8]

Relations between Nationalists and Communists worsened in 1927. After their capture of Shanghai in March 1927, the Nationalist Party dropped its policy of cooperation with the Communists. Large-scale arrests and killings of Communists and left-wing activists were carried out in Shanghai on 12 April and then in Canton on 15 April. In Canton, more than forty students were arrested at Zhongshan University. Lu Xun called an emergency meeting of department heads at the university on the day of the arrests to petition for their release. Dai Jitao refused to back them and Lu Xun, Xu Shouchang, and Xu Guangping all submitted their resignations on 21 April. The university authorities accepted the other resignations but were reluctant to accept his; various student representatives and members of staff also urged him to stay. Lu Xun's resignation was finally accepted on 6 June. Xu Shouchang left Canton in June, but Lu Xun and Xu Guangping stayed on at White Cloud Road. Neither of them had a regular job or steady income.

Over the summer Lu Xun wrote almost an essay a day, mostly expressing disillusion with the Nationalists and the student movement. In Canton he was knowingly in contact with the Communist Party (it is hard to tell if he was aware of the allegiances of his Communist students and visitors in Amoy). He suspected he was under surveillance and would confuse suspected spies with a flood of talk about literature.[9] Living together with Xu Guangping also created talk.[10] In July, Lu Xun and Xu Guangping decided to leave Canton, but Guangping first had to attend to some family affairs. Lu Xun and Xu Guangping attended a family anniversary at the Gaodi Street shrine in August, and a few days later they visited Xu Leping's husband and their children.

Lu Xun originally thought of returning to Peiping (as Peking was now named), but it would have been awkward for them to live there together openly.[11] On the other hand, his brother Jianren was living in Shanghai, there was easier access to books and a better market for his writing, and the International Settlement made Shanghai safer than either Canton or Peiping.[12] On 27 September they boarded the 'Shantung', headed for Shanghai via Hong Kong and Swatow. A few weeks later, on 11 December 1927, a new Canton Uprising took place and was repressed within a few days following a massacre of several thousand men, women, and children.[13]

Shortly before leaving, Lu Xun wrote a number of aphorisms, some of which have become slogans for their time.[14] They vary from political, to reflective, to personal:

> When you feel lonely, you can create; but once you feel cleansed, you cannot create any more, for you no longer feel any love.
>
> All creation is based on love . . .
>
> Although you say that creation expresses your own self, you always want other people to read it.
>
> Creation has a social nature.
>
> But sometimes it is enough if only one person reads it: a good friend, a lover.[15]

The 'Shantung' reached Shanghai on 3 October, and Lu Xun and Xu Guangping put up at Gonghe Hotel. On the evening of their arrival, they had a visit from Lin Yutang, who had left Amoy in the spring. The following day a group photograph was taken of Lu Xun and Xu Guangping with Jianren, Yutang, Fuyuan, and Fuyuan's younger brother, Fuxi; it has been called their 'wedding photograph'.[16] The next day Lu Xun and Xu Guangping met Yu Dafu's mistress Wang Yingxia for the first time at a dinner arranged by Li Xiaofeng. The day after the dinner, 6 October, Yu Dafu and Wang Yingxia paid a call on Lu Xun and Xu Guangping; Tao Yuanqing and Xu Qinwen also turned up, and Yu Dafu invited them all out to lunch.

Yu Dafu thought that Lu Xun had left Amoy because of his dispute with Lim Boon Keng, and had not paid much attention to Xu Guangping's presence in Shanghai. At the end of the meal when coffee was being served, however, he was startled to see Lu Xun advising 'Miss Xu' in a tender voice that she should not take coffee since she had a stomach upset but should have some fruit instead, and at once realized that Lu Xun was in love with her.[17]

Yu Dafu had met and fallen in love with Wang Yingxia in January 1927. He besieged her with ardent letters but she was doubtful about accepting the attentions of a man eleven years older with a wife and two children. In March she succumbed to his pledges of undying love and vowed to love him in return for the rest of his life. Shortly afterwards she happened to see some passages in his diary where he expressed his resentment of her failure to meet him or answer his letters, and where he admitted that he missed his wife and children.[18] Angered by his lies, she broke off their relationship. After more pleading on his part including a declaration that he would never publish his diary, she forgave him. By April their association had become a matter of public knowledge, to Yu Dafu's unconcealed satisfaction.[19] In June, he finally succeed in persuading his wife Sun Quan to agree to a formal separation, although there was never a divorce.[20] Nevertheless, Yu Dafu and Wang Yingxia celebrated their 'betrothal' the same month and began to live together openly. Some of the younger members of the Creation Society were shocked by his behaviour, and reacting to their criticisms Yu Dafu resigned in August 1927. In September he published his diaries without first consulting Wang Yingxia but managed again to soothe her anger. Lu Xun's arrival in Shanghai with a young mistress in October established another bond between the two writers, and the two couples saw each other regularly over the next few years.[21]

On 8 October Lu Xun and Xu Guangping moved to a three-storied Western-style house at No. 23 Jingyun Alley, off Donghengbing Road in Chapei. (8 October was subsequently described as the date they were 'married'.[22]) Chapei was a new and moderately prosperous district under direct Chinese rule.[23] Lu Xun and Xu Guangping soon discovered that one drawback of the neighbourhood was the noise, with mahjong-playing neighbours and a very lively street life at all times of the day and night. Gangs were also active in this area, and once a stray bullet pierced their glass window during a police raid nearby.[24] The main attraction of the house was its proximity to Jianren's apartment on one floor of No. 10 Jingyun Alley. Jianren was now living together with Wang Yunru and they had two daughters.[25] Yunru was also a graduate of Peiping Women's Normal College and a good friend of Xu Xiansu's. She had not previously met Lu Xun or Xu Guangping but they were soon on intimate terms.[26]

The premises at No. 23 were spacious: Lu Xun lived on the ground and first floor and Xu Guangping lived on the second floor. Xu Guangping later explained that this was because Lu Xun liked plenty of space.[27] Another reason could have been to conceal the fact that they were cohabiting. At first no one outside their immediate circle knew they were living together.[28] Among their friends there was a problem of how she should be addressed: Jiang Shaoyuan, who had known them both in Canton, suggested (possibly as a joke) that she should be called *shimu*, the usual title for one's teacher's wife.[29] Once the word got around, there was more scandal.[30] It was claimed, for instance, that Lu Xun had only separated from his wife because of Xu Guangping.

The news of their cohabitation seems to have been conveyed to Lu Xun's family in Peiping by the photograph of them together; Lu Rui accepted their relationship, probably without much surprise.[31] Zhu An was unhappy but acknowledged her husband's right to take a concubine. She told Yu Fang that she had always tried to be a good wife to Lu Xun despite his coldness to her, hoping that he would come to accept her. She compared herself to a snail, climbing slowly but steadily up a wall, but it was hopeless and she was not strong enough to keep climbing. Nevertheless, she expected to attend her mother-in-law until the old lady died, and for Lu Xun to continue to support her.[32] Zhou Zuoren disapproved of the liaison and refused to recognize it. Xu Guangping's family broke off relations with her.[33]

Lu Xun and Xu Guangping held no ceremony to mark their cohabitation in Shanghai, but in subtle ways they were more of a couple than they had been in Canton. They made joint decisions about their new life, resolving to live simply with one bed, one desk and two chairs per person. They would have no servant; they would eat with Jianren. In practice, they occasionally also borrowed Jianren's maid, and eventually added more furniture.[34] They also ate out a lot, sometimes at the home of a friend like Lin Yutang. According to Yu Dafu, Lin Yutang had asked him shortly after the couple's arrival in Shanghai if there was anything between Lu Xun and Xu Guangping, but Yu Dafu denied it. Yu Dafu also claimed that it was only when Xu Guangping was due to give birth that Lin Yutang finally realized the truth, but given Lin's close relations with Lu Xun and Xu Guangping in late 1927, Yu Dafu is probably exaggerating Lin's naivety.[35]

It was around this time that Lin Yutang referred to Lu Xun as a 'white elephant', meaning a rare national treasure as distinct from the ordinary run of grey elephants; it also means 'a burdensome or costly possession given by the kings of Siam to obnoxious courtiers in order to ruin them'. Lin Yutang was presumably aware of its associations,[36] although it is not altogether clear that Lu Xun and Xu Guangping understood. Xu Guangping later wrote that the name tickled their fancy and Lu Xun became to both of them 'Xiao bai xiang' [Little white elephant][37] or (in German) 'Elefant'. Xu Guangping in turn became 'Xiao ciwei' [Little hedgehog], but she never explained why.[38]

Xu Guangping now accompanied Lu Xun everywhere: the lunches, dinners, and parties, the visits to the cinema and the bookshops; Zhou Jianren and Xu Shouchang often joined them. That autumn, Lu Xun notes twice in his diary that he got very drunk, and at a grand party on New Year's Eve, he got so drunk that he threw up when they got home. To people like Yu Dafu who had known him as abstemious in Peiping, he seemed a changed man.[39]

Lu Xun had made the decision not to teach again but to live from his writing, although during these first months together in Shanghai he got little work done. Xu Guangping had thought of taking up teaching again and asked Xu Shouchang to find her a position, but Lu Xun had become dependent on her help and was not willing for her to go out to work. Instead, she and some friends set up a new journal, *Geming de funü* [Revolutionary women]. Lu Xun wanted her to learn Japanese, and found a textbook for her to study. In search of some Japanese literature to accompany the textbook, they discovered Uchiyama Bookshop three days after arriving in Shanghai. The proprietor, Uchiyama Kanzô, took a special interest in modern Chinese literature, and writers like Yu Dafu made a habit of dropping in. Uchiyama was very pleased to find that his new customer was the famous author Lu Xun.[40] Lu Xun told him he was married,[41] and the two families soon became close.

Not long after they arrived in Shanghai, *Thread of Talk* was closed down by the warlord Zhang Zuolin in Peiping, and the Shanghai branch of its publisher, Beixin Press, also closed. Li Xiaofeng re-established a Shanghai office and asked Lu Xun to take over as editor. Lu Xun agreed, and the next issue, which contained contributions from Zhou Zuoren as well as Lu Xun, was ready to print in December 1927. At the same time he co-operated with the Creation Society in re-establishing their periodical *Chuangzao zhoukan* [Creation Weekly].

In 1928 Lu Xun either stopped drinking heavily or failed to record it in his diary.[42] In April, he bought a copy of his translation of Kuriyagawa's *Symbols of*

Anguish as a present for Xu Guangping. That month Yu Dafu and Wang Yingxia held a 'wedding banquet' in Shanghai. It was a small-scale family affair and Lu Xun and Xu Guangping did not attend, but Lu Xun invited 'Yu Dafu and his wife' to a dinner on 5 April along with Lin Yutang and his wife and Li Xiaofeng and his wife.[43]

During the first half of 1928, relations between Lu Xun and the Creation Society deteriorated, and he found himself under attack from the left as well as from the right in the literary world, with *Thread of Talk* occupying the middle ground. It was partly as a result of these attacks that he began to take more seriously the study of Marxism. But Creation Society activists Cheng Fangwu and Feng Naichao also brought up Lu Xun's private life, criticizing him as ideologically backward for having left his wife to start an affair with his student.[44] There were also frequent references to his drunkenness, to which Lu Xun responded with his customary vigour. Their attacks formed another bond between Lu Xun and Yu Dafu, and the two men decided to collaborate on a new journal, *Benliu* [Torrents], mainly as a vehicle for translations.[45]

In July 1928 Lu Xun and Xu Guangping finally accepted a long-standing invitation from friends to spend a few days in Hangchow. Lu Xun arranged for Xu Qinwen (who was then teaching in Hangchow) to go to Shanghai a few days earlier so that he could accompany them on the train, and also for Qinwen to share their room at the guest-house overlooking West Lake; the reason was the political situation in Hangchow was very tense and he hoped in this way to offer some protection.[46] Zhang Tingqian and Sun Peiqun were there to meet them. Qinwen thought their main reason for coming was for Lu Xun to visit the antiquarian bookshops; Lu Xun joked that it was a belated honeymoon.[47] To Yu Dafu he complained of the heat, the mosquitoes, and the polluted water.[48] Unlike Yu Dafu, whom he liked, or Xu Zhimo, whom he disliked, Lu Xun had no time for transports of delight over nature: he was not a traveller, nor a nature worshipper. He did not return to Hangchow, nor did he take the opportunity to visit nearby Shaoxing, which he had last seen in 1919.[49]

It was also that summer that Lu Xun met Zhao Pingfu, who had audited his lectures at Peiping University on Chinese fiction and now wrote fiction himself under the pen-name Rou Shi.[50] By December Lu Xun had lost interest in *Thread of Talk*, and suggested closing it down. Since Li Xiaofeng was reluctant to do this, Lu Xun recommended Rou Shi as his replacement. In November, Rou Shi introduced Feng Xuefeng to Lu Xun, and Xuefeng (who unbeknown to Lu Xun was already a member of the Communist Party) stayed in Jianren's house for a few weeks.[51] Rou Shi and Feng Xuefeng visited Lu Xun and Xu Guangping almost every day, and often accompanied them on outings to the cinema or to restaurants.

Lu Xun's relationship with Xu Guangping was by now widely known in Shanghai, although there was no open admission to close friends elsewhere. When his latest collection of essays, *Er yi ji* [And that's that], came out in November 1928, he inscribed a copy to his '*airen* Guangping' (*airen*, literally 'beloved', at that time meant either lover or wife).[52] They planned to have a child, but one only and not yet, so at this time they practised birth control using a pessary.[53] When Xu Guangping became pregnant in January 1929 it was a surprise to both of them.[54] In

February they moved to No. 17, while Jianren and his family stayed at No. 18, and No. 23 was passed on to Rou Shi and his friends. Xu Guangping acquired a new nickname, becoming a 'little white elephant' too.

As Xu Guangping's condition became obvious, it was time to let their friends know. In March Lu Xun confirmed in a letter to Wei Suyuan that 'he had invited Miss Xu' to share a house with him and Xu Shouchang in Canton, and then to come to Shanghai with him where they were now living together.[55] 'In fact, I was in love with someone of the opposite sex but for a long while I did not dare follow through, because I was very much aware of my shortcomings and was afraid I was not worthy of her. But once I fell in love, once I got angry, I no longer cared about any of that.'[56] In April, Lu Xun expressed his views on love to Wei Suyuan: 'I believe that what is called romantic or sexual love is something apart from revolution. Revolutionary love resides in the masses, it is in essence the equivalent of food, and there can be no affection or sentiment involved, although there is some choice of partner.'[57] In May, Xu Guangping confided the news at much greater length to Chang Ruilin. Their respective families were not informed.

On 11 May, Lu Xun received a letter from his mother Lu Rui saying that she was ill and suggesting that he and Xu Guangping come to Peiping to see her.[58] Lu Xun bought a ticket to Peiping the next day and set forth the day after; Jianren, Rou Shi, and Cui Zhenwu went to see him off, while Guangping rested at home. He arrived in Peiping on the 15th, and immediately sent a telegram to Jianren.

This was their first separation since they had been reunited in Canton. Guangping was the first to write, following his progress on the railway timetable, and giving a report on her daily activities. She rested a lot, usually taking an afternoon nap, read books, and studied her Japanese grammar; she was also translating from the Japanese (under Lu Xun's supervision) Herminia Zur Mühlen's *Was Peterchens Freunde erzählen* (1921), a collection of fables written for the children of Hungarian workers.[59] She spent most of her time upstairs, but had her meals with Jianren, Yunru, and their baby daughter Ah Pu.[60]

When Lu Xun stepped down from his rickshaw outside West Third Alley, his mother immediately asked why Guangping had not accompanied him, but he did not give a direct reply. That evening he wrote a short letter to Guangping to report in more detail on his journey and to let her know that he was already missing her.[61] Xu Xiansu, who was living in the Tiger's Tail, was the first to hear about Guangping; although she had known about their affair, this was the first she knew that they had been living together. She offered to move to the south wing, and after some hesitation, Lu Xun moved back into his former bedroom.[62]

The next day he told Lu Rui that they had thought the vibrations from the train would not be good for the child: this was his first disclosure to his mother that Guangping was pregnant. As he duly related to Guangping,

> She was very happy, saying that she thought we should have one, because there should be a small child running up and down in the house. Although her reason for the 'should' is very different from our idea, nevertheless in short she is extremely happy.[63]

Lu Rui presumably felt that the child should be living with its grandmother.[64] Zhu An also welcomed the news: as Lu Xun's wife, she was by traditional custom the child's official mother, so that finally she could be accounted a good wife (i.e. one who continued her husband's family line either personally or by proxy) and there would be someone to carry out ancestral rites for her as well as for her husband.[65]

Lu Xun also reported on the changes he saw in his mother:

> In spirit and appearance my mother is much the same as three years ago, but it seems that her concerns have become much narrower.[66]

> My mother's memory has got worse and her powers of observation and attention have also deteriorated; sometimes she's cross like a small child. Her feelings towards us are very good.[67]

Xu Guangping was always polite about Lu Xun's mother. In this exchange she confines herself to remarking,

> Your mother is getting on in years and you are only home for a few days, it would be best if you were to spend more time with her, talking with her and keeping her spirits up.[68]

Still, it must be good to be in Peiping again, wrote Guangping, thinking back on their former life there:

> Peiping is not desolate at all, it's quite nice, because I look on it as my hometown too. I sometimes feel even fonder of it and miss it more than my real home, because there is still so much that reminds me of my former life there [24 May].[69]

Among the friends who came to visit were former classmates such as Lü Yunzhang and Lin Zhuofeng, and Lu Xun went out almost every day to see friends, frequently ending up at restaurants for lunch or dinner. Guangping commented:

> From your letter [21 May] your social life seems to be very hectic, which is also unavoidable. Not having been in Peiping for a long time it's also nice to see the people you know, and use up the whole day on this excuse. I sometimes fear you use up a lot of energy going back and forth but at other times I want you to go out since it gives you a change of scene and also some physical exercise. It's rather ridiculous, these two ideas are mutually contradictory, but you don't have much time in Peiping so it would be better to go out more.[70]

On 22 May Lu Xun gave a talk at Yenching University and another at Peiping University on 29 May; more than a thousand people showed up at the latter.[71] When the possibility of his coming to teach at Peiping or Yenching was raised, however, he promptly rejected the idea:

> I think it's better that these fine places invite those gentry types to hold jobs while we continue to drift.[72]

He received another job offer on 23 May and although he was naturally flattered, he wrote to Guangping that he prefers the turmoil in Shanghai to the tranquillity of Peiping, since Shanghai had a vitality that he missed in Peiping.[73] An unexpected encounter with Gu Jiegang, who according to Lu Xun was in Peiping looking for a transfer north, left Lu Xun feeling superior.[74] Lu Xun reverted to the subject of returning to Peiping in his last letter, claiming that certain people (such as

Gu Jiegang) feared that he was coming to steal their ricebowls.[75] He also defended his own academic writing as in no way inferior to the products of professional academics.

The chief difference between this batch of letters and their earlier exchanges is the way in which both of them repeatedly gave voice to their affection and concern.[76] Lu Xun and Xu Guangping address each other, sign themselves, and refer to each other and themselves with pet names, for example, that are too intimate and tender to leave in *Letters between Two*. On the eve of his departure for Shanghai, Lu Xun wondered if there were a place where they could simply be themselves, untouched by the outside world.[77] By a happy coincidence, Guangping had just been on an excursion with her Aunt Feng to just such an idyllic place.[78] Shanghai, however, was to remain their home for the few years left to Lu Xun, in which moments of peace would become increasingly rare.

7

Birth and Death: 1929–68

Their son was born on the morning of 27 September 1929.[1] Xu Guangping went into hospital the previous day and Lu Xun stayed with her during the night. It was a difficult birth: Xu Guangping was in labour for over 27 hours.[2] When the doctor asked whether he should save the child or the adult, Lu Xun replied the adult.[3] That afternoon, Lu Xun sent letters to Xie Dunnan (Chang Ruilin's husband) and Xu Xiansu. The next day, he visited Guangping at the hospital in the morning; in the afternoon he went to Uchiyama Bookshop and bought a pot of bamboo for her. He continued to visit every day. On 1 October they decided on the baby's name, Haiying [Shanghai infant], thinking that he could change it as he grew older (he never did).[4] The nurse called him Didi [Little brother], which they also adopted for a while. Their own pet-name for him was 'Xiao hong xiang' [Little red elephant], a play on their name for Lu Xun.[5]

Mother and child returned home on 7 October. They had the baby's portrait painted on 12 October, and he was photographed on 16 October. On 18 October Haiying had a slight cold and they took him to the hospital, but all that was needed was something to help him breathe a little more easily. More photographs were taken on 22 October, and copies sent to Chang Ruilin and Xu Xiansu. On 24 October Lu Xun presented the obstetrician with a bolt of silk. On 26 and 27 October, friends came with presents for the baby. During November Lu Xun took Haiying to the hospital every three or four days, and by the end of the month Xu Guangping went along too. Thereafter, Haiying appeared regularly in Lu Xun's diary, mainly on visits to the hospital, the barber, or the photographer.

The amah they hired to look after Haiying, Wang Ahua, was usually cheerful, but they noticed that from time to time she would appear anxious. In a curious echo of Lu Xun's story 'Zhufu' [New Year's sacrifice], it turned out that she had left Shaoxing and come to Shanghai to escape a brutal husband. In October, her husband managed to trace her to their house. Lu Xun and Xu Guangping decided to help Ahua divorce him; they hired a lawyer and in January 1930 they 'bought' her from him for 150 dollars. Ahua was relatively young and inexperienced, and in March Lu Xun and Xu Guangping replaced her with an older woman, Xu Wen.[6]

Xu Guangping continued to do the shopping, laundry, and cleaning. She also prepared food when there were guests, and saw to it that Lu Xun changed his clothes regularly. She made their cloth shoes, woolen jumpers, and other clothing.[7] When she went to bed, he would sit by her side while he had a last cigarette but she would fall asleep before he had finished.[8] When Lu Xun resumed his social life,

Xu Guangping tended to stay at home except on family outings to see a film, a play, or an exhibition,[9] or to see Jianren and his family. In return, Lu Xun frequently bought books as presents for her, and used a pen-name in his translations that incorporated or reflected her childhood name, Xu Xia.[10] Xu Guangping read but did not write, and Lu Xun acknowledged that her household duties stood in the way of her writing.[11]

There were also quarrels. Lu Xun was often irritable, and Xu Guangping did not always know how to answer his complaints. Sometimes they might go for a day or more without speaking to each other, but Lu Xun was usually the first to apologize for his bad temper.[12] Xu Guangping was particularly anxious to save every bit of paper on which Lu Xun had written something, even when he had thrown it out or left it in the lavatory as toilet paper; then he would become impatient when there was no paper in the lavatory.[13]

Xu Guangping continued to urge him to reduce his smoking and to buy higher grade tobacco. She also asked Yu Dafu's advice on how to lessen the damage to his health from drinking. At this point Lu Xun was fond of Shaoxing wine (the most famous kind of Yellow [rice] wine), Wujiapi (a medicinal liquor), beer, and brandy. Yu Dafu, a long-time heavy drinker, told her that he should stick to Yellow wine or beer (since their alcohol content was relatively low), or else leave the stopper off the Wujiapi bottle so that the alcohol could evaporate.[14] Lu Xun still drank heavily from time to time over the next few years. In August 1929, for instance, he got drunk and quarrelled with Lin Yutang, and the two families became estranged.[15]

Haiying was a source of both joy and trouble, as Lu Xun wrote in letters to friends and to his mother.[16] Sickly since birth, it seemed as if every day he had to be taken to hospital or to be dosed at home with medicine from the pharmacy.[17] At one point, when they were considering moving to Peiping, the possible bad effect on the child's health was one factor in deciding not to go.[18] In spite of all his troubles, Lu Xun took pleasure in exchanging banter with the young child, and frequently took him out for a walk to buy ice-cream.[19] They often took photographs of him to send to relatives and friends, such as the 'first one hundred days' photograph taken on 4 January 1930.[20] Lu Xun even remained indulgent when his son toddled into his study and disturbed his books.[21]

Lu Xun and Feng Xuefeng began a new journal, *Mengya* [The sprout] in late 1929, and the first issue appeared in January 1930. Unlike *Thread of Talk* and *Torrents*, *The Sprout* was strongly polemical, showing how far Lu Xun had moved to the left since 1927. On 2 March 1930, Lu Xun attended the secret inauguration of the League of Left-Wing Writers in Shanghai. Although not part of the small group controlling the League, he had a nominal position on the standing committee and contributed to many of its publications. When the League came to the attention of the authorities in March, he was obliged to seek a temporary refuge upstairs at Uchiyama's house from 19 March to 1 April. During this time, Xu Guangping came to visit him almost every day, sometimes with Haiying.[22] There were many other visitors as well, and Lu Xun frequently went out during the day for meals, to the hospital for dental treatment, to the photographers with Haiying, and to look for other lodgings. From 6 to 19 April he also lived away from home, still receiving guests, going to the dental hospital, having his hair cut, going out for dinner with Guangping, Jianren, and friends, and house-hunting. If he were wanted by the police, it seems that it would have been easy to find him.[23]

It was presumably for reasons of security that their next move, in May 1930, took them into 'Little Tokyo', the area around North Szechwan Road in Hongkew. The new flat was on the second floor of an apartment building at the end of North Szechwan Road. The other apartments were occupied by Japanese, and their balcony overlooked the headquarters of a Japanese naval station.[24]

According to the lunar calendar, Lu Xun's fiftieth birthday was on 24 September 1930. It was celebrated with a party for him, Guangping, and Haiying in the French Concession with twenty-two friends from the League of Left-wing Writers on 19 September.[25] The following afternoon Yu Dafu paid a visit. On the twenty-fourth, Guangping made special noodles, and the next day the three of them had their photograph taken. Jianren came over with a bottle of wine on the twenty-sixth, and there was more rejoicing on the twenty-seventh, Haiying's first birthday. On 6 October it was Mid-Autumn festival, and although Haiying was not well, Guangping prepared duck, ham, and special noodles for Rou Shi, Xuefeng, and Xuefeng's wife. From time to time Lu Xun had stomach upsets, sometimes taking the form of diarrhoea which he dosed with a preparation called 'Help', but he also indulged in crab feasts with Jianren and their respective families during the autumn. The year that had started badly ended on a pleasant note, with a morning visit from Yunru with *yuanxiao*, a lunch invitation from Wei Congwu to Lu Xun and Jianren, and the purchase of five books from Uchiyama Bookshop in the afternoon.

The new year started quietly but soon brought terrible news. Rou Shi paid a visit on 12 January. A few days later, he was arrested along with other members of the Communist Party (which he had joined only the previous year). Lu Xun, who knew several of them well, was himself in danger of arrest. With Uchiyama's help, Lu Xun, Guangping, Haiying, and Xu Wen moved into a Japanese inn at Huayuanzhuang, Huanglu Road, on 20 January.[26] Apart from occasional visits to Uchiyama Bookshop and to Jianren, this time they stayed mostly indoors and received few visitors. Rou Shi and his fellow-prisoners were executed on 7 February.

Lu Xun and his family returned home on 28 February. The following days were bleak, and it was a long time before they found any cause to rejoice. Xu Xiansu, who had been looking after his mother in Peiping, moved out of West Third Alley in spring 1931 to work as a teacher in Hopeh, and before she left, she passed over all her letters from Lu Xun to Zhu An for safe-keeping. Her role as the household's voice to the outside world was taken over by Song Zipei.[27] In Shanghai, Feng Xuefeng and his wife became their closest friends around this time,[28] while visits from Yu Dafu and Wang Yingxia became less frequent.[29] With two families to support and no guaranteed income, Lu Xun was often in financial difficulties. He continued to send an allowance to his mother and wife in Peiping,[30] but in Shanghai they became more frugal.[31]

On 28 January 1932, fighting broke out in Chapei between Japanese and Chinese forces. The apartment in North Szechwan Road was close to the fighting, and a bullet entered Lu Xun's study.[32] Jianren was arrested but was bailed out by Uchiyama. Both families, altogether ten people, then took refuge in Uchiyama Bookshop on 30 January, bringing only their clothes. There are no entries in Lu Xun's diary for the next week. On 6 February they moved to Uchiyama's branch shop in the International Settlement, where all ten of them shared a single room.[33] Because of the danger, they rarely went out, but on 16 February, the two families went out for a drink. The next day they went out again, and this time Lu Xun became slightly drunk. Afterwards they went to another bar where Lu Xun asked a prostitute to join them, giving her a dollar; the next two days he suffered from indigestion.

In March Haiying became ill, so Lu Xun and Xu Guangping moved to a hotel,[34] while Jianren and his family went to a friend's place in the French Concession. When they went to inspect their house they found it slightly damaged and some of their possessions stolen, but they moved back as soon as Haiying was discharged from hospital. Haiying was still not very well and over the next few months was taken to hospital almost every other day. Xu Wen left for other employment, and Xu Guangping was temporarily left with all the housework. Under the strain, both Lu Xun and Xu Guangping fell ill.[35]

By July the situation had become a lot calmer, and the three of them would often go out for a walk. Lu Xun met Qu Qiubai through Feng Xuefeng that summer, after they had been in correspondence. At the time, Qu Qiubai was the highest-ranking Communist of Lu Xun's acquaintance. In August they received the news from Peiping that Wei Suyuan had died; looking for his letters set them thinking about publishing their own correspondence. Then Guangping became ill, and when she was recovering, Lu Xun became ill in early September. In early October, after indulging as usual in crab feasts with his brother, he suffered indigestion, although a few nights later they ate crabs again with no ill effects. On 31 October, they finished sorting out their letters into three parts for publication.

On 9 November, Jianren came over with a telegram from Zuoren in Peiping saying that their mother was ill and that he should go there immediately. (Despite their estrangement, Lu Xun and Zuoren were obliged to remain in touch if only for the sake of their mother,[36] but relations between the two younger brothers were even cooler. Zuoren apparently did not have Lu Xun's address, however, and only knew how to reach him through Jianren or Uchiyama.[37]) Lu Xun bought a ticket the next morning and left the following day, arriving on 13 November. During his stay Lu Xun and Guangping exchanged letters almost every day.[38] Compared to the earlier letters, they show an even deeper level of affection and intimacy.

Xu Guangping wrote on the day he set out, addressing him as *ge* [elder brother; used affectionately by women for their lovers or husbands] and signed herself *gu* [girl]. She was mainly concerned about Haiying, who had been ill and was asking when his dad was coming back. In these letters both parents generally referred to Haiying as Goupi [Dogfart]. Chinese baby names are often derogatory, indicating to demons or other possible baby-stealers that the child is worthless, but in this case the parents were overdoing it, and Lu Rui asked him not to use this name.

Lu Xun wrote the day he arrived in Peiping, addressing her as *guai gu* [darling girl] and signing himself Xun (in other letters, he is *ge* or L). He reported that his mother's condition was not very serious after all, and in his next letter he explained that she had been having indigestion and fainting spells, probably because of old age and not eating well. He had no other business in Peiping except to look after her until she was better, and for the moment he could stay quietly at home. Alone in his study, he 'can't help thinking of the darling girl and the little darling girl [i.e. Haiying], although not to the extent of "wanting daddy" '. (Referring to a baby boy as a baby girl is also a way of averting misfortune.)

Xu Guangping's next letter, written 14 November, continued to keep Lu Xun informed on his son's stools and diet. As before, she passed on the details about manuscripts and other items that had come in the post. Jianren had heard from Zuoren that their mother was better, and she wished the old lady well. In her letter of 16 November she wrote that she was busy copying out their letters, and urged him not to drink and upset his digestion.

Lu Xun's letter of 15 November reported that he had received hers of 12 November, which made him very happy. The Japanese doctor he had called in explained that his mother's illness should respond well to treatment, and Lu Xun thought he might be able to leave in about a week. But the old lady was irritable, blaming the doctor for her not having made an immediate recovery. Although Lu Xun was not sleeping much, needing to tend to his mother at night, he felt well. In an added note written on 16 November, he noted that Peiping was very quiet in comparison to Shanghai—like another world altogether—and that perhaps the whole family should come for a month next spring. Even his wife showed her goodwill to them both, although Nobuko had tried to stir up trouble; Lu Rui, however, had restrained her. Nobuko was also upset about the rumour that Guangping was pregnant for a second time.[39] In her reply, Xu Guangping urged Lu Xun not to worry about Nobuko.

On 18 November, Xu Guangping reported that Haiying was better. Together with Wang Yunru, Apu, and the two maids, they went to see a film but Haiying was very naughty. She wondered if Lu Xun should use this opportunity to stay longer in the north and start work on the novel he had been planning to write, since in Shanghai it was impossible to get anything done with so much coming and going all the time. In his letter of 19 November, Lu Xun wrote that he had already been separated from his 'two darling girls' for nine days, and was very happy to hear that the little darling girl was better. His mother liked to talk to him about the old days twenty or thirty years ago, and though these stories had little interest for him he was obliged to listen. His mother was well-disposed towards him and Guangping, and had a photograph of Haiying by her bedside, while the photographs of Zuoren's children were on the wall; this made him a little uncomfortable until he realized it was a diplomatic gesture. On one of their visits to Lu Rui, Zuoren and Nobuko brought her parents along as well.

Xu Guangping wrote next on 20 November: Haiying was being good and his health had improved. Lu Xun's next letter was also dated 20 November; he was pleased that Haiying had been a good boy and had recovered from his illness. He reported that he was being careful about his health, confining himself to one cup of Yellow wine and one bowl of rice per meal. He was touched by the warm welcome he received from old friends, unlike the coldness he found in Shanghai.[40] Although his mother was not able to get out of bed she was feeling better, and he planned to leave by the end of the month.

Xu Guangping's next letter, 21 November, is mostly about Haiying and the continuing problem with Beixin Press, which Jianren was now handling in Lu Xun's absence. Lu Xun wrote again on 23 November. His lectures at Peiping University and Furen University had attracted large crowds, and Lu Xun reflected again on his warm reception in Peiping compared with Shanghai. However, at home he mostly passed the time reading old books, and he found himself unable to write fiction. He was still careful about his diet, and because he had to drink when he was invited to dinner, at home it was his habit to abstain.

Xu Guangping sent four more letters, dated 23, 24, 25, and 26 November. She wrote about sending Haiying to a kindergarten, where he could play with other children and enjoy more exercise than he got at home; what the doctor said about Haiying; what Haiying ate and excreted; and that she had got as far as Letter 84 in transcribing the manuscript of their published correspondence. Lu Xun's last letter is dated 26 November: getting ready to leave, he bought some toys for Haiying. He also related that it was not even particularly cold in Peiping and that he had been very glad to see his old friends, so that the thought of moving to Peiping was appealing; but he was afraid that if he did move, there would be too much pressure from students urging him to return to teaching. Nevertheless, it would be nice for the three of them to return to Peiping for a short holiday in the spring. He left on 28 November. It was to be his last visit to Peiping.

Lu Xun's personal library in Shanghai was by now so large that in March 1933 he rented a room in another building where he could house his books and write undisturbed.[41] The following month, Lu Xun, Xu Guangping, Haiying, and Amah Xu moved to 9 Dalu Xincun off Scott Road, also in Hongkew near the boundary with the International Settlement.[42] Their new home was also a foreign-style building but unlike their former apartment house it was set back from the street and had plenty of light.[43] There was a small garden inside the front gate, where Lu Xun planted a peach tree in memory of Rou Shi and the other writers executed in 1931. On the other side was a vegetable garden where they planted various kinds of squash.

Guests were usually entertained in the ground floor living room around the main table; Guangping's sewing machine and work table was to one side, and Haiying's toybox was in another corner. One of their new possessions was Qu Qiubai's roll-top desk, which he left with them when he went to the Communist base area in Kiangsu. There was also a small table with a hand-cranked gramophone. Beyond this room was a small room used for family meals.

Upstairs was a large room used by Lu Xun and Xu Guangping as a combined bedroom and study. On one side was an iron-frame double bed, with white bed curtains and linen. To one side was a glass-fronted bookcase where Lu Xun kept his translations. Next to it was a writing table, one of the original pieces of furniture they had bought on arriving in Shanghai, with a desk lamp given to them by Feng Xuefeng. Next to the desk was a battered old rattan reclining chair, much used by Lu Xun. Other furniture included a dressing table, a clothes cupboard and a tea-table. Also on this floor was a small boxroom.

On the second floor was a room shared by Haiying and Amah Xu, and a guest room. The sunniest room in the apartment was Haiying's bedroom, which had its own balcony, and it was here also that they put the best furniture, sold to them by their former landlady at North Szechwan Road when they moved.[44] Another elderly maid also lived on this floor.[45]

Although some of their chairs and tables were handsome enough, the general impression was spartan. There were no sofas or stuffed chairs, no carpets, no silk embroidered hangings. Apart from family photographs and some paintings, there were few decorations or ornaments. What they did have a lot of were books, kept in all kinds of book cases and book shelves. Even after the move to Scott Road, Lu Xun kept his main library separately, but there was still an overflow in the first and second floor bedrooms and also in the living room.

Some years later, Xu Guangping recalled that the number of visitors decreased in the early 1930s, and there were even fewer women who came to visit. Lu Xun was often out, leaving Guangping at home feeling lonely.[46] Jianren still came over most days, and Wang Yunru and one of their three daughters usually came on Saturdays. Yu Dafu had moved to Hangchow with Wang Yingxia and the children in April 1933,[47] and from then on there was only sporadic contact between the two couples. Lu Xun and Lin Yutang patched up their long-standing quarrel in 1933, although the reconciliation was not to last long.[48] On a visit to Shanghai on 29 December, Yu Dafu and Wang Yingxia dropped by to see them; Lu Xun wrote a poem for Wang Yingxia expressing disapproval of Dafu's retreat from active politics.[49] At the end of the year, Feng Xuefeng and Qu Qiubai both left for Communist headquarters in Kiangsu.

In the three years 1933–6, Lu Xun regained much of his former vigour as a writer. Financial and health reasons combined to reduce his drinking,[50] but the worsening political situation also made him more aggressive. When Lin Yutang had launched a new journal, *Lun yu* [Analects], in 1932, Lu Xun had contributed to it, although he had wondered if it might degenerate into inconsequentiality; but when *Analects* gave way to *Ren jian shi* [The human world] in 1934, jointly edited by Lin Yutang and Zhou Zuoren, he was openly contemptuous (Zuoren's involvement may have increased Lu Xun's ire).[51] Lu Xun's new friends also tended to be more militant: Hu Feng joined their circle in the autumn,[52] and Xiao Hong and Xiao Jun followed at the end of the year. Lu Xun was often ill, and Xiao Hong and Xiao Jun moved to be nearer in order to help; Xiao Hong would drop in once or twice a day. By the end of the year even his new friends were shocked by his appearance.[53]

The house in Scott Road at times resembled a salon from which invitations were issued like imperial edicts; Hu Feng's wife, Mei Zhi, recalls being summoned to appear with her infant child late one night in spite of high winds.[54] There was also an inner sanctum: Mei Zhi was once asked by Xu Guangping to help entertain

Xiao Hong downstairs while Lu Xun conferred with Feng Xuefeng and Hu Feng upstairs.[55] In company, Lu Xun still referred to Guangping as '*Misi* [Miss] Xu';[56] Guangping referred to him as *xiansheng*.[57]

When Lu Xun's compilation *Jiezi yuan huapu* [Illustrations from the Mustard Seed Garden] was published in December 1934, he presented Guangping with a copy on which he inscribed a poem celebrating their ten years together.[58] Her constant presence was by now indispensable. When some young women activists urged her in 1935 to spend more time outside on women's affairs, Lu Xun ordered her not to leave the house.[59] At one point (it is not clear just when), they thought of sending eight crates of books to Peiping for safekeeping, and Lu Xun's mother had hopes that this was an indication that they might return to live there. Disappointed, his mother proposed in March 1935 coming to live with them in Shanghai, with Yu Fang volunteering to be her travelling companion, but she fell ill again and the plan did not materialize (it is not clear what would happen to Zhu An).[60]

Qu Qiubai's execution in June 1935 was yet another heavy blow. The last major political activity in which Lu Xun took part was the 1936 dispute with Zhou Yang and Xu Maoyong over literary policy in the face of Japanese aggression. To Lu Xun, who had close Japanese friends, the main enemy was the Nationalist Party which had killed his students and associates, and he found it hard to fall in with the new Comintern directive on the formation of a United Front. Feng Xuefeng, returning from Communist headquarters in April 1936, had the task of reconciling the two sides.[61]

Lu Xun's condition suddenly worsened in March 1936, but he refused to go to hospital, and he was somewhat better in April. In May he had a relapse, and from then on he was mostly confined to his favourite cane chair. The doctors informed Xu Guangping (but not Lu Xun) that he had less than six months to live.[62] Friends and colleagues urged him to go abroad to seek medical treatment but he refused. In early June he could hardly move. There was a brief remission in early August, when he talked with Yu Dafu of going to Japan to recuperate,[63] but by late August he was spitting blood. On 8 September, he drafted a mock will in an essay entitled 'Si' [Death], spelling out his wish for a simple funeral and no commemorations, and remaining as intransigent as ever towards those he called his enemies.[64]

In early October Lu Xun weighed only 88 pounds, but was well enough to write to Peiping saying that he was feeling better.[65] On 6 October he went out to see a film with Guangping and Haiying, and on 17 October, he went for a walk in Hongkew Park, visited a Japanese friend, and dropped in at Uchiyama Bookshop. That evening he asked Jianren to help him find another apartment, this time in the French Concession. Although their home on Scott Road was comfortable and convenient, the likelihood of war between China and Japan made his continued residence in 'Little Tokyo' grounds for criticism.

Early on 18 October his condition deteriorated sharply. Xu Guangping went to tell Uchiyama, who came over with the Japanese doctor who had been treating him, but there was not much they could do. Xu Guangping and a nurse took turns to wash him and keep him comfortable. Over the last few days, Xu Guangping hardly left his side except to prepare his meals, attend to the constant flow of visitors and mail inquiring about him, and look after Haiying. When Haiying needed to go to the dentist, she took him there; when he wanted to see his father, she explained that he was ill and sent him to play outside with Amah Xu; when he wanted his father to tell him stories, she told him stories instead.[66] Lu Xun died at dawn on 19 October with Xu Guangping beside him.

Zhou Shuren was only 55 years old when he died. His life had been marked with illness, personal troubles, and the violent death of many friends and students. He was not an easy man to get along with. Apart from his job at the Ministry of Education, which lasted fourteen years but was towards the end a job in name only, his only other regular employment was as a teacher, but in none of his teaching jobs was he able to last for more than a few months. His difficulties with colleagues is well-recorded; less well-known is his impatience with students.[67] Similarly, none of the organizations he founded lasted more than a few months, and his publishing ventures were either still-born or short-lived, in part at least because of censorship. He fostered warm relationships with young writers most of his life, although when he felt they let him down his vindictiveness was intense.[68] He also quarrelled with most of his peers; Yu Dafu, Xu Shouchang, and his brother Jianren were among the very few people about whom he does not seem to have said an unkind word. Not everyone returned his enmity. Writing in 1938, Yu Dafu recorded discussions with people who revered Lu Xun in spite of his peculiar temper: apart from such old university colleagues as Qian Xuantong, Ma Yuzao, and the Shen brothers, these also included Hu Shi and Zhou Zuoren.

Lucian Pye has argued that 'even though the Chinese have been far less encumbered by other worldly and mystical inhibitions than any of the Asian peoples in becoming a part of the modern world, they have established a somewhat different, but functionally equivalent, set of inhibitions. They have tended to attach so much importance to "reality" that they have felt powerless to act against it. Also, and even more important, they have known that if their emotions are aroused, their condition could not have been self-induced but had to be the work of others. The individual should never properly seek self-stimulation, and, therefore, if one does feel the reality of one's emotion, the respectable assumption is that others have in fact been doing something to the self. In this manner the practice of denying the subjective and stressing the objective has the strange consequence of producing hypersentistive "realists", manifesting seemingly paranoid behaviour but with a great capacity for action whenever the cues are well defined.'[69] Lu Xun's letters from Amoy and his last letter from Peking in 1929 portray just such a denial of the subjective and stress of the objective. In Canton, Xu Guangping in Canton even suspected that Lu Xun was enjoying his feelings of impotent suffering.

Lu Xun's letters show him to be suspicious and quick to take offence. He excelled at sarcasm but was awkward at expressing good humour. Most of his attempts at humour in letters to Xu Guangping come across as clumsy and heavy-handed: most have to do with threatening to strike, beat, or whip her. He also found it difficult to tell Xu Guangping that he loved her, and he never managed to convey romantic passion; in his last letters, however, he shows great tenderness towards Guangping and their child. His diary entries show that in addition to his highly public role as a famous author and polemicist, in the last years of his life he also knew the pleasures and distractions of private life: going with Guangping to take Haiying to the hospital, then being accompanied by them when he was ill; but also going for walks, visiting family and friends, and going to Tarzan movies.[70]

Xu Guangping stayed at Lu Xun's bedside while Haiying was woken by Amah Xu, informed of his father's death, and taken to see him. Jianren was then informed, and sent a telegram to Zuoren in Peiping.[71] When his mother heard the news she did not weep but her legs gave way.[72] She was not able to travel to Shanghai for the funeral, and Zhu An was obliged to stay in Peiping to look after her.

Lu Xun's request for a simple funeral and no commemoration was of course ignored, and preparations were immediately undertaken to preserve Lu Xun's memory. A photograph of the dead body was taken, and another as it was conveyed that afternoon to the International Funeral Parlour where it was laid out.[73] On the same day Feng Xuefeng formed a funeral committee which included Mao Zedong, prominent writers, and old friends as well as Jianren and Zuoren. From 20 to 22 October, thousands of people came to pay their respects. Yu Dafu, on hearing the news, immediately left Fukien for Shanghai.[74] On 20 October, Xu Guangping, accompanied by Soong Chingling and Feng Xuefeng, went to the International Cemetery in Hongkew district to select a burial site. On 21 October, the corpse was placed in an expensive nanmu coffin paid for by Soong Chingling. A funeral ceremony was held on 22 October, followed by a procession from the funeral parlour to the International Cemetery; tens of thousands took part.[75]

Soon after Lu Xun's death, with Xiao Jun's help, Xu Guangping, Haiying, and Amah Xu moved to No. 64 Joffre Alley in the French Concession, taking with them the furniture from their old house. Xu Guangping decided to make the move because it had been Lu Xun's wish. The next problem was her financial situation, since she had no income of her own. There was a question about her and Haiying's legal rights to Lu Xun's royalties, but Lu Xun's publishers took the line that payments should go to her. The medical expenses incurred in Lu Xun's final days were heavy; Haiying was still sickly and needed constant medical treatment; and she felt obliged to continue the monthly remittance to Lu Rui and Zhu An.[76] The publication of Lu Xun's last works was not just a tribute to his memory, it was also a financial necessity for the whole family.

In December 1936, Xu Guangping made a public appeal for letters written by Lu Xun: over 800 resulted. A selection of sixty-seven of these letters appeared under the title *Lu Xun shujian* in 1937, followed by a volume of essays and other works. Xu Shouchang began compiling a chronology of Lu Xun's life. In 1937 he wrote to Guangping to apologize for having to mention Lu Xun's marriage to Zhu An and for using the term *tongju* [cohabitation] to describe their own life together in Shanghai, but Xu Guangping agreed on the need for historical accuracy and regarded her status as a mark of rebellion against tradition.[77]

Over the following years, Lu Rui wrote to Guangping several times.[78] Zhu An also wrote, mainly about the rights to Lu Xun's published work; she styled herself

Elder Sister and ended with wishes for Haiying's health. Towards the end of 1936, Jianren travelled to Peiping for his mother's eightieth birthday, bringing Yunru with him, but when they paid a visit to Badaowan, Yoshiko burst into tears, and their eldest son physically attacked his father.[79] Early in 1937, Xu Guangping thought of taking Haiying to Peiping to visit his grandmother, but Lu Rui was advised by Xu Shouchang and Song Zipei that Guangping would not be made welcome by Nobuko and Zhu An. Although Lu Rui thought that Zhu An would not be a problem, she was afraid that Guangping would get the same kind of reception as Yunru had from Badaowan.[80] Xu Guangping wrote back to say that the 'harmful mare' would not be as meek as Yunru, but in the end she did not go. Soon after, Xu Guangping wrote an affectionate tribute to Lu Xun's mother for publication.[81]

Since Haiying was still a child, the new head of the family was Zhou Zuoren. In that capacity Zuoren negotiated an agreement on the disposition of the Badaowan property between himself, Zhu An (as Lu Xun's heir), and Jianren in April 1937; Xu Guangping was neither advised nor consulted, and Yoshiko signed for Jianren without Jianren's knowledge. The first Guangping knew about these arrangements was from a letter from Zhu An to Haiying in 1946.[82]

In November 1937, the Japanese army occupied the Chinese sections of Shanghai, leaving the International Settlement and the French Concession as neutral territory, an 'orphan island' surrounded by the Japanese. Xu Guangping decided to stay on to protect Lu Xun's former possessions, declaring that they were not her private property but the common property of the Chinese people.[83] Limited political activity was still possible in the 'orphan island', and between 1937 and 1941, Xu Guangping was an active member of Shanghai's left-wing literary circles. Among other things, she contributed regularly to two women's journals.

Xu Guangping's main work continued to be compiling materials by and about Lu Xun. A 'complete works' was to have been edited by a committee organized by Xu Guangping, Xu Shouchang, and Tai Jingnong and including Zhou Zuoren. Because of the Japanese occupation of north China, Xu Guangping was not able to go to Peiping to make the final arrangements, and the editing instead took place in her house in Joffre Alley with the help of Zhou Jianren and others. The publisher was the Restoration Society [Fu she], recently formed to organize resistance by left-wing activists who had stayed in Shanghai after the outbreak of war.[84] The twenty-volume *Lu Xun quan ji* [Complete works of Lu Xun] appeared in September 1938.

In June 1938 there was a brief interruption to Xu Guangping's support for Lu Xun's mother and wife as the income from royalties was running low, but payments from the *Complete Works* started coming in the following month and she resumed their remittances.[85] Xu Guangping had shouldered the main burden of their upkeep for two years, but when she learnt from friends in Peiping that Zuoren's contributions to his mother's household were still comparatively meagre (but see also below), she wrote to Zuoren in October 1938 suggesting that they share the costs. Zuoren sent an answer through his mother that they should contribute equally. Xu Guangping continued to send money to Peiping while communications between the two cities remained possible.[86]

Haiying's health had been a worry since early childhood, and now the cost of medical care plus housing was putting a great strain on Xu Guangping. In 1939 she wrote to Yu Dafu discussing the possibility of joining him in Singapore, where the tropical climate would have been good for Haiying's weak chest, but their plans came to nothing. One consideration was still the need to look after Lu Xun's belongings in Shanghai.[87]

The 'orphan island' period came to an end after the Japanese bombing of Pearl Harbour in December 1941, when the Chinese puppet government took over the whole city. Xu Guangping was one of the first in the literary world to be picked up by the Kempeitai. In her own account of her sufferings during the war, she describes how Japanese soldiers raided her house on the morning of 15 December 1941, collecting papers and journals including her manuscript of Lu Xun's diary, and shredding her son's stamp collection. While they were searching the house, she got Haiying out of bed and gave him his instructions to seek refuge with friends and to warn the others. Then she was arrested and taken to Japanese military headquarters where she was interrogated about the Shanghai literary world, but when she refused to cooperate she was beaten, whipped, and given electric shocks. In January she was transferred to another prison where conditions were slightly better, and she was finally released on 1 March 1942 into the care of Uchiyama Kanzô. When she made her way back to Jianren's house, she found Haiying living there under the name Zhou Yuan.[88]

Xu Guangping resumed contact with Zhu An in 1944. Lu Xun's mother had died in April the previous year, but Guangping had not been able to attend the funeral. In accordance with his mother's last wishes, Zuoren had transferred to Zhu An the allowance he had been sending to Lu Rui,[89] but without Guangping's remittances, Zhu An was finding it hard to survive. On Zuoren's advice, she made plans to sell the books Lu Xun had left in Peiping. Guangping only learnt of this when Zuoren arranged for catalogues to be made of Lu Xun's library and distributed copies to potential buyers. Xu Guangping then issued a notice in September 1944 saying that she would not recognize the validity of any sale. Two of her Shanghai friends, Tang Tao and Li Zhemin, went to Peiping to explain to Zhu An the reason for Guangping's reluctance to sell Lu Xun's library and her guarantee that she would take full responsibility for Zhu An's income.[90]

Victory over Japan was announced in Shanghai on 10 August 1945. There were many problems facing Shanghai residents, chiefly soaring inflation and political conflict. Haiying was sent to live in Hong Kong, for the climate and also to be out of harm's way.[91] By this time Xu Guangping had become a prominent activist, supporting herself from her writing and editing. Apart from publicising Lu Xun's life and works, she took part in the women's movement and was one of the founding members of the Association for the Promotion of Democracy in China [Zhongguo minzhu cujin hui] in December 1945. She and Zhou Jianren were also appointed members of a committee to investigate Chinese collaborators in the Shanghai literary world.[92]

Nationally, one of the most prominent collaborators was her brother-in-law, Zhou Zuoren. In 1945 he was taken to Nanking where he was tried and convicted the following year of collaborating with the Japanese. In his defence, Hu Shi pointed out that he used his position to protect Peiping University.[93] He was sentenced to fourteen years' imprisonment (later reduced to ten) and transferred to serve his term in Shanghai. His property, including his share in Badaowan, was confiscated, causing great difficulty to his dependents, including Zhu An. Shortly before he died, Zhou Zuoren claimed that the main reason he stayed in Peiping under Japanese occupation was his financial obligation as head of his extended family: apart from himself and his wife, his son, his daughter, and his daughter's two sons, he also supported his mother, his elder brother's widow, and his younger brother's abandoned wife, two sons and a daughter.[94] In 1945, when the Nationalist Party made a huge grant to Zhu An in the name of commemorating Lu Xun, Xu Guangping made a public appeal to her asking her to return the money (it is not recorded whether she did so or not).[95]

The tenth anniversary of Lu Xun's death was marked by a rally attended by over 2000 people in Shanghai on 19 October 1946. The actress Bai Yang read aloud a tribute from Xu Guangping; Zhou Enlai was among those present. The next day, Xu Guangping took Haiying to visit his father's grave in the company of prominent left-wing writers including Mao Dun.[96] Xu Guangping returned to Peiping for the first time in twenty years on 22 October 1946, travelling by air because hostilities between the Nationalists and Communists made the rail journey unsafe. After putting Lu Xun's library in order she collected some last papers and manuscripts and flew back to Shanghai.[97] Her month-long visit gave Zhu An and Xu Guangping their first opportunity to talk together informally and at length, and although Zhu An found it difficult to talk freely, she wrote to Guangping shortly afterwards to express her appreciation of Guangping's generosity.[98] She also told a visitor that Xu Guangping had been very good to her, although because of inflation she still suffered privations in postwar Peiping.

Zhu An died in June 1947. Shortly before her death, she made arrangements for Haiying to be identified as Lu Xun's legal heir.[99] Xu Guangping sent money from Shanghai for the funeral.[100] Zhu An was buried not by her husband's side, as she had wished, but next to her mother-in-law.[101]

Zhu An was ignored by most mainland critics up until the 1980s. Xu Guangping was routinely described as Lu Xun's wife although they were never married, and mention of his actual wife was taboo. The Chinese literary, academic, and political establishment tried to forget her very existence, as if she was some socially embarrassing disease Lu Xun had accidentally contracted. Lu Xun accepted his financial and social obligations to her but bore her a lifelong grudge, even after his escape from the celibacy he had chosen since his marriage. Zhu An, who had no means of escape, spent thirty years as her mother-in-law's companion and a final four years as a lonely widow, on distant terms with the families of her brothers-in-law and with few friends. The first time her personal name was ever written down was by Xu Guangping in her notes to Xu Shouchang for his chronology of Lu Xun's life in 1937.[102] Nevertheless, she maintained her own dignity, sense of duty, and feelings.

Her one confidant seems to have been Yu Fang, whose curiosity overcame her manners and prompted the few personal comments by Zhu An about her life that have been recorded.

In March 1948, along with six other people, Xu Guangping made her first visit to Shaoxing to see Lu Xun's old home. In October 1948 the CCP arranged for her to travel via Hong Kong to north-east China in order to take part in a meeting of the provisional government of the soon-to-be-established People's Republic of China. Communist forces entered Peiping in January 1949, and she arrived there in February. The same month, Zhou Zuoren was released from jail under a general amnesty. He stayed in Shanghai, attempting to arrange a passage to Taiwan, but Communist forces entered Shanghai before this could be done. Zuoren then returned to his former home in Badaowan, rejoining his wife and family.[103]

In April 1949, Xu Guangping was given the honour of being on a delegation to Prague, on her first ever journey outside China, as a delegate to the World Peace Congress; in June she was sent to Shanghai to organize the Shanghai branch of the Women's Federation. In July, she was elected a member of the council of the new Chinese National Federation of Writers and Artists; in September she was elected to the Chinese People's Political Consultative Conference as a member of one of the eight democratic parties. In 1950 Xu Guangping moved to Peking (as it was renamed in October 1949). As a member of the standing committee of the CPPCC, she was entitled to four members of staff but accepted only a car and the services of a chauffeur; she paid herself for the other members of her staff. Her surroundings were still spartan, furnished with second-hand furniture bought in Peking.[104]

Plans for a major commemoration in October 1949 of the thirteenth anniversary of Lu Xun's death included erecting statues of Lu Xun in Peking and Shanghai and turning his former homes into museums. Xu Guangping now enjoyed rights over all of Lu Xun's property. She donated the house in West Third Lane for use as a museum in July 1950, and the following month donated Lu Xun's Shanghai belongings to a Lu Xun Memorial Hall at the Scott Road house, which was established in January 1951. (This included the furniture she had taken to Joffre Avenue, along with the calendar that was hanging in their bedroom at the time of Lu Xun's death.[105]) In October 1951 she passed over all rights and royalties from the publication of Lu Xun's works to the nation. She also contributed to establishing a Lu Xun Memorial Hall in Shaoxing.

Throughout the 1950s Xu Guangping's main activities were devoted to upholding Lu Xun's place as modern China's foremost writer and to confirming his revolutionary aspirations. Many of her earlier essays, written before Mao Zedoug's 1940s glorification of Lu Xun as 'not only a great man of letters but a great thinker and revolutionary', were personal and intimate, even domestic. Over time, she became more cautious in what she wrote, giving particular emphasis to the left-wing contacts and writings of his later years.[106]

In October 1956, on the twentieth anniversary of Lu Xun's death, Xu Guangping paid a visit to Shaoxing with Haiying and his wife, Ma Xinyun, and then went on to Shanghai, where the main ceremony was being held. To great public display,

Lu Xun's remains were translated from the International Cemetery to Hongkew Park, where a huge memorial had been erected.[107]

Xu Guangping became a member of the Communist Party in 1960. She had previously applied to join but had not been accepted, presumably since the Party regarded her role as a non-Party supporter as more useful. It is not clear when she left the Nationalist Party (probably in the late 1920s or early 1930s) but it seems unlikely that her early allegiance was held against her. The same year Tianma Film Studio in Shanghai drew up plans for *Lu Xun zhuan*, a film biography, under the guidance of an advisory group including Xu Guangping and Mao Dun. The script writing group included Chen Baichen, Tang Tao, and He Ling; Zhao Dan was cast as Lu Xun and Yu Lan as Xu Guangping. The director, Chen Liting, fell ill in 1961, and progress was slow. A new directive in 1963 that films should concentrate on the years since 1949 finally caused the plan to be abandoned.[108] Between December 1960 and June 1961, Yu Lan met Xu Guangping four times, but whether due to lapses in the latter's memory, in Yu Lan's notes or in her subsequent writing-up, the details of her early life given in Yu Lan's undated published account differ greatly from Xu Guangping's own earlier memoirs.[109]

Xu Guangping had visited Japan in August 1956 as a member of a peace delegation, and in March 1961 paid her second visit there at the head of a Women's Federation delegation. According to reports, *Letters between Two* was especially popular among Japanese readers.[110]

Lu Xun's reputation was given a new boost by the Cultural Revolution (1966–76). A characteristic for which he received particular praise was the unrestrained vituperation in his attacks on his colleagues from the time of the Women's Normal College onwards. Xu Guangping was protected through him, although she witnessed the downfall of old friends as well as enemies. The thirtieth anniversary of Lu Xun's death was commemorated with a rally on 31 October 1966, attended by more than 70,000 people; Zhou Enlai was one of the many Party leaders present. The speeches by Chen Bota, Xu Guangping, Guo Moruo, and several Red Guards were printed in a pamphlet under the title *Jinian women de wenhua geming xianqu Lu Xun* [Commemorating our forerunner of the cultural revolution, Lu Xun].[111] In her speech, Xu Guangping echoed the standard adulation of Mao Zedong and the equally standard denunciation of Zhou Yang, Tian Han, Xia Yan, and Yang Hansheng; the only noteworthy passage is where she is obliged to defend her own reminiscences which (according to critics in the Soviet Union) portrayed Lu Xun as a great humanitarian.

Despite having spent much of the past seventeen years writing about his elder brother, Zhou Zuoren was subjected to new attacks on the outbreak of the Cultural Revolution.[112] It is likely that persecution hastened his death in May 1967.[113] Shortly after, in an article for *People's Daily* commemorating Lu Xun's anniversary, Xu Guangping claimed that he had been protected by high Party officials like Zhou Yang and Hu Qiaomu, who had also authorized the purchase of his personal diary for the Lu Xun Museum in Peking.[114] In 1968, there was an incident involving the misappropriation of Lu Xun manuscripts from the Lu Xun Museum for Jiang

Qing's use, and Xu Guangping was also asked to hand over papers relating to Lu Xun. Under stress from these acts, Xu Guangping suffered a sudden heart attack on 3 March 1968. She was taken to Peking Hospital where she died the same day. Zhou Enlai was one of the chief mourners at her funeral. Her ashes were scattered near Lu Xun's grave in Hongkew Park, and a memorial tablet was set up in Peking's Babaoshan Cemetery.

From her correspondence, Xu Guangping's chief characteristic was her determination. Only once in her letters does she falter, when she sees Lu Xun slipping away from her in his fear of condemnation in the eyes of the world. For her part, she refused to be deterred by obstacles, whether expulsion from college or her lover's marriage. With Lu Xun behind her, she was willing to face down Duan Qirui's government in the 1920s and the Nationalist government in the 1930s; alone with her child, she also survived the Japanese occupation. Although she spent thirty years playing the role of the great writer's relic with great energy, it was not her only claim to public recognition: throughout her life she was also active in the Chinese women's movement. Some of her former classmates found her arrogant; this would not come as a surprise to anyone who reads her unexpurgated letters.

Xu Guangping loved to be where the action was, and her drive and enthusiasm for left-wing causes not only helped her win China's most famous writer but also propelled him into a life of public protest. As he once hinted, the consummation of their affair was a factor in the loss of his creative impulse; it was also a major factor in his abandonment of 'trench warfare' for active political participation.

Xu Guangping was intensely loyal. She never fully overcame her respect for Lu Xun as her teacher, and although she debated issues with him she never seriously disagreed with or objected to anything he said or wanted. She was affectionate and loving, putting up with his endless complaints and bad temper with warmth and understanding, and willingly sacrificed her career for the sake of his. As a mother she devotedly fussed over her child, but she resumed her own career when it was possible to do so, thanks to the long-serving Amah Xu and friends.

The latter part of Xu Guangping's life was almost entirely in the public realm: like most left-wing intellectuals, she made the passage from dissident to cadre with no outward indication of unease. Her will is a purely political document, with no mention of any member of her family, and among the many reminiscences that followed her death, there is nothing from any of her own relatives. It could be said that she abandoned her privacy when she set up house with Lu Xun, and yet in the decade that followed she reverted to a semi-traditional role as housewife. Like all prominent figures, however, she found that private revelations were increasingly discouraged throughout the 1950s and 1960s, so that even had she wanted to lower the barriers between her public and private lives there was no appropriate space in which to do so.

Xu Guangping's most attractive characteristics were her humour and imagination. Once their relationship was secure, she was able to tease Lu Xun, and her letters show an ability to be playful and tender at the same time. Always in Lu Xun's shadow even after his death, this is one aspect where her own personality still shines.

Part II

Real and Imagined Letters

The letter was one moment in her hand, then in her lap and then in pocket; and she looked as if she knew not what she did . . . As soon as she dared leave the table she hurried away to her own room; but the housemaids were busy in it, and she was obliged to come down again. She turned into the drawing room for privacy . . .

Jane Austen, *Northanger Abbey*

The rules about reading other people's letters were fairly well defined. If you left your letters lying about and somebody read them, then it was your fault, and you were not justified in retaliation. If somebody rifled your desk or locker and read them then it was their fault, and you were justified in taking vengeance.

L. P. Hartley, *The Go-Between*

8

Traditional Chinese and Western Letters

When Xu Guangping wrote her first letter to Lu Xun in 1925, a section of the Chinese literary world had already become fascinated by the literary possibilities of letter-writing. On the one hand, a group of young women at Peking Women's Normal College were experimenting with epistolary fiction; on the other hand, several literary couples were preparing to open their private correspondence to the public. For Lu Xun, the long tradition of letter-writing in China was probably most important in shaping the form, style, and to some extent even the content of his letters. Both Lu Xun and Xu Guangping were also aware of contemporary Western practice. At the same time, although much of letter-writing generally is learnt behaviour, a great deal is also spontaneous and unique to the letter-writers themselves in any setting, so that it is impossible to detect with any precision which elements in the correspondence between Lu Xun and Xu Guangping are owed to earlier examples. A brief sketch of letter-writing in China and Western countries follows below, with particular attention to published letters, love-letters, and letters in literature:[1] it was against this background that Lu Xun and Xu Guangping drew for their own practice.

There are many ways in which to define letters: with reference to the materials with which they are written, to the formulae which apply at the opening or close, or to the functions they perform.[2] As a literary or semi-literary genre, their most important feature to modern critics is their dialogic nature. Although some letter-writers may be fully absorbed with their own concerns, even to the extent of not presupposing a reply, or not sending a completed letter, it is more common for letter-writers to anticipate responses, imagining the impact of the letter on the other, and looking forward to a continuing exchange. It is in this respect that letters differ most from the other main genre of private writing, diaries.[3] In Virginia Woolf's case, for example, her diaries and letters were complementary, almost nothing being repeated from one to the other: 'Reflections and self-analysis and toying with ideas and phrases were the characteristics of the diary; the purpose of the letters was to communicate and entertain.'[4] Lu Xun's diary, by contrast, serves mainly as a record of the weather, visitors to his home and his calls on other people, letters received and sent, and his salary payments. In his letters to Xu Guangping he was never completely unguarded, but they contain some of his most personal expressions. The correspondence between them is also a fine example of their mutual interaction: only by reading both sides is it possible to understand the influence that each exerted on the other.

The history of letter-writing in China is thought to have its origins in the questions to and answers from the spirits in oracle bone divinations. Some of the documents in the *Shu jing* [Book of documents] can also be seen as public letters with conventionalized openings and closing salutations.[5] The most common word for 'letter' (in the meaning 'epistle') throughout Chinese history has been *shu*, which has the basic meaning of 'writing' and can also mean 'document' and 'book'; it has been recorded in the *Zuo zhuan* [Zuo commentary] in its meaning 'letter'.[6] More specific terms used in ancient times include *du*, *tie*, and *jian*, derived from the materials used for writing letters: *du* were wooden tablets or strips, *tie* were pieces of silk, *jian* were bamboo sections. Wooden letter strips came in pairs, each one *chi* long (hence *chidu* as a generic name for letters as well as denoting a sub-genre of personal letters); the top strip was used to record the names of the addressee and sender, and the strip underneath bore the text of the message. Combinations of these and other terms for the physical stuff of correspondence formed a rich variety of synonyms for letters; at the same time, as more specific words developed for uses of *shu* apart from letters, the meaning 'letter' became more central to the word *shu*.[7]

Most of the earliest surviving examples of Chinese letters were written about public affairs by members of the educated élite; early personal letters from obscure individuals (often dictated to scribes) were not intentionally preserved. The development in literary self-awareness characteristic of the third and fourth centuries can be seen in letters by famous literary figures such as the brothers Cao Pi (187–226) and Cao Zhi (192–232).[8] The earliest extant manual of letter-writing dates from the third century,[9] and the expression *shu xin* [to write a letter] was recorded in use around the fifth century.[10] Liu Xie (ca. 465–522), the author of the first comprehensive study of literary criticism, *Wen xin diao long* [The literary mind carves dragons], defined the nature of *shuji* ('letter records'; also translated as 'epistolary writing') as 'to pour out one's mind in words and display them on bamboo or wooden strips' and 'to state in words without reserve'. These definitions indicate the familiar letter, and Liu Xie gives examples of this type; but he introduces confusion with a long list of sub-types which have little to do with his own definitions.[11] The earliest anthology of literature, *Wen xuan*, also includes a section on letters.[12]

In the tenth century, exchanges of letters between lovers, friends, and family were recorded in fiction and poetry as a normal part of everyday life. Du Fu uses the expression *jia shu* [family letter] in his famous poem 'Chun wang' [Spring scene];[13] the term *jia xin* [family letters] also occurs in the Tang dynasty.[14] Authentic letters by literary scholars and poets such as Han Yu (768–824) and Su Shi (1036–101), written in classical Chinese, were routinely included in their posthumous collections (although their more personal letters, which may have been written in a more colloquial language, were not always thought suitable for inclusion).[15] Women's letters are recorded but not as often preserved.[16] Calligraphic skills were highly valued, and copies were circulated on the basis of artistic merit as much as literary skills or the letters' origins or content. Highly conventionalized formats and vocabularies were developed to signify the relative standing of writer and recipient.

A courier service for official documents including mail dates back at least to the time of Confucius.[17] During the Ming dynasty, it was explicitly forbidden to use the courier service (which was operated by the military) to send private letters or other documents.[18] To cater for commercial and personal mail in urban centres, letter agencies [*min xin ju*], usually connected with a remittance bank or other business enterprise with distance operations, made their appearance in the fifteenth century.[19] The standing of letters as a literary genre was enhanced by the publication of letter anthologies, which began in earnest towards the end of the sixteenth century,[20] more or less coincidental with the rise of the full-length, fully fictional novel. It was also around this time that the line separating formal from informal prose writing became blurred; letters were classed as 'small pieces' [*xiao pin*] along with essays, biographies, and diaries.[21] Qing scholars could expect posthumous publication of their correspondence as a matter of course, and publication during one's lifetime was also commonplace.

Amid this enthusiasm for circulating authentic personal letters in the public realm, the absence of love-letters is notable: whether one-sided or as an exchange, written by men or by women, and circulated during their lifetimes or posthumously, the collection and publication of authentic love-letters was not favoured in pre-modern China. The one apparent exception, love-letters published in the seventeenth century, turn out to be more ritualized and possibly fictional than personal and intimate.[22]

The major characteristics of letters in pre-modern China can be summarized as follows:

(1) letters were frequently published, mostly posthumously but sometimes during the writer's and/or recipient's lifetimes;
(2) personal letters were mostly excluded and love-letters rarely included in collections of letters by public figures before the eighteenth century;
(3) letters by public figures, especially literary figures, were more likely to be preserved than the letters of the humble and obscure;
(4) manuals for letter-writing fostered but simultaneously subverted the notion that sincerity and spontaneity are desirable attributes in personal letters;
(5) as women's writing became more publishable in late Imperial China, there was a tendency to regard women as having a natural affinity with letter-writing;
(6) there was a close association between letter-writing and literature, with letters (especially love-letters) often figuring in fiction and drama;
(7) calligraphic skills led to publication in facsimile versions in modern times;
(8) letters were also valued as a medium of personal revelation, moral guides, and historical records.

Lu Xun does not appear to have taken any special interest in older Chinese letters as a genre, but as a scholar of Chinese prose literature and a busy letter-writer himself, he would have been aware of these characteristics. Xu Guangping did not share Lu Xun's antiquarian tastes but as an educated woman would also be familiar with their history.

Private letter-writing in the West is commonly traced back to Greek times, although its more distant ancestor is in ancient Mesopotamia.[23] The English vocabulary for letters and letter-writing has its roots in Greek and Latin. The word 'epistle' has a Greek root meaning 'missive' or 'sending' from which was derived the Latin *epistola*. An early specialist use of the word is found in the New Testament, where it is used for the letters of the apostles. Its earliest use in English dates back to 893. Over time it came to be used of letters of a public character or addressed to a body of persons rather than an individual, and it is now used only playfully or ironically.[24] In Roman times the terms *tabullae*, *tabellae*, and *codicilli* came into use, referring to the small wooden tablets on which letters were written. The English word 'letter' comes from the Roman *littera*, meaning a letter of the alphabet, which in its plural form *litterae* means written documents or records in general and also epistles; 'letter' in English meaning epistle goes back to 1225.[25]

Already in antiquity letter-writing had developed as a genre with its own conventions in form and content. A list of 19 'epistolary commonplaces' includes charges of not reciprocating letters, the letter as the expression of a friend's soul or character, grief or suffering over the recipient's absence, the joyful experience of receiving or reading a letter, the letter as a substitute for personal presence, and wishes for health or well-being. These commonplaces continue to appear in letters written up to the present day, and are as characteristic of Chinese letters as of Greek or Roman or modern English letters. The only item which is more of a rhetorical figure than a devout wish in modern letters is the prayer or obeisance to the gods for well-being.[26] As with other forms of writing or speech-making, there were manuals for letter-writing, the earliest of which dates from the first century BC.

It is a commonplace observation that all literary works are a kind of letter to a reader.[27] Whether to lend a sense of authenticity and intensity to the expression of sentiment or passion, or simply to display the author's virtuosity, the use of letters as a compositional technique appears throughout Western literary history, and the function and style of love-letters were considered particularly suitable for literary adaptation.[28] The *locus classicus* for the first literary work composed entirely in letter form is *Heroides*, a series of fifteen letters in verse by Ovid (43–18 BC) purporting to be written by women lamenting their seduction, betrayal, or abandonment.[29] Predating the publication of Cicero's letters, Ovid's models were presumably taken from life as well as from earlier literary sources and suggest that the practice of writing love-letters whether in verse or prose was well-established in Roman life.

The earliest and most famous example of a published exchange of love-letters is the correspondence between Abelard (1079–1142) and Heloise (1101–64), written in Latin prose on waxed tablets and preserved on parchment.[30] In the popular imagination, the two-sided correspondence between Abelard and Heloise remains as the standard of a lovers' dialogue against which all others are measured.[31]

The growth of literacy, the increase in leisure, the rise of a unified postal system and new ideologies of subjectivity are factors in the flowering of private, public, and fictional letters in eighteenth-century Europe[32] in novels such as *Clarissa* (1747–8) by Samuel Richardson, *Julie, ou la Nouvelle Héloïse* (1761) by Jean-Jacques

Rousseau, and *Die Leiden des jungen Werthers* (1774; rev. ed. 1787) by Johann Wolfgang von Goethe. The novels dwell on the perils of courtship, and the letters are a device to focus the reader's attention on the emotions and ideas held by the letter-writers. Despite this common ground, the differences between the novels show the flexibility of the format. Although epistolary fiction and letter-writing in general were sometimes seen as a woman's genre (written by women for women), many of its eminent authors were male and, it can be assumed, many of its readers as well. In the words of the young heroine of *Northanger Abbey*, 'I should no more lay it down as a general rule that women write better letters than men, than that they sing better duets, or draw better landscapes. In every power, of which taste is the foundation, excellence is pretty fairly divided between the sexes.'[33]

From being the most popular and widely practised fictional form of its time, the full-scale epistolary novel lost its central position during Romantic and Victorian times never to regain it.[34] Jane Austen's juvenilia, including the first version of *Sense and Sensibility*, were mostly in the form of corrrespondence, but it was a sign of the times that none of her published novels took this form. Unsuited for nineteenth- and twentieth-century plot-driven adventure or detective fiction,[35] epistolary fiction was not easily adaptable either to the late nineteenth- and early twentieth-century modernist vision of fragmented selves and unstable realities, as if the device of shifting perspectives had become too mechanical.[36] Although epistolary fiction continued to be written, other technical devices were developed to provide the assumed authenticity, intensity, subjectivity, and dialogic exchange, which the letter format had contributed to the novel.

The decline of epistolary fiction did not affect letter-writing or the publication of letter manuals, letter collections, and the *Life-and-Letters* class of biography, all of which flourished in nineteenth- and twentieth-century Europe and America. A newly reformed postal system in Britain, introduced in 1840, became a model for other countries, including China. Far more people could now afford to use the post, and far more became literate enough to do so.[37] Dickens claimed in 1847 to be writing a hundred letters a day, and there were twelve mail deliveries in central London as well as servants to dispatch them.[38]

The public or open letter has its own history in life and literature, but the boundaries between authentic letters written for a single recipient or limited circulation and letters written for general publication have always been uncertain. Even intentionally public letters allowed the writer to address the reader with a greater degree of informality than is common in public prose, in the expectation that informality and personal testimony will prove persuasive, and with the flattering implication that the reader is invited to join in a dialogue with the writer. Thanks to the proliferation of newpapers and magazines in the nineteenth century, the intentionally open single letter, of which Zola's 'J' accuse' is a prime example, became a powerful tool for influencing public opinion.[39] Newspaper letter pages also opened up an inexhaustible field for trivia as well as national debate.

As letters became more commonplace in everyday life, correspondence to or from public figures was passed around or published either occasionally or in collections without regard for the feelings of the original author. Inconsistency, if not downright hypocrisy, was rife: Walt Whitman damned in highly inflammatory language his publisher, Park Benjamin, for publishing private letters without their writer's consent in 1846, but less than ten years on he published a private letter of praise to him by Ralph Waldo Emerson without obtaining his permission; Emerson was deeply offended.[40] By the nineteenth century, letters to or by any public figure, especially a professional writer, inevitably fell under suspicion of being written with an eye to future publication.[41] Almost immediately following a writer's death, in some cases, his or her letters would be collected for publication in the complete works, released to biographers for their research, and sometimes sold for great profit.[42]

Remarkable love-letters in the nineteenth and twentieth centuries, posthumously published as exchanges between the two parties, start with the letters between Elizabeth Barrett Browning and Robert Browning.[43] The correspondence between George Bernard Shaw and Ellen Terry, published after her death with his consent and a Preface, is justly called 'intimate' by him, but the two were not lovers and indeed hardly met.[44] One-sided collections include Leo Tolstoy's letters to his fiancée Valeria Asenev in 1856 and 1857, translated by S. S. Koteliansky and Virginia Woolf for The Hogarth Press in 1923: they show great passion when the couple first fell in love and a gradual cooling before the engagement was broken off.[45] Oscar Wilde's love-letters to Alfred Douglas make especially painful reading. The early letters, dating from 1893, were read out in court and became a topic of public ridicule. In prison, when Wilde heard that Douglas was planning to publish his more recent letters, he responded with the anguished plea that was published in part as *De Profundis*.[46]

The most comprehensive history of English letters is George Saintsbury's Introduction to his anthology *A Letter Book*, written in 1921.[47] Saintsbury begins with a brief glance at ancient Chinese, Hebrew, Greek, and Roman letters[48] but his chief subject is letters written in English. He sees England and France as the two countries in Europe where the art and practice of letter-writing were most advanced, and attributes its eighteenth-century flourishing to the literacy, stability, informality, and leisure enjoyed by the upper-classes;[49] but the appearance of letters 'written for publication' he traces back to the seventeenth century.[50] In his own times, he notes, there is a common saying that the penny post has killed letter-writing,[51] although he rather thinks that newspapers are more to blame.[52] Sainstbury's testimony is particularly useful, partly because it is so close in time to the interest in epistolary fiction and published love-letters in China, and partly also because it appears to have been the last general work on the subject.[53]

Despite Sainstbury, an ordinarily literate person in early to mid-twentieth-century Europe and America might still be expected in a lifetime of writing (fifty or sixty years) to dispatch about 18,000 letters; long-lived professional writers such as George Bernard Shaw could be responsible for several tens of thousands;[54] Henry James and Virginia Woolf mention writing up to six or seven letters in one evening.[55] (By contrast, although writing and receiving letters took up much of Mme de Sévigné's life, her extant letters number only 1372.[56])

The decline of the personal letter is hard to date. Henry James questioned in 1875 whether 'we any longer write letters in the real sense at all. We scribble off notes and jot down abbreviated dispatches and memoranda, and at last the postal card has come to seem to us the ideal epistolary form'.[57] Over a century later, Steiner wrote that 'ours is not or no longer a letter-writing culture' and thought it was related to the decline in handwriting after the introduction of the typewriter as well as the telephone.[58] Nevertheless, in the face of electronic competition, the rise of mass communications and the ease of travel in the twentieth century, letters of all kinds continue to be written and valued by their recipients. Personal letters of all kinds from earlier times still catch the public interest, including letters unearthed from family archives by people whose lives are otherwise obscure, and letters that are clearly spontaneous as well as those that read as if copied from a draft.[59]

Features associated with Western letter-writing which differ from older Chinese letters include the following:

(1) personal letters, even love-letters, are generally included in posthumous collections, especially in modern times, although often in edited versions;
(2) dialogic collections of love-letters became a recognized genre after the publication of the correspondence between Abelard and Heloise;
(3) letters, especially love-letters, have formed the main compositional frame or structure in a significant body of poems and novels since Roman times, with the flourishing of the epistolary novel in Europe in the eighteenth century as the most notable episode;
(4) the boundaries between public and personal letters and between authentic and fictional letters have always been blurred;
(5) the physical appearance and aesthetic qualities of letters have not attracted much interest among general readers;
(6) interest in the intimate disclosures of the humble and obscure as well as those of figures in public life appears to be inexhaustible, especially in modern times.

When Chinese writers and readers looked westwards in the early twentieth century, they quickly assimilated all of these features except the last.

Of particular relevance to the letters written and then published by Xu Guangping and Lu Xun are the porous borders between personal and open letters, between love-letters and other kinds of intimate confessions, and between authentic and imagined letters. There is no evidence, however, that Lu Xun or Xu Guangping themselves took any particular interest in Western letters, although it is reasonable to assume that they knew about the story of Abelard and Heloise, the Barrett–Browning correspondence, Tolstoy's love-letters, and Saintsbury's anthology. They would certainly have read at least one version of Goethe's *Werther*, most probably in Guo Moruo's translation, and by 1935 Lu Xun had read (or read of) Oscar Wilde's *De Profundis*.[60] Their chief acquaintance with epistolary fiction and the love-letters of literary couples, however, would have been from contemporary examples in China.

9

Modern Chinese Letters and Epistolary Fiction

Older conventions governing epistolary form were still in place in the 1910s and 1920s.[1] These included an elaborate structure for terms to be used in the greeting or opening salutation, the complimentary opening, references to oneself and to one's respondent in the body of the letter, the complimentary close (taking a new line), the valediction or closing salutation (also on a new line, usually indented) and the signature (lower margin), varying according to the status and profession of the recipient and sender.[2] Dates (often including the time of day) were always given at the end of the letter. The place of writing is also sometimes indicated at the foot of a letter. Apart from the date and place coming at the end rather than at the head of the letter, these conventions correspond to those in formal letters in English in the early twentieth century.[3] In both places, these conventions eventually gave way to more relaxed forms of exchange, but the process was slow and gradual.

The appearance of modern love-letters in China dates back to 1915, with the publication of a manual claiming to offer advice and models for courtship by letters composed in classical Chinese but influenced by European and American letters under the title *Seqing chidu* [Love-letters].[4] It is not clear why the compiler chose to invent a new terminology for the genre, but the word *seqing* emphasizes that sexual love was involved. A volume of model love-letters that became widely known (and an object of Lu Xun's sarcasm) was *Hua yue chidu* [Flower and moon letters] by the novelist Xu Zhenya (1889–1937).[5] The same writer's even more popular novel, *Yu li hun* [Jade pear spirit], incorporated love-letters in its storyline, and the transition to epistolary fiction was under way.[6] The terms *shuxin* [uncountable noun] and *xin* [countable noun] became standard, but *chidu* soon became obsolete;[7] *qingshu* remained in common use.

The movement for a new literature, using vernacular Chinese in forms largely borrowed from Western literature, was not immediately reflected in private letter exchanges. The accepted starting point for literary reform, an article by Hu Shi published in the magazine *New Youth* in 1917, was his own adaptation of a letter he wrote to the editor in October 1916; like the article, the letter was written in modernized classical Chinese, and Hu Shi addressed it with the formula 'Duxiu *xiansheng zuxia*'.[8] An early joke about the startling effect of using the vernacular for private letters occurs in a one-act play written by Ding Xilin in 1923, where a young man writes down a letter at his mother's dictation but alarms her greatly when she discovers that her actual words are being recorded.[9] One of the most original letters in the period 1917–21 is Yu Dafu's letter to Hu Shi dated 13 October 1919, addressed simply to 'Hu *xiansheng*', signed by a pseudonym, 'James Daff Yowen', and requesting that Hu Shi reply in English.[10]

Like the popular fiction magazines which preceded them, the new literary magazines in the first half of the century fostered a sense of a shared public realm between contributors and readers. Debates were conducted in the form of letters between readers and readers as well as between readers and editor, and writers received fan mail which could lead to friendship or even marriage, as in the case of Ba Jin.[11] An early example of published correspondence between literary men is *Sanye ji* [Trefoil]: these letters by Guo Moruo, Tian Han, and Zong Baihua in 1919 and early 1920 consist mostly of literary discussion, and the speed with which they reached publication in May 1920 suggests that they were intended for a wider audience from the beginning, despite Tian Han's disclaimer.[12] Bing Xin's series 'To Young Readers' in *Chenbao fukan* [Morning post supplement], starting in 1923, reintroduced a personal note to published letters but was still firmly in the public realm.[13]

The fiction inspired by the new literary movement included in its earliest phase a stream of epistolary short stories and novels. Much of it was produced by students and staff at Peking Women's Normal College: Huang Luyin, Shi Pingmei, Feng Yuanjun, Lu Xiuzhen, and Su Xuelin.[14] Huang Luyin was not a personal friend of Xu Guangping's (and is not mentioned in *Letters between Two*), but both Lu Xun and Xu Guangping were on close terms with Shi Pingmei and Lu Xiuzhen. Lu Xiuzhen was one of the main editors of the students' *Women's Weekly*, which provided an early testing ground for the eventual publication of epistolary fiction in New Culture journals and other venues such as *Xiaoshuo yuebao* [Short Story Monthly] and *Chuangzao jikan* [Creation Quarterly].[15] Bing Xin, who also wrote epistolary fiction, was not a member of this group but was part of Lu Xun's wider circle of literary acquaintances.

Two stories by Xu Zuzheng, both published in 1926, had particular revelance to Lu Xun and Xu Guangping. Xu Zuzheng (1895–1978) was a colleague of Lu Xun's at Peking University and Peking Women's Normal College in the 1920s. Yu Dafu greatly admired his 'Lansheng di de riji' [The diary of brother Lansheng],[16] which is written in the form of a single long letter based on Lansheng's diary, although Yu pointed out a customary fault of the form, that we only reach a full understanding of the narrator's 'Innigkeit' [sic], while the other party remains beyond our grasp.[17] Xu Guangping read it on board ship to Canton and comments on it in her letter to Lu Xun. Lansheng reappears in 'Song nan xing de Aier jun' [A letter to L. on his journey south].[18] The letter is from Luo Lansheng, a university teacher in Peking, and the addressee is his former student, L., who is about to go south (i.e. to Canton to work under the Nationalist government); embedded in his letter, which is written over a day and a half, are two letters addressed to him, one from L. and one from a friend around his own age. One of the main themes is the transition of a student–teacher bond into friendship. Lu Xun points out to Xu Guangping in their correspondence that L. is Li Yu'an, a young writer whose motives he finds suspicious, and Lansheng himself also alludes to the semi-fictional nature of his letter.[19]

The new epistolary fiction in China, unlike its immediate predecessor in China or its more distant cousin in eighteenth-century Europe, tended to emphasize thoughts and feelings rather than plot and to tease readers with apparent autobiographical reference. Possibly for this reason, the vogue for publishing imagined letters soon gave way to publishing one's own: in a bizarre phenomenon that appears to be unmatched in other countries, young Chinese literary couples from the late 1920s to the early 1930s began to publish their love-letters.[20] Lu Xun and Xu Guangping were among the readers of these published love-letters, whose writers were also among their acquaintances and inhabited overlapping literary circles.

Zhou Zuoren did not publish his own love-letters (if indeed he ever wrote any),[21] nor did he write epistolary fiction, although he saw himself as something of an authority on the history of Chinese letters.[22] Mixed motives appear to be behind his decision to publish his own letters from the 1920s and early 1930s in 1933.[23] The collection begins with a prefatory letter written within a few days of the publication of *Liang di shu* and addressed to Li Xiaofeng, publisher to both Zhou brothers.[24] In what seems like an attack on Lu Xun's choice of title, he defined the term *shu* as letters of the kind that might be included in a public figure's official collected works, whereas *chidu* or *xin* were private letters (*si shu*) not originally intended for publication.[25] The evidence does not support Zhou's contention, but the passage shows that to Zhou Zuoren at least, the word *si* [private] did not necessarily have a negative connotation. In another passage in the same introduction, Zhou Zuoren equated *si hua* [private talk] (a characteristic of *xin* rather than *shu*) with *zhen hua* [true talk], further elevating the quality of *si* [private].[26] He points out that the private letters in his own collection, which included both types, were neither *qingshu* nor manifestos but simply letters to friends; and he concludes with a stinging attack on men past the age of forty who give way to selfish desires despite their age and ugliness.[27] A notable omission from the collection is his separation letter to Lu Xun of 18 July 1923.[28]

Zhou Zuoren was especially fond of reading diaries and letters, which he thought showed the writer's individuality [*gexing*] even more than literary works such as poetry, fiction, and drama since they were not written for a third person's eyes. Apart from their qualities of directness and intimacy, he especially enjoyed reading about the small details of daily life. In his own correspondence he even felt that writing letters himself was too intimate [*simi*].[29] In the 1920s he saw himself as a connoisseur of letters, buying tattered collections at second-hand bookshops, and writing about them with copious excerpts. His main interest was in letters written by men from the Shaoxing area and vicinity in pre-modern times; he was also interested in letters by Japanese writers from Bashô to Natsume Sôseki. He does not seem to have taken the same interest in Western letter-writers.[30] In an essay written in November 1928, Zhou Zuoren shows an intuitive understanding of one function of privacy when he advocates reading in one's room behind closed doors as a cheap and safe way of alleviating anxiety.[31]

Zhou Zuoren's distinction between *shu* and *xin* was not generally observed, and the word *qingshu* continued in common use, from Ding Ling's 'Bu suan qingshu' [Not a love-letter], published in *Wenxue* [Literature] in 1933, to the present day. *Chidu*, on the other hand, is now a rather formal word used to describe letters as a genre, for example in library catalogues. One reason that Zhou Zuoren's directives were ignored was that his influence began to decline in the 1930s, and from the end of the war against Japan to the 1990s, the only works of his that were widely read were his biographical and critical sketches of Lu Xun and his works. Another reason may have been that his remarks in this essay were inspired more by jealousy of his brother than by distinctions recognized at the time.

In choosing to publish their correspondence in 1933, Lu Xun and Xu Guangping were not doing anything particularly remarkable at the time. As the only example of published letters to remain in print up to and including the present, however, *Letters between Two* has been endowed with a misleading aura of uniqueness in this respect. Unique they are, but for other reasons.

10

The Making of *Letters between Two*

Lu Xun was a frequent and somewhat obsessive letter writer, noting in his diary all letters received, replied to, and written; he often replied to a letter the same day as he received it. According to his diary, he wrote over 5600 letters between 1912 and 1936.[1] This was not a particularly large number, compared to Western literary figures of the same period: Lu Xun's ill-health and short career as a writer are reasons for a comparatively meagre output. Although he routinely destroyed ordinary letters once he had replied, and several times made bonfires of accumulated letters, he took great care of the letters he decided to keep for a longer time, sometimes making special envelopes for them.[2] Like most educated men at the time, he invariably wrote with a brush.[3]

As Lu Xun became a famous author, the volume of his mail increased accordingly. Partly for this reason and partly also for reasons of personal security after 1927, he developed the habit of not giving out his home postal address. Letters from his family in Peking and some close friends were sent care of Zhou Jianren at the Commercial Press;[4] other mail was sent care of Uchiyama Bookshop, where Lu Xun would pay a regular call in the afternoon or evening.

Lu Xun was aware of the possibilities of publishing parts of his correspondence with Xu Guangping at an early stage, especially after he began to edit and publish his own journals. In a letter written in June 1925, Xu Guangping suggested publishing passages from his first letter to her in the form of an article in *The Wilderness*,[5] and although her suggestion was not accepted, some of his letters to her from Amoy in 1926 appeared there. Apart from *Letters between Two*, Lu Xun continued to publish occasionally his letters in magazines edited by himself or his friends; it is not clear if they were intended for publication at the time of writing. He defends the publication of letters originally intended for a single reader in his preface to Kong Lingjing's *Dangdai wenren chidu chao* [Personal letters by contemporary writers], as responding to readers' wish to know the whole person rather than to prurience.[6] He does not mention any other collection or anthology of letters but refers to Wilde's *De Profundis* and Romain Rolland's diaries as examples of these authors' reticence in not sanctioning publication during their own lifetimes—unlike Chinese authors, whom he does not name.

After Lu Xun's death, work began almost immediately on preparing his other letters for publication. The first compilation, consisting of only 69 letters, was published in June 1937; by 1946, there were 855 letters.[7] The collection continued to expand: in the 1981 edition of Lu Xun's complete works there are 1333 letters to Chinese respondents and 112 to foreigners, in addition to the letters in *Letters between Two* or otherwise published separately.[8] A survival rate of roughly 20 per cent needs no special explanation. Just as Lu Xun destroyed letters to him, many of his respondents may have acted in the same way for the same reasons, despite the sender's fame. According to records in his diary, Lu Xun sent Xu Xiansu altogether 104 letters and 6 postcards between 1921 and 1930; when she left Peking in 1931 she gave them to Zhu An for safe-keeping, but they later disappeared.[9] It is also possible that some letters, which have been preserved, have not been included in the published collections, such as his letters to Yu Fen and Wang Shunqing. Letters that were discarded are likely to be shorter and more informal than the ones that were preserved.

Of Xu Guangping's separate correspondence before, during, and after her relationship with Lu Xun, only those letters which bear on their relationship have been printed.[10] In her letters to Lu Xun she almost invariably uses a fountain pen,[11] and her clumsiness when she does write with a brush suggests it was not common for her do so.

The Origins of *Letters between Two*

The decision by Lu Xun and Xu Guangping to publish their correspondence was made in 1932, when the vogue for published love-letters by literary couples was at its height, but there is no hard evidence that they read any other collection of Chinese or Western letters or letter-manuals.[12] In his own account, the immediate trigger for *Letters between Two* was a letter to Lu Xun from the Unnamed Society in Peking in August 1932, informing him of the death of Wei Suyuan and the intention of his friends to collect his papers for a memorial volume. Looking in vain for Wei Suyuan's letters, Lu Xun came across his own correspondence with Xu Guangping, and decided to put their letters into print.[13]

An unacknowledged reason behind the decision to publish their letters was financial need. Lu Xun's income at this time depended chiefly on royalties, Xu Guangping was confined to acting as his assistant and housekeeper, and there was a sickly three-year-old child and a maid at home as well as his mother and wife and their servant in Peking to support. The popularity of love-letters and his own literary standing made it likely that the book would sell. Another reason, which may only have developed fully during the process of editing, is that it gave him an opportunity to speak out on issues that still occupied his attention, from the still-pervasive 'dark atmosphere' of the age to the sense of injury he still nourished at his betrayal by former protégés.

As hinted in the reference to their child, publication of the letters was in part provoked by the rumours that still surrounded their relationship. By showing its development in a heavily edited version, Lu Xun and Xu Guangping controlled the story of their affair and made it respectable in the eyes of the world. Up until this time, Lu Xun and Xu Guangping had not attempted any form of public recognition of their liaison, letting it become known only gradually and to close personal friends and family; by going public now, they sacrificed part of their privacy in order to preserve it.

Compiling *Letters between Two*

The task of collation went slowly at first, interrupted by illness on both sides, and it was not until the end of October that they finished sorting out the letters into three parts according to the places where they were living at the time of writing. They had preserved their letters carefully: only one from the period 1925–9 had been placed elsewhere and was missing.[14] Six letters (two from Lu Xun, four from Xu Guangping, all from June–July 1925) were omitted for reasons that will be discussed below; 135 remained to form the published collection.[15]

In November 1932, when Lu Xun made another short visit to Peking to see his mother, Xu Guangping assumed the task of copyist.[16] By the time of his return, she had completed more than half of the manuscript, which had been given the working title *Liang di ji* [Between two]. Meanwhile in Peking, Lu Xun asked Li Jiye, a close colleague in the Unnamed Society, if he thought there would be an audience for *qingshu yi kun* [a bunch of love-letters]. According to Li Jiye's reminiscences, the Unnamed group disapproved of Zhang Yiping's *Qingshu yi shu* [A bundle of love-letters] and recognized that Lu Xun's use of the word *kun* was satiric. Guessing that he was referring to his correspondence with Xu Guangping, they assured Lu Xun of their support and predicted that it would have more readers than *Outcry* (of which 8000 copies had been sold by this time).[17]

The 'title' *qingshu yi kun* never existed as more than a joke. The actual working and final titles were as typically bland as Lu Xun's essay collection titles.[18] Of the two Chinese words for 'two', *er* can act as a prenominal in titles such as Lu Xun's collection *Er xin ji* [Two hearts], published in 1932, but *liang* is more common as a prenominal and additionally has a close aural and visual link with *lia* [couple]. The most common meaning of *di* is 'place', and *liang di* is often read as 'two places', but these letters are sent from more than two places, and the more accurate meaning of the title is 'letters between two [people who are living] apart'. Older Chinese readers may catch an echo of a recommended formula in letters from a husband to his wife, as in *san qiu kuo bie, liang di kui wei* [for three autumns long parted, in two places far away],[19] but the relationship need not be marital or even between two people of the opposite sex. No explanation is needed for favouring *shu* over *xin*, the two common words for letters.

Xu Guangping finished the copying and put the letters in sequence. In order to complete the task quickly, they decided not to include the seven letters from Lu Xun and the eleven letters from Xu Guangping they exchanged during November 1932. In December Lu Xun re-copied the manuscript on high quality paper, writing neatly and with great care (there are no corrections).[20] Before doing this, he carried out the extensive editing that makes *Letters between Two* an unreliable guide to the authors' thoughts and emotions at the time of writing.

Authorship and Copyright

When the book was published, it appeared as jointly authored by Lu Xun and Jing Song (his name preceding hers). When he sent copies to friends, in at least one case, he acknowledged joint authorship by not signing it with his name (as was his custom) but using the expression *zhuzhe* [author/s].[21] Nevertheless, it has customarily been regarded as part of Lu Xun's opus without due recognition of her contribution.

The question of copyright on *Letters between Two* came under scrutiny in 1997 when Zhou Haiying complained that his mother's copyright was being ignored: unauthorized compilers had been republishing Lu Xun's letters without Xu Guangping's since 1986, on the grounds that fifty years after his death Lu Xun's copyright had run out.[22] Lu Xun scholars were sympathetic to Zhou Haiying's claim and subsequent correspondence broadly supported him.[23] A distinction between a co-authored work and an edited work was made, but since there is no irrefutable evidence to show whether or not Lu Xun was the sole editor, the ambiguity remains. Wang Dehou even declared that as a co-authored work, *Letters between Two* should not be included in Lu Xun's *Complete Works*.[24]

Although we may assume that Xu Guangping was consulted during the editing, the extent of her contribution to the final manuscript cannot be established. In his Preface, Lu Xun refers to himself only as editor, and two of his three general comments on the nature of the correspondence refer only to his own letters. It is also noticeable in *Letters between Two* that when letters from both are sent on the same day or if they cross in the mail, his letters take precedence over hers.[25] Again, *her* letters are most heavily edited for changes in expression and suffer the greater number and bulk of deletions and recensions, while *his* letters have the greater number and bulk of additional material. This tendency lends weight to the assumption that Lu Xun is the main if not sole editor.

Xu Guangping, typically, may have settled for less discretion as editor. According to Wang Shiqing, Xu Guangping handed over the original letters to the Lu Xun Musuem in 1956, saying that because they contained many passionate passages she was not planning to have them published during her own lifetime.[26] According to Haiying, on the other hand, Xu Guangping repeatedly instructed him after his father's death that all of Lu Xun's writings, including the original letters for *Letters between Two*, could be published.[27] Whether this is due to a pious wish that her teacher's every word should be preserved or to a more rebellious desire that her own words should be heard more clearly is impossible to tell.

Editing *Letters between Two*

The transformation of the original correspondence (OC) into *Letters between Two* involves words, phrases, extended passages, and entire letters; many changes are minor, others are very substantial. The four processes for editorial decision were deletion, recension, retention, and addition: the special function of each of these will be examined below. We do not know the extent to which Lu Xun pondered over his editing at any point, and the only explanation he offered the reader for deletions and recensions, as will be shown below, was at the very least misleading.

In editorial terms, there is little difference between *deletions* and *recensions*: both have the same function of removing sensitive material from the text. Lu Xun's *retentions*, by contrast, reveal what kind of material he did not regard as too sensitive to expose to a public reading; the most significant of these are probably his references to his bad temper and his urinary habits in Amoy. The extent of his *additions* is particularly noteworthy.[28] Whereas the other processes are common practices when letters are prepared for publication,[29] I know of no other case where the original writer has added a substantial amount of new material. In part this can be attributed to the rarity of cases where both original and published versions of a correspondence can be compared. In *Letters between Two*, the additions are clearly related to the image of himself that Lu Xun wished to present in the 1930s.

A more straightforward function of some recensions and additions is to make the text easier to understand by third-party readers. For example, the phrase 'earlier made an announcement that she was going to Europe but now I hear' is added to his postcript about Ouyang Lan to make it clear that it was expected that she would be leaving Peking.[30] Another example is to a letter by Xu Guangping where Lu Xun adds the expression 'who published their statement' to identify more clearly the seven teachers who supported the students.[31] Some recensions, by contrast, such as the use of initials in Part III, hint to an acute reader of withheld intimacies.

The extent and nature of the editing are fairly consistent over the four years covered by the correspondence, even to the extent of disguising changes in the way they thought and wrote about issues such as privacy. Lu Xun is careful to maintain internal consistency, presumably to conceal from readers the extent of the changes. For example, at the end of his last letter the expression 'this page' is changed to 'two pages' because of the long additions to the text in the revised version.[32] A few anomalies remain. Lu Xun retains a rather mysterious reference to 'breathing under money', his response to a remark of hers deleted from a previous letter.[33] Xu Guangping's reference to a letter she is writing to 'Yushu'[34] is retained, although the reader is not to know who Yushu is and what the letter was about. Lu Xun's reference to 'young gentlemen' to whom they should or should not send money is also confusing to readers.[35]

The missing letters in *Letters between Two* fall into two categories: the one that was not preserved and those that were preserved but not included. Lu Xun indicates where a letter, several letters or a part of a letter were missing, all without further explanation, so that readers are at a loss to know (but can try to guess) for what reason certain letters are being withheld. According to Lu Xun's Preface, the loss of the missing letter 'was through my own carelessness . . . and not because of any official or military misadventure'.[36]

Third-party readers of authentic letters, unless they are very brief, are typically presented with considerable difficulties. I have not seen a case where one partner to an exchange complains about the other's handwriting, but editors of letter manuscripts frequently run into difficulties. In the case of the OC, for example, Wang

Dehou's readings occasionally differ from those by other editors. Even more of a problem, for editors and other unintended readers, is the elliptical style natural to letter-writing: the writers refer to events which are common knowledge to both, or even to their contemporaries, but which soon pass from public knowledge. Some historical events can be reconstructed but many private events remain obscure to even the most diligent researchers. When the original writer is editor, he or she has an easier task, but the unpublished letters still hold many traps for later interpretation. For over seven decades, despite the diligence of several editors, many passages in both the OC and *Letters between Two* are still ambiguous or obscure.

The Preface to *Letters between Two*

In the Preface, dated 16 December 1932, Lu Xun takes the opportunity to express his ideas on letters as a literary product. He forestalls expectations that this correspondence bears any resemblance to the love-letter genre: 'There is no passion for "Life" or "Death!", nor fine words such as "Flowers!" or "Moon!" We did not study "the essence of epistolary art" or "rules of correspondence" for our diction but let our words flow from our pens, ignoring rules of grammar . . . If the book must be praised for having a special quality then I'm afraid it will have to be on account of being ordinary.'[37] Similar claims for 'ordinariness' are commonly made by writers who publish their letters, including Zhou Zuoren. Lu Xun's sneer about 'flowers' and 'moon' is presumably directed at Xu Zhenya's collection.

Lu Xun sets out by claiming that they did not regard their own letters as particularly precious and the reasons for not destroying them was that 'time was very limited in those days' and 'our letters could only involve ourselves at most'. The first reason is hard to believe; the second reason is manifestly untrue. In his following paragraph, Lu Xun concedes that since the letters 'lay in the line of fire on the battlefield for three or four weeks yet suffered not the slightest harm' then 'we feel there is something special, something appealing, about them.'[38] In the context of his other misleading remarks, we need not feel obliged to believe that the letters' survival through the White Terror of the late 1920s and early 1930s was the only source of their value to the authors.

Lu Xun also denies, with disingenuous sarcasm, that their correspondence has any revolutionary flavour, and goes on to make a more startling claim: 'one often hears that letters are the most unembellished and truthful kind of writing, but that is not the case with me. No matter to whom I am writing, I am always very noncommittal to start off with, and what I say is not what is in my mind. In this instance, there are important places where even afterwards I would still write with deliberate ambiguity, because we are living in a country where local officials, post offices, headmasters . . . can censor our letters at will. But there is also, of course, a fair amount of plain speaking.'[39] These remarks appear to be a deliberate attempt by Lu Xun to distinguish their correspondence from conventional love-letter collections as well as to display his usual fondness for challenging conventional attitudes.

The goal of seeking to achieve (or to find) 'naturalness' in letter-writing has been very persistent,[40] but the evidence tends to side with Lu Xun. Many letter-writers undoubtedly wish to reveal their emotions, but others write to mislead or deceive whether for personal advantage, fear of unintended readers or just to protect one's own privacy.[41] From the sustained note of banter in Virginia Woolf's letters, for example, even her intimate friends would be unable to guess at the bouts of severe depression that are simultaneously recorded in her diary.[42] There is also a great contrast between Yu Dafu's diary entries recording a visit to a prostitute and going to an opium den with her the following morning, and his letter a few days later to Wang Yingxia asking her to choose between life as household slave [i.e. marriage] or as 'queen of freedom' [i.e. his mistress].[43] In another letter, Yu Dafu lied to Wang Yingxia, claiming that he had only lived together with Sun Quan for a total of six months between 1920 and 1927.[44]

Lu Xun also conveys the impression, contrary to the opening paragraph, that compiling and editing the letters was only a task they undertook 'when the mosquitoes would not let us write in peace' and that he was not himself over-anxious to go public: 'In the end, however, the strange thing was that a bookshop would be willing to print this book. Since they wanted to, then I let them print it, it was something that did not really concern me . . .'[45] The charitable interpretation of these remarks is that Lu Xun's readers would share the joke in his mock-modest statement (and, like him, ignore the role of Xu Guangping in ownership of the letters).

In his penultimate paragraph, Lu Xun refers to changes he has made to peoples' names, giving two reasons: 'One is because I'm afraid of causing inconvenience to those who appear in our letters; the other is solely for selfish reasons, to avoid such trouble as being summoned to court for libel.'[46] This paragraph is also less than frank. Lu Xun makes no mention of any of the other revisions to the letters, and refuses to admit that the revised text (including the often provocative additions) could give cause for offence. The reference to 'libel' comes from a letter written by Gu Jiegang in 1927 warning Lu Xun that he would seek redress in court for Lu Xun's hints that Gu Jiegang had been responsible for the expulsion of rebellious Amoy students. What remains surprising is that none of the other vilified figures in the letters ever threatened to take Lu Xun to court, and that others (like the long-suffering Sun Fuyuan) continued to put up with him at all.[47]

In his final paragraph, Lu Xun spells out three reasons for publishing the correspondence: as a memento for their own sakes; to thank friends; and to leave for their son a true impression of his parents' experiences. The third reason, if taken literally, is especially bogus, since the revisions mean that the impression left by *Letters between Two* of the couple's relationship is anything but 'true'; but since Haiying also inherited the original letters he was able to construct a more accurate account of his parents' thoughts and emotions. It is the third-party readership from 1933 onwards that Lu Xun thus deceived. The unspoken purposes of publication are examined further below.

Printing and Publishing

Half the manuscript for what was now being called *Letters between Two* was completed and dispatched on 14 January 1933 (the other half is not mentioned in Lu Xun's diary, and may have been sent already by Xu Guangping). The publisher was Qing guang Press, the temporary operational name for Beixin Press, which had been closed down by the Nationalist government. The proofs came on 6 April, and on 19 April they received twenty free copies of *Letters between Two* plus another twenty copies for $14. According to Lu Xun's diary entries, 3000 copies were sold during 1933, for which he received $750, and another 1500 copies were printed in 1934.[48] *Letters between Two* was included in Lu Xun's *Complete Works* compiled by the Lu Xun quan ji chubanshe in 1941 and reissued twice in the 1940s, and has since been a standard part of Lu Xun's works.

Lu Xun's unhappy marriage, his rift with his younger brother, his youngest brother's complicated marital affairs, and his own friendships with younger women had all attracted talk even before his affair with Xu Guangping became common gossip in Peking and Shanghai.[49] Aware of this background, some readers felt let down on the publication of *Letters between Two* in 1933. It was claimed for instance that the published letters are not real love-letters since they lack the frisson of true passion.[50] In a letter to Xiao Jun and Xiao Hong in 1934, Lu Xun claimed that *Letters between Two* was not a collection of love-letters, first, because the couple were not lovers when the correspondence started, and also because their ages and the circumstances restrained displays of strong emotion.[51] The argument on age is unconvincing: consciousness of middle-age seemed to have fanned rather than dampened the flames in the case of the British Prime Minister, H. H. Asquith,[52] or old age in the case of Liang Shiqiu.[53] Lu Xun's temperament is perhaps the key, along with his dominance in the relationship and its expected eventual outcome. His native caution impressed itself on Xu Guangping from the start: her most passionate letter is her first; thereafter, her restraint echoes his, or is edited out. In somewhat similar circumstances, Luo Jialun's letters to Zhang Weishen, which can be characterized as courtship letters to a future wife rather than love-letters to a potential or current mistress, are even more restrained.[54]

Writing in 1980, Tang Tao recalled that *Letters between Two* appeared at the time of a debate on differences in character between Westerners and Asians. Some Chinese intellectuals claimed, for instance, that Asian and especially Chinese people were less apt to show their feelings openly, while others thought there was no great difference. The appearance of published love-letters in the late 1920s and early 1930s seemed to support the latter, but *Letters between Two* was held to be an example of Chinese emotional restraint, especially in the correspondents' forms of address. Tang Tao does not mention that *Letters between Two* was extensively revised for publication, so that it can be seen as evidence that Chinese people do reveal their feelings but not in public.[55]

Financially, publication of *Letters between Two* was a worthwhile venture. One of the first critiques to appear even suggested that it had single-handedly rehabilitated the discredited *qingshu* genre.[56] If one of their aims was to still the rumours about their relationship, however, they were not entirely successful. In October 1935, it was claimed in a newspaper that Lu Xun's *xiao airen* [concubine, i.e. Xu Guangping] was in Peking, although she did not return to Peking until after Lu Xun's death.[57] One voice was missing from *Letters between Two*: when the book was published, Zhu An was silent but not yet entirely to be ignored.[58] Nevertheless, Xu Guangping was generally conceded the status of a wife in the early 1930s and was treated as Lu Xun's widow after his death in 1936. The publication of *Letters between Two* undoubtedly played a part in their public acceptance as a couple.

11

Frequency, Appearance, and Terms of Address

The letters between Lu Xun and Xu Guangping from 1925 to 1929 shared many formal characteristics of love-letters by other couples and of letter-writing in general in the early twentieth century. Their frequency was due to the efficiency of the post office as well as to their own feelings; they were as careful or carefully slapdash respectively in the appearance of their letters as in their language use; and they began by using the conventional forms of address only to abandon them as their intimacy increased.

Frequency

A typical feature in lovers' correspondence is its frequency: lovers tend to write every day or every other day, regardless of how often they send their letters or receive letters in return. The speed, cheapness, and reliability of the post office in Britain's main cities in the early twentieth century increased the rate at which exchanges could take place. Lydia Lopokova in London and John Maynard Keynes in London or Cambridge in the 1920s wrote to each other almost every day, and it did not seem to bother them that their letters often crossed.[1] In Leonard Woolf's rare absences from home in the 1920s, Virginia Woolf wrote to him every day; in her letters to others, she often mentions the low cost of postage as a reason for them to write (but on occasion suggests that they telephone since the post is not always delivered in one day). In a letter written in 1928, Woolf complains that a letter sent from Berlin took four days to reach their country house in Sussex (it would now take about a week).[2]

Mail deliveries in Peking and other major cities in the 1920s and 1930s were frequent, regular, and cheap. In spring 1927, Yu Dafu wrote almost every day to Wang Yingxia, whether she was in Shanghai or in Hangchow; and when she was in Hangchow, they often sent their letters by express mail. In March he apologized for having let a day pass without having written to her. In April he suggested that she need not write to him every day, while he might not write every day either; but in May, he was apologetic again about not having written the previous day and assured her that from then on he would write every day. When the postal service between Hangchow and Shanghai was disrupted by political turmoil in April, however, he asked friends such as Jiang Guangci to carry mail for them.[3] By May 1927, the situation had deteriorated further, and he suspected that mail was being opened by censors.[4] Although he produces no grounds for believing that mail was being intercepted, his letters became less frequent and ceased altogether by the end of the month.

While they were living in Peking in 1925, Lu Xun and Xu Guangping exchanged over forty letters in just over four and a half months even although they saw each other every few days.[5] Letters sent one morning would arrive the same afternoon or the following morning. Neither of them mentions the cost of postage. Their letters rarely cross: at this stage they usually wait for a letter from the other before sending their next. The response is usually immediate, unless events intervene, although in her reply to Lu Xun's first letter to her, Xu Guangping notes that it has taken her three days to answer.[6] Their need to write is explained in their own letters: especially in the beginning, they rarely meet alone, and only in letters can they express themselves fully and intimately. These are letters of courtship; and when the courtship is completed, letters are no longer needed and the correspondence stops.

The frequency of their letters between Canton and Amoy in 1926 is higher: except in special circumstances, they write almost every day, and put a letter in the post every two or three days. But now their letters often cross, and their frustration is explicit. They are obliged to rely on the mail for any communication at all (except for visitors carrying letters), but the distance between them and delays caused by civil war make deliveries slow (up to ten days) and uncertain (although no letters fail to arrive). The blame lies with themselves and with others: they make foolish decisions on when and where to send mail; Xu Guangping's fondness for using different forms of Lu Xun's name on her envelopes may or may not be causing delays; but the staff at the post office or at the school are lazy and/or incompetent, and express mail takes even longer than ordinary mail. The uncertainty of their future together exacerbates the pain caused by poor communications. These are letters by engaged lovers still hesitating before full commitment.

Although the country is still in a state of civil war in 1929, the postal service between Shanghai and Peking is more reliable and rather swifter than in the south (letters take about five days). Again they write almost every day and mail a letter every two days or so. Letters posted on different days sometimes arrive together, but their mutual trust allows them to make light of crossed mail and delays. These are letters of loving partnership, short only of legal marriage. Their unpublished correspondence of November 1932 consists of daily letters, their son's health adding to their need to be in touch. They are parents now, and their letters are primarily domestic.

Although Lu Xun wrote almost as often from Amoy to his brother Jianren, Xu Xiansu, and Wei Suyuan, the attention given in their letters to their letters (see later) suggests that to Lu Xun and Xu Guangping writing and receiving their letters became one of the most important events in their daily life. Some letters take up an hour or more of their time to write.[7] Although at times the demands on Lu Xun's time were heavier and the total volume of his correspondence much greater, the original correspondence shows them as equal contributors to the exchange.

Appearance

In appearance, Xu Guangping's first letter to Lu Xun on 11 March 1925 is surprisingly slapdash.[8] It was written with a fountain pen, and although it starts off neatly enough, by the second and third pages the handwriting has degenerated into a scribble, and the fourth page is even messier as she tries to squeeze in a footnote without starting a new page. There are several interlinear corrections and additions, and Xu Guangping evidently did not bother to make a fair copy. She used standard writing paper with ruled vertical columns, and ignored the margin lines provided at the top of the page for the date and page number. A possible explanation for her carelessness is a wish to appear spontaneous and straightforward; consciously or otherwise, she may have sensed that this kind of approach would arouse her respondent's attention.

Lu Xun's reply is written with a brush on slightly more elegant notepaper, with ruled vertical columns rounded at the top and bottom to resemble bamboo strips. His script is neat and regular, and there are two errors corrected at the time of writing. Abashed by his example, Xu Guangping started her second letter carefully, but she soon got carried away and the last pages are even more careless than those in her first letter. This contrast between their writing styles remained constant throughout the correspondence.

By April 1925 Xu Guangping's letters are getting so long that she starts to use page numbers and frequently runs out of ink. Around the same time, Lu Xun changes his notepaper to one less fancy, and his calligraphy becomes more idiosyncratic: sometimes larger, sometimes smaller, not always contained within the ruled columns. In May she tries using a brush for the first time, on squared paper; in reply, his handwriting becomes more unrestrained, and he writes on unlined paper. The calligraphy in his letter denying drunkenness (2 June) is particularly vigorous. She uses a brush again, but the effect is not impressive. On 29 June, his handwriting is much bolder than usual, and on 9 July he signs off with an uncharacteristic flourish.

The letters between Canton and Amoy are more regular in appearance. Xu Guangping switches between using a pen on horizontally lined paper (writing from right to left) and a brush on vertically ruled paper. Lu Xun returns to his original small, neat script, and adds sketches of the buildings in Amoy to show where he is living; he also sends a postcard with an asterisk marking his room. In turn she sketches her living quarters at her school in Canton. Starting from 20 September, he uses notepaper supplied by Amoy University, overwriting the upper and lower margins and not bothering to stay within the lined columns. Both of them tend to write to the foot of the last page and to reduce the size of their writing rather than take a new page.[9] In October, she draws his attention to the number of errors in her letter that she has corrected on rereading it (deleted from *Letters between Two*).[10] The short note from Xu Guangping dated 17 November is written with a brush on vertically lined paper and is addressed to 'Xun *shi*' [Teacher Xun] rather than her usual 'My dear teacher'. As from 28 November, Lu Xun stops using the university's notepaper, and in December, as the time for his departure approaches, his handwriting becomes bolder and larger again.

The main difference in the third stage of the correspondence (Shanghai-Peking, 1929) is on Lu Xun's side. Apart from two letters written with a brush, Xu Guangping still uses a pen on horizontally lined paper; her handwriting has become a little more regular, and there is less sign of (or need for) interlinear corrections and additions. Lu Xun still uses a brush, but his script is lighter, larger, and more flowing than in his letters from Amoy. He now writes on unlined paper decorated with line drawings of lotus flowers and pods, a delicate reference to her pregnancy (see his letters of 23 and 27 May for his selection and purchase of the paper at Liulichang). At the foot of his first letter, in place of his signature, he draws a small odd-looking animal with a long neck, evidently intended to represent the 'elephant' of her pet name for him (see below). In response to this letter, she sketches an even odder-looking animal with an elephant's trunk, a camel's hump, and a horse's tail in front of her address, with a note reproving him for his inaccuracy. He tries other variations of his long-necked or long-trunked elephant in the remainder of his letters from Peking in 1929. These embellishments disappear in *Letters between Two*. Similar signature sketches appear in the correspondence between Winston and Clementine Churchill: she as a cat, he as a pugdog, a pig, and a lion.[11]

In the last phase of their correspondence, the unpublished letters of 1932, Lu Xun uses a brush on unlined paper; Xu Guangping uses a pen on vertically ruled paper; and they dispense with playful flourishes.

Punctuation at the time was very much in flux, and Lu Xun regularizes it in his editing. For reasons that are not clear, the straight and wavy lines used in the letters alongside characters to indicate names and book titles are omitted in the manuscript and printed versions of *Letters between Two*.

Forms of address

Men writing to men in 1910s and 1920s China routinely addressed them by their personal names or styles, usually followed by the title *xiansheng* or *xiong* (occasionally *jun*). In this context, *xiansheng* roughly corresponds to 'Mr', but there is no equivalent in English to either *xiong* or *jun*, both common polite but informal salutations between men. The full meaning of *xiong* is 'elder brother', and even when it is not to be taken literally in either the sense of 'older' or 'male sibling', it is normally restricted to discourse between men.[12] The translation 'brother' is appropriate because it assumes discourse between men on terms of social equality. Men writing to women and women writing to men or women tended to use the recipient's personal name alone.[13] Men and women both routinely signed themselves simply by their full names or personal names only; if *xiong* is used in the opening salutation, *di* [younger brother] is often used with the sender's personal name.

The term *qin'ai de*, the standard Chinese translation of the English word 'dear',[14] was not common at this time: Yu Dafu, for example, uses the salutation *qin'ai zhi* only once, to his brother and sister-in-law in 1916.[15] In 1927, writing to Wang Yingxia, he begins by addressing her as 'Wang *nüshi*' and thereafter adopts 'Yingxia *jun*' or 'Xia *jun*' as his standard greeting; only after they become lovers does he begin to address her as 'Yingxia, *qin'ai de* Yingxia'. Luo Jialun, writing from the United States in the early 1920s to Zhang Weizhen, the woman he hoped to marry, addressed her as 'Weizhen *wu you*' [my friend Weizhen] and signed himself at first '*di* Jialun' and then simply 'Zhixi' (his style); he did not bother about a complimentary opening but always included a complimentary close.[16] Two of Zhu Xiang's four letters to his wife in the 1936 posthumous collection of his letters use the salutation *Wo ai* [My love]; *Qin'ai de Ni meimei* [Dearly beloved sister Ni] and *Ni meimei wo de Meng mu* [Sister Ni my Mencius's mother] are each used once only. This combination suggests that in the late 1920s when these letters were written, *qin'ai* is much stronger in feeling than 'Dear'.[17] The use of *ni de* [Your] in the valediction, which Lu Xun and Xu Guangping use in their Canton–Amoy exchanges, became accepted during the 1920s.[18]

Lu Xun's early correspondence used the conventional forms of his time. His first letter to his friend and contemporary Xu Shouchang, dated 15 August 1910, addressed him by his *zi* [courtesy name] Jifu, followed by *jun,* and *jian* meaning 'inspect' or 'watch'); it was signed Shu, preceded by *pu* (a conventional term meaning something like 'your servant') and followed by *shang* ([sent] upwards) and the date. Lu Xun retained these forms, with minor variations, to friends for several years. His patron Cai Yuanpei, on the other hand, he addressed in 1917 by his *zi*, followed by the title *xiansheng* and the honorific for one man of letters to another, *zuoyou*, and signed with his full name Zhou Shuren, preceded by *wan* [late (born)] and followed by *qin shang* [respectfully (sent) upwards] and the date.[19] The first of his published letters in which Lu Xun used the expression *xiong* was to Qian Xuantong on 5 July 1918; this letter was also signed 'Lu Xun', the first example of this signature. In 1925 he generally addressed his letters to people by their full name, personal name or *zi*, followed by *xiansheng* or *xiong*, and signed himself 'Lu Xun' or 'Xun', sometimes followed by the honorific *dun shou* [literally, touching one's head on the ground], and the date. In letters to his mother, however, he retained a very formal, old-fashioned style.[20]

No examples of Xu Guangping's letters before her correspondence with Lu Xun have been published. Given the gap in their ages, it could be supposed she would be more informal than he in her general epistolary style to friends of her own age and social standing; on the other hand, in her first letter to her teacher, a famous writer, about a major scandal at her school, she could be expected to be more formal.

Xu Guangping starts her first letter with a simple 'Lu Xun *xiansheng*' [Mr Lu Xun], but her complimentary close, valediction, and signature are very formal: 'With best wishes for your literary work, A humble student under your instruction, Xu Guangping'. In a final touch of playfulness, however, she adds a postscript explaining why she does not use the word 'female' before the word 'student', and then explains that it's a joke.

Lu Xun chooses to answer with the salutation 'Guangping *xiong*', omits the complimentary opening, closing, and valediction, and ends with the unadorned signature 'Lu Xun'. Xu Guangping appears to offer a rebuke in the very formal salutation in her reply: 'Lu Xun *xiansheng zuoyou*' [My respected teacher, Mr Lu Xun], and signs off equally formally, 'With best wishes for your writing, Respectfully, Your humble student Xu Guangping'. In the body of the letter she questions his use of *xiong* [elder brother] to a female student. In his reply, Lu Xun defends the use of *xiong*, claiming that it only means 'elder' and saying that he uses it with all his close friends. This is not a convincing justification, if only because Lu Xun does not yet know Xu Guangping outside the classroom.

It is clear from Xu Guangping's reaction as well as the examples mentioned above that Lu Xun departed from the norm in addressing a young woman as *xiong*, and it is unfortunate that none of his letters to other young women are available for comparison. It would be an exaggeration to characterize his inappropriate use of *xiong* at this point as a deliberate, sexually charged instance of gender and age reversal, yet in the light of the repeated instances of self-conscious gender reversal in their subsequent correspondence and in Xu Guangping's essays about their affair, it seems prophetic. It could also be due to Lu Xun's awkwardness with female students, or to a wish to establish relations of sexual as well as generational equality with his students.

Lu Xun continued to address Xu Guangping as 'Guangping *xiong*' for the remainder of their correspondence in 1925 and 1926. He also continued to sign himself 'Lu Xun' until 2 June, when he changed to the more intimate 'Xun'.

Xu Guangping maintained her formality throughout March but became more relaxed in April. After employing the salutation 'My respected teacher, Mr Lu Xun' on 20 March, she changed to the simpler 'Lu Xun *shi*' [Teacher Lu Xun] for the rest of the 1925 letters (with the exceptions noted below). Also on 20 March, Xu Guangping (for reasons that are not clear) reverted to a more formal signature, 'Offered by Mr Lu Xun's student Xu Guangping'. In one of his rare editorial interventions in this area, Lu Xun reduced this to the more usual 'Offered by your student, Xu Guangping' in *Letters between Two*.[21]

The term 'young devil' was first used by Xu Guangping of herself in her 20 March letter and again in her 26 March letter; Lu Xun confers his approval in his 22 March and 8 April letters. On 10 April, she signed herself 'The young devil (a name acknowledged by Mr Lu Xun), Xu Guangping', and continued to use her new nickname without further adornment (with the exceptions noted below) as her valediction for the remainder of the 1925 Peking correspondence.

Lu Xun from the beginning refers to himself in the first person but frequently uses the third person in various formulations for Xu Guangping; at first this seems like a formality, later it seems more like affection. (Tolstoy also refers to himself in the third person in his letters to his fiancée.)

Xu Guangping avoids the use of first and second person in her first letter, but from her second letter on she uses the first person freely, and when she uses expressions like *dizi* [disciple] for herself, it is more as a joke than in deference. From her third letter on, she often refers to herself by her nickname 'young devil'. She also often uses the term 'my teacher' in the vocative case and as a substitute for 'you' in the 1925 Peking letters. Xu Guangping's coy reference to herself as *laoren* [old person] in her 30 April letter is changed to *wo* [me/my] in *Letters between Two*.[22]

From mid-June until the end of the 1925 exchange, both give way to a playful mockery of the conventions. Xu Guangping inserts the complimentary close 'Respectfully awaiting denunciation!!!!' on 12 June, and on 17 June she reverts to the salutation 'Respected Teacher, Mr Lu Xun'. In the first part of his 28 June letter (omitted from *Letters between Two*), Lu Xun omits the usual opening salutation and begins with the stern *Xun ci* [Instructions], and signs himself '*Laoshi*' ['Your teacher']. On 9 July, he addresses her as 'Your excellency, my dear elder brother [*xiong*] Guangping' and signs off 'Respectfully advising of my kind regards to "the good talker", With sincere admonitions from "Your teacher"'. On 13 July (letter omitted from *Letters between Two*), she calls him *nen di* [sweet little brother] and signs off with *yu xiong shou le* [hand-inscribed by his foolish elder brother]; her next letter (15 July; omitted from *Letters between Two*) is addressed to *nen didi* [sweet little brother] and signed *yu xiong le* [inscribed by his foolish elder brother]. Lu Xun finally responds on 16 July (letter omitted from *Letters between Two*) by addressing her as *yu xiong*. This facetious usage is typical of the letters exchanged in June and July; it is also an early example where Xu Guangping, following his example, reverses gender and age differences. His last letter to her, dated 15 August (omitted from *Letters between Two*), uses the salutation '"Miss" Jing Song *xue xi cheng men*' and the complimentary close (or valediction) and signature 'Respectfully offered by Teacher Lu Xun'.

Gender reversal often figures in salutations between lovers, like the use of pet names (see below), and is another indication of the changed relationship between Lu Xun and Xu Guangping that had begun a year earlier. An example from premodern China, of which they were not likely to be aware, is the signature '*di*' [younger brother] or *nü di* [female younger brother] used by the Ming courtesan Liu Rushi.[23] An even more striking use of gender reversal in opening salutations occurs in the letters from Princess Mary (1662–94) and Princess Anne (1695–1714) to their friend Frances Apsely, referred to as their 'husband'.[24] There is no reason to regard any of these instances as learnt behaviour rather than spontaneous invention.

In the Amoy–Canton exchange of 1926–7, Lu Xun and Xu Guangping drop the remaining traces of formal epistolary conventions along with their former facetiousness. Lu Xun mostly kept to the salutation 'Guangping *xiong*' and the signature 'Xun' or 'L. S.' (from Lu Sun, the romanized form of his name that he then used), with no complimentary close or valediction.[25]

Xu Guangping was typically more playful. From the start she adopted English expressions in the opening and closing salutations: 'My Dear Teacher' and 'Your H. M' (changed to 'MY DEAR TEACHER' and 'YOUR H. M.' in *Letters between Two*).[26] (Neither of them ever used the expression *qin'ai de*.) 'H. M' or '*hai ma*' stands for *hai qun zhi ma* [the horse which harms the herd], an epithet given to Xu Guangping by Yang Yinyu at the time of her expulsion in 1925; Lu Xun used it to refer to her in his 30 May letter, she took it up (after a slight delay) in her 5 June letter, and his mother then adopted it as a pet name for her as well. Xu Guangping's use of English in her salutations, like her use of formal epistolary style and the allusions to classical writers in her Peking letters, comes across as a mixture of pretentiousness and self-mockery.[27]

Lu Xun has his moments of playfulness as well. On 1 November, he addresses Xu Guangping as ' "Lin" *xiong*' [Brother 'Lin'] (changed to 'Guangping *xiong*' in *Letters between Two*), and on another four occasions he takes on her identity, signing himself 'H. M.' (changed in *Letters between Two* to 'L. S.'); for this and other examples of gender or identification reversal, see below.

They retain third person terms for themselves and for each other in the body of their letters, but when Lu Xun uses 'my friend' or 'H. M.' instead of 'you', again his use of the third person is intimate, not formal.[28] When Xu Guangping refers to him as 'Ah Q' she expresses a very playful form of affection.[29]

In their Shanghai–Peking exchange of 1929, Lu Xun and Xu Guangping use endearments freely in the salutations, signatures, and body of the letters. Many of these are in the form of pet names, which, it is clear from the context, were coined before Lu Xun's visit to Peking.[30] Lu Xun's first letter from Peking is addressed to 'Guai gu! Xiao ciwei!' [Darling girl! Little hedgehog!], and is signed with an odd drawing of a beast with a long neck;[31] variations of this drawing sign off all his letters from Peking in 1929. When she receives this letter, Xu Guangping responds with an opening salutation consisting of a drawing of an odd-looking beast and a criticism of his draughtsmanship.[32] The other letters in this exchange all have variations on these terms, and complimentary openings and closes are dispensed with. In *Letters between Two*, the drawings disappear, replaced by 'EL', 'ELEF.' 'L.' or 'Xun'; Xu Guangping's opening salutations are reduced to variations on the form 'B. EL' and 'EL DEAR', and her signature reverts to the former 'H. M.'[33]

In the body of her letters, Xu Guangping similarly refers to herself as 'Little Hedgehog' (changed to 'I' in *Letters between Two*) and to him as 'Little White Elephant' but she also regularly uses 'I/me' and 'you'.[34] Lu Xun more often prefers 'darling girl' and/or 'Little Hedgehog' over 'you' (changed to D.G. and L.H. or 'you' in the published versions),[35] when he is quoting his mother, he retains her nickname for Xu Guangping, 'the harmful mare',[36] and he also uses other third person reference for her (retained as a pronoun or initial letter).[37]

The use of animal pet names is spontaneous and universal among lovers. An early example in which it is taken to extremes is in a 1780 exchange between Erasmus Darwin (1731–1802) and Anna Seward (1747–1809), whose letters are written in the voices of two cats, Mr Snow and Miss Po Felina.[38] Virginia Woolf addresses Leonard Woolf as 'Dearest Mongoose' and signs herself with variations on the name Mandril, sometimes abbreviated.[39] Simone de Beauvoir calls Nelson Algren 'crocodile' and refers to herself as 'frog' (although these names occur mainly in the body of the letters and not so much in the opening and closing salutations).[40] Other kinds of baby-talk are also common, as in Swift's complimentary close to Stella in January 1710: 'So good night, myownlittledearsaucyinsolentrogues'.[41] Swift also refers to Stella in the third person as MD and to himself as 'Presto'.[42] Swift, Woolf, and de Beauvoir did not edit their letters for publication, and we have no means of knowing if they would have permitted their pet names to become public knowledge.

The terms of address 'Gu ge' [Girl's elder brother] for Lu Xun[43] and 'Ge gu' [Elder brother's girl] for Xu Guangping[44] are used both in the opening salutations and also in the body of the letters in preference to 'you'. The word *ge* [elder brother] sounds more affectionate in Chinese than in English translation: it is traditionally the term by which a young woman addressed her lover or husband.[45] The use of *gu* [aunt, sister-in-law, unmarried woman] in this context is not so common, while the expressions *gu ge* and *ge gu* are their own inventions and sound quite peculiar in Chinese as in English. The word *guai* is often used to praise or scold a child, and can mean both 'naughty, stubborn' and 'clever, obedient'. These terms of address, like the pet names, are deleted in *Letters between Two*.

Endearments continue in a simplified form in the unpublished letters of November 1932, where Xu Guangping invariably addresses Lu Xun as 'Ge' and signs herself 'Gu', while Lu Xun's address to her is invariably 'Guai gu', and he signs himself Xun, L. or 'Ge'.[46]

It is easy to track the openings and closings in the OC and the changes made to them in *Letters between Two*. No such precision, short of a full-scale concordance, is possible for the language used in the body of the letters, and few generalizations about style in the original correspondence apply to the published version (or vice versa), so many and extensive are the revisions. (For further discussion of language use see below in Part III.)

Summary

From the very beginning of their correspondence Xu Guangping and Lu Xun fall into the habit of writing to each other almost every day, and at length. They are formal with each other at first, and uncertainty introduces an uneasy facetiousness, which in turn becomes exuberance after they become lovers. Their first separation brings pain and renewed uncertainty, but when Lu Xun finally decides to join Xu Guangping in Canton, a sense of liberation can be seen in his handwriting. Second separation allows tenderness to be expressed without constraint; for once, Lu Xun becomes the more playful of the two. For reasons that are not entirely clear, some letters dating from the first stage of their correspondence, when they were both living in Peking, are missing, but thereafter they are careful to keep every letter and card. Although at the time they do not discuss how and why they preserve them so carefully, it is likely that there was all along some thought of publication; but another reason was likely to be as a talisman or charm for the present and as a memento for the future.

12

Defining Identities, Testing Roles

Lu Xun touched on the main themes of the correspondence in his Preface: they are not about tempestuous or romantic passion but about very ordinary things.[1] The chief of these 'ordinary things' is the correspondence itself; courtship and separation are closely connected. Lu Xun and Xu Guangping also exchange views on literature, the current political situation, gender issues, and life in general. Some of these topics, most notably their sexual relationship and political views, are subject to massive editorial intervention in *Letters between Two* and will be treated at greater length in Part III; this section focuses on the themes that are retained more or less intact. The dominant tone in the first phase and throughout most of the second phase of the OC and *Letters between Two* is mutual testing: they define and redefine their identities, exposing their expectations of the other and themselves; as they advance and retreat, masks are donned and lifted. Towards the end of the second phase and throughout the third, the tone is more relaxed, and mutual assurances of affection predominate.

The Letters Themselves

One of the most common topics in letters, especially in love-letters, is the letters themselves. The correspondence between Lu Xun and Xu Guangping typically starts off with an account of letters received, letters sent, delays caused by the authors, and delays caused by external forces (abbreviated in *Letters between Two*). They refer to the appearance and language as well as the content of the immediate last letter, to the physical act of writing the current letter, to the impact that the letters might have on the recipient and to the next letter they will write or expect to receive. They attract return letters by stressing the pleasure that letters give them and by mild reproaches when expected letters do not arrive. They reread the letters they receive and refer to them in their next letters, but they do not make copies of their letters and they frequently repeat themselves.[2]

All of this falls within the normal conduct of letter-writing. Cicero imagines the impact of his letters on Atticus and urges him to reply.[3] Heloise's first letter to Abelard is about letters, quoting Seneca to Lucilius on letters.[4] Swift writes to Stella on January 1710: 'As hope saved, nothing gives Presto [Swift] any sort of dream of happiness, but a letter now and then from his own dearest MD [Stella]. I love the expectation of it, and it does not come, I comfort myself, that I have it yet to be happy with. Yes, faith, and when I write to MD, I am happy too; it is just as if methinks you were here, and I prating to you, and telling you where

I have been: Well, says you, Presto, come, where have you been to-day? come, let's hear now. And so then I answer . . .'[5] de Sévigné repeatedly stresses the pleasure she receives from her daughter's replies, the encouragement her daughter gives to her to continue writing at great length, and her own need to write to her.[6] In the most famous unsent love-letter in history, Beethoven's 1812 letter to his 'immortal beloved', Beethoven twice refers to the postal service, and laments, 'I weep when I think that probably you will not receive the first news of me until Saturday'.[7] Edith Wharton describes how love-letters are read: 'the first glance to see how many pages there are, the second to see how it ends, the breathless first reading, the slow lingering over each phrase and each word, the taking possession, the absorbing of them, one by one, and finally the choosing of the one that will be carried in one's thoughts all day'.[8] Franz Kafka's love-letters to Felice Bauer are mostly about writing, sending, and receiving letters.[9] George Bernard Shaw, in his Preface to the collected correspondence between him and Ellen Terry, notes that they 'were both comedians, each acting as audience to the other, and each desiring to please and amuse the other without ulterior motives or what matchmaking mothers call intentions'.[10] Yu Dafu repeatedly begins his letters to Wang Yingxia by detailing the letters he has sent and received from her, or her lack of response. When she finally relents and asks him to write to her, he claims to have become so excited that he drops her letter to take up his pen on the spot.[11]

Much of Xu Guangping's first letter to Lu Xun is taken up by her explanation for writing;[12] in her second she discusses his reply, but her explanation for not replying until after an interval of two days is deleted in *Letters between Two*.[13] In her third letter, Xu Guangping apologizes for taking up his time;[14] Lu Xun merely notes in reply that if not writing to her he would not be doing anything else.[15] In April, Xu Guangping worries again that writing long letters and posting magazines to her are taking up too much of his time;[16] in reply, Lu Xun is still offhand: 'Although I speak of being busy, in fact it's only a "verbal tic". I always have time every day to sit around and talk about nothing, and it is no great hardship to write a letter.'[17]

In June, Xu Guangping suspects that their mail might be intercepted:

I received your letter of the 31st but before opening it I had an uneasy feeling that the enemy [i.e. the College; changed to 'they' in *Letters between Two*] has apparently gone so far as opening the mail! This situation has existed before, but on this occasion I received two letters at the same time, and the bottom half of both envelopes had been broken open and re-sealed, so that the marks of the original seal were lost. This can also be counted as 'knocking against a wall' [sentence deleted in *Letters between Two*]. Naturally I argued with them over it, but what was the use! I wonder if we could avoid this abuse by asking someone to deliver our mail for us. But I also wonder why I should bother to evade them at all, I may just as well denounce them freely in my letter and let them read it. But what crime has my teacher committed that he should be implicated in this way?[18]

Lu Xun offers partial reassurance:

In the case of the opened letter, maybe they have been falsely accused, because it may have been me who opened the letter of the 31st. It was late at night and I had written many letters, so I don't remember clearly, I only remember having opened one of them (from the bottom) to add a brief note on the first page. If there is a small note on your first page, then it was actually I who opened it. As for the other letter, however, I cannot act in their defence. In fact, opening mail is an old custom in China, and I have been expecting it for some time.[19]

This is the only mention in the correspondence of mail being intercepted. Lu Xun's misgivings were to be substantiated with the introduction of postal censorship in 1933, but there was no call to assume that the Chinese government was uniquely duplicitous. The post office in eighteenth-century Britain was a major organ for the transmission, collection, and creation of intelligence, and letters, chiefly diplomatic but also political and criminal, could be opened freely 'on suspicion'. Following protests from the House of Commons, the practice was reduced during the nineteenth century but did not cease altogether.[20]

During the first separation between Lu Xun and Xu Guangping, from September 1926 to January 1927, correspondence becomes their sole means of communication and is consequently of even greater importance to them. She fusses about the money he spends on postage for sending her his new book, *Hesitation*, and Blok's *The Twelve*, and is rebuked.[21] In her next letter, which is the first of many to refer to the new problems of letters crossing in the post or being lost *en route*, she writes that she knows he is waiting for her letters, so she sends hers even though she has not received one from him.[22] A few days later, she is even more anxious that some letters may have gone missing.[23] On the same day, Lu Xun writes, 'I think I should receive a letter within a day or two, but I'll post this one tomorrow'.[24] In his next letter he expresses anger because one of her letters must have lain in the mailboat for a full week.[25] His letter to her dated 18 October also lies in the post office in Amoy for a couple of days, but at least hers of the fifteenth has arrived.[26] It is a pleasure for her to receive on 18 October his of the 10th that she has been waiting for since dawn.[27]

Much of Lu Xun's frustration is vented on the post office. He is dismayed to find that at Amoy University there is only a postal agency, which is closed on Saturday afternoons and Sundays, and he finds the staff lazy and dumb.[28] Xu Guangping does not make it easier by her playful habit of addressing the envelopes using a variety of names for Lu Xun (Zhou Shuren, Yu Cai, Lu Xun) and for herself as sender (Jing, Song, Xu).[29] There is no convenient post office branch near Xu Guangping's school, and she gives the mail to a school servant to post, but when she finds that the servants do not take her letters straight to the post office she takes over herself. The school porter is also remiss in not passing over letters to her.

Counting the days between letters, Xu Guangping finds that three days without one seems a long time: 'At first I was planning to write, but then I thought I might wait for a couple of days until I heard from you, but then I got provoked into taking up my pen to pour out my woes to you.'[30] The next day, 'I felt I might get one today, and when I went to the office this morning there was your letter on my desk, which I read with pleasure'.[31] A further comment, on the time it takes for mail to travel between Canton and Amoy although the two cities are not far away, is deleted from her original letter.[32]

Lu Xun reports that now the semester has started the postal agency stays open half-day on Sunday,[33] but complains again about poor service by the mailboats.[34] Worried about his response to the invitation from Zhongshan University, she sends three express letters in a row, on 19, 20, and 23 October[35] and frets when she still gets no reply. When he realizes, Lu Xun explains that her (ordinary) letter of 22 October arrived that morning, but that he was only handed the express letter of 23 October after he had mailed his reply to the letter of 22 October; and he goes on at length on the bureaucratic confusion governing express and registered mail.[36]

By November, the tension caused by the uncertainty of communication and misunderstanding abates a little, but their impulse to write and their expectation of a reply have by now become a part of their lives that is almost beyond their control. Xu Guangping starts one letter: 'Now that I have a little free time I was thinking of answering a letter from Mr Xie, when suddenly I was swept by a strong impulse to write to you. So I stopped in the middle of that letter and started a new page for you.'[37] That was at 8:30 in the evening. After writing a few more letters she felt sleepy but she still had dormitory supervision to attend to. Instead she took out a photograph from Peking, thinking how much better it would be to have the reality than the image. Then she thought of a few more things to write to him about, and finished the letter at ten o'clock. (This second half is deleted in *Letters between Two*.[38]) She also writes that it is a great comfort to find a letter from him sooner than she had expected.[39]

Lu Xun is just as obsessive:

> I just sent off a letter today which may arrive at the same time as this. It might occur to you when you first see this one that it contains something important, but in fact it doesn't, it's just inconsequential chatter. The first letter I put in the postbox around midnight; there are two postboxes here, and one is inside the building but you can't get to it after five, so at night you have to use the one outside. But the present postal agency clerk is a recent newcomer who looks quite dumb, and I feel that he may not even remember to open the outside box, and so I'm not sure whether my letter was sent on to the general post office or not. So I am writing a few more lines and will put it into the inside postbox tomorrow morning.[40]

This provoked an 'order' from Xu Guangping that he was not permitted to go out at night to post letters since 'a blind horse could stumble into a ditch at the dead of night', and that in any case the letter posted in the outside box arrived before the letter posted in the inside box.[41] Lu Xun then joked in his reply about her 'order' being 'really terrible'.[42]

When Xu Guangping moves out of the school she sends him her home address in Gaodi Street,[43] but the letter does not arrive until the afternoon of 23 December. On the morning of that day Lu Xun thought her letter to him with the new address must have got lost, so he wrote two letters, one to Gaodi Street and one (registered) to the school.[44] Explaining this, he remarks, 'It's really a peculiar postal service'.[45]

In the 1929 Shanghai–Peking letters, Xu Guangping starts to write the same day that Lu Xun departs.[46] Even when she has nothing to write about she still writes.[47] In a separate letter written later the same day, she describes how she tells the others that she is going out shopping as a pretext for taking her letters to the post office: she does not want anyone else to know.[48] A few days later, she expresses joy when a letter arrives unexpectedly early: 'such a clever post office'.[49]

Lu Xun writes to her as soon as he arrives in Peking. He mostly writes at night, staying up until midnight or later.[50] He frets that the mail will be delayed because the post office is closed for Sun Yat-sen's reburial ceremonies.[51] When there is no letter from her, he writes, 'Although I felt a little depressed at not getting a letter today, I know the reason for the delay and so had no trouble falling asleep. I wish Little Hedgehog ['you' in *Letters between Two*] also a sound sleep in Shanghai'.[52] When a letter arrives, he writes, 'I returned from a visit to Wei Shuyuan at the Western Hills at 2 pm on the 30th to find Little Hedgehog's ['your' in *Letters between Two*] letters of the twenty-third and twenty-fifth. In both cases the post office played tricks with them, sending one early and the other late, it really makes me angry. But I know Little Hedgehog ['you' in *Letters between Two*] has received my letter and was somewhat comforted by it, which is also some comfort for me'.[53]

Lu Xun's last letter from Peking is in three parts, written between 1 and 1:30 a.m. on the night of 30 May, at 3 a.m. on 1 June and at 5 a.m. the same day. He had already posted a letter on 30 May but still felt like writing; nothing happened on 31 May but he wrote early the next morning because he could not get to sleep. In the original version he concludes, 'My little lotus pod with lotus seeds, you mustn't think that I always have such stupid thoughts in my mind here, it's not at all like this. It's just that I have had enough sleep and also I'm rather happy, so I am just rambling on . . . The lower edge of the envelope is like this because I opened it myself to add one more page'.[54]

Courtship

Living apart, or unable to speak freely when they meet, lovers can find in letters an ideal medium for the mutual definition of their roles.[55] The correspondence between Abelard and Heloise began when they were living in the same house; she sets out to define their relationship in her early letters to him.[56] Elizabeth Barrett and Robert Browning both lived in London, and Lydia Lopokova and Manyard Keynes met frequently; each couple still felt the need to express and to analyse their emotions in writing. Virginia Woolf, even during short absences, felt the need to send her husband constant reassurances of love.[57] Letters are the means by which Yu Dafu makes assignations with Wang Yingxia, passionate declarations of his willingness to sacrifice all for her sake, and elaborate and repeated apologies when she takes offence at his diary entries about her. The dialogic function of letter-writing is especially evident as lovers test their expectations of themselves and of the other. The following section explores aspects of Lu Xun and Xu Guangping's courtship from this perspective.

Students and Teachers

As letter-writers whose affair developed from a student–teacher relationship, Xu Guangping and Lu Xun had many predecessors, including Heloise and

Abelard, Charlotte Brontë and Constantin Heger,[58] and Hannah Arendt and Martin Heidegger.[59] In each case, the student is female, younger, sexually unattached, and relatively inexperienced, while the teacher is male, older, and usually married or otherwise unable or unwilling to bring the relationship to a happy ending. In China, where the student–teacher bond is particularly strong,[60] even between two men a formal transition towards friendship needed to be marked in some way.[61] When the student is female and the teacher male, as is more common than the other way round, the submissive–dominant mentality tends to persist throughout the relationship.

The letters between Xu Guangping and Lu Xun start off as a student–teacher exchange on the topics of education, the student protest, their writings, and their philosophies of life.[62] Xu Guangping's address to Lu Xun in 1925 and 1926 almost invariably includes a word for teacher; in 1929 he is an 'elephant' (to her 'hedgehog'), and in 1932 he is her 'elder brother'. Her signatures at first hint at rebellion: from 'your humble student' to 'young devil' (in 1925) and thence to 'H.M.' (in 1926) are quite considerable steps, from which 'hedgehog' and 'girl' in 1929 seem like a retreat.

On his side, Lu Xun was accustomed to having disciples who sought his advice, young women as well as young men, and he took his role of teacher and guide seriously. Of all the hundreds of letters he wrote, his letters to Xu Guangping up to the time of the Dragon Boat Day incident are among those containing the most guidance.[63] At the same time, he seems uncertain how to handle this talented but unruly student, being by turns patronizing, clumsy, and facetious, or issuing mock-violent threats to bring her to order. She enjoys teasing him and does not avoid archness; but she also questions his advice and is not always content with his answers.

In Canton, among her family and in her first job, Xu Guangping gains confidence and writes at length about her activities, but he is still patronizing about her writing,[64] her teaching career, and her ability to study: 'Probably for the reason that you have less worldly experience than I, it seems as if your thinking is a little more lucid than mine, and more decisive; nevertheless, that carelessness of yours needs correcting' (changed in *Letters between Two* to 'Probably because you have less worldly experience than I, your thinking although fairly simple is also fairly lucid; nevertheless, . . .').[65] 'Somewhere else where you are a disadvantage is in not being able to read foreign books. What would be most beneficial for you, I think, would be to study Japanese. Starting from next year I should order you to study, and meet resistance with brute force.'[66] (Lu Xun brushes up his German without a teacher.[67])

The First Approach

On the surface the letters do not mention love,[68] but they soon become the means by which Lu Xun and Xu Guangping explore their developing relationship. The first stage in their intimacy comes after her first visit to his home on 12 April. Lu Xun starts by explaining that 'There was much I could have said in answer to you the other day but there were always guests sitting here from morning to night, and so I could only talk about the weather . . . Because although it would only have been an ordinary conversation, if someone were accidentally to overhear he might easily misunderstand and create gossip out of it. For this reason it is better to continue to answer you by letter'.[69] (In fact, the gossip started immediately after the visit, but they did not discover this until more than a year later.)

Xu Guangping's reply is more uninhibited, conjuring up a romantic fantasy around the silent figure she imagines sitting alone in his room (and, it is implied, thinking of her).[70] Xu Guangping is also the first to introduce sexual teasing and gender reversal into the correspondence (discussed further in Part III). The intimacy between them deepens after her expulsion from Women's Normal College: they both drop their arch manner and return to the seriousness of the early letters. The missing letters around the time of the Dragon Boat Day incident indicate a further stage in their intimacy, and the few that are included in *Letters between Two* give way to facetiousness again. Although it is still some months before they consummate their affair, all but two of the July letters are so intimate in tone that they cannot be edited for inclusion.

Separation

Separation is another constant theme of letter-writers: what led to it, when it started, when it might finish, and the frustration to which it gives rise.[71] Letters alleviate the loneliness of separation but at the same time they draw attention to it. John Keats (1795–1821) had at times an almost morbid fear of letters. To his friend Charles Brown he wrote, 'I am afraid to write to her [Fanny Brawne]—to receive a letter from her—to see her hand writing would break my heart—even to hear of her any how, to see her name written would be more than I can bear'.[72] Aware of his sensitivity, Leigh Hunt writes to Joseph Severn, 'I have sent no letters to [Keats in] Rome, because I was aware of the effect they would have on Keats's mind; and in Italy I remember his telling me upon one occasion that, in his sick moments, he never wished to receive another letter, or ever to see another face, however friendly'.[73] William and Mary Wordsworth, by contrast, used the distance between them during separation to affirm the strength of their feelings, and noted that their correspondence could serve as a bequest to the one who survived.[74]

The difficulty in expressing one's feelings in letters is the theme of one of Kafka's most famous letters:

> Actually I don't have to apologize for my not having written, after all, you know how much I hate letters. All my misfortune in life—I don't want to complain, just make a generally instructive observation—derives, one might say, from letters or the possibility of writing letters. People have hardly ever deceived me, but letters always have, and as a matter of fact not those of other people, but my own. In my case this is a particular misfortune that I do not want to discuss further, but it is nevertheless also a general one. The easy possibility of writing letters—from a purely theoretical point of view—must have brought wrack and

ruin to the souls of the world. Writing letters is actually an intercourse with ghosts and by no means just with the ghost of the addressee but also with one's own ghost, which secretly evolves inside the letter one is writing or even in a whole series of letters, where one letter corroborates another and can refer to it as witness. How did people ever get the idea they could communicate with one another by letter![75]

Dora Carrington writing to Gerald Brenan two years later expresses a similar wretchedness in a more down-to-earth way: 'Sometimes it seems impossible to write letters. Everything is too frail, and intangeable [sic] to put in paper. I confess my head aches so I *will* go indoors and take an aspirin.'[76]

The theme of separation occurs constantly throughout Lu Xun and Xu Guangping's Canton–Amoy and Shanghai–Peking exchanges. (Further details are given below in Part III.) In the Canton–Amoy letters the problem is particularly acute since there is so much uncertainty about the length of their separation. Their expressions of emotion at parting are restrained, and in Lu Xun's case oblique. In November, Xu Guangping suggests travelling to Amoy to see him 'to fill up your void—no—or should I say, only by exchanging your cup of wine for a cup of water will you be roused' (changed to 'you seem to be extremely lonely' in *Letters between Two*).[77] In his reply, he denies there is a void in his heart and gives sensible reasons for not encouraging this visit.[78] He shows instead that he understands her frustration by being very tender: 'Naturally it is a consolation to know that there is still someone, and also this makes me much braver' (changed to 'Naturally it is a consolation to know that there is still someone who will be my companion, and also this makes me strive harder' in *Letters between Two*).[79]

This kind of tension is missing from the 1929 Shanghai–Peking exchange, but if anything both parties are more impatient for reunion than before. Towards the end of his stay, there is much discussion about his return journey, whether by train or Japanese boat, possible delay or danger because of the civil war, and relative speed and cost. But despite cross words from Lu Xun on the postal service, neither here nor in the 1932 exchange does either of them express the frustration of the Amoy–Canton letters.

Exchanging Views

Many love-letters stick to a single subject: the pursuit of love; Yu Dafu, for instance, rarely strays from that topic. Simone de Beauvoir is more prolix, taking pleasure in relating literary gossip and speculating on current political and philosophical issues. In the first and to a lesser extent in the second phases of the correspondence, Lu Xun and Xu Guangping exchange opinions and comments on a wide range of topics, but as they make plans to meet again in Canton, and in their Shanghai–Peking exchange, their personal situation becomes their main focus. Most of their remarks on education, literature, current events, gender issues, and life in general are retained in *Letters between Two*, and a selection of these will be discussed below. Passages relating to the Chinese Communist Party, the Nationalist Party, and

Xu Guangping's political activities in Canton, however, are invariably deleted or rewritten, and will be discussed in Part III.

Education

The letters start off on the topic of education: as a teacher in training, Xu Guangping is both professionally and personally involved, but Lu Xun is generally detached and almost indifferent to wider issues. Xu Guangping wonders if education would be improved if schools were located outside 'the clamour of the city and the influence of political currents',[80] but Lu Xun points out that 'Students are only a little sheltered from unpleasant news at school, but when they pass through the school gates and come into contact with society, they will still suffer and degenerate, it is just a question of sooner rather than later . . . it is probably better to be in town, where degeneration sets in without delay and suffering comes speedily'.[81] In response to her request for guidance on how to respond to the principal's scheming and the students' apathy or corruption, Lu Xun advises her not to set her expectations too high: 'To talk of the educational sector as pure and lofty is basically camouflage, in fact it is the same as any other; it is not easy to change human nature, and a few years at university has no effect on it.'[82]

Xu Guangping returns with questions about the goals of education, whether it should encourage people to adapt to their environment at the risk of damaging their individuality, 'or is it better to think of ways to preserve each person's individuality?'[83] It is clear that her sympathies lie with educational reform along the lines advocated by followers of Dewey such as Cai Yuanpei and Hu Shi. But her letter immediately descends again to complaints against her fellow-students for their frivolity, bookishness, or political ambition.

In reply, Lu Xun rebukes her naivety and severity:

> What passes for 'education' at the present time, in no matter what country across the world, is in fact nothing more than a method of turning out machines which will adapt to their environment. The time has not yet come, and perhaps never will, when it will be properly adapted to the individual to develop each person's individuality. I suspect that in the golden age of the future, renegades will still be condemned to death, and everyone will still consider it the proper business of a golden age; the problem being that everyone is different and can't be made to conform to one standard like a printed book. Anyone who tries to destroy utterly this general trend easily turns into an 'individual anarchist like Shevyryov in *The Worker Shevyryov*. The destiny of such a character at the present time—though perhaps it's in the future—is that he wants to save the masses but is persecuted by the masses and ends up a solitary figure; in an excess of fury and frustration, he does an about-turn, regards everyone as his enemy, and opens fire indiscriminately, destroying himself in the process'.
>
> Society embraces an infinite variety of the strange and curious, and all things are included in it. In schools and universities, people who only carry thread-bound books or hope for handsome diplomas are still fairly decent even if fundamentally they do not venture beyond 'profit or loss'.[84]

The letters then turn to the authors' attitudes towards life in general (see later), to machinations in the Ministry of Education, and then to the student protest movement at Women's Normal College and Xu Guangping's role in it.[85] Although the student protest remains a frequent topic from the end of March to the end of June 1925, there are no further remarks on general educational theory or practice.

In Canton, Xu Guangping's remarks about education are about her immediate problems as a teacher, where she finds it difficult to sustain her left-wing sympathies towards students when they attack her from a right-wing position. She complains about the demands on her time from her varied duties, which include attending plays and organising patriotic activities, but she does not venture general remarks on education from her new perspective. Her sole reference to education in the abstract is her playful response to Lu Xun's encounter with the barbed wire fence outside his building: as an educator, she advocates guidance rather than repression (reworded to a more general formula in *Letters between Two*).[86] Despite her ignominious retreat from Girls' Normal in November 1926, Xu Guangping did not abandon teaching as her profession but looked for other teaching appointments even after Lu Xun offered her a job at Zhongshan University as his assistant.

In Amoy, Lu Xun also confines himself to remarks on his immediate surroundings, although his battle is with his colleagues and the chancellor rather than the students. His letters reveal his increasing alienation from academic life, but without another obvious source of income he agrees to replace Guo Moruo at Zhongshan University from the beginning of 1927. He shows no particular interest in educational theory or practice, and shuns executive or administrative responsibilities.[87] In the end he only stays at Zhongshan University a few months; it turns out to be his last teaching post.

When they moved to Shanghai in 1927, she intended to look for a teaching position, and it was apparently at Lu Xun's insistence that she gave up teaching to act as his 'private assistant'; she never returned to her original profession. Lu Xun's visit to Peking in 1929 renews gossip that he might still be seeking an academic position,[88] but Lu Xun turns down possible offers from Yenching University[89] and Peking University.[90] He remains interested in academic writing[91] but states that teaching is not for him. The reason given is that 'I've been on the run for several years and I've grown careless and superficial'.[92] Evidence from the Amoy letters also suggests that reasons include claims on his time by students, competition among his colleagues, and possibly also incompatibility between academic work and the kind of writing he was committed to. What is meant by the latter is not spelt out, but the indications are that Lu Xun still thought of himself primarily as a writer. Despite the financial insecurity, he therefore decided to go freelance.

LITERATURE

A subject on which both Lu Xun and Xu Guangping remain relatively silent is literature, although this was a common theme in the love-letter collections of 1924–33.[93] In view of Lu Xun's standing as the most prominent writer of his time, this may seem anomalous, but Lu Xun is not alone in not wanting to discuss his own writing in letters to a lover or friend: other examples are Charlotte Brontë,[94] Lord Byron, and Virginia Woolf. Like them, he is more likely to dwell on the professional aspects of writing and editing than to discuss his current work or speculate on literary theories. There is a great deal of gossip in the correspondence about other writers and Lu Xun's relationships with them, and about the mechanics of publishing magazines, books, and academic articles.

During the period of the letters, Lu Xun was writing the prose poems that were eventually collected as *Weeds*, the reminiscences collected as *Dawn Blossoms Plucked at Dusk*, the fables collected as *Old Tales Retold*, and miscellaneous essays. From the evidence in the letters, there is no reason to think that Lu Xun had consciously abandoned writing creative fiction (his last original story was written in November 1925), and he evidently took pleasure in writing essays. On the other hand, he frequently complains about the over-abundance of contributions in fiction and poetry to *The Wilderness*, and this might have affected his own attitude towards writing fiction:

The condition of literature in China at the present time is really quite poor, though there are indeed some people who can write poetry and fiction. What we lack most are 'critics of civilisation' and 'critics of society'. My getting people together in *The Wilderness* to raise a clamour is mostly to attract henceforth new critics of this kind; although my tongue may be cut out, there are still people who will speak out and continue to rip the mask from the old society. Unfortunately most of the manuscripts we have received up to now are still fiction.[95]

However, our own *The Wilderness* is very hard-pressed. Most of what is submitted is fiction or poetry, and critical articles are few. If I'm not careful it is also likely to turn into a literary magazine.[96]

When material is submitted to *The Wilderness* there is too much fiction and too little discussion. Now even fiction is scarce, probably because everyone is concentrating on patriotism, they want to 'go among the people' and therefore aren't writing.[97]

As to why your masterpieces are frequently accepted, it is really because *The Wilderness* is in the grip of famine. What I want to print more of is discussion, but what comes in is fiction and poetry. Formerly it was sham 'Flowers!' and 'Love!' poetry, now it is sham 'Death!' and 'Blood!' poetry. Oh, it is such a headache![98]

Another passage also suggests that he is turning away from fiction:

If my tongue were cut out, then: in the first instance, I'd avoid teaching; in the second instance, I'd avoid entertaining guests; in the third instance, I'd avoid being an official; in the fourth instance, I'd avoid social intercourse; and in the fifth instance, I'd avoid giving speeches; and henceforth I should be able to concentrate on writing for journals, something I should not find uncongenial.[99]

Following Xu Guangping's expulsion from the college, and despite his own intervention in the public debate that followed, Lu Xun shows even more ambivalence about writing in general:

At present I am more and more convinced that those who speak and write are people who serve no function; no matter how reasonably you speak or how much your writing moves people, all is in vain. No matter how unreasonable they are, in real life, however, they will win in the end. And yet surely the world is not really just like this? I want to resist, and make a try.[100]

In response to her criticism that the second issue of *The Wilderness* was 'sedate'[101] and that the third 'seems to have a tendency to tread in cloth shoes and peer through thick glasses',[102] Lu Xun, probably correctly, took her remarks to refer to him:

The Wilderness really does have a tendency to tread in cloth shoes, and does not carry articles that fly into a rage and create terrible scenes, it really can't be helped. I am in the habit of writing obscurely, and I can't correct myself quickly. When I take up my pen I am determined to be clear, but I always wind up with an obscure ending, it is really extremely annoying![103]

The most extended passage in which Lu Xun offers a critical perspective on literature comes in response to Xu Guangping's request to evaluate a friend's poem which she sends him in June 1925 (it is possible that the poem was written by Xu Guangping herself):

It is not that the poem lacks vitality but such a violent attack is only appropriate in prose, like the 'random thought' type of essay, and you still need to be indirect in your phrasing or you run the risk of provoking the opposite response. Poetry has more of an eternal nature and so is not particularly well suited to writing on this kind of subject.

After the Shanghai incident the weeklies were full of extremely stern and serious poems, but in fact they were meaningless; feelings change with circumstances, and they have the flavour of chewing wax. I believe that when feelings are at their most violent is not the right time for writing poetry; the passions are too openly exposed and can kill off 'poetic beauty'. This poem suffers from the latter defect.

I am no poet myself, this is just my opinion. Editors as a rule don't offer criticism on the manuscripts they receive, but I have ventured a few remarks now in obedience to the command in your letter; but if the person who submitted the poem has no wish to know my opinion, I hope it is not necessary to inform her.[104]

His views here are conventionally Late Victorian and add little to our understanding of his own poems.

One topic on which Lu Xun was challenged by Xu Guangping to define his views was on whether writing by women possesses special characteristics. In 1925, an article called 'The Unrest in Women's Normal College' signed by 'A Female Reader' appeared in *Contemporary Review*, No. 15 (21 March); suspecting that the principal had written it, Xu Guangping wrote a denunciation in *Peking Gazette Supplement* of 24 March, using the penname 'Speaking the Truth' without the title 'Miss' so as not to influence the editor's decision.[105] Lu Xun responded that 'looking at the style and structure I suspect [the article by 'A Female Reader'] was written by a man, so your guess may not be correct'.[106] Later in the same letter, he writes about her own article,

Although you don't sign your articles 'Miss' this or that and I even address you as 'brother' in my letters, nevertheless the article I felt had a definite feminine quality. I have not made a careful study of this but, generally speaking, it would seem that the sentence arrangement in a 'Miss's' speech is different from a 'Mr's', so when it is written down on paper one can spot the difference immediately.[107]

In her reply, Xu Guangping is at first conciliatory:

You suspect the article by 'A Female Reader' was written by a man. That is of course one opinion, and I have heard that many of the people who write for *Contemporary Review* are in the same party as our principal and exert themselves on her behalf. But as a matter of fact some of the school personnel also have 'A Female Reader's' ungrammatical writing style, so that my guess even if mistaken is not a random shot in the dark.[108]

Further down, she returns more belligerently to the topic:

Words are symbols which express one's inner feelings, and what one writes or says is always affected by one's individual nature, but owing to the influence of the environment and from what we see and hear, naturally there are many differences between 'Misses' and 'Misters' in their 'arrangements of sentences in speech.' It seems to me that the petty details of one's way of speaking is no great matter, but I am very willing to enlarge my vision and expand my mind, to cast off the 'Miss' style of speech, and so I beg my teacher to instruct me. Also, is the point of difference in the 'Miss style' of writing a fondness for words like 'alas', 'ah' and 'oh', or is that the sentence structure is too poeticized and there is no clear leading idea? I hope you will guide me so that I can improve.[109]

Lu Xun's reply provides an insight into his own preferred style:

What I call 'feminine writing' is not primarily a matter of too many 'alas', 'ah' and 'oh'. In lyrical writing, it means such things as using a lot of fine phrases, introducing a great deal of scenery, showing great concern for family, becoming broken-hearted at the sight of flowers in autumn, shedding tears before a bright moon and so on. In polemical writing, it is particularly easy to distinguish. It is citing in succession each point made by one's opponent and refuting each of them in turn, which may be incisive but is not weighty; also, it rarely inflicts a mortal wound by striking directly at the crux of 'the enemy's' argument with a single blow. In short, it is having a mild venom but not an acute venom, and being good at writing long articles but not skilful at short ones.[110]

Xu Guangping responds with a mixture of truculence and diffidence:

Talking about scenery is the speciality of literary men and elevated scholars, and grieving over flowers and the moon is a disease from which young men and women both suffer; why should one who makes her home wherever she happens to be concern herself overly with such matters; while the ones who are concerned now with such things as 'in a mother's bosom . . . in the cradle', I should think, say one thing but mean another. It's true that lyrical writing full of 'fine phrases' [. . .] is now called characteristic of women writers (?)—the most obvious examples are [Shi] Pingmei's prose and poetry, Jingqing [Lu Xiuzhen]'s poems, Bing Xin, [Huang] Luyin and Tingmei [?] all have this flavour. [The names are omitted in *Letters between Two*.] Fortunately, I have neither the qualification nor the desire to be a writer, and I would not be able to compose a single sentence in this style. I have, however, in fact perpetrated unwittingly the style which 'is particularly easy to distinguish' in polemical writing. I did not exercise due caution, and now that I have been seen through by my teacher, I am deeply ashamed and fully persuaded of my guilt. But my reason for 'refuting each argument in turn' is that otherwise, I believe, I won't leave my opponent a mass of bruises. This is also a matter of some regret to me, and is probably due to the lingering influence of Mencius and Su Dongpo, which I have been so long accustomed to that I am hardly conscious of when I first began to suffer from it. As for such things as 'rarely striking directly at the crux of the enemy's argument' and 'being good at writing long articles but not so skilful at short ones', they are perhaps because women have not yet been able to enjoy equality of training in reason, judgment and logic, plus the fact the long-standing practices die hard; henceforth we must try to find a way to change all this. 'Not so skilful at short ones', in addition to the above-mentioned causes, is perhaps a matter of degree. Generally, when one is learning to write, one suffers from an inability to convey one's meaning; then when one is able to convey meaning, one becomes too verbose; and then one progresses to the next stage, succinctness; these are related to one's age and educational level, and I very much wish henceforth to cleanse my writing. [. . .] But without a mirror one cannot perceive one's faults, and in addition to my own efforts I await correction. If teacher proceeds on occasion to instruct me, how very fortunate I shall be.[111]

In his response, Lu Xun sidesteps any further mention of a 'feminine' style of writing or argument:

Views on writing differ as do people. Because I'm good at writing short pieces and at using irony, taking every opportunity to argue the point and going headlong on the attack, casting caution to the winds, I consider any opinion that differs from my method must be wrong. In fact, there are some advantages in employing an easily readable style, and it is not necessary to reduce the wording deliberately (though if it is verbose then you should pare it down). For example, [Qian] Xuantong tends to be diffuse with little content, so that readers have no trouble in reading his work. To be intentionally explicit, on the other hand, is appropriate and makes one's writing very effective. My pieces, however, often arouse misunderstandings, sometimes going far beyond anything I could have anticipated, so you can see that when you put your meaning very succinctly, unless you are quite careful, it is easy to slip into obscurity, and the disadvantage is that it does not yield to scrutiny (the expression 'does not yield to scrutiny' is rather faulty, but for the moment I cannot think of the right word, so I'll leave it as it is; the meaning is just that 'the disadvantage is rather great').[112]

Xu Guangping does not respond to this directly, and in his following letter Lu Xun makes another assertion on his ability to recognize 'feminine' poetry in the context of Ouyang Lan's various pseudonyms.[113] Xu Guangping still does not respond and the matter is dropped.

Preparing for the launch of *The Wilderness* in March 1925, Lu Xun found editorial work a heavy chore: 'I am always looking at articles nowadays, not only does it leave me little spare time but one gets too tired. From now on I won't do any reading for others, apart from a few close friends.'[114] One of these friends was Xu Guangping, whose writings he continued to correct.

Xu Guangping's writing is mostly in the form of articles and letters, and as is suggested above she is not particularly interested in the formal or technical aspects of literature. She mistakes the article 'The World in a Cotton-Padded Gown' in the first issue of *The Wilderness* as being by Lu Xun, which is not unreasonable since young writers like the actual author, Gao Changhong, were much influenced by Lu Xun, and Lu Xun as editor may have had a hand in its final version. Her remarks about it, however, relate solely to her worry that there is a guarded message in it critical of people like herself.[115]

At Lu Xun's express invitation,[116] Xu Guangping submitted several articles to *The Wilderness* in 1925. The first was received with politeness: 'I also received today a manuscript and had the pleasure of reading it. The last three paragraphs are good but the opening paragraph is a little involved, so I will see how the pages look and I may delete this paragraph.'[117] Next was 'Doubt', submitted and accepted with a minimum of teasing.[118] In contrast, her accompanying letter for 'Alcohol Addiction', written after the Peking demonstrations following the 30 May Incident, is embellished with self-derogatory remarks in pseudo-classical style.[119] Lu Xun's acceptance is fairly matter-of-fact: 'There are too many fine words in your masterpiece; I propose to delete some of them and then grant it a place in issue X of *The Wilderness*.'[120] Another article is similarly accepted with little fuss.[121] In July, in contrast, Lu Xun's praise becomes embarrassingly facetious:

I have the honour to inform you that I have had the pleasure of receiving the masterpiece you so kindly submitted . . . The conclusion is too much lacking in strength, and therefore I have added a few sentences, which presumably will not necessarily be contrary to the author's intentions . . . Do not employ the arts of 'in-laws at battle' but . . . revert to your original practice of sending us your manuscripts to illumine our wretched paper, to our immeasurably good fortune!

. . . Once you have been writing longer, you must show some signs of progress in your level, and if you allow yourself to grow lazy and perfunctory, I will have to attack you with violence: so be careful![122]

A few weeks later he decides to reject another of her articles, a 'masterpiece' on swearing, giving the following grounds:

This subject, in fact, at present is something only I can write on, because it will probably be attacked. That wouldn't worry me. First, I have my own ways of attacking, and second, it now seems a rather detestable thing to be 'a literary figure'; it seems you have to turn into a machine, and therefore I am quite willing to take a tumble from 'the literary arena'. As for you young ladies from the Face-cream Party, you actually belong to the 'tender' type, there is no need for you to write an article which would invite attack and misunderstanding, and end in 'tears falling to wet your lapels'.[123]

Perhaps because of reactions such as these, Xu Guangping stopped submitting articles for publication in *The Wilderness*. Altogether she had eight essays published there between May and October 1925, all under the pen-name Jing Song.

There is much less discussion of literary matters in the 1926 letters. On board her boat to Canton, Xu Guangping refers to the book she is reading, *A Bundle of Love-letters*, by Zhang Yiping, and remarks that the story 'Taose de yishang' [Peach-coloured rainment] is particularly artificial; in *Letters between Two*, the title of the book is changed to 'fiction', and the disparaging comment is deleted.[124] Lu Xun also deleted a reference further down in the same letter where Xu Guangping compares the protagonist in 'Peach-coloured rainment' unfavourably to Lansheng in 'The Diary of Brother Lansheng' by Xu Zuzheng. She also started reading *Tan hua* [Charcoal Sketches] by Henryk Sienkiewicz in Zhou Zuoren's translation but did not finish it because it was in Classical Chinese, and *Ye ku* [Weeping at night] by Jiao Juyin, which she thought was 'a complete mess'.[125]

In Canton Xu Guangping had less time for reading. With one exception (i.e. their discussion of Xu Zuzheng's story, 'Seeing off Mr L on a Journey South', initiated by Lu Xun because of his suspicions of Li Yu'an[126]), there are no more references to other works of fiction (other than by him) in her side of the correspondence. Instead she requests him to send her a book on composition and essays by Yosano Akiko.[127] Her only original work of this period is 'Xin Guangdong de xin nüxing' [The new female in the new Kwangtung], published in December 1926, an article she is commissioned to write by Zhang Xichen (through Zhou Jianren and thence Lu Xun) for *The New Female*, which she undertakes again with hesitation and on which she asks for his guidance.[128] His judgment on her composition returns to an earlier theme: 'It looks to me as if the article will do. But some of the sentence structures are inappropriate, a common fault among young ladies. The root of this fault is carelessness; they most likely don't read it through after it's done. I'll correct it in a day or two and send it on.'[129] If he has abandoned creative fiction, she does not know: she still refers to him as 'a writer of fiction' and assumes that he can write himself out of suffering.[130] She remarks that she does not have a 'literary' pen-name like Bing Xin, [Shi] Pingmei, and Jingqing [Lu Xiuzhen], and that she is beginning to dislike her pen-name Jing Song, suggesting perhaps that she still has some literary ambitions (these remarks are deleted in *Letters between Two*).[131]

Lu Xun found his editorial and publishing responsibilities even more onerous in 1926. At one point he threatened to close down *The Wilderness* because of disputes between Wei Suyuan, the editor, and the contributors Xiang Peiliang and Gao Changhong,[132] but when he found out about Gao Changhong's attacks on him, he withdrew the threat and gave Wei Suyuan his full support. He complained at length about being used by younger writers and resented being turned into a 'puppet'.[133] On the other hand, he is not bothered by 'things like proof-reading',[134] although he still does odd jobs for the local student magazines.[135] Instead, he devotes much attention to his academic work, writing up his lecture notes, and compiling old fiction. Although he discusses at some length in 1926 the conflict that he feels exists between writing and teaching, his interest in academic writing continues after he gives up teaching as a career in 1927, as he reaffirms in 1929. In 1929 the only remark on his writing is about a projected academic work that does not come to fruition (see earlier).

Current Events

Lu Xun and Xu Guangping were witness to major events in modern Chinese history. Apart from her role in the Women's Normal College protests, Xu Guangping was also an enthusiastic participant in the Peking demonstrations following the May Thirtieth Incident in 1925. She wrote a long description of the first of these demonstrations to Lu Xun, including some critical remarks on the competition between student leaders for the public attention (softened in *Letters between Two*).[136] Typically he did not take part, and his remarks are more critical of the futility of

Chinese reactions than of the foreign perpetrators.[137] Again, he lectures her about 'meaningless sacrifice':

Young people in China tend to suffer greatly from the fault of 'impatience' (the young devil being one of them) and hence find it difficult to sustain their momentum (they are apt to exhaust their strength by being too rash at the outset). They are also likely to run into obstacles, incur losses and lose their tempers. Such has been stated by this writer on three or four occasions and indeed has even been personally experienced by him.[138]

Xu Guangping is not convinced, although she avoids directly contradicting him:

Teacher never wants to discourage the younger generation or let them lose hope, and so in his conversation he is always devising ways to find words that offer a way out or hope; in fact, however, it is not so easy or simple. There are some people who of course still dare not relax even when they listen to words of comfort, but there are always many who take this as grounds for feeling at ease and therefore relaxing their guard. I beg teacher to keep this in mind.[139]

Lu Xun is obliged to justify his attitude in a footnote:

The papers say that Zhang Shizhao will resign and Qu Yangguang will succeed him. The latter is a famous Chekiang personality 'who hasn't supped with the others for a long time'. He amounts to being the same as Shizhao, or perhaps not even up to him. Therefore my general opinion is that unless internal government is reformed nothing good will ever come about, no matter how many marches and demonstrations there are.[140]

In Canton, Xu Guangping wrote at length about political developments in Nationalist headquarters and the university, but because of its sensitive nature (and her own role as a member of the Nationalist Party), much of this is deleted in *Letters between Two*. Also omitted is a long account of her attempts to intervene in the affairs of her home county, Panyu. Lu Xun, on the other hand, although he follows closely the military progress of the Northern Expedition, is preoccupied with his unhappy relations with the students, staff, and administration at Amoy University and with his former students and associates in literary circles.

The letters between Shanghai and Peking in 1929 are dominated by their domestic affairs, although Lu Xun expresses anger at what he sees as his exclusion from academic life by his academic inferiors.[141] The Shanghai–Peking letters of 1932 are almost wholly domestic, mostly about the health of their son.

Gender Issues

Xu Guangping's debate with Lu Xun on the question of special characteristics in women's writing has been noted above. She also challenged his provocative remark about 'leading female students on a tour' (see below, Chapter 14) but temporarily ignored his teasing follow-up, 'I have heard that young ladies are given to dissolving in tears'.[142] Gender issues also surfaced in regard to the Women's Normal College protest: both Xu Guangping and Lu Xun considered that the argument that a women's college should be headed by a woman principal as bogus.[143] In Lu Xun's case, his attitude may have been influenced by the fact that his old friend, Xu Shouchang, had been ousted in order to make room for Yang Yinyun.

From an early age Xu Guangping had identified with male heroes and the women revolutionaries who emulated them.[144] By extension, she was scornful of her fellow-students: 'when they get together they either talk about dresses or discuss parties, or else they talk about going to the theatre.'[145] Lu Xun counsels her again not to set her expectations too high: 'As I see it, female students are still not too bad, the reason they only talk about things like dresses and parties is probably because they haven't yet come into much contact with the outside world.'[146] Xu Guangping was also critical of the women's groups in Peking at the time and of the women activists Tang Qunying, Shen Peizhen, Shi Shuqing, and Wan Pu (whose personal names are scored out in *Letters between Two*): 'The only one among them who comes near to living up to expectations is Qiu Jin.'[147] Lu Xun makes no further comment.

Xu Guangping had personal experience of the problems faced by a career woman in the 1920s:

> Present-day society is really dark. When a woman conducts business, everywhere she really encounters difficulties. I am not timid, but because I would prefer to avoid trouble, I often ask others to make enquiries on my behalf. I had not expected that the press in intellectual circles were also such treacherous devils—not giving the place for signing up was itself suspicious—they were also like this. It really makes people who advance boldly very conscious of so many obstructions and delaying tactics everywhere. 'Who made you born a woman?' Faced with this query, indeed I have no answer to offer venerable gentlemen and their wives.[148]

In Canton, Xu Guangping continued to be hard on her students: 'Girls are not generally known for their brilliance and this together with direction coming from outside puts them in the same category as a Yang Yinyu. It's really a shame.'[149] She goes on, 'Luckily, if I work hard myself I may not necessarily end in failure, and even if I fail, women have equality with men in Kwangtung now, so there are other places where I can go; it's not like other parts of the country [i.e. Peking] where once you are attacked you will find it extremely difficult to establish yourself back in society.'[150] In December 1926, Xu Guangping was asked by the training office of the Department of Women's Affairs in the provincial government to give a three-week course on women in relations to economics and politics; she knew she was not qualified but was persuaded to accept anyway and carried out her duties conscientiously.[151] Lu Xun's reaction was not encouraging,[152] but through activities such as these, Xu Guangping took the first steps in her second career, as an activist in the women's movement after Lu Xun's death.

In Shanghai, Xu Guangping did not take paid employment during Lu Xun's lifetime. Apart from some translating work, she also acted as his editorial assistant. It was only after Lu Xun's death that her second career began to complement her status as Lu Xun's former partner.

Philosophy of Life

In the early letters, Xu Guangping and Lu Xun debate their general outlook on life. These discussions continue into 1926 but become less frequent and intense as they become more familiar with each other.

Xu Guangping's first letter asks for guidance about the crisis at Women's Normal College and about life in general: 'How may one add a little sugar to bitter medicine, so that people will not feel the bitterness of bitterness? And will sugar make it absolutely free from bitterness?'[153] Lu Xun responds with remarkable openness, showing reluctance to offer leadership and expressing pessimism about China's future:

I think that suffering is an inevitable component of human life, but there is one time when it leaves and that is in the realm of sleep. When you are awake, if you want some relief from suffering, the old Chinese way is by 'pride' and 'cynicism'; I feel I have this fault myself, which is not too good. When you put sugar into bitter tea, the amount of bitterness remains the same, it only tastes a little better than without any sugar at all. But even this sugar is not easy to find; I do not know where it is. On this point I can only hand in a blank paper.[154]

Lu Xun then tries to be a little more specific, in what has become the most quoted passage from *Letters between Two*:

Firstly, when you travel the long road of 'life', you are most likely to encounter two major difficulties. The first is 'a fork in the road'. In the case of Mr Mo Di, tradition has it that he wept bitterly and turned back. But I neither weep nor turn back: I first sit down at the fork in the road, rest a while or take a nap, and then I select a road that looks passable. If I meet an honest fellow I may snatch some food from him to satisfy my hunger but I do not ask him the way because I assume he will not know either. If I meet a tiger, I climb a tree and only climb down when it gets hungry and goes away. If it does not go away I will starve to death in the tree, but I would first tie myself fast with my belt and not let it have my corpse to feed on. But what if there is no tree? Then there is no choice, I may as well ask the tiger to eat me, although there would be no harm in me taking a mouthful of it in return. The second is 'no thoroughfare'. It is said that Mr Ruan Ji also cried loudly and returned home, but I would use the same method as with the fork in the road: I would step forward and try to force a way through the thorns for a while. But I have not yet found a place where thorns made the way totally impassable. I do not know whether this is because there is no such thing anywhere as a 'no thoroughfare' or whether I am just fortunate in not having come across one.

Secondly, when it comes to waging war on society, I do not stand up to be counted myself, and this is why I do not exhort others to sacrifice themselves. During the European conflict, the main emphasis was on 'trench warfare', where the soldiers lay low in ditches, sometimes smoking or singing, playing cards, drinking or even putting on art exhibitions in the trenches, but sometimes they would suddenly fire a few shots at the enemy. In China, where ambush is frequent and heroes who stand up are apt to lose their lives, this kind of warfare is also essential. But I'm afraid that there will be times when close combat cannot be avoided and at such times there is no solution but to engage in hand-to-hand fighting.

In short, my way of dealing with anguish is to make trouble for the suffering that assails us, to regard underhand tricks as victory, and to persist in singing songs of triumph as a kind of pleasure: this is perhaps the sugar. But in the end it still comes down to 'having no solution'. This is truly no solution!

This is all I can say about my own way of dealing with life; it is more like a game than a steady march along the true path of life (there may be a true path in life, but I don't know). I believe that writing it down may not necessarily be of much use to you but it is all I can do.[155]

Xu Guangping replies by quoting from his prose poem, 'Guoke' [The passer-by],[156] whose protagonist asks about the road ahead:

[he] may not see either graves or flowers as described to him but something quite different again—but there is no harm in asking and the question still seems to be worth putting. . . . . Not a day has passed when I have not been accused of being 'proud' and 'cynical'. Sometimes I also feel that this is 'not proper conduct' (and, in reality, I am aware that I do not have enough to be proud about), but I cannot wallow in the mire with others, and so I always end up getting worsted.[157]

She likens herself to Confucius' most impatient disciple, Zilu, who lets himself 'be chopped up into mince-meat' and is incapable of 'trench warfare'.[158]

Lu Xun's next letter contains another well-known passage:

China is probably too old, and everything in society, large or small, is intolerably vile, it's like a vat of black dye in which even new things come out pitch-black. However, there is nothing we can do except to think of ways of reform. All idealists, it seems to me, either hark back to the 'past' or find hope in the 'future', but on the question of the 'present' all of them hand in blank papers, because no-one can prescribe a remedy. All the best remedies turn out to be 'hope for the future'.

Although we can't know what this thing called the future will be like, one thing is certain, it will certainly come. What concerns me is that when that time comes it will be the then 'present'. However, people don't have to be so pessimistic, as long as the 'then present' is a little better than the 'present present' then it is fine, it is progress.

These idle fancies can't be proved to be fancies, and so they can be considered a kind of consolation in life, just like the god of believers. It seems you are always reading my works, but my works are too dark, because I always feel that only 'darkness and emptiness' are 'real', and yet I persist in waging a hopeless battle against them, and therefore there is much that has an extremist tone. Actually, this may be a matter of my age and experience, and is not necessarily true, because after all I can't prove that only darkness and emptiness are real. Therefore I think that in youth you should be indignant at injustice and not pessimistic; you must always fight back and at the same time defend yourself. If there are thorny paths that must be trodden, then you must tread them, but if there is no necessity to tread them, then don't tread them anyway. This is the reason that I advocate 'trench warfare', it is simply so that we can keep a few more soldiers to win a few more battles. Mr Zilu was certainly a brave warrior, but I have always felt it somewhat pedantic of him 'to tie his cap-strings before dying' just because 'the gentleman facing death does not allow his cap of office to be taken off'. What is wrong with allowing your hat to fall off? To be so solemn about it is really to be taken in by Mr Confucius. Mr Confucius himself 'was in difficulties in Chen and Cai' but he certainly did not starve to death; he was really possessed of considerable cunning. If Mr Zilu had not believed his nonsense but had begun to fight bare-headed with his hair streaming loose, perhaps he would not have ended up dying. But this way of fighting, with your hair streaming loose, also belongs to what I would call 'trench warfare'.[159]

The debate on 'trench warfare' and the darkness of society continues over the next few letters: she is typically rash, he is typically cautious.

After her expulsion from Women's Normal College, Xu Guangping confides her thoughts on the meaning of life and death, referring to her attempted suicide (omitted in *Letters between Two*).[160] Lu Xun responds with equal gravity, distressed to hear that she regarded herself as 'waste matter' and explaining his own vacillation between humanism and individualism:

To be candid, the line 'Surely the world is not really like this' was actually 'directed at the young devil'. What I say is often not the same as what I think; as for why it is like this, as I have said in the Preface to *Outcry*, I do not want to infect others with my own ideas. The reason I am unwilling is because my ideas are too dark, and I myself ultimately cannot know with certainty if I am right. As for 'I still want to resist', it is true, but I know my 'reason for resistance' is acutely different from the young devil's. Doesn't your resistance come from hope for a better future? I should think it must. But my resistance only amounts to making trouble for the forces of darkness. There are probably many of my opinions that the young devil does not fully comprehend; this is because of differences in age, experience, environment and so on, and is hardly surprising. For instance, I curse 'human suffering' but do not find 'death' repugnant, because there are ways in which 'suffering' may be alleviated whereas 'death' is inevitable. Although one speaks of 'the bitter end', it is not in itself tragic. But you are unhappy with this kind of talk—yet why do you look on fine living beings as 'waste matter'? This is more to be 'chastized' than not to have written articles which could 'wring the heart'. Again, your letter says that whenever people die who have some connection with me, I hate those who have no connection with me—, but I am just the opposite; I am uneasy when those who are connected with me are alive, and I relax once they are dead. I have touched on this idea in 'The Passer-By', and it is quite different from the young devil's. In fact, my outlook for the time being is not easy to comprehend, because it embraces many contradictions. If you ask me to explain, there is perhaps a fluctuation or alternation between two ways of thinking, humanism and individualism. At one moment I love man, at the next I hate him. When I work, sometimes it is really on behalf of others, sometimes it is just to amuse myself, and sometimes, because I hope to wear down my life more swiftly, I deliberately work to the point of exhaustion. Whatever other reasons there may be apart from these I do not myself fully comprehend, but to others I generally choose to speak of the brighter ones. However, my guard occasionally slips to reveal thoughts that the King of Hell would not oppose, but which 'the young devil' is not happy at. In a word, my perspective is not the same for myself as it is for others. The reason is that my thinking is too dark, but ultimately whether it is right I have no way of knowing; therefore I can only try myself, I do not dare invite others. Actually, when the young devil hopes for eternal life for her brother and father, regards herself as 'waste material' and stubbornly pleads on behalf of the masses, she is for the most part also like this.[161]

In 1926, their reflections on life tend to be more closely related to their personal affairs and are subject to editorial intervention; for more detail, see Part III. In 1929, they rarely discuss general issues.

The Uses of Love-Letters

The absence of passion in *Letters between Two*, and its relative unimportance in the original correspondence (OC), caused some readers to wonder if they should be regarded as love-letters at all. A functional analysis of love-letters show that even *Letters between Two* indubitably falls into this category. The most fundamental function of love-letters is to create two fictional personae: the idealized figure of the lover (the writer) and the beloved (the recipient), so that for the duration of the correspondence, these two inhabit a fictional world. Athough Lu Xun and Xu Guangping allow the real world untypically frequent access, when they clear a space in their lives to write to each other, the world that is most vivid to them is the one they create around themselves. The difference that letters can make to a loving relationship, or the value they bring to it, lies chiefly in this extra dimension.

A second function is to explore the identity, especially the sexual identity, of the writer: this is evident in the OC but obscured in *Letters between Two*. A related function, to explore the changing relationships between the lovers, is common to both versions. Lu Xun, however, preoccupied by worries about his adultery and the gossip it caused, often failed to notice that their relationship had changed since they first wrote as teacher and student; Xu Guangping, most worried about whether he would abandon it altogether, was more perceptive.

Both writers were fully aware of another function: the pleasure of unburdening one's soul to the beloved. Lu Xun and Xu Guangping both reveal the emotions of joy and sorrow as well as the details of their daily life, knowing without needing to say that their feelings will be understood and that no detail is too trivial to be treasured by the recipient. Both are also conscious that letters can be used to manipulate the beloved's feelings: to provoke feelings of love, jealousy, pity, and so on. This kind of manipulation is most evident in their letters from Amoy and Canton.

Letters can also act as a kind of talisman: to carry with one, to learn off by heart, to hide in an intimate place, and, after the death of the other, to keep memories alive. We do not know if Lu Xun or Xu Guangping carried each other's letters on their person or where they hid them when they were separated; we do know that although other letters were burned or carelessly lost, these letters were very carefully preserved.

Finally, letters, especially love-letters, can be used to make money. One way is by blackmail; another is to publish them, with or without the consent of the other. *Letters between Two* was published by joint consent; the OC finally appeared in print with the implied consent of the longer-lived and less famous half.

Summary

The correspondence between Xu Guangping and Lu Xun shows the changes in their relationship from student–teacher to unwed partners, in which Lu Xun's dominance is challenged but not overcome. In their first exchanges, she typically offers her views for his confirmation or criticism; he responds with extensive guidance. During their first separation, she relates in detail her thoughts and activities in regard to the student protest in her school and the factional struggles in the Nationalist Party and government; he grumbles about his colleagues and sends information about the Northern Expedition. Second separation, in 1929, shows them largely preoccupied with their own affairs.

As a source of biographical information about Lu Xun between 1925 and 1932, the original letters are invaluable. They also give some insight into the political, intellectual, and literary history of the time, but with rare exceptions, usually deleted in *Letters between Two*, they add little to other documentation. Some passages showing Lu Xun's views on literature and life have become well-known, but his critical opinions on his colleagues, derogatory comments on his own projects, provocative remarks on women's writing, and commonplace remarks on poetry are usually passed over. Xu Guangping's opinions and the possibility that they had some influence on Lu Xun's way of thinking have never been systematically explored.

Part III

Searching for Privacy

Whom Heav'n would bless it does from pomps remove,
And makes their wealth in privacy and love.

Dryden

Happy is the civilization which can breed men accustomed from infancy to regard certain at least of the ego's natural activities as unthinkable. This training, which in happy circumstances can be of life-long efficacy, is however seen to be superficial when horror breaks in: in war, in concentration camps, in the awful privacy of family and marriage.

Iris Murdoch, *The Black Prince*

13

Mapping Personal Space

When people are asked what privacy means to them, they first volunteer information about what things, events, or experiences they consider are or should be private. When comparisons are made between two or more groups' concepts of privacy, it is usually in reference to these differences or similarities in content, and when defenders of one cultural tradition accuse members of another of trying to impose concepts of privacy, the imposition is usually thought of in terms of content. Most definitions of privacy are also based primarily or solely on content. For a fully rounded understanding of privacy, whether in regard to a culture or a limited body of texts, other aspects of privacy that should also be considered are its mechanisms, functions, and values. Finally, it might be asked whether or not an articulated concept of privacy is present in the material under examination.

A comparison between the original and published versions of their correspondence yields apparently incontrovertible evidence of what Lu Xun, with the presumed assent of Xu Guangping, regarded as private. In practice, however, the evidence is not entirely straightforward. Since both texts are open to different interpretations, the differences between them are similarly open to dispute. As will appear below, Wang Dehou and I differ in our readings of specific instances and in overall interpretation of the original correspondence (OC) and the nature of the editorial interventions in *Letters between Two*. In large part, these variations can be attributed to differences in our respective goals. In compiling his minutely detailed comparison, Wang Dehou's aim was to reach a comprehensive understanding of Lu Xun's life, creative work, and thinking.[1] My own interest is both broader and narrower: to examine concepts of privacy as expressed or implied by both parties in their correspondence and by the editorial process of preparing it for publication. It is commonly believed that letters express the true self. Wang Dehou also tends to believe that what the letter-writers say is always a true expression of their feelings at the time of writing, and that while the editorial interventions may be prompted by unavoidable caution, they may also on the whole be accepted at face value. As suggested above, there is little evidence to support this belief, and Lu Xun's warning that 'one often hears that letters are the most unembellished and truthful kind of writing, but that is not the case with me' should be taken seriously.

There is a common belief that concepts of privacy are properties of national cultures, although even a cursory examination of the evidence shows how unlikely this would be.[2] In countries with a small and homogeneous population, it may be relatively easy to find instances of shared conduct peculiar to that country.

For example, it is common in the Netherlands for people not to draw their curtains in the evenings, allowing passers-by to look into their living rooms. However, it would be nonsense to conclude from that one instance that the Dutch are less jealous of their privacy than the English whose lace curtains are only ever twitched to observe others. It is even more implausible to make claims about much larger countries, for example, that certain instances of Chinese behaviour, like standing very close to each other in queues (or not queuing), demonstrates some truths about the Chinese sense of privacy. Isolated instances of behaviour in regard to privacy issues do not add up to concepts of privacy but need to be examined within a general framework such as that suggested in the Introduction above. It has nowhere been demonstrated that any single country in Europe or America has a nationally unique concept of privacy, even less one that can be considered characteristic of Western countries generally. How much less again is it likely that a country as large and heterogeneous as China should have a concept of privacy accepted throughout the whole nation. Even among people of the same age, social background, educational level, and nationality there can be a huge range of different views: attached to a large body of generally shared opinion, we can also expect to find a long tail of minority opinions as well as opinions which are mutually contradictory.[3] It seems inherently unlikely that there could be a single Chinese concept of privacy, or even a single set, just as there is no single Western concept of privacy. To date, systematic studies by Chinese scholars are few, however, and there is no history or sociology of privacy in China even in general terms.

In cross-cultural comparisons of concepts of privacy, the problem of terminology is a crucial issue. According to Charles Taylor, it is an error to suppose that in cross-cultural comparisons the language of understanding (or sympathy) has to be either ours, theirs or a supposedly 'neutral' or scientific language: what is needed is a language of 'perspicuous contrast'.[4] 'Such a language of contrast might show their language of understanding to be distorted or inadequate in some respects, or it might show ours to be so (in which case, we might find that understanding them leads to an alteration of our self-understanding, and hence our form of life—a far from unknown process in history); or it might show both to be so.'[5] 'It is a language which enables us to give an account of the procedures of both societies in terms of the same cluster of possibilities . . . [but] it does not involve projecting our own gamut of activities on to the agents of the other society. It allows for the fact that their range of activities may be crucially different from ours, that they may have activities that have no correspondent in ours; which in fact they turn out to do. But . . . it does not just accept that their particular activities will be incommensurable with ours, and must somehow be understood on their own terms or not at all. On the contrary, it searches for a language of perspicuous contrast in which we can understand their practices in relation to ours.'[6]

In practice, to create this new language might prove more confusing than helpful. A contrary view is proposed by Bakhtin: 'There exists a very strong, but one-sided and thus untrustworthy, idea that in order better to understand a foreign culture, one must enter into it, forgetting one's own, and view the world through the eyes of this foreign culture', Bakhtin begins. 'This step is necessary, but it if is viewed as a goal, the research becomes "mere duplication and would not entail anything new or enriching" for either side . . .' '*Creative understanding* does not renounce itself, its own place in time, its own culture; and it forgets nothing. In order to understand, it is immensely important for the person who understands to be *located outside* the object of his or her creative understanding—in time, in space, in culture. For one cannot even really see one's own exterior and comprehend it as a whole, and no mirrors or photographs can help; our real exterior can be seen and understood only by other people, because they are located outside us in space and because they are *others*.'[7]

Zhang Longxi warns against negative definitions in cross-cultural comparisons, of the type 'there is no word for X in Chinese'.[8] English-speakers point out there is no word for 'privacy' in Chinese without being aware that the word 'private' in English is problematic and its history complex. The words 'private' and 'privacy' come from the Latin *privatus*, meaning 'withdrawn from public life, deprived of office, peculiar to oneself', and the generally negative sense is continued into the definitions of the English word 'private' (whose first recorded appearance goes back to 1450).[9] By the end of the nineteenth century, 'privacy' became related to legal and political rights, associated with modernity and advanced civilization, and attributed relatively or very high value.[10] Near-synonyms for 'private' as a descriptor in English in different contexts include 'individual', 'personal', 'familiar', 'family', 'domestic', 'secluded', 'secret', 'confidential', 'secure', 'inner', 'interior', and 'intimate'.

The Chinese word most commonly given as the equivalent of 'private' is *si*, although like English it has a wide range of near-synonyms such as *nei* [inner] and *geren* [individual].[11] Also like 'privacy', *si* is commonly paired with its antonym *gong* [public], and commonly has a negative connotation in modern Chinese, the main associations being with selfishness and unwanted solitude rather than intimacy and desired solitude.[12] Nevertheless, over its long history, *si* has a wide range of meanings in Chinese, including combinations where *si* is combined with positive words like *jia* [family] as well as the expressions *qin* and *ni*, denoting intimacy.[13]

Differences in denotation or connotation do not invalidate the proposition that concepts of privacy exist in equivalent ways among English-speakers and Chinese-speakers. Few English-speakers who are aware that there is no exact equivalent of the word 'privacy' in several European languages would wish to deny on linguistic grounds that concepts of privacy exist in the Netherlands, France, Italy, Sweden, or Finland.[14] If, as argued by Steven Pinker, mental life goes on independently of particular languages,[15] a sense of privacy and concepts of privacy can exist equally in cultures despite lexical differences.

Even more crucial is the need to avoid imposing predetermined definitions of privacy on the interpretation of the texts. One danger is that there are too many existing definitions in English (over a hundred), so that arguments can be shaped by choice of definition or by the creation of new definitions. More seriously, there is a constant danger of shaping our understanding of Chinese concepts of privacy by imposing Western definitions on Chinese experiences. Chinese definitions might be seen as an alternative starting point, but in the absence of systematic studies of privacy in China, this alternative is not likely to be promising. The profusion of English-language definitions of privacy also suggests that other approaches may be more fruitful. What can result, however, from cross-cultural comparisons is vital. To return to Taylor: 'What I have been trying to sketch above is the way in which understanding another society can make us challenge our self-definitions. It can force us to do this, because we cannot get an adequate explanatory account of them until we understand their self-definitions, and these may be different enough from ours to force us to extend our language of human possibilities.'[16]

Complete avoidance of linguistic and definitional traps may be an impossible ideal. In the following chapters I propose to postpone provisionally both the use of the word 'privacy' and its definitions. Instead, the term 'personal space'[17] will be used to designate the differences created by Lu Xun between the OC and *Letters between Two*; anything referred to in the OC which Lu Xun conceals from the reader of *Letters between Two* by deletions or recensions will be designated as 'personal', while Lu Xun's retentions and additions will also be examined as evidence for what is considered, at the very least, not very personal. The OC will also be examined for the presence or absence of references that might indicate a difference of attitude between Lu Xun and Xu Guangping on personal space.

Chapters 14–22 examine the instances that make up the content of Lu Xun and Xu Guangping's personal space in the correspondence. These instances can be divided into nine categories:

(1) The love affair between Lu Xun and Xu Guangping, and their sexual relationships with others;
(2) Their own bodies and bodily activities and functions;
(3) Their domestic and working life and habits;
(4) Their family relationships;
(5) Their relationships with other people, including former and current students and colleagues;
(6) Their political beliefs, activities, and observations;
(7) Their intimate thoughts and feelings;
(8) Rumour and gossip;
(9) Secrecy, seclusion, and private/selfish interests.

These categories are neither rigid nor exclusive; certain instances can be identified as belonging to more than one category.

Neither the instances nor the categories will be compared systematically against other sources, but the overall content will be considered against definitions of privacy in Chapter 23. Chapter 23 also examines the mechanisms, functions, and values of the personal space revealed in the texts, and whether or not Lu Xun and Xu Guangping can be said to have unique, shared, or culturally specific concepts of privacy.

14

Sex and Sexual Relationships

The salient issue on which Lu Xun and Xu Guangping were most reticent was sex. Arendt observes that 'love, in distinction from friendship, is killed, or rather extinguished, the moment it is displayed in public'.[1] While this is far from a universal truth, it may help to explain their reticence. Even in the original correspondence (OC) there is very little direct reference to their physical attraction to each other, the consummation of their affair, their cohabitation, or the accidental conception of their son. There is a fairly substantial amount of indirect reference in the OC to these things, but only a small part is left in *Letters between Two*. Similarly, there is very little reference to any sexual relationship they may have had with other people, or to the subject of sex in general.

Initial Attraction

From the beginning of their correspondence, Xu Guangping was highly emotional in her attitude to Lu Xun, although it is unlikely that she regarded him as a possible sexual partner from the very beginning. The first hint that she was attracted to him sexually comes in her letters after her first visit to his home in 1925. In letters dated 16 and 25 April, she refers to his home as a *mimi wo* [secret nest]; on 17 June in the context of a joke about their relationship, she uses the expression again.[2] In *Letters between Two*, Lu Xun avoids the suggestion of intimacy by changing the expression first to *zun fu* [honourable residence], deleting the second instance, and in the third, replacing it with *jia* [home].[3]

In Xu Guangping's letter of 16 April she also makes a remark about enjoying the lectures in his classes on 'physiology'; if Wang Dehou is correct in his guess that this refers to instruction on basic human sexuality that Lu Xun introduced into his lectures on literature, then her remark can be seen as provocative as well as possibly damaging to Lu Xun's reputation as a teacher. Its deletion from *Letters between Two* suggests that it conveys some sense of impropriety.[4]

The strongest hint that there might be more between them than ordinary friendship comes in Xu Guangping's reflections in May on her suicide attempt: 'This is a matter in which the mind controls the body and emotion overcomes reason, and nothing can be done about it. Of course, I do not regard this as "good fortune", but neither do I feel it is so terrible. If such a day should come, then my hope is that the person by my side will give me an iron pill or a holy injection'; 'the person by my side' is changed to 'someone' in *Letters between Two*.[5] The expression seems innocent enough, but it does suggest that by June he was more to her than simply her teacher, an impression he apparently preferred to avoid giving others.

There is no indication in any of Lu Xun's 1925 letters that her sexual attraction to him is reciprocated at this stage.

Missing Letters

As editor, Lu Xun chose to let readers know that certain letters were missing from *Letters between Two* without indicating whether they were lost or deliberately omitted. One of the lost letters, written by Xu Guangping on 25 or 26 June concerns the incident on Dragon Boat Day.[6] The omission of the first half of Lu Xun's reply[7] clearly suggests to readers that her letter was too personal to be made public, an impression reinforced in his letter the following day.[8] Xu Guangping's letter of 28 June also seems to have been lost; from Lu Xun's reply, it can be guessed that Xu Guangping blames herself for having urged him to drink and apologizes at length. Lu Xun refers to his landladies (i.e. the Yu sisters) in this letter, but in *Letters between Two* quotation marks are added around 'landladies': with or without quotation marks, the term would mystify readers who were not intimate enough with Lu Xun's affairs to know the the landladies were the Yu sisters (or who the Yu sisters were). Apart from the references to Lu Xun's excessive drinking and his aggressive behaviour that afternoon, Wang Dehou believes that the tone of intimacy in these letters suggest that it was at this time that the couple first acknowledged their feelings for each other.

Another editorial note indicates that several letters are missing between 29 June and 9 July, the exact number being unclear: the only one of these that has been preserved is Xu Guangping's letter of 30 June which refers to the omitted first half of Lu Xun's earlier letter.[9] Another note indicates that five or six letters are missing between 9 July and 29 July; in fact, five unpublished letters from this period have been preserved but are omitted because their facetiousness and other indications of intimacy make them much too personal even to be included in part.[10] For the remaining months of 1925 and into 1926, meeting frequently and alone, Lu Xun and Xu Guangping no longer needed letters.

Irregular Unions

A significant deletion occurs in Xu Guangping's first letter after they parted in Shanghai in 1926: in a passage describing what she is reading on board the boat to Canton, her mention of Zhang Yiping's *A Bundle of Love-letters* is omitted.[11] Not only was Zhang Yiping by 1932 regarded as having spied on them in Peking but his book about love-letters was an unwelcome reminder that their relationship was only one of several irregular affairs among literary couples at the time; references to him and his book, therefore, had to go. Similarly, Lu Xun's remark on the similarity between his situation and his brother's (both married, both conducting affairs with former students) was deleted from *Letters between Two*.[12] This kind of deletion suggests that Lu Xun wanted to give the impression that their affair only began in 1927, either in Canton or in Shanghai.

Straying Eyes

An exchange that is retained almost in full starts with Lu Xun's admission that he has five girl students in his class but that he has decided that his eyes will not stray from the straight and narrow path until after he has left Amoy.[13] Her reply takes the form of a rebuke at his attempt to provoke her jealousy: 'The letter especially is sheer "childishness", it's just as well I received it. What is so important about "straying eyes", the usual problem isn't "straying eyes", I believe, but possibly a stare which catches you off guard.'[14] Up to this point, the exchange is retained in full in *Letters between Two*, but her next remark, 'Like this, a person who welcomes a stare, who appreciates a stare, must be someone who can also stare, but even if there is someone like this, what does it matter?' is deleted.[15] Lu Xun's retort, 'If I don't dare let my eyes "stray", how can I presume "to stare"', is retained.[16] Also retained in both letters are their remarks about Peking University's 'Dr Sex', Zhang Jingsheng, and his theories of sex as an aesthetic activity that should not evoke possessiveness or jealousy. The situation implied in these passages is that Xu Guangping was once caught off guard by Lu Xun staring at her in class, but she welcomed the stare and returned it. Lu Xun is not too prudish to admit in public to an interest in his female students but draws the line when it comes to his flirtation with Xu Guangping in class. In revealing that the possibility of sexual jealousy and possessiveness existed between them, however, Lu Xun here acknowledges what elsewhere he conceals.

Age and Gender Reversal

One of the chief markers of their sexual relationship is their repeated reversal of gender and age terms for themselves and each other, especially in the 1926 letters. The origin lies in Lu Xun's initial address to Xu Guangping as *xiong*, which at the time seemed innocent enough but which became the basis of teasing salutations in letters between them in July 1925.[17] Gender reversal in the letters also occurs after he has been persuaded to take the class on an excursion to the History Museum at Meridian Gate: after his complaint that 'leading female students on a tour' is a far cry from 'leading troops into plunder and looting',[18] she suggests that if he is uncomfortable about being a male leading a group of females he should practise Buddhist transubstantiation and transform himself into a woman.[19] He responds by referring to her as a 'young gentleman', and they debate the issue to and fro until their mood changes when she is expelled from the school.[20] These passages are mostly retained.

Xu Guangping reintroduces the practice after their separation in September 1926, admonishing him to be a 'good little boy' so that 'your elder brother can stop worrying'.[21] Lu Xun responds by signing the first part of his reply with her nickname, 'H. M.',[22] and repeats the gesture a couple of weeks later.[23] Taking up the challenge, she writes 'For the crime of making "my dear little brother" anxious, ah, I deserve to be slapped'.[24] To this Lu Xun replies, 'The crime of calling me "dear little brother" is also noted in the books'.[25] A few weeks later he addresses her as '"Lin" *xiong*',[26] possibly in reference to the pen-name Ping Lin she used for her 1926 prose poems about their affair, 'Fellow-travellers' and 'Aeolus is My Love'. Both of these prose poems play with gender reversal, presenting the narrator [Xu Guangping] as male and the beloved [Lu Xun] as female.[27] Gender reversal is also extended to Xu Xiansu: in a letter from Peking, Lu Xun refers to her as 'your little brother'.[28] All of these instances of age and gender reversal (except *xiong*) are deleted or disguised in *Letters between Two*; the sexual teasing they convey is part of their personal space.

Sitting and Thinking in Silence

In her letter of 16 April, following her first visit to his home, Xu Guangping conjures up an image of Lu Xun 'sitting in silence'; the words 'in silence' are deleted in *Letters between Two*.[29] This deletion turns an innocent expression with origins in Neo-Confucian meditational practice into one that has a particular and covert significance. In the 1926 letters, the expressions 'sitting in silence' or 'thinking in silence' appear as censored code words for imagining or recalling their love-making, perhaps accompanied by solitary masturbation. Towards the end of October, Xu Guangping writes, 'Can you sit quietly and think in silence of XX? He too likes to think in silence...' where 'XX' and 'he' both refer to Guangping.[30] Lu Xun replies that now he can relax 'and think in silence of a certain person, especially when I sit alone under the lamplight and a strong wind howls outside the window.'[31] In reply she asks, 'What is the simpleton doing in silence under the lamp? He should be slapped for not studying or working properly!'[32] To this he replies, 'Sitting in silence under the lamp should still be counted as what interests me, why should I be "slapped"? Is it possible that "thinking in silence" is incorrect?'[33] At the end of November, hearing that the central government had moved to Wuchang, she writes that her heart flew after them, but that once she had 'thought in silence' she decided to not to leave Canton.[34] In early December, after noting that he can get through the remaining time apart easily enough, he writes, 'Not to mention there is still thinking in silence, but the degree of thinking in silence has a tendency to increase, I don't know why, it seems that in the end that person has still conquered.'[35] Each of these instances is deleted or changed in *Letters between Two*, suggesting that like the gender reversals they incorporate they are indirect references to their sexual relationship.

Hitting and Being Hit

A practice with sexual undertones that started after the Dragon Boat Day incident in June 1925 is remarks about hitting or being hit. In his letter describing the

Dragon Boat Day incident, Lu Xun's admission that he shook his fist at the Yu sisters is retained, but his reference to having pressed down Xu Guangping's head is deleted.[36] In his next letter, his mock-threat 'I will have to attack you with violence' is retained, evidently because it is not serious.[37] There are no grounds for believing that Lu Xun ever hit Xu Guangping, but it seems that on this occasion he used her roughly.

References to hitting or being hit in the Amoy–Canton exchange are only occasionally deleted. In her 28 September letter, Xu Guangping's expression 'I deserve to be slapped' is retained,[38] and his response repeating the expression is also retained.[39] The deletions begin in November 1926: after enumerating the letters and journals she has recently received from him, she writes that he should be slapped for having muddled up the dates in his diary,[40] and the exchange quoted above about slapping and 'sitting in silence' ensues. A final remark from him as he prepares to leave Amoy, that she deserves to be slapped for thinking of going to Wuchang, is also deleted from *Letters between Two*.[41] The proximity of the remarks about slapping to the sexually charged term 'sitting in silence' together with their deletion suggests that they too have a certain sexual significance.

Love Tokens

An apparently innocent exchange about a piece of cloth in which she wraps the seal stick she sends him from Canton is only given significance by its deletion. She asks if he has noticed that the cloth she has used as a wrapping is one that was bought and regularly used in Peking;[42] he responds, 'It is a pity that I did not examine carefully at the time the wrapping around the seal stick, because attention has shifted to the white wrapping, where it still persists. I had actually sensed immediately that it had been used'.[43] Wang Dehou believes that the wrapping was a piece of cloth that Lu Xun had casually given her in Peking but which she had treasured, and that sending it back with the seal stick was a reminder to him of that occasion. The cloth could also have been part of their love-making in Peking. Whatever its intimate significance, this cloth appears to be the only love token they exchanged during their courtship.

Photographs of the beloved afforded great consolation to Jane Carlyle in the 1850s,[44] Luo Jialun in the 1920s[45] and Zhu Xiang in the 1930s,[46] but they occur only once in the OC, when Xu Guangping takes out a photograph from Peking; what it portrays is not specified, but mention of it is deleted.[47]

Lu Xun seems not to have had, and in any case does not mention, any material object that might remind him of Xu Guangping. However, he seems pleased with her gift of the seal stick and the vest she has knitted for him. After having thanked her earlier for them, in December he writes that he wears the vest over his undershirt, because it's warmer than wearing it over his gown, 'but perhaps there may also be another reason'; these remarks are deleted.[48] Behind his deletions may be a wish to conceal a certain imbalance or simply any sign of sentimentality.

Pain at Separation

Although their frustration at being apart in 1926 is allowed to show in *Letters between Two*, the full extent of the tensions developing between them over their future together is glossed over. In her letter written between the first and sixth of September, she wonders if she will be able to keep to the pact they made before parting, and feels 'something pressing on my heart', so that 'I would get very upset, wondering what it would be like in the days following our separation'.[49] In the original version of the same letter, she writes: 'Thy house is near at hand but thou art far away!!! It is really hard to write letters, to write this way is not convenient, and to write that way is not suitable.'[50] For example, her question in early October, 'If you can't stay longer in that place, where would you go?',[51] and his answer that he has no intention of leaving Amoy immediately,[52] are both deleted in *Letters between Two*. Other changes create the misleading impression that they are relatively indifferent to each other's plans: Lu Xun's phrase that he does not see any need to rush down to Canton is an addition to *Letters between Two* (his original comment was a reflection that Zhongshan University may not want him and that he should not place too much hope on being invited),[53] and her remark in reply that she may be too busy to write for a while sounds unnecessarily curt (in the original letter she explains more clearly that the troubles at the school will be taking up all her time).[54]

By December, hurt because the papers say he is coming to Canton while he refuses to confirm it, she criticizes his reluctance to cut himself free of his 'inheritance of suffering' from the old society, and remarks that 'you are sacrificing yourself for the sake of a single person'.[55] Without the latter remark, which is deleted in *Letters between Two*, it is difficult for a reader to understand that the expression 'inheritance of suffering', which is retained, refers to Zhu An (although readers who knew he was married might be able to guess). In his response, Lu Xun acknowledges that she is the more decisive of the two, and agrees that he should dare all. In his following letter, Lu Xun confesses his indecisiveness over the past month, saying that his emotions have been up and down like waves, but recently he has calmed down, and at least he will go to Canton at the end of the semester, and then return to Amoy to finish out the year; all of this is deleted.[56]

The situation is only finally resolved in his reply on 28 November to her letter of 21 and 22 November: '[the third way] would be safer than what we discussed in Peking, but without having discussed it face to face, for the time being I won't make a decision'.[57] This is changed in *Letters between Two* to 'and by being a little careful one can be fairly safe, so for the time being I won't make a decision'. Both versions are still discreet, but the original indicates that Lu Xun is now proposing to continue their affair but without openly living together (in Peking they had apparently discussed living together). His next letter, therefore, begins with an indirect but unmistakable reference to her being a reason that he wants to go to Canton (retained in *Letters between Two*).[58]

Before receiving this reassurance, Xu Guangping is close to despair: 'My heart is in turmoil, I can't find the right words, and I am afraid that what I say will give you some new queer impressions, but if I don't write a few lines, I fear you will be waiting for a letter, I feel it's very unpleasant communicating through letters, it takes time and is totally inadequate in conveying anything. KU is naturally not an ideal place for sacrificing yourself, so that when you speak of staying on at AU, I find it difficult to say more. But I still think that writing cannot represent one's thoughts, and as for where exactly you will end up, if you were to ask me, I think it would be best if we could talk about this in person and go over it exhaustively.'[59] In *Letters between Two* this becomes: 'I am deeply troubled. KU is of course not an ideal university and therefore if you want to stay on at AU I find it difficult to say much. But if I don't write a few lines, I'm afraid you will be waiting for an answer, and if I do speak out, I can't find the right words, and I'm afraid you will get some new queer impressions. I feel it's really very unpleasant sending letters back and forth, it's both time-consuming and totally inadequate in conveying anything. And this letter is no exception.'[60] The differences here are subtle, but they could be seen as disguising the depths of her despair, while the final added comment sounds almost as if it is meant to discredit what goes before.

The contrast with her next letter is extreme: having by now received his assurances, it is her glee that is deleted: 'I think "an increase in sitting in silence" is because the time is drawing near. Little children always seem to getting into tiffs like this just before the New Year celebrations. At whose hands have you suffered defeat? You have truly not acquitted yourself splendidly at all.'[61]

Similar expressions of eagerness to see each other again and reassure each other of their constancy, too numerous to be given in detail, are deleted or reworded in the remainder of Part II of *Letters between Two*. One of the most revealing deletions is her remark that she might keep her dormitory room at the school because it is easier to move to another place from the school than from home, suggesting that in spite of his reluctance for them to live together openly she is expecting to move in with him after his arrival in Canton.[62] Sometimes the editing is inconsistent. In one letter Lu Xun deletes his remark that he will 'lay his head at someone's feet', but goes on to add a joking remark that he is 'deeply troubled' about taking orders from her.[63]

In Xu Guangping's last letter from Canton, prompted by his 'Preface to *The Grave*', she charges him with having revealed to the world 'the news of spring'; this uncharacteristically frank reference to their affair is made more discreet and politicized in *Letters between Two*: 'it is you coming out of the trenches'.[64] Lu Xun's last letter from Amoy is an odd mixture of very intimate retentions ('I had once in a while thought of love, but always immediately after felt ashamed, fearing I didn't deserve it'); melodramatic and revelatory revisions and additions (from 'I will tell the news, and see what they can do about me' to 'I will take off my armour: let's see what form their second strike will take'; and from 'it made me feel I was by no means a bad man' to 'it made me believe that I am not the kind of man who has to devalue himself to such an extent, and I could fall in love!'); and deletions of some of his most moving declarations ('I love my owl, snake, ghost or monster [Xu Guangping], and I will give it the right to trample on me').[65]

Missing Each Other

Expressions of missing each other dominate the 1929 letters, which express affection rather than sexual passion (although it is impossible to draw a strict line between these two). For example, Lu Xun deletes his May 1929 wish that it would soon be the end of the month so that he can return; Wang Dehou comments that he is even more impatient than in Amoy: they have barely been parted and yet he longs for home.[66] His fond admission a few days later that as he sits at his desk he thinks of 'a certain person' is even fonder when he uses her nickname, 'Little Hedgehog'.[67] The same effect occurs four days later, when Lu Xun writes, 'Everything is as it used to be in the back room, but I feel very discontented because the Little Hedgehog is not sitting on the bed'; this is changed to 'Everything is as it used to be in the plaster hut, only slightly more desolate. When I sit here alone at night I sometimes feel much too gloomy'.[68] Further on, 'I estimate that when this letter arrives, the day when I leave here won't be far off. This makes me happy. But I am still quiet and looking after myself, and I don't get upset, the Little Hedgehog should be at ease and concentrate on taking care of herself' is changed to 'Here I can only wish you from a distance a natural and peaceful sleep, and that you take good care of yourself'.[69]

Similarly, Xu Guangping's admission that she was 'so happy I shed tears' at getting his letter is changed to 'my joy cannot be expressed in words', and a whole paragraph affectionately enjoining him to look after himself is deleted.[70] Her expression 'I truly do miss you' is weakened to 'how I miss you', and a curiously formal final salutation is added.[71] Another curious addition is where her reference to fond memories [i.e. of him] in Peking is made even stronger.[72]

Cohabitation

Since their sexual relationship was about to become public with the birth of their child, there was no reason to suppress reference to it in Part III of *Letters between Two*, where deletions and revisions conceal its nature rather than its existence. Even so, Lu Xun is reluctant to admit in public to their cohabitation: in Xu Guangping's first letter, 'since we've been living together' is changed to 'since we've come to Shanghai' and 'after I saw you off at the door' is changed to 'after we parted': in each case the OC is more concrete and intimate.[73]

Their affair now stabilized, there are few references in the OC to their sexual relations. The only area where they are relatively uninhibited is in their nicknames and other terms of endearment. Despite Xu Guangping's explanation of the pet name 'White Elephant' for Lu Xun as meaning a national treasure (see above), it is also possible that for them 'elephant' has a sexual connotation, for example, in their jokes about cold noses (or trunks), which are deleted in *Letters between Two*.[74] Certainly, the drawings of elephant-like creatures that adorn their original correspondence emphasize the beast's long trunk.[75] Her pet name, 'Little Hedgehog', may be a reference to her prickly temperament or equally to their love-making.

After Lu Xun writes to her on notepaper with a drawing of a lotus pod in an affectionate reference to her pregnancy, Xu Guangping reverses it to refer to his fertility, calling him 'Little Lotus, because you are a bit short. Darling Lotus!'[76] In response, Lu Xun calls her 'Little Hedgehog = Little Lotus Pod = Little Lotus Seeds'.[77] All of these terms are replaced with pronouns or deleted in *Letters between Two*.

He is similarly reticent about their unborn child, deleting all of his references to their 'Little White Elephant',[78] although when the manuscript was being edited their son was already three years old.

Reflections on the Future

For both of them, their temporary separation in May 1929 after four years acquaintance and eighteen months living together provides a pause for reflection on their past and future relationship. A significant deletion of such reflections begins with Xu Guangping's reference to a letter she is writing to Yushu [Chang Ruilin] about her relationship with Lu Xun; she sends a copy to him thinking that he would like to know what she writes.[79] The letter to Chang Ruilin starts with an apology for not having been more frank with her earlier. Going back to the time of the school strike, Xu Guangping describes the importance of Lu Xun's support, which he offered without any private interest whatsoever; even when he became ill and was advised by his doctor to rest he still continued his activities. She then explains, somewhat less than frankly, that when he came to Canton, she became his teaching assistant, and since they have been in Shanghai she has been his private assistant. Now they have little money but they love each other and have a joyous private life. Although his marriage of more than ten years has just been an empty form, he does not want to publicize his estrangement from his wife. Now he has gone to Peking to see his mother; she had intended accompanying him and then going to Heilongjiang to see Ruilin, but this became impractical since she is in her fifth month of pregnancy. Finally, she asks Ruilin not to tell people, since even her own family does not know. This is the first letter in which Xu Guangping discusses her relationship with Lu Xun (whom she refers to as 'Mr Zhou').

In reply Lu Xun writes: 'The letter you wrote to Xie [Chang Ruilin] is very good, but you are a bit too kind to me. Judging from the situation at present, there seem to be no hindrances whatsoever to our future, but even if there were, I would certainly want to leap over them and advance with Little Hedgehog, with absolutely no shrinking back.'[80] Lu Xun also has some gossip to pass on: 'Lin Zhuofeng asked little brother [Xu Xiansu] that she'd heard that Lu Xun had a favourite person, and have they married or not? But she did not ask who the "person" was. Little brother replied that she did not know. This is a trifling matter, not worth deep consideration, and we can talk of it at our leisure.'[81] The third and final reference to Chang Ruilin is also deleted: Xu Guangping has received a letter from Ruilin in which Ruilin relates that her sister in Tientsin sends the news that Xu Guangping is now married to Lu Xun.[82]

In his last letter from Peking, Lu Xun stays up until five in the morning in order to express his thoughts fully. After reflecting on his 'inexperience' in previously having struggled against 'the upright gentlemen' in Peking, he continues in a passage which he deletes from *Letters between Two*, 'Little Hedgehog, there are indeed profound reasons behind our living together, and how could people who pry into our affairs and speculate about us on the basis of their own thinking understand. Looking at it from here, I know more firmly than ever that we are by no means infinitesimal'.[83]

In the final section of this letter, where Lu Xun returns to the question of his relations with 'the upright gentlemen' and how this relates to her, one deleted passage runs: 'But sometimes I also feel that only for this am I worthy of my Little Lotus Pod and Little Hedgehog. Hereafter, rather than make a row in all directions, it would be better to be nice and quiet for a spell, but to write a dispassionate specialized book would be a problem. Luckily we will meet soon and can discuss it then.'

Other Relationships

Lu Xun is silent on any other sexual relationship he may have had. It is claimed that his marriage with Zhu An was unconsummated, and she is only mentioned directly by him once in the OC (deleted in *Letters between Two*: see below). Although he may have been sexually attracted to Hata Nobuko, there is no evidence that there was ever an affair between them, and she is only referred to with disgust in *Letters between Two*. Apart from Xu Guangping, his closest woman friend was Xu Xiansu: demonstrating their intimacy by age and gender reversal, he refers to her three times in the letters as 'your little brother'.[84] Lu Xun also reworded a reference to the women in Amoy which might seem to indicate excessive interest in their physical appearance.[85]

Xu Guangping is almost as reticent: her affair with Li Xiaohui is not mentioned directly in the correspondence, although her attempts at suicide are referred to twice (both times deleted in *Letters between Two*). In the first instance, she writes: 'Although the first year I was at Women's Normal because I and a fellow-student were vomiting blood in a bout of scarlet fever, very stupidly I took some rattan-yellow, in the end funnily enough I was saved.'[86] This is changed to 'The first year I was at Women's Normal, I also almost died of scarlet fever'[87] and in Lu Xun's subsequent references to her 'taking rattan-yellow', the phrase 'regard [oneself] as "waste matter"' is substituted.[88] A related passage in 1926, referring to her earlier attempt at suicide is also deleted.[89] Whether or not Xu Guangping's attempts at suicide were wholly serious or not, it is hardly surprising that they do not appear in *Letters between Two*. Virginia Woolf freely mentions her bouts of madness to friends but there is only one reference to her suicide, and it arises in response to her correspondent's despair.[90]

Summary

Throughout their correspondence, Lu Xun and Xu Guangping were discreet about their sexual relationship, possibly fearing that their letters might be intercepted or seized. In 1925, Xu Guangping was not above making frank and even provocative remarks about the budding sexual attraction she felt for her teacher, while Lu Xun responded rather feebly. The gap between them in this regard disappears once they become lovers. In 1926, their use of gender and age reversals and their remarks about sitting in silence or slapping one another are evenly balanced, both in what is retained and what is deleted. In another respect, by referring even indirectly to her other sexual relationships in 1925 and 1926, Xu Guangping again shows less need for personal space, although she stops short of revealing the details; Lu Xun never even hints at being attracted to any other woman.

Nevertheless, Lu Xun still found much to delete or disguise for publication: when and how their affair began; their reversals of self-identification; her love tokens and gifts to him; the agreed length of their separation; their intention to live together in Canton; their cohabitation in Shanghai; their love-making; their future as a couple; Lu Xun's possible sexual interest in other women; Xu Guangping's earlier sexual relationships and the two attempts at suicide that occurred as a result; and their as-yet unborn child. Less personal are references to Lu Xun's sexual awareness of other women, including his students; hitting and being hit; their frustration about being apart and the misunderstandings that thereby arose; and the pet-names they used for themselves and for each other.

15

Bodies, Bodily Functions and Activities, and Hygiene

Bodies are a mixed realm of public and private. According to Arendt, 'it is striking that from the beginning of history to our own time it has always been the bodily part of human existence that needed to be hidden in privacy'.[1] This is not wholly true, since eating and drinking have commonly been social activities. On the other hand, copulation, excretion, childbirth, illness, and death are commonly carried out in seclusion (to the extent that circumstances permit) by humans and even some animals. Carl D. Schneider relates the sense of privacy to the sense of shame[2] and lists phenomena where privacy is related to dignity: 'the use of nicknames or formal names; the names of relatives; things that carry the weight of the individual's identity or autonomy [. . .]; faces and other body parts; things needed to care for the body such as soap, towels and combs.[3] The open display of bodily functions (defecating, great pain, the process of dying) threatens the dignity of the individual, revealing an individual vulnerable to being reduced to his bodily existence; the function of shame is to preserve wholeness and integrity.[4] Bodily functions (sexual activities, sleep and excretion; illness, suffering, and eating) are rarely physiological processes alone. We invest all our activities with meanings, so that the physiological is invariably permeated with the human; the obscene is a deliberate violation of the sense of shame and privacy.[5] All social interaction involves risk to the self; the problem of shame and the private realm is the problem of human vulnerability. Human relationships demand both a protecting of and risking of this vulnerability through a pattern of mutual and measured self-disclosure.'[6]

When they first started to write to each other, Lu Xun and Xu Guangping rarely discussed bodies, bodily functions or activities, or personal hygiene, apart from his drinking and smoking. In 1926, by contrast, they exchanged much detailed information about a wide range of bodily activities, while in 1929 they confined their remarks mainly to getting adequate rest and good diets. Some of their attitudes changed over time: in her first letters, Xu Guangping tends to glamourize his smoking and drinking but she becomes more wifely after the Dragon Boat Day incident; he becomes more inclined to boast of sobriety than his drinking capacity after 1926.

Resting and Sleeping

There are few references to resting or sleeping in 1925: Lu Xun does not discuss his insomnia with her, and she only mentions her habits in order to assert her normality: 'the young devil is really an ordinary person who eats and sleeps well, who laughs and enjoys herself just like everyone else' (retained).[7]

In 1926, she often fusses about his sleeping, and he just as often assures that he is sleeping well, better than in Peking: these comments are also mostly retained.[8] In contrast, detail about her bedtime habits is deleted,[9] as also a reference to her bedding not being wet by a leaky roof.[10]

In 1929, her need for rest and sleep, important during the early months of her pregnancy, is frequently discussed; their remarks are mostly deleted,[11] although enough remains to demonstrate his concern, her reassurances, and his own ability to sleep soundly.[12] Her description of how her sleep patterns in Shanghai are still determined by his habit of working late into the night is also deleted, presumably as too personal.[13] But trivial detail about him, as when he sets his alarm at 9 a.m. for his dental appointment at 10 a.m., is retained.[14]

Bathing and Personal Hygiene

There is not much reference to personal hygiene in the letters. In Amoy and Shanghai, Lu Xun notes in his diary his visits to bathhouses, but his only reference in the correspondence is soon after his arrival in Amoy, where he declares that he will not go sea-bathing since the university has a bathhouse.[15] In Canton and Shanghai, Xu Guangping seems to have washed herself at home, but the two references in her letters to taking a bath are both deleted.[16]

Foot-washing [*zhuo zu*] then and now often refers to a medicinal practice carried out in special clinics or other premises outside the home. Lu Xun notes in his diary when he has this treatment from 1928 on, but he does not mention in his letters the occasion during his visit to Peking in 1929.[17] Xu Guangping refers once to washing her feet [*xi jiao*]: this appears to be ordinary bathing and like the examples mentioned above is deleted in *Letters between Two*.[18]

Xu Guangping's reference to sweating in class while she is teaching is retained,[19] as is Lu Xun's description of himself sweating in the Amoy sunshine.[20] He deletes her reference to picking her nose, a habit she learned in Peking and continued in Canton, as also a reference to being bitten by mosquitoes in the same letter.[21] At no time does she ever refer to menstruation in these letters.[22] (Virginia Woolf discusses her and her sister's menstrual problems in letters to her sister, and in letters to her brother-in-law she also mentions Lydia Lopokova's use of sanitary towels; but writing to a sister and writing to a lover—especially before there has been any cohabitation—involve confidences of a very different kind.[23])

Excretion

Reference to excretion is relatively rare in modern letters, especially in love-letters. European writers were not always as reticent, however; Mozart's famously scatalogical letters to his cousin continue a long-standing custom in eighteenth-century letters.[24] (Mozart's mentions of shitting and so on are mostly word-plays of various kinds, such as nicknames, and rarely refer to his or others' actual excretion.) Virginia Woolf promoted a revival of frankness in her letters to her sister and other close friends, which contain several mentions of lavatories, WCs, earth closets, and chamber pots. A letter to her sister's partner appears to have been written while Woolf was sitting in the lavatory and another compares letter-writing to shitting.[25] In her love-letters, however, there is no trace of this deliberate vulgarity.

References to excretion appear to be even rarer in modern Chinese letters. In his letters to Wang Yingxia, for instance, the normally frank Yu Dafu makes a single, discreetly worded reference to 'washing his hands' in the courtyard after a meal and looking up at the moon.[26] In actual conduct, Chinese men are not always so bashful. A relatively common sight in central China, not so evident in the north or south, is men urinating in the street during daylight hours as well as at night, their backs turned away from pedestrians but their urination nonetheless public; signs saying 'Do not pee here!' are ignored. Shaoxing, Lu Xun's hometown, is one of several towns where this practice is rife, and one of the most striking markers of Lu Xun's letters to Xu Guangping in 1926 is his introduction of information about his urinary habits.

The first passage where Lu Xun raises the topic is very explicitly in the context of confirming their intimacy: his frequent trips to the postal agency on campus to collect her letters are no imposition, he writes, since it is on his way to the lavatory; then he goes on to remark that because the lavatory is so far away, after dark he generally relieves himself on the lawn downstairs.[27] In another letter he mentions that at night he sometimes uses a chamber pot which he then empties out of the window when there's no one around.[28] Both of these passages are retained in *Letters between Two*, with the additional remark that it was only at midnight that he emptied the pot (as if to assure readers of his discretion).[29]

Xu Guangping, in contrast, never mentions her urinary habits. The nearest she comes to the topic is her reference in 1929 to their servant 'emptying the bucket' (presumably a slop bucket) first thing in the morning. This is changed to 'opening the back gate': a loss of concrete detail about a daily event familiar to all contemporary readers.[30]

The gender difference suggested by these instances is corroborated by evidence from 1930s Shanghai. According to Hanchao Lu, the nightstool was commonly kept in the back corner of a room, curtained off with a cotton drape for privacy or placed behind a piece of furniture, or else underneath a stairwell. But adult males often preferred to use a public lavatory; as in rural areas, using the nightstool if there was a public lavatory nearby was considered somewhat sissified.[31]

Defecation (except their infant son's) is nowhere mentioned by either Lu Xun or Xu Guangping.

Diet and Digestion

Lu Xun also had trouble with his digestion, and his diet is a frequent matter of concern in 1926.[32] According to Xu Guangping, his indigestion went back to his student days in Nanking; too poor to buy padded clothing for the winter, he kept himself warm by eating chillis.[33] In Canton, Xu Guangping is at her most wifely, worried that 'some people in Peking' [his mother?] thought that bananas and pomelos were hard to digest.[34] He responds in turn with reassurance and teasing but seems to appreciate her advice.[35] All of this exchange is retained. Lu Xun also writes that he will cut down on chilli powder and that he drinks less tea (because it is inconvenient to get hot water);[36] this is repeated a few days later, except that he writes cayenne pepper instead of chilli powder;[37] eventually he buys a spirit kettle and so can make tea.[38] All of this information is retained. Since his student days in Tokyo, Lu Xun had always been fond of pastries, and he was eager to try the local variety, but problems with ants getting at his food stores occupy his attention and her concern throughout September and October: some of the detail is kept but later much is deleted,[39] presumably to avoid boring third-party readers.

General references to food and meals occur in almost every letter in 1926, and they exchange information about the local delicacies in Amoy and Canton.[40] Nevertheless, Lu Xun is anxious for them not to appear self-indulgent. Xu Guangping's remark that in Shanghai 'That day I saw you take fried rice with shrimps and egg with your wine, you did not take a meat dish' is changed to: 'That day I saw you take fried rice with your wine'.[41] Wang Dehou claims that the change makes it clearer that Lu Xun did not drink without taking food, but it also shows Lu Xun as more abstemious. In the same letter, Xu Guangping describes a meal she had on board that consisted of a cup of coffee with milk and three pieces of bread; this is changed to a cup of coffee and two slices of bread. Wang Dehou suggests that two for three is a slip of the pen, but it also makes Guangping sound less greedy.[42] In her next letter, her complaints about the food and accommodation on board are deleted, possibly to avoid showing her as too interested in material comforts.[43]

References to food and meals are rather less common in 1929, and most are retained.[44]

General Health and Appearance

In 1926, Lu Xun is at pains to reassure Xu Guangping that he is looking after his health and general appearance: he assures her that he will not go swimming in Amoy[45] and that although that he has not cut his hair he has trimmed his moustache.[46] Despite her long hours and the strains of her new job, Xu Guangping is generally in good health, apart from a slight chill,[47] and once mentions getting her hair cut.[48] These remarks are all retained. Xu Guangping worries that he might catch cold (retained),[49] and both of them describe what they wear as the weather changes (usually retained;[50] one deletion, for no obvious reason[51]). Lu Xun remarks that he is wearing fur clothing although padded clothes would be enough, because he's too lazy (? to go and buy a new outfit): this is retained since there is no disgrace in the 1930s (or in China now) in wearing animal fur.[52]

Lu Xun's favourite proprietary medicine is Sanatogen;[53] he also takes quinine[54] and cod-liver oil.[55] All references to these medicines are retained. Her advice to him not to take indigestion tablets in Peking in 1929 is deleted (to avoid her appearing over-anxious about him?) but his report that he has taken three tablets is retained.[56] Her health is of great importance in 1929, and now she is at pains to let him know that she is well: some of the detail is deleted[57] but much is retained.[58] In return, he tells her that he is well, and that a visit to his dentist has been successful (retained).[59]

Weight and height are more personal. In 1926, Lu Xun expresses concern about her losing weight,[60] and later mentions that some people say he is fatter.[61] Both of these remarks relate to health rather than appearance and are retained. Her remark that she will be a fatty when he comes to Canton is apparently too personal to be kept,[62] however, as also some joking remarks about putting on weight in expectation of his arrival.[63] Her report on her weight gain in 1929 is retained.[64] By 1929 she is familiar enough to tease Lu Xun about his short stature, but 'a small person' (i.e. Lu Xun) becomes 'a person',[65] and her remark that she declares him to be 'a little lotus, because you are short' is deleted.[66]

Smoking

When Xu Guangping first visited Lu Xun at home, she found a mysterious allure in the tobacco smoke which wreathed above his head.[67] In 1926, smoking is a health risk about which she lectures him (deleted in one letter,[68] retained in another[69]). Lu Xun admits to smoking more heavily in Amoy,[70] and in another letter mentions a hand tremor, the result of thirty cigarettes a day, refers to 'trouble in Peking when [someone] tried to moderate it', and confesses to lack of self-control in this respect: these remarks are all retained.[71] He deletes remarks about how she tried to stop his smoking in Peking and how he lost his temper with her at the time, as also his hopes that next year someone will control his smoking and that he is willing to be controlled.[72] When Xu Guangping expresses concern about his hand tremor, he replies that it has stopped (retained).[73] There are no references to his smoking in 1929; presumably both had by then given up hopes of his ever reforming. There is never any suggestion that Xu Guangping might take up the habit; few educated women smoked at that time.

Drinking

Lu Xun's drinking was a much more complicated matter. In her first reference to his 'indulgence in alcohol', she softens the implied criticism by adding 'But the young devil also often indulges in alcohol'.[74] It shows the growing intimacy between them that she can raise the matter even indirectly. Although her criticism is allowed to stand, her confession (which is probably an exaggeration) is deleted.[75] In response, he makes two references to drinking as a problem, hers as well as his; somewhat inconsistently, both are retained in full.[76] Her next reference (retained) seems to condone the use of alcohol as a solace: '. . . please dismiss it with a smile and quaff another cup.'[77]

Her concern about his drinking intensified after Dragon Boat Day in June 1925. On 28 June, he wrote an elaborate and unconvincing denial of having been drunk that day.[78] Xu Guangping's letter of the same date is missing, but from Lu Xun's reply the next day (retained), it can be inferred that Xu Guangping blames herself for having urged him to drink and apologizes at length, but again he insists that 'I know myself that I was not in the least drunk that day, even less to the point of being stupid'.[79]

In Amoy, Lu Xun claims to have stopped drinking,[80] but although this is later shown to be only temporary, the remarks are retained. Xu Guangping was not convinced and urged him to be more abstemious (retained in one letter,[81] deleted in another[82]). Lu Xun even set fire to himself in Amoy by falling asleep while drunk with his cigarette still alight. Zhang Tingqian had come over for a meal, and Lu Xun, who had had rather a lot to drink, dozed off after Zhang had left. The gown he was wearing was patched by Zhang's servant, and Lu Xun continued to wear it for many years after.[83]

Lu Xun drank heavily after their arrival in Shanghai in 1927, and Xu Guangping continued to worry about the effect on his health. In 1929, however, the only reference to alcohol is when Lu Xun writes that he is not drinking much and has not even opened a bottle of Fen liquor that someone had given him.[84] The sentence in his last letter on stories spread by the Creation Society on his wealth and drinking is a later addition.[85]

Summary

Above we have seen how Lu Xun and Xu Guangping refer to sexual acts only in very indirect ways; other parts of the body or bodily functions about which they are reticent range from resting and sleeping to bathing and excretion. Xu Guangping tends be more frank about her body than he is about his, but her references are more likely to be deleted than his are. She makes more references to sleeping and bathing than he does; hers but not his are deleted. Neither admits to defecation and menstruation is not mentioned, but his urinary habits are disclosed while hers are not. She does not mention any dietary problems of her own (she may not have any); his can be exposed but not in full and repeated detail. His shortness may not be mentioned in public; their weight gains may be, but not in all instances. She is the only one to refer to sweating and to picking her nose; the former is retained, the latter deleted. Interest in food is acceptable for third-party readers except where it may give rise to suspicion of greed. His smoking was not a personal matter, but her lectures about his habit and his response are too personal for publication. Remarks about their respective drinking habits are retained except where it may indicate serious alcoholism on his part, and his claims to sobriety are invariably retained or added.

16

Domestic Life and Habits

The deletion or recensions of references to bodily functions is generally due to their intimate nature; deletions and recensions about other aspects of their daily life are more likely to be due to their limited interest to the general public. For the same reasons, there are few additions in this category.

The only significant addition in regard to Lu Xun's domestic habits in Peking occurs after Xu Guangping asks in alarm why he keeps a knife under his mattress in his bedroom at West Third Lane.[1] In his reply he fails to respond, but in *Letters between Two* he adds a short passage about the knife being 'only for use against thieves in the night'.[2] Wang Dehou comments that the addition avoids giving an impression of discourtesy in not having replied; it also makes Lu Xun appear more aggressive, although whether or not Lu Xun actually expected to be burgled, and would have confronted the burglars with the knife, is not clear. The two short descriptions of his room (one set by Lu Xun as a test of her powers of observation) after her April visit are pruned by Lu Xun to make them sound less intimate, such as her references to his 'secret nest', 'sitting in silence' and his cigarette smoke (see above). Another change is given significance only by its recension, where her description of the lamp as *hongxue* [blood-red] is changed to *tonghong* [bright red]: the former is presumably seen as overdramatic.[3]

In 1926, both describe their new accommodation in great detail; some of this is deleted as either too personal[4] or trivial[5] (including all of their sketches and floor maps). One deletion that is hard to explain (unless because its expression is clumsy) is a passage in which Lu Xun notes that some people might get envious because he has more furniture than other members of staff: you must have adequate 'living expenses' or 'living' becomes too difficult, but 'expenses' without the 'living' (i.e. working) is even worse.[6] Although some of her complaints about her accommodation and her neighbours are retained, others are deleted, possibly to avoid making her sound difficult.[7] She is very interested in his domestic arrangements, and suggests that he bring his servant[8] and his cooking utensils[9] to Canton; he appears pleased at her interest and agrees.[10] All this is retained, but it is not clear why he should later decide to add the spirit stove to the list of his utensils.[11]

In Amoy, Canton, Shanghai, and Peking there are always servants in their employ. Problems with them are often mentioned in Lu Xun's letters from Amoy,[12] but there are only two such mentions in 1929.[13] Some of their harsher remarks are deleted or softened,[14] not so much because their opinions have changed but because such criticism has become somewhat less acceptable. To contemporary readers there would have been nothing odd in the many and mostly disparaging references to servants in their letters. In China and in most Western countries at that time the wages of domestic servants were so low that even families on limited incomes could afford them; Virginia Woolf's letters to her sister are dominated by stories about her servants (including one who refused to leave her employ), and Woolf confessed that she was 'fascinated' by servant problems.[15] There are similar deletions in regard to workmen (see later). Although Lu Xun and Xu Guangping regularly travelled by rickshaw, the reference to Xu Guangping having taken one in 1925 is deleted[16] while the references to Yang Yinyu[17] and to Lu Xun[18] travelling by rickshaw are retained.

Although they and their families can afford servants and rickshaws, Lu Xun and Xu Guangping are not wealthy and she does a lot of housework herself. From Canton, despite being very busy at her new job, she offers to help him: in *Letters between Two*, Lu Xun adds 'with clothing, food or copying mss', thereby subtly indicating intimacy in their domestic life as well as in their work.[19] She makes clothes for herself and for the baby (retained),[20] and knits for herself and for him (retained).[21] (The vest and cardigan he is wearing in photographs taken in 1933 appear to be hand-knitted.) She often mentions shopping (retained);[22] he never does, except for books and notepaper,[23] and, occasionally, presents[24] (although he asks Xu Xiansu to buy a wedding present from him to an old friend.)[25] He has no domestic hobbies of any kind, and 'is quite incapable of cooking anything' (retained).[26] Details of their personal finances are frequently abbreviated or deleted;[27] some of the deletions are of a trivial nature, although some trivial detail is also retained.

Summary

Deletions and recensions about domestic matters are mainly carried out on trivial detail and repetition, and quite a lot of detail is retained. The only other areas where there are extensive deletions are passages such as her description of his bedroom when she is still his student, and their critical remarks about their or their institutions' servants.

17

Family Matters

Xu Guangping is also the less inhibited of the two in family matters, referring to both her own family members and his in her 1925 letters. Lu Xun only begins to discuss family matters with her in 1926, while she talks freely about her relatives' problems in Canton. In 1929, the main family references are to Lu Xun's mother and her feelings towards them. Remarks that are critical of family members are deleted or rewritten; the only critical remarks that are retained are about Lu Xun's sister-in-law, Hata Nobuko, but her identity is disguised.

Xu Guangping on her Relations, 1925–6

Xu Guangping takes the lead in introducing family matters into the correspondence by mentioning her eldest brother's nationalist fervour[1] and the deaths of her father and her brother[2] (both retained). In September 1926, having just left Shanghai, Xu Guangping notes that her relatives there have treated her rather better than before, and speculates playfully on the reason.[3] The implication is that she is being given more respect as the famous writer's disciple or travelling companion (these relatives would be unaware of her true relationship with Lu Xun), and the passage is deleted either as not being of anyone else's concern, or else as approaching sensitive ground.

Xu Guangping discussed her family problems with Lu Xun before they left Peking,[4] although the general reader is not to know that they were on such intimate terms. Another reference to her grief on hearing of her brother's death is deleted,[5] and a description of her father as being so 'stupid' (i.e. upright) that he left his children in poverty is changed in *Letters between Two* to 'father and mother': given Xu Guangping's coldness towards her mother, this addition may have been Lu Xun's idea.[6]

Still living at her old home in Canton in 1926 were Xu Guangping's younger sister, her widowed sister-in-law, the latter's four sons, and the widow's younger sister. Their situation is described by Xu Guangping as 'lonely and sad' (retained),[7] but Lu Xun deletes her repeated and detailed accounts of how her sister-in-law is pressing her for money for the boys' schooling and even for her own sister; a visit from Guangping's brother Chonghuan increases the pressure on her; and other relatives also see her as a source of income.[8] More detail would need to be added to make these passages comprehensible to an outsider, and it is not surprising that the decision is taken instead to reduce or delete them.

Xu Guangping's influential relatives in Canton are also treated with some caution, perhaps because she does not want to cause them trouble, or else to de-emphasize her family's social standing and political connections.[9] She is particularly careful about her cousin Xu Chongqing: in her description of a banquet he gives on the birth of a son, her references to him as the twentieth member in her generation and director of the department of education are deleted,[10] as is also another passage about his intervention in the school's affairs.[11]

Chen Yanxin, the husband of her cousin Li Xueying, is given the same protection: he is first referred to as Chen Xiangting in *Letters between Two*,[12] and his name is deleted as her source of information on conditions for assistant teachers at Zhongshan University.[13] On the other hand, it would be for other reasons that the information is withheld that Chen Yanxin stayed the night at his dormitory while Guangping slept in the same bed with Xueying after a family excursion.[14]

Lu Xun on Xu Guangping's Family, 1926

Lu Xun is generally sympathetic to Xu Guangping's accounts of her family problems, merely counselling her not to sacrifice herself; as with the accounts themselves, these remarks are generally deleted in *Letters between Two* or else generalized. For example, a reply by Lu Xun on her family problems is reworded in *Letters between Two* so that it refers not to her family but to 'self-styled revolutionaries and writers', while Lu Xun's sarcastic remarks on how this kind of person will write about your room, clothes, and so on are all later additions.[15] His concession that she should after all help her nephews, if she can do so without wearing herself out, is retained.[16]

Xu Guangping on Lu Xun's Family, 1925–6

In March 1925, Xu Guangping, who knew Zhou Zuoren as a teacher at the Women's Normal College as well as a prominent May Fourth writer, was probably unaware of the brothers' rupture, and her reference (which was deleted) to the well-known predilection of 'the elder and younger Zhou brothers' for irony was probably quite innocent.[17] In June she refers to a letter by Mr Qiming [Zhou Zuoren] attacking Yang Yinyu which *Peking Gazette Supplement* failed to print; this is also deleted.[18] In September 1926, passing on news about Women's Normal College, Xu Guangping reports that two teachers still at the school, Mr Qiming and Mr Zuzheng, were falsely accused of having turned 'red' [left-wing or communist], and in October she refers to an article by Mr Qiming in *Thread of Talk* about Women's Normal: both of these references are retained.[19] However, when Xu Guangping refers to one of her colleagues in Canton as an admirer of 'the two Zhous' [i.e. Lu Xun and Zhou Zuoren], this remark is deleted.[20] It is possible that Xu Guangping knew little or nothing about the brothers' rupture until much later (the fact that she does not mention Zhou Zuoren in her 1929 letters suggests that she may have known by then).

Xu Guangping only makes one reference to Zhu An in 1926, and although it is very indirect ('a single person' for whom he sacrifices himself), it is still deleted.[21] Although she had got to know Lu Xun's mother quite well during 1925, she draws back from any direct mention of her in 1926: a brief reference to 'someone' in Peking who cautioned Lu Xun against eating bananas and pomelos could be either his wife or mother, but more probably his mother.[22]

Lu Xun on his Family, 1926

Lu Xun does not mention members of his family in letters to Xu Guangping until 1926. The first to appear is Zhou Jianren, whom Xu Guangping met when they passed through Shanghai. From the reference by Lu Xun to the similarity in the two brothers' affairs, it is clear that she was familiar with Jianren's situation.[23] This comparison, which is also the first admission on Lu Xun's part about their own relationship, is deleted in *Letters between Two*. The reference to 'Keshi' (Jianren in the OC) telling him about Sun Fuyuan's rumours is retained, but an uninformed reader would assume Keshi to be a friend. Also deleted are Lu Xun's concern at his brother's low salary at the Commercial Press and fondness for *baigan* (a cheap and very strong liquor; Lu Xun persuaded him to switch to grape wine).[24]

Not surprisingly, a reference by Lu Xun to Jianren asking in a letter for too much money is deleted.[25] In her response, Xu Guangping refers to Jianren as *San xiansheng* [Third master], but instead of her response being deleted, 'Third Master' is changed in *Letters between Two* to 'a young gentleman',[26] as also in Lu Xun's reply to her letter.[27] As Wang Dehou notes, readers would be hard-put to guess the point of these references to young gentlemen.[28] Also deleted are a reference to 'his friend' [Wang Yunru] visiting Shanghai[29] and Jianren's plans to visit Peking in the summer (and the remark that he would not spread rumours about them).[30]

The first letter in which Lu Xun mentions his mother directly is in 1926 when he links her with Xu Guangping as his only loyal supporters: 'were I to lose my footing, the only ones to grieve for me would be my mother and a friend'.[31] The remark is replaced by a short passage about the disloyalty of unnamed former supporters (who from the context include Gao Changhong) once the repressive measures of Duan Qirui and Zhang Shizhao took force. He writes more realistically about his mother's difficult position between two estranged brothers at the end of his stay in Amoy when he finally reveals to Xu Guangping his suspicions about how the rumours about them got started. His grumble that his mother 'was very much in disagreement [about Xu Xiansu's attempts at gardening] and went to Badaowan to complain' is softened to 'felt it was a pity and wasn't very happy about it'.[32] The more disparaging comment, 'Now there is a very intimate association [between Badaowan and West Third Lane], and the old lady [his mother] is easily taken in', is deleted, while the line 'I tried very hard to make peace with Madam Yan, but all I got was more filth' is added. Madam Yan is Hata Nobuko; only people in the know would be able to identify her.

Two references to West Third Lane are also reworded, in one case to 'Peking',[33] in another to 'my old home'.[34] Lu Xun may have suppressed his home address to protect his mother and wife from curious visitors.

Lu Xun's Family in 1929

In his first letter from Peking in May 1929, Lu Xun writes that immediately on his arrival home, 'She [his mother] asked why the Harmful Mare did not come with me, and I answered that she was not so well. In fact, it occurred to me on the train that the reverberations would not have been suitable for the darling girl'. This passage is deleted in *Letters between Two*.[35] Lu Xun continues that his mother only wants to talk about Badaowan (where his brother, his two sisters-in-law, and their children still live) a subject that is 'of no interest to him'; 'Badaowan' is changed to 'neighbourhood affairs'.[36]

In his next letter, Lu Xun writes: 'This morning, your younger brother [Xu Xiansu] told me a story. She said that about one or two months ago, Mrs X [Zhu An] told mother that she had a dream, that I came back home with a child, and she was very angry about it. Mother told her that she shouldn't be angry, and told her there are there were various stories around, and what did she think of them. She said she already knew. Mother asked how did she know. She said, Second Mistress [Hata Nobuko] told her. I think Senior Mistress [Zhu An] probably heard it from Second Mistress.' This passage, with the only direct mention of Zhu An in the correspondence, is deleted from *Letters between Two*.[37] After it comes a passage about the rumours surrounding their relationship, which is retained. Lu Xun then continues, 'When I told younger brother [Xu Xiansu] about the Little White Elephant [the expected baby], she wasn't surprised, she said she expected it. The same morning, I spoke to my mother, telling her that we would have a Little White Elephant in August.'[38] The first sentence in the above passage is deleted, and the last sentence is changed to 'When I arrived home the day before yesterday my mother immediately asked me why the Harmful Mare hadn't accompanied me. I was busy paying the rickshaw fare and answered in haste that you were a little unwell, but yesterday I told her that the vibrations of the train would not be good for the child, and she was very happy, saying that she thought we should have one, because there should have been a small child in the house running up and down a long time ago.' In the revised version, Lu Xun gives a positive gloss on his mother's reception of the news of his child.

In her second letter, Xu Guangping respectfully enquires after 'my teacher's mother' [Lu Rui] and 'the others' [Zhu An],[39] and later reminds him that since 'Mother' is advanced in age Lu Xun should spend more time with her.[40] She is so discreet that all these references are retained.

Repeated references to Zhou Jianren, Wang Yunru, and their children in Shanghai are much reduced in *Letters between Two*. Lu Xun now refers to Jianren more familiarly as Youngest Brother (retained)[41] but mention of him as an intermediary for their letters is usually deleted,[42] as are also passages about money and other personal affairs. Xu Guangping still calls Jianren Third Master, but with one exception[43] either the reference is deleted[44] or the name replaced with something vague such as 'they' or 'the others'.[45] A reference to Third Master reading foreign newspapers for news on China is deleted,[46] possibly because of the implication that the foreign press is more reliable. Wang Yunru is referred to as Mrs Wang in one letter[47] and as Yunru in another:[48] the uninitiated would not be able to guess that this is the same person, or her relationship to the family.

Lu Xun makes only one direct reference to Zhou Zuoren in the whole correspondence, reporting that Ma Yuzao claimed he had heard rumours about them from Zhou Zuoren;[49] this passage is deleted in *Letters between Two*. Even at this stage of their intimacy, Xu Guangping refrains from commenting, nor does she ever make any remarks about his sister-in-law.

Xu Guangping's Family in 1929

When she moved to Shanghai, Xu Guangping's family cut off relations with her, and in her letter to Chang Ruilin in May 1929 she mentions that they do not know about her pregnancy (see earlier). But reconciliation was at hand: her Shanghai uncle, Xu Bing'ao, and his daughter had just sent her some presents along with some family news, including a forthcoming visit from her Aunt Feng.[50] Xu Guangping by this time was visibly pregnant and concluded that it was time to let her family know; in his response, Lu Xun agrees that she should take the initiative and tell her aunt herself.[51] Both of these passages are deleted, as also a further reference by Lu Xun recommending that her cousin, who has not been well, take fish liver oil, and that Guangping should buy some for her out of the money he is sending her because his generation has plenty and hers not enough.

Xu Guangping continues with the family news relayed by Aunt Feng, an account of a cousin's birthday party (Xu Chongqing's elder brother) she attended, and a gift by her to Aunt Feng of twenty dollars, almost all of which is deleted.[52] A detailed description of her excursion with Aunt Feng the following day,[53] however, is mostly retained; the main deletions are some family detail about Aunt Feng's son (a local school principal), and a long conversation about her relationship with Lu Xun, at the end of which Aunt Feng promises to tell the rest of the family about Xu Guangping's pregnancy to spare her the burden.

Summary

Lu Xun systematically deletes remarks that are critical of family members or touch on their personal lives, such as his youngest brother's affair with his student, his finances, and his drinking problem. The deletions in regard to his younger brother are of a rather different nature: all of the five references to Zhou Zuoren by Xu Guangping are innocuous, but only two are retained. This suggests that Lu Xun is not protecting him but prefers not to have his name mentioned. Tellingly, Xu Guangping does not mention Zhou Zuoren once in her 1929 letters, although this is the only occasion on which Lu Xun refers to him; it could be argued that the rupture is one of the most personal matters in the letters since neither Lu Xun nor Xu Guangping ever mentions it directly. Details of family addresses, either for correspondence or visits, are also suppressed. The revisions show that Lu Xun and Xu Guangping extend to relatives the same kind of personal space as they desire for themselves.

18

Friends and Enemies

Lu Xun's circle, apart from family, consisted of former fellow-students, ministry colleagues, former and current students and university colleagues, writers, and political activists. As was usual for the time, it did not extend beyond the educated élite. The same was true of Xu Guangping except that she had relatively closer contact with members of the government in Canton through family connections (see Chapter 17). References to friends and associates are mainly by Lu Xun; they are relatively few in 1925, increase greatly in 1926, and decrease again in 1929.

Lu Xun's Colleagues and Students in 1925

One of the first colleagues mentioned in the letters is Zhang Xichen, a contributor to *Women's Magazine*; in *Letters between Two*, Lu Xun changes *hutu* [nonsensical] to describe Zhang's advice column to the less harsh *mohu* [confused] to avoid giving offence and being too critical about a progressive journal.[1] Another fellow-teacher, Zhu Xizu, is also treated gently: Lu Xun tempers his criticism of his former classmate's 'theory on pseudonyms', by changing 'wrong' to 'irresponsible',[2] and in another letter adds the expression *ouran* [accidental, by chance].[3] The main beneficiaries of editorial kindness are the students at Women's Normal, especially Lu Xiuzhen and other participants in the complicated affair of Ouyang Lan's activities, although the deletion of much of the detail is probably due to its triviality.[4]

Lu Xun and Sun Fuyuan, 1925–6

One of Lu Xun's closest colleagues in the 1920s was his former student Sun Fuyuan, but Lu Xun's long-standing irritation at him is only partially concealed in the editing. For example, Sun's name is deleted from a critical reference to his good relations with the *Contemporary Review* group, but the context anyway reveals Sun's identity.[5] Lu Xun's criticism of Sun became more acerbic in 1926, after Lu Xun became aware that Sun was spreading stories about their journey together from Peking to Shanghai. Usually this is softened in *Letters between Two*,[6] but Xu Guangping's sneer at his eating habits is retained,[7] and Lu Xun even adds the scornful epithet 'ordinary' to describe him.[8] Wang Dehou comments that in both versions of this letter the impression left of Sun Fuyuan is unfavourable. Nevertheless, Lu Xun continued to expect Sun Fuyuan to carry out commissions for him in Canton and elsewhere.

Lu Xun in Amoy

Although Lu Xun was often impatient with Lin Yutang in Amoy, he also appreciated his kindness and good intentions, and they remained good friends in Shanghai from 1927 up to their falling out in 1929. By the early 1930s, however, they had patched up their quarrel,[9] and Lu Xun takes considerable efforts to spare his feelings: his constant carping at Lin and his brothers in the original correspondence (OC) is either deleted or softened.[10] One of the changes is curious: a description of Lin Yutang as *jilie* [enthusiastic] is changed to *ji'an* [elated].[11]

Shen Jianshi, his colleague in both Peking and Amoy, comes in for less criticism, and even mildly critical remarks are deleted or softened in *Letters between Two*.[12] Others who are mentioned favourably both in the OC and in *Letters between Two* include Yu Shude,[13] Ma Yuzao,[14] and Liu Bannong.[15] In the case of old friends like Xu Shouchang,[16] Qi Zongyi,[17] Xu Xiansu,[18] and Gu Mengyu,[19] some remarks are deleted because they could be seen as intrusive or not of general significance. Sometimes a reference to a friend is disguised in order to spare possible embarrassment: Lu Xun changes Zhu Jianhua (the acting head of Zhongshan University) to Zu,[20] while a reference to 'speaking to Chuan Dao' [Zhang Tingqian] to enquire about the source of rumours about them is changed to 'writing to Guling'.[21] A passage about Tao Yuanqing, who designed the cover of several of Lu Xun's books, is augmented to emphasize Tao's ability.[22] Possibly copying his example, Xu Guangping also complained about her 'intolerable' colleagues in Canton, and these remarks are also watered down in *Letters between Two*.[23]

Lu Xun and Xu Guangping's Friends in 1929

Lu Xun deletes several of his references to the personal affairs of friends, such as Tai Jingnong and Wei Congwu's girlfriends,[24] and the price of his wedding present to Li Bingzhong.[25] The identity of Xu Guangping's closest friend, Chang Ruilin, is disguised.[26] Two references to another close friend, Lin Zhuofeng, are deleted, presumably because both refer to their relationship. Lu Xun had mentioned that Lin had wondered if Lu Xun and Xu Guangping had married; Xu Guangping replied: 'Lin Zhuofeng has a good nature and has been good to me; if she mentions me, why not tell her I am in Shanghai. It's sad about her illness, in which her friends are involved.'[27] Xu Guangping's nickname for Yu Dafu is changed from Yu *fuzi* [Master Yu] to the more respectful Dafu *xiansheng* [Mr Dafu].[28]

From Friend to Enemy

One of the most striking examples of editorial intervention in *Letters between Two* is Lu Xun's rewriting of references to friends or disciples whom he subsequently regarded as disloyal: chief among these are the young writers Gao Changhong and Xiang Peiliang. His description of Xiang Peiliang as 'my student' in April 1925, for example, is deleted since Xiang Peiliang was associated with Gao Changhong's transgressions.[29] In his next letter, he had described Gao Changhong as an anarchist; but in *Letters between Two* he adds the modification 'seems to be', exercising prudence although he has no reason to expect that Gao would start a libel action against him; he may have been reluctant to land Gao Changhong in serious trouble with the authorities.[30] In June 1925, he expressed frustration at being used by his former students; in revising, he adds the sentence 'Sometimes the other party abuses you anyway, and if he doesn't you should be grateful for this great favour',[31] although Gao Changhong's hostility had not yet become apparent.

Rather oddly, Xu Guangping's critical remarks on Gao Changhong's poetry in her reply on 17 June are deleted.[32] Perhaps Lu Xun did not want it known that she was so judgemental, or perhaps he did not share her opinion. Xu Guangping's criticism casts doubt on a suggestion subsequently made by Gao Changhong that she admired his poetry. Writing in 1940, Gao claimed that Xu Guangping had written to him asking to buy a copy of one of his poetry collections and that they then exchanged eight or nine letters before they had even met. Eventually he met her at Lu Xun's house, but realizing that Lu Xun was very attached to her, he broke off the correspondence. Gao Changhong does not date the episode precisely but suggests that it took place in 1925.[33]

Lu Xun first wrote to Xu Guangping about a quarrel between Gao Changhong and *The Wilderness* group in Peking in October 1926; this account is slightly reworded, and abusive lines are added about Xiang Peiliang.[34] He took up the subject of Gao Changhong's trouble-making again a few days later, but in *Letters between Two* he transforms his remarks about Xu Guangping's importunate relatives into a denunciation of 'self-styled revolutionaries and writers' who might now wish to call on her.[35] Xu Guangping's advice about ignoring the 'young gentlemen's quarrelling' is revised to transform it from a question of tactics to a matter of right or wrong,[36] that is, making her more perspicacious, while Lu Xun's critical remarks about *The Wilderness* group are deleted, presumably to make him appear less even-handed in the quarrel between the two groups.[37] Lu Xun continued his attack on Gao Changhong into early November, extending it to cover Li Xiaofeng as well, but in the *Letters between Two* version their names are deleted and Lu Xun's rage is both generalized and augmented: 'Much of my life has already been frittered away on doing things for others, like correcting and reading their manuscripts, editing their books and doing their proof-reading. But there are some people who for this very reason see themselves as my master and shower recriminations if there's something not to their liking.'[38]

Lu Xun's suspicions about former disciples for a while also included Li Yu'an (referred to in *Letters between Two* as Li Fengji), who wrote to him in early October about his plans to go from Talien to Canton.[39] Xu Guangping agreed to look after Sun Fuyuan and Li Yu'an on their arrival although she asked Lu Xun to warn them that she was very busy.[40] Lu Xun then complained that Li Yu'an appeared to have misled him about the extent of his contacts in Canton.[41] Before receiving this letter, Xu Guangping wrote to say she had invited Li to come and see her, adding that 'he's a decent sort of person.'[42] In reply, Lu Xun was more forceful about Li's duplicity, but in the revision some detail about his grounds for concern is deleted.[43] Xu Guangping quickly withdrew her support for Li Yu'an, and her further remarks about him are revised or deleted.[44] Lu Xun finally warned her that he suspected that Li Yu'an was trying to find out if she was really living and working in Canton (not in Amoy with him).[45] In the end Lu Xun did not break off his own correspondence with Li Yu'an,[46] and the whole episode may have been caused by jealousy rather than fear of rumour. Xu Guangping's responses reassure him of her loyalty, and he eventually decided that Li Yu'an was not directly involved in the rumours; it may have been for this reason that he subsequently suppresses of some of his accusations.

Lu Xun launched another attack on Gao Changhong on 15 November: most of this is retained and one sentence is added: 'In short, now that he has discarded the mask of having met me "no less than a hundred times", I need to keep a careful watch', making himself appear more prescient and aggressive about the trouble still to come.[47] On 20 November, Lu Xun informed Xu Guangping that he was going to make a public stand against Gao Changhong, placing notices in several journals to denounce what he regarded as slander; changes in *Letters between Two* make the text more colloquial and also more damning.[48] However, he deletes Xu Guangping's response that she had tried to warn him in Peking against the 'bloodsucking young gentlemen': she noted that he had understood what she meant but had still wanted to help them.[49] The following day, 21 November, Lu Xun sent off his 'Announcement concerning the so-called "pioneer among thinking people"' to Wei Suyuan for publication in the December issue of *The Wilderness*.[50] In an accompanying letter to Wei Suyuan, Lu Xun complained that his environment in Amoy was like the Dead Sea but did not continue his attacks on Gao Changhong or mention any rumours.[51] In his next letter to Xu Guangping, Lu Xun confined himself to irate remarks about the 'impudence' of young writers (retained).[52]

On 13 December,[53] Lu Xun received a letter from Wei Suyuan in which Wei told him about 'Ji . . . [To . . .]', a poem Gao Changhong had written and published in *The Tempest*, No. 7.[54] The poem describes the competition between the sun (Changhong) and the night (Lu Xun) for the love of the moon (Guangping). In his letter a few days later to Xu Guangping, Lu Xun expressed irritation again but did not disclose the cause; in revision, he adds much more than he deletes, his anger having grown over the years.[55] The additions to this letter include inflammatory terms about having been 'enslaved' and 'slandered' by members of the Tempest Society. He mentions that Xiang Peiliang 'still wants to make use of me', and adds the following remark about another Tempest writer, Shang Yue: 'he was wrong to have abused me earlier and from now on he will stop doing so. He also encloses an unpublished article abusing me, asking me to burn it after I've read it.' There are too many additions in this letter to cite in full, but the following two are characteristic:

> I am not going to look for a place, nor will I take anything for the series, nor will I look at the article, nor will I burn it, nor will I write a reply; I will close my doors and please myself reading, smoking and sleeping . . .

> I believe that people who have drunk my blood should clear off when they see there is no more blood left to drink. They should not mark me down as a blood debtor and even try to kill me before they go, and not only that but also wipe out the record of their debentures and burn down my poor plaster hut. In fact I make no claim to be a creditor but nor do I have any debentures.

Lu Xun kept up his sniping over the next few letters to Xu Guangping, although he deletes his remark that Gao Changhong wants to make a name for himself by toppling Lu Xun, perhaps because it sounded boastful.[56]

Lu Xun's retaliation against Gao Changhong took the form of a fable, 'Ben yue' [Flight to the moon], in which the famous archer Yi (Lu Xun) is viciously attacked in his old age by his former pupil, Feng Meng (Changhong); while they are engaged in battle, Yi's wife, the lovely but dissatisfied Chang E (Guangping), steals Yi's elixir of immortality and flies to the moon. The story ends with Yi's resolve to obtain another flask and join her.[57] Dated December 1926, the story echoes Lu Xun's resolve to join Xu Guangping in Canton.

Around the same time as writing 'Flight to the Moon', Lu Xun wrote to Zhang Tingqian to make enquiries about the sources of the Peking rumours.[58] According to the account he eventually passed on to Xu Guangping, the main propagators were Wang Guizhen, Sun Fuyuan, Zhang Yiping, Li Xiaofeng, and Hata Nobuko. He conceded that Sun Fuyuan was not among those who claimed that Xu Guangping was secretly living in Amoy, but blamed the people who had seen them off in August (probably referring to Xiang Peiliang and Gao Ge).[59]

More rumours arrived in Amoy when Huang Jian returned from a visit to Peking in mid-December;[60] first Huang Jian and then Chen Wanli spread the story that Lu Xun's reluctance to stay in Amoy was due to the absence of the 'moon'. In a letter to Wei Suyuan some two years later, Lu Xun claimed that he had not been aware of the full extent of the rumours about them until after Zhang Tingqian's arrival in Amoy on 24 December 1926,[61] when Zhang was clearly taken aback to find Lu Xun living there alone.[62] (Lu Xun chose not to take Zhang into his confidence.[63])

Lu Xun read Gao's poem for the first time on 29 December. In his letter to Wei Suyuan the same day, he claims that up till then he had believed that the only reason for Gao's attacks on him had been the quarrel over *The Wilderness*. In the same letter, he also mentions that he has heard the rumour that 'Mourning the Dead' is the story of his affair with Xu Guangping, which he treats as a joke.[64]

In his letter to Xu Guangping on 29 December, Lu Xun disclosed that there were rumours about them in Peking, similar to those in Shanghai, which were behind Gao Changhong's disloyalty (retained),[65] adding afterwards that it was 'unexpected'.[66] His next letter contained a long passage on how Gao Changhong attacked him because he thought that Lu Xun was exhausted and alone on an island, despite all the help that Lu Xun had previously given him; this is deleted in *Letters between Two*.[67] Three days later he wrote that the students in Amoy, flourishing a copy of *The Tempest*, had urged him to return Changhong's abuse.[68] Lu Xun's last letter from Amoy finally revealed the full story behind the rumours, Gao Changhong's jealousy, and his own new determination not to lose the one love of his life.[69]

Relatively little is deleted from this letter; added is a remark about Zhang Yiping 'looking like a rat' when he searched for signs of Xu Guangping's presence at West Third Lane in 1925.

Transparent Libels

In references to friends, Lu Xun sometimes made minor changes such as not retaining their full or their real names; when it came to people he thoroughly disliked, this was a regular practice which was presumably connected to fear of being sued for libel. Name changes are most apparent in his references to his colleagues at Amoy University, where Gu Jiegang is called Zhu Shangen, Huang Jian is Bai Guo, and so on. In fact, any reader who was interested could readily establish the true identities of these people. Believing himself protected, however, Lu Xun made many changes or additions that make him sound more aggressive, especially in the early letters from Amoy.[70] In one passage which refers to Lin Yutang, Shen Jianshi, and Gu Jiegang, critical remarks about each of the three men are deleted, but two other phrases about Gu Jiegang are altered, from 'the people he's recommended' to 'the entourage he's arranged' and from 'he has me in his sights' to 'he is already trying to drive me out'.[71] One particularly gratuitous addition is a remark that Gu Jiegang stutters in class.[72] A deletion that might have been prompted by caution is his remark on the refusal of the authorities in Canton to pay attention to a warning about Gu Jiegang's opposition to the Nationalist Party.[73] Lu Xun also deletes gossip he heard in Peking that Yenching University has declined to appoint Gu Jiegang (still referred to as Zhu Shangen) because it is hoped that Lu Xun will come, although other unpleasant remarks about Gu are retained.[74]

Summary

Most of the changes to remarks about their friends and colleagues occur in Lu Xun's letters or relate to his circle. Critical remarks about students and friends are frequently softened or deleted, but friends who have proved to be disloyal are subjected to added abuse, especially in the case of Gao Changhong. Both friends and enemies have their identities disguised, but in the case of Gu Jiegang and his associates the use of pseudonyms seems to have given Lu Xun license to attack them even more ferociously in *Letters between Two*.

19

Political Opinions, Observations, and Activities

Lu Xun's animus against colleagues such as Gu Jiegang appears, at least in part, to be motivated by personal dislike or jealousy, but in many cases it also had political overtones, and it is often difficult to distinguish between his personal and political opinions. Xu Guangping was more directly involved in political action and intrigued by political gossip, although this is less obvious in *Letters between Two*. Distinctions between literary or academic groups and institutions on the one hand, and political groups, parties, and institutions on the other, are largely blurred in the letters. The instances listed below are inclusive, covering references to literary, academic, and political groups, parties, and institutions, on the grounds that editorial decisions made by Lu Xun about these matters were largely prompted by political considerations. The range of their observations is noticeably much wider in 1926 than in 1925 or 1929.

Xu Guangping's Political Views in 1925

In 1925 Xu Guangping expressed her opinions to her teacher freely and without caution, and Lu Xun took some pains in making her appear more logical and also more politically advanced. For example, her charge against her fellow-students as acting 'not for the sake of reason but for emotion' is changed to 'not on behalf of the masses but for themselves'.[1] Following her observation that the present time cannot be considered a golden age, Lu Xun adds 'although many people already regard it as fine', making her appear more critical of her contemporaries.[2] Passages in which she seems to be advocating assassination are deleted,[3] making her appear less irresponsible, as also statements of dubious accuracy, such as her reference to Zhang Shizhao and Yang Yinyu's connection with the Research clique.[4]

An important set of deletions begins where she describes her reluctance to join any political party, or for that matter any large organization;[5] his answer, that the choice is up to her, is also deleted.[6] Lu Xun goes on to advise that if she wishes to preserve her freedom of thought and independence of action, it would not be fitting for her to join a political party, but it would be all right if she were willing to sacrifice certain of her own opinions. In present-day China, he continues, only the anarchists were without regulations, and they were in fact quite scarce (all of this is deleted). Xu Guangping returned to the matter with the following passage: 'Take for instance the unrest at our College: at the time of the winter vacation,

I really dared not say that the people who began it did not in fact have a certain colour [i.e. red, for communists] and so I just stood at the sidelines with my arms folded. Even now I dare not say that they certainly had no colour, but the opposition was really in such a frightful state! I was driven beyond endurance and must make the first move—attack—before considering the second—construction.'[7] Lu Xun changed 'colour' to 'ulterior motives' in both instances and 'opposition' to 'College', thereby suppressing her implied criticism of the Chinese Communist Party as well as his own reluctance to join a political party and his tolerance towards anarchism, both unacceptable in the polarized political world of the 1930s. Wang Dehou claims that the original version shows that Lu Xun and Xu Guangping both approved of the Communist Party's role in the student movement; the letters can also be interpreted as showing strong reservations.

Xu Guangping concludes her account of the May Thirtieth demonstration in Peking with the remark: 'Even when the country is on the brink of defeat, they [the student leaders] still can't sacrifice their private ambition to become a commander, a chairman . . .!'[8] This is deleted, as also her remark to the effect that the Soviet Union would not intervene to help China in the event of an outbreak of war in the Far East.[9] Here Lu Xun makes her appear her as less critical and more left-wing in the 1930s than she was in the 1920s.

Lu Xun on Worthy Causes, 1925

Lu Xun also suppressed his own criticism of worthy causes. Describing an article that appeared in the student journal *Women's Weekly* as 'ridiculous', Lu Xun deleted the information that identified the article and also softened the terms of his ridicule by changing *shizai* [really] to *jianzhi* [simply].[10] In response to her criticism of the students at Women's Normal College, he remarks that 'It is a long-established fact that the masses [i.e. the students] are just as you say, and in the future they will still be just as you say' but tones down his pessimism by adding the expression *kongpa* [I'm afraid] after 'in the future'.[11]

Writing on the May Thirtieth Incident, Lu Xun cites the Chinese translation of a Reuters report that 'a certain number of people *were left unconscious*' [emphasis in the original] as an example of 'the cleverness of the Chinese language' in leaving it unclear whether these people were dead or alive. By changing 'a certain number of people' to 'Chinese people',[12] Lu Xun emphasizes the racial aspect of the Incident. He also distorts the record in both original and edited versions: the newspaper account states that 'Among the demonstrators ten were seriously wounded and six were left unconscious'. Commenting on this letter, Wang Dehou notes that Lu Xun's additions make his letters sound more militant, transforming them from merely private letters [*siren xinjian*].

In the same letter, Lu Xun compares the ruthlessness of the Yongle emperor with supporters of the present government such as Chen Yuan. In the original version, Lu Xun states that 'if the present generation had their way, [university] departments and provinces would also be exterminated', to which he subsequently adds 'not only clans but also' before 'departments',[13] emphasizing the comparison between Chen Yuan and the Yongle emperor.

Lu Xun in Amoy

The scope of the correspondence in 1926 is widened as Lu Xun and Xu Guangping relate their separate activities to each other in writing. Some of the changes reflect the need for caution in the repressive environment of the 1930s: for example, the Research clique becomes either the *Contemporary Review* group (thus diverting the focus from politics to literature)[14] or else 'the gentry' (a fairly innocuous term).[15] Other changes are the reduction or deletion of events that would not be of general interest in the 1930s (e.g. on the reorganization of Women's Normal College in Peking after their departure).[16]

In general, Lu Xun emerges from the revisions as more intransigent, aggressive, and left-wing, although apart from the progress of the Northern Expedition, his concerns are mainly restricted to the activities of his colleagues at Amoy University. For example, Lu Xun changes the wording about an invitation to attend a banquet for a visiting Buddhist monk from 'They invited me to accompany him and demanded that I go' to 'They wanted me to accompany him and insisted that I go'.[17] A line in the same letter describing the clothes he wore to the banquet (a blue gown in traditional style with no hat, avoiding modern dress) is deleted.[18] A remark a week later that before he leaves he would like to write an article for the Institute's quarterly and to give a public lecture is deleted, perhaps because it undermines his image of opposing the authorities.[19] An anecdote about a mendacious Chinese student in Tokyo is elaborated to be more accurate and also to show his indignation.[20] In one letter he inserts his recollection of the contemptible views he attributes to a Western-educated professor at Amoy:[21] Wang Dehou comments that to remember this encounter six years later shows the deep impression it left on Lu Xun; alternatively, the addition could be completely fictional, depicting by implication Lu Xun as aggressively anti-Western.

Again, Lu Xun's editorial practice is not consistent. His description of the situation at Amoy University as similar to *Shuihu zhuan* [Water margin]—a novel about bandits—is changed to *San guo zhi yan yi* [Romance of the three kingdoms]—a novel about kings and generals[22]—and critical remarks about the students and their activities in Amoy are generally softened.[23] He tones down a criticism of Amoy University from 'It's like a missionary school or a school run by the British' to 'It's really pointless',[24] and deletes a comment that the chancellor of the university is not like a Chinese but like an Englishman.[25] His ambivalence is shown in remarks after he has made up his mind to go to Canton: the original 'AU is rubbish' is changed to 'I have to abandon AU', but he makes himself sound more militant by changing 'My main reason for coming here was to have a rest' to 'Although it was to escape temporarily from the oppression of warlords, bureaucrats and "upright gentlemen" that I came to AU, a minor part was also to get some rest'.[26]

Xu Guangping in Canton

Lu Xun makes drastic deletions to the detailed accounts in Xu Guangping's letters of the student movement in her own school,[27] the right and left factions at Zhongshan University,[28] the internal struggles within the Nationalist government in Canton,[29] and local politics in her home county, Panyu.[30] Wang Dehou notes that in the original version of her letters, Xu Guangping appears more politically active, informed, and perspicacious than in *Letters between Two*.[31]

Xu Guangping is also made to appear less militant by significant deletions of her statements of beliefs.[32] Her description of the protesting students at her school as 'right-wing' or 'expelled reactionaries' is changed throughout to 'belonging to the old faction' or 'stubborn',[33] the latter term indicating the students' temperament rather than their political allegiance and showing Xu Guangping as being sympathetic even to the students who demonstrated against her. Although from time to time Xu Guangping is depressed about the problems facing her at school, there are also times when she relishes the fight, but while her remarks about being depressed are retained, her enthusiasm for battle, previously in Peking as well as currently in Canton, is very much toned down;[34] her statement that she herself was a cause of the student protest is reversed into a denial in *Letters between Two*.[35] Her criticisms of Amoy are also very much diluted; for example, 'In Amoy there are cow demons and snake spirits, how could you live there for long, it would be much better for you to move elsewhere' is changed to 'It would be hard to stay in Amoy for a long time'.[36]

Reference to Xu Guangping's membership of the Nationalist Party and teaching Nationalist doctrine at the school is suppressed throughout.[37] Wang Dehou comments that Xu Guangping's remark that her heart flies out to the new government in Wuchang (deleted) shows her commitment to Lu Xun,[38] but it also shows her scarcely less fervent commitment to the Nationalist Party. Both Xu Guangping and Lu Xun felt that the Canton government was excessively lenient towards the workers in the matter of holidays and other social welfare, but their attitude does not survive the editing.[39]

Xu Guangping's references to the Communist Party in 1926 are still less than respectful and show some distance between her and Communist activists.[40] When Xu Guangping writes that 'people in Canton generally do not welcome the Communist Party; how strange!' (deleted), Wang suggests that the original remark shows that both Xu Guangping and Lu Xun welcome the Communist Party, but it is possible to read it otherwise.[41] Xu Guangping was especially sensitive to the charge that she was a running dog for the Communist Party: references to her intimacy with the school principal and with Deng Yingchao are deleted in *Letters between Two*[42] as well as the charge itself.[43] Wang Dehou comments merely that in the 1930s it was safer not to name known Communists.[44] Similarly, Lu Xun deletes Xu Guangping's suggestion that from Canton they might go to Russia, since it's easy there to get a scholarship to Russia.[45]

Lu Xun in Peking, 1929

The great majority of political deletions from the 1929 letters are in Lu Xun's letters and relate to his old adversaries' projected fear of his possible return to teach in Peking.[46] Again there are additions which make Lu Xun appear more militant and dramatize the occasion of his visit.[47] An example of political correctness in hindsight is the change from 'dwarf' to 'Japanese'.[48]

An odd inconsistency appears in Lu Xun's editorial decisions on references to Guo Moruo and the Creation Society. In 1926, Xu Guangping's expression 'Arts faculty Guo has terminated his contract' is changed to the more respectful 'Arts faculty dean Guo has gone off to be an official',[49] and her remark that 'Since Guo Moruo became left-wing, people regard him as a communist' is softened to 'Since Guo Moruo's become an official, people say he's a leftist, some even regard him as a communist'.[50]

On the other hand, Lu Xun adds a remark expressing concern that the Creation Society might take offence if he publishes one of its former authors, and Cheng Fangwu might abuse him.[51] He then deletes from a 1929 letter his reference to cursing everyone 'from Cheng Fangwu down to Xu Zhimo',[52] but adds the following passage in which he acknowledges the mutual hostility between himself and Creation Society members: 'Where should I go, however? In Shanghai the people in the Creation Society on the one hand spread stories about how rich I am and how much I drink, at the same time using "A Letter from Tokyo" [by Guo Moruo] to print libels about me proposing to slaughter youth. These are simply plots against my life, and I can't go on living there. I could actually live in Peking, and there are a lot of old books in the library, but because of past associations, some people have to make me offers of a rice bowl and other people will then suspect me of coming to steal their rice bowls. You mustn't put your shoes on in a melon patch, but it is difficult to make people believe that you never put your shoes on unless you run away. Think, D. H., where should we go? Why don't we go to some small village incognito, not telling a single soul, and just enjoy ourselves.'[53] This addition serves as Lu Xun's belated response to the wishes expressed in Xu Guangping's last letter for more seclusion in their personal life; it might also serve to divert public attention to his still active participation in left-wing literary circles in the 1930s.

Summary

The deletions cover a wide range of political observations and views, ranging from remarks about the warlord government in Peking, the Nationalist Party and government in Canton, the Communist Party and its activities and the involvement of people they knew, to detailed accounts of day-by-day manoeuvrings connected with institutions such as Women's Normal College and Zhongshan University. The volume of deletions and recensions is significantly greater in Xu Guangping's letters, while most of the additions are to Lu Xun's letters; the result is that Lu Xun appears to be the more militant of the two in *Letters between Two*.

20

Thoughts and Emotions

More than any other subject, their correspondence is about their intimate thoughts and emotions, and most of this exchange is retained in *Letters between Two*. There is, however, an inner level of personal feeling and expression that they shield from public view. There are many such passages, and only a few examples are given below.

Xu Guangping's Emotional Outbursts

Lu Xun repeatedly disguises Xu Guangping's sentiments towards him in 1925, making her appear more in control of her emotions and less passionate towards her famous teacher. For example, Xu Guangping's remark in her first letter that she always sits in the front row at his lectures at Women's Normal College is deleted.[1] Since she was tall and apparently did not suffer from defective hearing or eyesight, either she wanted to make an impression, hoping he would notice her, or she is over-anxious not to lose a single precious word. This letter also ends very emotionally with repeated appeals to her 'Teacher!' to save her from the danger of losing her resolve; these are also deleted. Following her complaint that it has taken his first letter three days to arrive, she notes that it has taken her three days to answer, so deeply was she affected;[2] this remark is deleted. In the salutation to her fourth letter, she refers to his letters as 'impolite' and to herself as 'smiling with closed eyes': both remarks are deleted, presumably as too familiar.[3]

In making changes, Lu Xun may have paid attention to the overall tone of each letter, deleting some expressions not necessarily because of any intrinsic intimacy but with an eye to the total effect, as when her references to dreaming about what he is doing in Amoy (which are not to be taken literally) are changed to 'speculate' or deleted altogether.[4] Her sympathetic image about his isolation in Amoy, 'I'm afraid you won't be able to bear other people's insults, you being alone and depressed, with no-one by your side to comfort you', is changed to the much weaker 'I'm afraid you won't be able to bear insults, alone and depressed with no-one to encourage you from the side'.[5]

Lu Xun's Emotional Prudery

Lu Xun's customary caution in expressing his emotions is most evident in Part I of *Letters between Two*, so that as editor he is not obliged to censor himself. In Part II, his emotional outbursts are few, and since most of them are expressions of anger or frustration they are allowed to remain more or less intact, while the absence of passion in Part III is more likely due to his new state of being at ease with himself. In his general reticence, Lu Xun resembles Gorky, a writer he greatly admired. As Gorky wrote to Andreev, 'I have never allowed anyone to touch upon my private life and I don't intend to start now. I am I, and it is no business of anyone else where I hurt, if indeed I do hurt. To reveal one's wounds to the world, to scratch them in public, to bathe in pus, to squirt one's bile into people's eyes, as many have done—the most disgusting being our evil genius Fedor Dostoevsky—is a vile occupation, and a harmful one, of course'.[6]

Xu Guangping's Expulsion from Women's Normal College

In Xu Guangping's first letter to Lu Xun after her expulsion, some of her expressions of indignation are toned down or deleted, including excessive use of intensifying adverbs and exclamation marks, so that she is made to appear more controlled and focused.[7] In the same letter, the explanation she gives for her pen-name Fei Xin, that the two characters combined into one forms *bei* [tragic], and that it is part of a four-character expression *shi fei zhi xin* [a heart/mind that knows right from wrong], is deleted, possibly regarded as too personal.[8] On the other hand, the second letter that Xu Guangping writes about her expulsion, coming directly after Lu Xun's first public condemnation of the College authorities, is the only letter in the collection where not a word has been altered: for the first and only time, Lu Xun chooses to reveal Xu Guangping's anguish entirely in her own words.[9] It is followed by the letter in which she talks about her suicide: here, as shown above, her personal revelations are substantially reduced.[10]

Lu Xun's Future Path

From Amoy, Lu Xun several times wrote to Xu Guangping expressing uncertainty about his future direction. Following his long-delayed promise at the beginning of November to go to Canton at the end of the first semester, he ponders whether in the future he should choose between teaching and writing (retained).[11] In her reply on 11 November, she avoids giving advice apart from general remarks that he should try and have a good time occasionally, not mix with people he does not like, and not waste energy thinking about the Research clique and Huang Jian (all deleted).[12]

Continuing his reflections on his future in his next letter, Lu Xun hesitates again about leaving Amoy for Canton, in part at least because 'a friend of mine might go to Swatow'.[13] He sees three paths before him: (1) accumulate a little cash, not do any work at all in future, and live in hardship; (2) no longer care about himself, work for the sake of others, even if it means going hungry in future, and even if it means putting up with others' abuse; (3) continue to work (unavoidably being used by others at times), and should colleagues scorn him, then for the sake of existence, daring to do anything but not being willing to lose his friend [Xu Guangping]. (In *Letters between Two*, the wording of this passage is changed to make it clearer and stronger; for example, the words 'and retaliating' are added after 'existing'.[14])

The first path he rejects outright; the second path, which he has taken for two years now, is too stupid; the third path is dangerous, and there is no assurance of success (in life), so that it is hard make up his mind, and so he wants to write and discuss it with his friend, and ask for a ray of light (slightly revised).[15]

This time Xu Guangping answers in detail (21 and 22 November), but her letter is drastically reduced in *Letters between Two*, amounting to over two pages of deleted and revised text.[16] For the first time Xu Guangping raises the subject of his wife ('his inheritance'), but the deletions make the reference even more obscure (although not to those in the know).[17] She rejects both the first path (as in Amoy) as not working out, and the second path (as formerly in Peking), as self-destructive, whereas the first and third paths are at least on the side of life. Only the general drift of her impassioned plea for their future together is retained in *Letters between Two*.

Having just received her non-committal letter of 11 November, Lu Xun then concedes, 'You probably already know that I have two contradictory ways of thinking, one is to do something for society, the other is to have a good time . . .' (deleted; this remark hardly fits in with his image of being very dedicated).[18] He also writes that 'I've suddenly developed a distaste for teaching lately, and I don't even want to be on close terms with the students. When I have the students over, I don't feel very friendly or sincere' (retained).[19] In his next letter, replying to her provocative remark that the road they should take is still being reclaimed [from wasteland] (i.e. living together as a couple without being married), Lu Xun claims he is very willing but that present circumstances do not permit; both her challenge[20] and his response[21] are made more ambiguous in *Letters between Two*. The remainder of the discussion about his future is diverted to the question of their relationship rather than his professional future.

In 1929, Lu Xun and Xu Guangping have no doubts about their future together as a couple (see above) but there is still some uncertainty about whether Lu Xun should accept any of the offers he receives on his visit from universities in Peking and the urgings of his colleagues and students to return to the capital. His self-mockery about not being able to be an academic any more is retained, possibly as a mark of defiance,[22] but the answer he gave to students is deleted: 'The L[u Xun] of today is not the L of three years ago, the reason I shall not speak of it for the moment, however, it will be clear in the future, but in short I no longer want to be a professor.'[23]

Mutual Praise and Criticism

Lu Xun regularly deletes or revises both praise and criticism of him by Xu Guangping, which mainly occur in the 1926 letters. Her praise in 1925 for his lectures and her description of him as 'a genius' are deleted,[24] and her slightly facetious rebuke that 'People with great aspirations [Lu Xun] tend to exaggerate, and often drift into dishonesty, and as a result it doesn't fit with the facts at all, and words do not match actions' is cut off after 'exaggerate'.[25] Lu Xun's reference to 'the child's over-sensitivity' is retained (for an older man to call a young woman a child was perfectly acceptable),[26] but when Xu Guangping picks up the expression to refer to herself, it is changed in *Letters between Two* to 'my over-sensitivity', as if the former was too intimate.[27] Her admonition that he should not risk his health for the sake of students, because 'you can only love others if you love yourself', is praise of a subdued kind and is retained.[28] In response to his description about hurting himself jumping over barbed wire (retained),[29] she writes, 'Silently in my breast floated a picture of a child jumping back and forth, I was afraid he would hurt himself, but I couldn't help but enjoy his liveliness. If this is "a reprimand", then the educational principles are wrong. Children like activity by nature, it is right to guide them but it's not right to suppress them. I am an educationalist, and this is what I advocate'.[30] This passage is much more affectionate than in *Letters between Two*.

As the correspondence continues, she becomes more frank, and remarks such as the following are deleted: 'You used to be so silly, you never knew personal pleasure, you wore yourself out for the young gentlemen, now you have reached realization, this is your good point.'[31] Her remark that 'Your temperament is peculiar, so that you are not like ordinary people. Ordinary people at AU are quite satisfied, so you naturally are restless and uneasy' is changed to 'Your temperament is too peculiar, once you take a dislike to something you can't bear it, you get restless and uneasy',[32] and her exclamation, 'Don't be absurd!' is deleted.[33] Her quite serious criticism that 'it really seems completely hollow to chop and change like this' is modified by the addition of quotation marks around the word 'hollow'.[34] When she calls him 'a stupid child' [*sha haizi*], which is as much affection as rebuke, this is changed to a milder 'simpleton' [*shazi*] in *Letters between Two*.[35]

Lu Xun typically refrains from praising her, although his patronising remarks about her educational shortcomings are retained in full.[36] The following remark, from his last letter, is more affection than praise, and the praise is in any case scored out: 'The Little Hedgehog . . . is getting ready for the Tiny White Elephant, she's really awfully clever' is changed to 'You . . . are getting everything ready, I do feel a bit wretched'.[37]

Self-Analysis and Self-Criticism

Lu Xun's letters frequently refer to his personal defects, such as complacency, laziness, and irritability: some of this is retained, some deleted or revised.[38] Following his confession that his wish to protect people he knows personally is a 'fatal disease' about which he can do nothing, his further remark, 'nor do I wish to', is deleted, avoiding an impression of complacency.[39] His letters from Amoy repeatedly show irritation at his colleagues and intolerance of the ordinary pressures of academic life: most of this is retained or even exaggerated, as if Lu Xun found his bad temper admirable,[40] and only in one instance is his irritability toned down.[41] In 1929, although he is still unpleasant about his former colleagues, he seems much more at ease with himself[42] and only once admits to bad temper (retained).[43]

Xu Guangping's occasional confessions of laziness are more likely to be deleted;[44] it is of course possible that they were not meant to be taken very seriously at the time. An uncharacteristic submissiveness on her part ('best you decide the rules and I'll put them into effect') is deleted.[45]

Language and Style

The terms of address used by Lu Xun and Xu Guangping in their openings and closures and their references to themselves in the body of the letters vividly illustrate the development in their relationship from 1925 to 1929. Lu Xun makes only minor changes in this respect to the original letters in March–June 1925, since both authors were at that stage relatively restrained in their language, but some changes in 1926 are very significant, and the number and significance of changes increase substantially in 1929. Details of these changes are given above in Chapters 12 and 14.

One of the few generalizations that can be sustained in regard to general language use is only to be expected: that is, the language used by both authors becomes more relaxed and less formal as the correspondence proceeds. In the same manner, at the beginning of the correspondence they both dignify their writing with frequent allusions to the Confucian classics and other standard works of famous scholars and writers,[46] while references to Western or contemporary Chinese literature are rare: the allusions are there to impress, not for information. In the Canton–Amoy correspondence, the number of classical allusions is much lower, and they disappear altogether from the 1929 letters.

Xu Guangping aptly describes her letter of 10 April 1925 as 'a confused rambling, neither ass nor donkey, neither literary nor colloquial, and it should be consigned to the flames', but she adds, 'Conversely, it is also possible to say that it is in the most modern school of writing (I am surely able to manage that much)'.[47] Modern or not, Lu Xun made substantial changes. In Canton, Xu Guangping refers to her letters as 'scribble', apologizing for writing in haste and when she is tired at the end of the day. This self-deprecatory mode, while accurate enough, continues an honourable tradition which is not always merely polite, from Bai Juyi to Yuan Zhen in 817 and Queen Elizabeth I to James IV in 1588.[48]

Most of the changes Lu Xun made to vocabulary and grammar are to Xu Guangping's letters. Sometimes Lu Xun chooses a more standard form of an expression, such as changing *wo xin zhong xiang* to *wo xin li xiang* (both meaning 'I thought [to myself]')[49] and *bugao* to *baogao* (both meaning 'to announce, report').[50] Especially in the letters from Canton, where Xu Guangping tends to revert to Cantonese idioms, Lu Xun corrects to northern style: for example, *shi fan* is changed to *chi fan* (both meaning 'to eat') and *shang tang* is changed to *shang ke* (both meaning 'to teach' or 'go to class').[51] Sometimes she writes in a compressed *wenyan* style, which is rephrased to make it more readily comprehensible.[52] In one letter which Xu Guangping wrote on three separate topics without dividing the text into paragraphs, Lu Xun not only constructs paragraphs but also changes their order, presumably to make her sound more logical.[53]

Lu Xun is also careful about his own style. Changing *shehui li* to *shehui shang* (both meaning 'in society') is a shift from his native central Chinese to northern Chinese.[54]

In one of his early letters, he changes the expression *qian yi hui* to *qian hui* (both meaning 'the previous issue'), and adds the adverb *ze*, indicating consequence;[55] the effect is to make the sentence less colloquial, which may in turn affect the reader's impression of their intimacy at this early stage. In 1926 formality can be relaxed: in one of his first letters from Amoy, he changes *sihu* in three places to *haoxiang*, which sounds more colloquial; in the same letter, he changes *bing bu huai* to *sihu hai hao* to avoid the use of *hao* twice in a four-character expression.[56] In a December letter, he changes *liang jin chaye* to *chaye liang jin* (both meaning 'two catties of tea leaves'), the latter sounding slightly less colloquial.[57] In a January letter, the changes are in grammar as well as style: *guan wo qian hui fushang zhi* becomes *kan wo qian ci fushang de* [looking at what I attached previously]; *dan zheyang shi ji shao de shi* [but this kind is a rare thing] becomes *dan zheyang de shi shi hen shao jian de* [but this kind of thing is rarely seen];[58] *dan wulun ruhe* becomes *wulun zenyang* [no matter how]; *sihu* [it seems] becomes *dayue* [probably]; *xianzai zhengzai* becomes *xian zhengzai* [just now]; *dayue* becomes *dagai* [probably]; *zhe xie* [these] becomes *na xie* [those];[59] *ziran* [naturally] becomes *dangran* [of course], and *yao* [want] becomes *xiang* [would like].[60] In the last letter in *Letters between Two*, a very rare example of a wrong character, *zong4ji4*, is corrected to *zong3ji4* [total],[61] but *zhe xinfeng* [this envelope] is changed to *zhe feng xin* [this letter], although the former makes more sense.[62]

In writing to Xu Guangping, Lu Xun appears conscious throughout of his standing as a professional writer, and his language use reflects his pursuit of accuracy as well as his emotional and political caution. With many years of experience behind him, and being by nature cautious in expression (except in abusing his enemies), Lu Xun had relatively little need to correct or otherwise change his language use or style as he edited *Letters between Two*. While Xu Guangping may have wondered if her letters to him might one day reach the public eye, there is no indication that she practised self-restraint in her language on this account any more than she concerned herself about her handwriting; it might even be supposed that Xu Guangping deliberately aimed at an impression of spontaneity. Xu Guangping was much less experienced as well as much more emotional than Lu Xun, and Lu Xun takes considerable pains to disguise this. With an illiterate wife in Peking as a silent 'third voice' in this correspondence, Lu Xun had every reason to display his partner's literacy and literary sensibility as comparable to his own.

Summary

Lu Xun and Xu Guangping are less secretive about their intimate thoughts and emotions than might be expected: the main areas of personal space are the language in which they express their mutual affection, his indecision about their future, and their wish to have time in which to relax in each other's company. Contrary to what might be expected, his bad temper is only marginally protected from exposure and sometimes even exaggerated, while direct praise and criticisms of him are both suppressed. Changes to and from a more colloquial to a more formal style sometimes appear to be made at random, but the general effect is to make the earlier letters (especially hers) more formal and the letters in 1926 and 1929 more colloquial.

21

Rumour and Gossip

The concepts 'rumour' and 'gossip', like 'privacy', tend to draw the attention of social scientists rather than literary scholars and critics.[1] In literature, rumour and gossip are mostly limited to serving as a plot device, revealing character, and introducing vivid language and imagery in dialogue. In life, writers, like other public figures, are also a target and a source of talk. Rumour, for instance, was famously blamed by Lu Xun for the suicides of two Shanghai film stars (see below). Rumour, less dramatically, appears to have first delayed and then prompted the decision by Lu Xun and Xu Guangping to admit to their adulterous relationship and live together openly. It is little wonder that rumour and gossip are prominent topics in their correspondence.

There is a similar distinction in English and Chinese between the terms 'rumour' [*yaoyan, yaozhuan, chuanyan*] and 'gossip' [*xiantan, liaotian*]. Rumour is generally characterized as unverified and often false information of a scurrilous nature: the early stories about Clinton's affair, for instance, were true and scurrilous, while hagiographic stories, like George Washington and his cherry tree, are more usually known as legends or myths.[2] The sources of rumour are anonymous, diffuse, and multiple, and include governments or celebrities who plant stories. Gossip refers to trivial or personal stories or exchanges, often from an identifiable source and about a specific person, and not necessarily malicious or untrue.[3] Both expressions in English generally carry a negative connotation, although the Chinese *xiantan* and *liaotian* lack a pejorative sense. Yu Dafu writing to Wang Yingxia in 1927 frequently refers to *yaoyan* but the term invariably indicates rumours about the political situation in Shanghai and Hangchow.[4] Far from being bothered by gossip about them (which he never refers to as such), he appears pleased when notices about their affair appear in the Shanghai press.[5] The term most often used by Lu Xun and Xu Guangping to describe the talk about them is *liuyan*, which is less pejorative than *yaoyan* but not as innocent as *xiantan*: either 'rumour' or 'gossip' is an appropriate English translation of *liuyan*. The stories circulating about the affair between Lu Xun and Xu Guangping, as it happens, were personal, largely true, and came from verifiable sources.

Gossip is seen typically as an unwanted intrusion into other people's personal lives, and women are often depicted as its perpetrators and victims. Rumour tends to be in the male, public domain.[6] The domains overlap when rumours are spread in public about the private lives (including sexual activities) of public men and women. In Lu Xun's 1935 essay, 'Lun "ren yan ke wei"' [On 'what people say is fearful'], he identifies the main victims of gossip as women and the main perpetrators as old women and journalists.[7]

Defenders of gossip maintain that as an unofficial way of expressing community concerns about its members, it may even protect individual privacy by forestalling official intervention into the community's affairs.[8] An example of this kind in fiction is Edith Wharton's *The Age of Innocence* (1920), where gossip alerts the wronged wife and enables her to prevent her husband from deserting her and committing adultery. Gossip, according to analysts who see social cohesion as positive, provides groups with means of self-control and emotional stability, circulates information and evaluation, facilitates self-knowledge by offering bases for comparison, constitutes a form of wish-fulfilment, helps to control competition, generates power among subordinates, and provides opportunity for self-disclosure and for examination of moral decisions.[9]

Across the centuries, letters have been an ideal medium for gossip. Notable epistolary gossips in English include Lady Mary Wortley Montagu, Jane Austen, and the Bloomsbury set.[10] The most heroic gossip of them all in English letters is Horace Walpole (1717–97), whose correspondence, written for publication, filled forty-eight volumes.[11] Condemnation of gossip is also a topic in letters: an early example occurs in a Han dynasty letter from Ma Yuan to his nephews.[12]

Gossip about other people's affairs does not often figure as a topic in love-letters: one exception is Simone de Beauvoir writing to Nelson Algren. There are very few instances of this in the correspondence between Lu Xun and Xu Guangping where they gossip about other people's affairs. Given the illicit relationship between them, however, they themselves were vulnerable to gossip, and their letters repeatedly refer to gossip in general as well as to the specific rumours about them.

Dawning Awareness, 1925

Following her first visit to his home in West Third Lane in April 1925, Lu Xun felt obliged in his next letter to Xu Guangping to warn her that the other two people present that day, Li Xiaofeng and Zhang Yiping, might easily misconstrue their quite ordinary conversation.[13] In *Letters between Two*, he adds 'and thus create gossip [*yaoyan*]'. The addition reveals that six years after hearing about the gossip spread by these two men he is still offended by it.

Lu Xun also expresses contempt for the 'rumour' [*liuyan*] on which Chen Yuan claimed to have based his attack on Lu Xun's part in the student protest.[14] It is not clear exactly what this rumour was, but Lu Xun is justified in claiming that he did nothing to incite the protest movement (he had counselled 'trench warfare' to Xu Guangping). On the other hand, throughout his public defence of the students, Lu Xun concealed his special relationship with Xu Guangping, one of the student leaders. In this instance, his fear of losing the moral high ground lay behind his condemnation of rumour. His own vulnerability made him less than honest in this exchange.

Mounting Anger, 1926

Gossip about their journey together from Peking to Shanghai becomes almost immediately a topic in their 1926 letters. On the eve of his departure from Shanghai, Zhou Jianren had come to see his brother off: 'When we talked about my affairs, I learned that Fuyuan has been spreading rumours (how skilled he is at speculation surprises even me), so now lots of people in Shanghai, seeing my travel arrangements, are more inclined to see it that way, and believe what Fuyuan has been saying. Jianren said that it's quite good, it saves us having to announce it later on.'[15] This is changed in *Letters between Two* to 'We talked a lot before I went on board and I learned then that Fuyuan has been spreading rumours about my affairs everywhere, along with some elaborations of his own. So when some people in Shanghai saw that we'd travelled there on the same train, they became even more convinced that Fuyuan's stories were true, although they didn't see anything very peculiar about it'. The changes suggest that six years later Lu Xun is even more irritated by Sun Fuyuan's gossip than he was at the time, and also more careful about what he reveals; he implies that they only 'travelled in the same train' (they also stayed in the same hotel) and that Fuyuan's account was inaccurate (the original correctly implies the opposite). Answering a question from Xu Guangping on the substance of the rumours,[16] Lu Xun replies with details that are deleted in *Letters between Two*. 'There are not only many male students at L's home, there are also female students, and two of them are most familiar, but L loves the tall one. He loves talent, and she is the one with most talent, so he loves her. But in Shanghai, I heard that these comments were not considered strange.'[17] The matter was then dropped. It was not necessary to say in so many words that the taller female was Xu Guangping and the other was Xu Xiansu.[18]

Lu Xun need not have been so irritated: there seems nothing malicious in the information spread by Sun Fuyuan nor is there any adverse reaction to it from his friends. Zhou Jianren, who had passed on the stories, seemed to have an intuitive understanding of this when he counselled his brother not to be too upset at the gossip about them, since it saved Lu Xun the embarrassment of having to inform friends himself. After all, by this time Xu Guangping was no longer Lu Xun's student, and none of his friends, with the possible exception of the Yu sisters, had ever been friendly with his wife.

Gao Changhong's poem about being in competition with Lu Xun over Xu Guangping, published in November, had the effect of bringing rumours circulating in Peking to Lu Xun's attention.[19] According to Lu Xun's enquiries, Zhang Yiping and Li Xiaofeng were claiming that Xu Guangping was living secretly in Amoy; Lu Xun also thought Hata Nobuko was involved.[20] Lu Xun's retaliation against Gao Changhong took the form of a fable, 'Flight to the moon', which echoes his decision, after much hesitation, to ignore the rumours and to join Xu Guangping in Canton. Newly emboldened, Lu Xun decided to employ Xu Guangping as his teaching assistant in Canton: 'Who cares what other people think.'[21] It is Xu Guangping's turn to worry: she warns that they should still be on their guard lest working together become an occasion for talk.[22] In his final letter from Amoy, Lu Xun comments that she should not worry about being his assistant or she will become the prisoner of rumour [*liuyan*]; and to emphasize the point adds to *Letters between Two* five years on 'and the rumour-mongers will have won'.[23]

Relaxing their Guard, 1929

By 1929, Lu Xun and Xu Guangping are much less bothered by the stories circulating about their relationship.[24] The extent to which it was known in Lu Xun's circle but yet unmentionable to his face is nicely shown where he describes the student agitation at Yenching University for him to come and teach in Peking: '[Wei] Congwu said, with much hemming and hawing, that the head of the Chinese department (Youyu's younger brother, but not Ma Heng) doubted that I would be willing to go, because in the south there was mumble mumble mumble . . . I answered that the reason was not because "in the south there is mumble mumble mumble", that *it* could also come north with me, but the reason that I decline is because I don't want to be a teacher. So then I told them about Changhong's rumours when I was in Amoy and also you now being in Shanghai; only the matter of the Little White Elephant is still secret and has not been spread'.[25] In *Letters between Two*, the reference to Changhong's rumours and to the Little White Elephant are both omitted: Lu Xun is still unwilling to discuss the rumours or even to mention their (then still unborn) son in public. In their place, a jovial remark is added: '*it* was not a great tree that couldn't be moved.'

Xu Guangping's response, which is rather confused, is deleted: 'As for our affairs, if some people are hard on us, I'd really prefer it, what I fear most is being soft, which makes it difficult emotionally; I'm the sort who fears softness rather than hardness, talking about feelings rather than talking about reason.'[26]

Lu Xun's final reference to the gossip about them, made in connection with the impending visit of Aunt Feng, is also deleted: 'In regard to all outside rumours [*chuanyan*], I don't even dispute the most negative . . . I don't bother about whether they are right or wrong, in the end we have our Little White Elephant.'[27]

From Peking, Lu Xun passes on a tidbit of gossip from Wei Congwu about Gao Changhong and Bing Xin. Changhong had been writing love-letters to Bing Xin for three years, and when she married this year, she handed them over to her husband who tossed them into the sea as he read them. This anecdote is deleted from *Letters between Two*, possibly in deference to Bing Xin's feelings, possibly because Lu Xun does not wish to be seen to be a gossip himself.[28]

Summary

At the time the first batch of letters were written, Lu Xun and Xu Guangping were unaware that gossip had already begun to circulate about them, so that when Lu Xun rewrote the text he added comments to castigate the gossip-mongers, whom he now regarded as having plotted against him, and to indicate his abhorrence of gossip. In 1926, as the rumours increase, so do his ire and her concern, and they become a major topic in their letters, fully represented in *Letters between Two* although the concrete detail is missing. By 1929, both are more relaxed about gossip and can even joke about it, but the detail is still deleted.

22

Secrecy, Seclusion, and Private/Selfish Interests

Secrets and Secrecy

The study of secrecy by Western sociologists begins with Georg Simmel's *Soziologie, Untersuchungen über die Formen der Vergesellschaftung* (1908),which has become the canonical source on the topic since its English translation in 1950.[1] Simmel regarded secrecy, 'the hiding of realities by negative or positive means, [as] one of man's greatest achievements . . . The secret offers, so to speak, the possibility of a second world alongside the manifest world; and the latter is decisively influenced by the former . . . For even where one of the two does not notice the existence of a secret, the behavior of the concealer, and hence the whole relationship, is certainly modified by it'.[2] He pointed out that 'the secret is often ethically negative; for, the secret is a general sociological form which stands in neutrality above the value functions of its contents. It may absorb the highest values—as, for instance, in the case of the noble individual whose subtle shame makes him conceal his best in order not to have it remunerated by eulogy and other rewards; for, otherwise, he would possess the remuneration, as it were, but no longer the value itself. On the other hand, although the secret has no immediate connection with evil, evil has an immediate connection with secrecy: the immoral hides itself for obvious reasons even where its content meets with no social stigma as, for instance, in the case of certain sexual delinquencies'.[3]

Simmel captures the attraction of secrecy beyond its immediate instrumental use: 'In the first place, the strongly emphasized exclusion of all outsiders makes for a correspondingly strong feeling of possession. For many individuals, property does not fully gain its significance with mere ownership, but only with the consciousness that others must do without it . . . . Moreover, since the others are excluded from the possession—particularly when it is very valuable—the converse suggests itself psychologically, namely, that what is denied to many must have special value.'[4] At an even deeper level, he explores our fascination with secrets and the sense of pleasure associated with concealment, disclosure, and betrayal: 'The secret puts a barrier between men but, at the same time, it creates the tempting challenge to break through it, by gossip or confession—and this challenge accompanies its psychology like a constant overtone.'[5]

The mystery surrounding secrecy is imaginatively transferred to the study of everyday transactions in Erving Goffman's *The Presentation of Self in Everyday*

Life (1969). According to Goffman, secrecy is one form of 'backstage behaviour' that establishes intimacy between a couple or among a group. He distinguishes between three kinds of secrecy: dark, strategic, and inside; inside secrets may not be very dark but simply trivial or domestic.[6] In similar fashion, Inness (1992) differentiates between intimate and non-intimate secrets.[7]

In contrast, Carol Warren and Barbara Laslett dispel this appreciation of the pleasures, licit and illicit, of secrecy in their 'Privacy and Secrecy: A Conceptual Comparison' (1997).[8] Drawing on 'a considerable body of sociological and social psychological literature on secrecy' since Simmel, they distinguish between 'privacy' (concealment of intimate facts or relationships that are morally neutral or acceptable), 'private-life secrecy' (concealment of behaviour in private life that is an actual or potential threat to the moral or political order), and 'public-life secrecy' political or business related (including journalism) secrecy.[9] They point out that secrets can be individual, shared by a couple, shared by a family, or shared by a large unit such as a government department.[10] Comparing privacy and secrecy, they conclude that privacy is more likely to be available to adults, the healthy, and socially privileged, while secrecy is more likely to be practised by children, the ill, the morally stigmatized, the lower socio-economic class, and by those with high public visibility.[11] Again, 'Privacy is consensual; the behaviour it protects is socially legitimated and seen as nonthreatening to others. Secrecy is nonconsensual; the behaviours it protects are seen as illegitimate and as involving the interests of the excluded'.

Stanton Tefft reaches a similar conclusion by analysing secrecy according to conflict theory (1980):[12] 'Individuals and the organisations to which they belong determine the rewards or costs of secrecy in terms of their own self-interests as the conflict with outsiders intensifies or dissipates . . . . Secrecy is a social resource which opponents can use defensively or offensively during social conflicts.'[13] 'To the extent that secrecy denies social actors information which might reveal that they are exploited, or manipulated by others, to that extent then secrecy promotes order. For the most part, however, secrecy furthers social antagonisms and tensions . . . Each of us, by choice or by the requirements of certain group memberships, pursue our interests through both concealing information and disclosing it . . . . Secrecy enables the powerful to escape accountability for their exploitation and manipulation of the weak and enables the weak to escape coercion by the powerful and to oppose them.'[14]

By ignoring the magical properties of secrecy and its function in creating intimacy, Warren and Laslett and Tefft end up with impoverished appraisals of secrets.[15] The balance is somewhat restored by Sissela Bok, whose previous work includes *Lying* (1978). Although Bok indicates aspects of life where both secrecy and privacy can be undesirable in *Secrets: On the Ethics of Concealment and Revelation* (1984), she takes a minority view in upholding secrecy as deserving protection in law.[16] Undifferentiated secrecy, however, is not generally given a strong positive value in Western countries, and laws on privacy do not grant a fundamental right to secrecy.

The terms *mi* or *mimi* [secret] are used sparingly in Lu Xun's and Xu Guangping's correspondence, and their secrets are domestic and intimate rather than dark or strategic. But their secrets created 'a second world' to which they deny access to others. When Xu Guangping calls his home a *mimi wo*,[17] and when Lu Xun says that he has told his friends in Peking about their affair and cohabitation but not about their *mi* (i.e. her pregnancy),[18] these cherished secrets are kept secret by deletion before publication.

In their conduct and in words, Lu Xun and Xu Guangping shared a belief that letters were confidential to sender and recipient unless agreed for public release by joint consent. In her early letters to Lu Xun, who was already a famous and influential figure in the literary scene, Xu Guangping would have been conscious that at some point her letters to him, and almost certainly his letters to her, might reach publication. She is the first to anticipate this, writing in June 1925 to suggest that some passages in his letters could be patched together for publication in his journal *The wilderness*.[19] At this stage in their correspondence Lu Xun was still very cautious in what he put on paper, and publication of these excerpts without prior editing would not have revealed much that was personal, nothing that was secret. Nevertheless, Lu Xun did not then adopt her suggestion.

Their expectation that personal letters should be regarded as secret is articulated in an exchange in 1925, when Xu Guangping had been expelled from Women's Normal College but had refused to move out of her dormitory. Xu Guangping begins her letter by expressing her anxiety that 'the enemy' [changed to 'they' in *Letters between Two*] may have opened his last letter to her.[20] It is implied first that letters should not be read by third parties, and second that if anyone has tampered with the mail it must have been the College authorities. Lu Xun's response, especially his admitted carelessness in sealing his letters, suggests that he also takes it for granted that letters should be not be opened and read by third parties and that there is no postal censorship in China at that time.[21] He remarks that *si zhe hanjian* [tampering with the mail] is a custom in China and that he had been expecting something like this to happen. The meaning of *si* in this context is not entirely clear, but it may suggest that the tamperers are individuals or institutions rather than official agencies; in any case, *si* has a negative connotation, suggesting something underhand or illicit. In Amoy, Lu Xun finds the post office regulations for preserving the secrecy of registered letters merely ridiculous.[22]

Despite her intimacy with Zhou Jianren's family in Shanghai, Xu Guangping still preferred to conceal from them her expeditions to the the post office in 1929 to mail her letters to Lu Xun in Peking, and even tried to prevent letting the postal clerks suspect how frequent her letters were. Making a joke of her secretiveness, she writes: 'I realize that it's not important if people know but naturally it seems as if I feel there is something secret about it.'[23] In *Letters between Two*, the first part of the sentence is changed to 'I realize that it's not a secret matter', perhaps indicating that these playful and affectionate 'secrets' can now be made public.

Like letters, the content of diaries are also expected to be secret, although there is no reason not to refer to their existence. The first reference to their diaries is when Lu Xun checks his diary about mail he has sent to her from Amoy.[24] Xu Guangping's teasing rebuke for having muddled the dates in his diary is deleted but probably only because it comes in a longer passage about missing journal issues.[25] Xu Guangping's single mention of her 'simple diary' is retained.[26] Visiting Peking in 1929, Lu Xun gets very agitated when a cousin staying at West Third Lane in his absence has been reading his old diaries, uninformative as they are.[27] This reminds Xu Guangping to remind him to collect adequate supplies of the right kind of notebooks for his diaries.[28] Neither of these remarks requires editorial intervention.

Editing the letters in 1932, Lu Xun denied that he had any secrets. When he left Amoy to take up a professorship at Zhongshan University, he suspected that one of the students accompanying him had been sent by the Amoy University authorities to find out his real reason for breaking his contract. He mentioned his suspicions in a letter to Xu Guangping written on board, and for the published version he added, 'Although I don't indeed have any secrets [*mimi*], nevertheless it is irritating to have to put up with this kind of thing'.[29] This *post hoc* denial is unconvincing, since despite the gossip about them Lu Xun and Xu Guangping were still attempting to conceal their relationship, and neither at the time nor subsequently was Lu Xun prepared to admit that his main reason for going to Canton was to rejoin Xu Guangping. Alternatively, Lu Xun's editorial addition might be meant to signify that he had no hidden political mission in going to Canton.

The general impression from the correspondence is that although Lu Xun and Xu Guangping felt justified in regarding the contents of letters and dairies as secret, they felt vaguely embarrassed about admitting to sharing secrets or having secret lives. Their ambivalence corresponds to the kinds of ambiguity about secrets described by Goffman, Inness, and Bok. As described above, some of their secrets (or talk about secrets) have the function of creating or confirming intimacy between them; others, such as the contents of Lu Xun's diary or their letters, suggest that these personal documents, innocuous though they may be, are nevertheless not for the public gaze except at the authors' choosing. A third possibility is that information released not by consent may cause trouble to the authors or to a third party.

Solitude and Seclusion

The relationship between seclusion and privacy is close. In one Dutch–English/English–Dutch dictionary, the translation for 'privacy' is given as *afzondering*, but the translation of *afzondering* is given as 'seclusion'.[30] If the connotations of *si* in Chinese tend to be negative, the word *you* [seclusion] is almost always agreeable. In Du Fu's 'General He' poems (a set of fifteen poems on Du Fu's visit to the retired general's estate), the concept of seclusion is the key to the whole set, even to the extent that the word *you* appears eleven times in the fifteen poems.[31] The reader understands that the poet, as the guest of General He, is accompanied in this desirable seclusion by his host and probably other guests as well, and the poem itself is an exercise in sociability. Nonetheless the poet's longing for seclusion (a home of his own far from the troubles of official life) can be regarded as entirely sincere. Neither in English nor in Chinese is seclusion necessarily solitude.

Neither Lu Xun nor Xu Guangping discuss their attitude towards solitude or seclusion in any kind of systematic way, and there is no particular vocabulary they use for it. Most of their remarks are negative expressions about the intrusion of other people on their time and personal space: Lu Xun introduces the topic and sets the tone. These passages occur only in Part II of the correspondence, that is, in the context of confirming their intimacy.

Before moving to Amoy, Lu Xun had not experienced living on campus, and he found it hard to get accustomed to frequent claims on his time from colleagues and students. His letters from Amoy are full of irritation about having nowhere to hide from unwelcome visitors at Amoy University[32] and hopes of being free from such intrusions in Canton.[33] These passages are retained in *Letters between Two*, suggesting that Lu Xun refused to be embarrassed by his lack of sociability; he concealed his irritation at students, however, referring to them as 'visitors' in *Letters between Two*.[34] Lu Xun recognized that his need for privacy in Canton, in order to have time alone with Xu Guangping, would be more imperative than in Amoy; possibly to disguise this, Lu Xun's expressed wish to avoid to visitors on campus is made to sound more reasonable.[35]

Lu Xun also expresses exasperation at having to take part in the normal round of social activities in Amoy. In one letter he claims that his main reason (changed in *Letters between Two* to a 'minor part' of his reason) for leaving Peking was to get some rest from this kind of intrusion on his time;[36] in describing the farewells that precede his leaving Amoy, he even adds the extra line: 'This kind of boring socialising is really the enemy of life'.[37] This kind of attitudinizing is conventional among academics and writers and need not be taken too literally.

Xu Guangping is probably influenced, nonetheless, by his rhetoric. In a passage retained in *Letters between Two*, for instance, she echoes his condemnation of 'wasteful' social intercourse, although in other passages she appears to enjoy outings with friends and colleagues.[38] Not being famous, of course, spares her the excessive attention paid to Lu Xun. In another passage, she complains that her exploitative family regard her as a *dushen zhuyi-zhe* [an alone-ist], a charge to which she lamely responds that she is not any kind of 'ist'.[39] This passage is deleted from *Letters between Two*, presumably because of the unfavourable light it casts on her relatives.

In 1929, circumstances have changed: together as a couple, they no longer find the company of others oppressive, nor do they live in a campus dormitory. On his brief visit to Peking, Lu Xun takes pleasure in looking up his old friends and spending time with them, and Xu Guangping encourages him to make best use of this opportunity. Still, as the time approaches for them to be reunited, they express their longing to spend time alone together, perhaps in some peaceful rural setting. Lu Xun reports that Peking is very tranquil [*chen jing*],[40] almost like an 'other-worldly Peach Blossom Spring'.[41] A few days later, Xu Guangping describes to him an excursion with her Aunt Feng to a small country town not far from Shanghai that is 'extremely tranquil and secluded' [*ji wei qing you*] and 'a true other-worldly Peach Blossom Spring, the very acme of tranquillity' [*qing jing zhi zhi*].[42] Lu Xun, who did not receive this letter in time to reply to it, deleted the latter phrase from

Letters between Two[43] and added the following passage to his last letter from Peking: 'Why don't we go to some small village incognito, not telling a single soul, and just enjoy ourselves';[44] it is as if he transferred the responsibility for their shared desire for seclusion from her to him. These were the only occasions where either of them associated seclusion with the countryside. It is noticeable that the setting described by Xu Guangping is only semi-rural, and that Lu Xun was bored by country towns such as Amoy, Hangchow, or Shaoxing. Unlike Rousseau, Lu Xun did not seek personal privacy in nature.[45]

From the above, it can be seen that Lu Xun and Xu Guangping understood solitude as an opportunity for them to be together, or (if they were apart) at least to be free from the distraction of third parties so that they could think about each other. Although their expressed dislike of social intercourse need not be taken too literally, it is implied that only in seclusion (whether alone or together) can their authentic selves find rest and renewal.

Private/Selfish Interests

In the customary pairing of *gong* and *si*, the terms correspond to 'the public interest(s)' and 'private and/or selfish interest(s)' rather than 'the public sphere' and 'the private sphere' or 'privacy'.[46] For the purpose of the present analysis, *si* is not automatically equivalent to the concept 'personal space' as previously defined.[47] The meanings and associations of Lu Xun's use of *si* changed over the period of his correspondence with Xu Guangping; hers also changed, but to a lesser degree.

In their 1925 letters, Lu Xun and Xu Guangping paid little attention to the matter of the public interest versus private/selfish interests; to the extent it is mentioned, both accept the conventional view that only the former is honourable.[48] Xu Guangping worries briefly about using a public cause for private ends when she gives way to the impulse to denounce the principal of Women's Normal College during a demonstration against the May Thirtieth Incident, but both causes are in the public political domain, and the passage is retained in full in *Letters between Two*.[49] In the same letter, Xu Guangping castigates the student leaders for not subordinating their private ambitions [*si jian*] for the sake of the cause; this passage is weakened in *Letters between Two*, presumably because Lu Xun wished to avoid showing Xu Guangping as being overcritical of the student movement.[50] There is no indication that either of them is aware of any serious conflict between public and private interests in their own lives.

By 1926, in contrast, the conflict between public and private interests becomes a problematic topic in their letters as Lu Xun fails to match Xu Guangping's determination that they resume their relationship as lovers sooner rather than later (or not at all). This new aspect of the *gong/si* dilemma is preceded by a semi-facetious exchange about whether or not Lu Xun is sexually attracted to his female students in Amoy. Responding to his remark that he keeps his eyes from 'straying', Xu Guangping pretends to take umbrage at the suggestion that she might be jealous, arguing that 'the desire for private possession [*si you*] would naturally disappear' once people raised their educational levels.[51] To this, Lu Xun replies that 'Judging from my own example, I know that the elimination of the idea of private property [*si you zhi nian*] will probably have to wait for the twenty-fifth century'.[52] Both remarks are retained in *Letters between Two*, showing that Lu Xun is willing in the 1930s to label Xu Guangping as his 'private property'; 'private property' here, of course, punningly refers to a private (i.e. intimate) relationship.

Writing in the same letter about his aborted plan to go to Canton in October with Sun Fuyuan, Lu Xun is more serious: 'Part of the reason I was going to go with him was naturally for private purposes, but the main reason was in the public interest' [*xiao ban ziran ye you xie si xin, dan da bufen que shi wei gong*]; this remark is retained in *Letters between Two*.[53] A week later, he expresses his new plans to leave Amoy for Canton somewhat differently: 'I am naturally determined to go, although not wholly for the public cause'; this is changed to 'I should certainly be very happy to go there now' in *Letters between Two*.[54] These two passages show some ambivalence on Lu Xun's part, but it is notable that he is willing to admit that 'private purposes' related to his personal life are part of his motivation in wanting to pay a visit to Canton and possibly also to accept a new postion there.

By December 1926, Lu Xun has finally made up his mind to break his contract with Amoy and come to Canton. Since her own job in Canton has become intolerable, Xu Guangping needs to look for other work herself, and remarks self-deprecatingly, 'I'm really not much good for anything, I do a bit of this and that and then I feel like stopping, it's better from a private point of view [*zi si fangmian*], I suppose you would agree?'[55] Here Xu Guangping hints that she does not wish to become engaged in any work that might interfere with their reunion; the meaning of 'private' is here closer to 'intimate' rather than 'selfish'. The remark is deleted in *Letters between Two*, presumably because it refers to the imminent resumption of their previous intimacy.

By the end of his stay in Amoy, Lu Xun has come to reject the elevation of the public over private interest. Reacting to the suggestion by his students that he is not 'just himself' any more, Lu Xun writes, 'This caused me some alarm, and I thought to myself that I have become an object in the public domain. This is disastrous and I won't agree to it. It is worse than being overthrown, which would be much more comfortable'.[56] Lu Xun retains this disclaimer of his public role in *Letters between Two*, thus affirming that this private interest—his wish to live with Xu Guangping—will take precedence over any duty he might owe his students in Amoy, or over any potential harm his adultery might inflict on his political or moral authority.

In 1929, the conflict between public and private interests has disappeared as a topic in their letters. It is no longer an issue: the resumption of their relationship has caused gossip, but it does not seem to have damaged Lu Xun's political influence or moral standing. Xu Guangping has by now also shifted her position. In a letter to Chang Ruilin, a copy of which she sends to Lu Xun in Peking, she uses the word *si* in three different senses. Referring to the school protest in 1925, she describes the importance of Lu Xun's support, which he offered *dique hao wu si xin* [without any private interest whatsoever]: here, the term *si xin* means 'selfish interests'. She then explains, somewhat less than frankly, that when he came to Canton, she became his teaching assistant, and when they came to Shanghai she was his private assistant (*siren zhushou*): here, *siren* means only that she is not then employed in the public sphere. She concludes by saying that now they have little money but they love each other and have a joyous private life (*si xing shenghuo*): here, *si* refers to a treasured intimate relationship.[57]

Summary

The meanings and associations in Lu Xun and Xu Guangping's use of *si* changed over the period 1925–9, corresponding to the change in their circumstances. As their future as a couple became assured, they shifted the balance between private and public interests in their lives towards favouring the private, although in *Letters between Two* this is only clear in Lu Xun's case. In editing *Letters between Two* for publication, Lu Xun revealed to readers that he and Xu Guangping desired secrecy and seclusion in their lives as a couple and also individually in regard to their letters and diaries. Only a few specific references to secrecy in the early stages of their relationship are suppressed, while just as much is added to indicate their wish for seclusion. The place of *si* in their lives will be considered again below in the context of their conceptualization of personal space.

23

Personal Space as Privacy

The preceding chapters have shown a wide range of instances where personal space is established by Lu Xun through his editorial interventions, chiefly deletions and recensions. There are no comparable texts against which these specific instances or categories of personal space can be systematically measured: the richness of the evidence in the original and edited versions of Lu Xun and Xu Guangping's correspondence is unparalleled. Instead, this chapter will investigate how the content, mechanisms, functions, and values of Lu Xun and Xu Guangping's personal space correspond to existing definitions of privacy. In the absence of comprehensive works by Chinese scholars on privacy, two Western writers are cited as representative.[1]

Alan F. Westin's *Privacy and Freedom* (1967) is one of the first postwar works specifically on the theme of privacy, and his delineation of four basic states of individual privacy (anonymity, reserve, solitude, and intimacy) is widely quoted by later writers.[2] The functions of privacy are grouped under another four headings: personal autonomy, emotional release, self-evaluation, and limited and protected communication.[3] Julie C. Inness, in *Privacy, Intimacy, and Isolation* (1992), takes her data from cases under US tort and constitutional law. She specifically limits her findings to the US only, but the framework she uses is more systematic than Westin's and is readily adaptable to other countries and disciplines. Whereas Westin and later writers distinguish the content of privacy from its functions, their discussion of values tends to be perfunctory, and they overlook the category of mechanisms. Inness also draws attention to feminist perspectives on privacy, noting that protection of privacy may function as a social control mechanism to maintain the dominance of groups or individuals in power and enforce silence and helplessness on others.[4]

According to Inness, privacy covers (1) access to intimate information about the agent, (2) access to intimate aspects of the agent's person, and (3) autonomy in the agent's decisions about intimate matters.[5] Intimacy, in this context, refers to situations that involve liking, love, and care for oneself or others as well as situations where the body is physically vulnerable such as during sexual intercourse, excretion, and personal hygiene.[6] The first and third kinds of privacy are both relevant to Lu Xun and Xu Guangping's correspondence.

Contents

For the *contents* of Lu Xun and Xu Guangping's personal space as demonstrated by their correspondence, the relevant area is access to intimate information about the agent or agents. The kinds of information in Lu Xun's personal space can be summarized as follows, arranged in a descending order of importance as indicated first by the extent of changes to the text and supported by references within the text:

(1) the nature and extent of their intimacy in 1925 and 1926;
(2) the nature of their intimacy in 1929;
(3) their intimate secrets, their longing for seclusion, and their ambivalence towards private/selfish interests;
(4) their fear of gossip and the content of the gossip about them;
(5) episodes whose recollection is painful;
(6) episodes or expressions which show them as immature, impolite, or imprudent;
(7) episodes or expressions which leave them open to criticism or prosecution on moral, legal, or political grounds;
(8) details of their bodily functions, domestic habits, and financial affairs;
(9) the situation of members of their respective families, whether liked or disliked;
(10) details that might cause inconvenience or embarrassment to liked or respected students or colleagues;
(11) criticism of disliked former students or colleagues;
(12) errors or irregularities in grammar, script, or expression that might leave them open to criticism on educational or aesthetic grounds;
(13) detail that might prove boring to third parties;
(14) passages that might prove obscure to third parties.

All but the last two of these items come within Inness's definition of privacy. The items at the top of the list may be more relevant to privacy than those lower down, but only the last two are not indisputably related to privacy. The contents of Lu Xun's personal space, therefore, can be redefined as areas of privacy (as conceptualized by a modern American philosopher). The two items that are not related to privacy are matters of editorial decision that are independent of privacy issues.

Mechanisms

Without necessarily being conscious of doing so, Lu Xun and Xu Guangping construct intimacy in their correspondence by means of 'backstage behaviour': this includes such things as derogation of the absent, expressions of irritability, use of nicknames, descriptions of biological needs, and listing trivial and domestic matters.[7] Reticence encourages limited or protected communication, while privacy keeps emotions and acts from being trivialized: what is important is kept private (e.g. lovemaking).[8] Love-letters are a prime example of backstage behaviour: lovers go out of their way to expose themselves as foolish, as if vulnerability were a measure of sincerity. Examples of backstage behaviour are especially frequent in the 1926 letters, when Lu Xun and Xu Guangping are still establishing their intimacy, and in turn take a different form in the 1929 letters when their intimacy is acknowledged.

Control mechanisms are introduced when backstage behaviour is transformed into 'front region behaviour'.[9] When personal letters are published, control is established by rewriting the text; publication of intimate information, transformed by substantial intervention, in this way becomes a *mechanism* for obtaining personal space. Given their fear of gossip and longing for seclusion, it seems paradoxical that Lu Xun and Xu Guangping chose to publish their intimate correspondence at all.

The three reasons given in Lu Xun's Preface for publishing the correspondence are to serve as a memento for their own sakes; to thank friends; and to leave for their son a true impression of his parents' experiences. As suggested above, financial gain, circulating their current views on issues raised in the letters, and halting the gossip about them were also important reasons. The solution to the paradox lay in Lu Xun's editorial and fiction-writing skills. Gossip and rumour-mongering could be seen as the attempts by others to appropriate their story; by rewriting their story and making public some part of their private affairs, they regained control over their love story and preserved their privacy. The appearance of *Letters between Two* declared that the relationship between these two had all along been serious and proper, not a matter of libertine indulgence, and that they wished their personal space to be respected. Publishing their love-letters was their equivalent of a marriage rite.

More specifically, their mechanisms for asserting control over their personal space through publishing their correspondence were deletions, recensions, retentions, and additions. With the exception of concealing the early extent of their intimacy, there is no particular pattern in the distribution of these mechanisms over time.

Deletions and Recensions

The deletions and recensions in *Letters between Two* are primarily negative; they deny, in part or wholly, access to information which ranges from highly personal (such as their sexual relationship) to less personal (such as their domestic habits) and not very personal (such as events that might not be of interest to readers). In some cases, fine distinctions can be made in their uses of these mechanisms. For example, by deleting or otherwise rewriting passages on their sexual relationship, they drew a line between *Letters between Two* and the love-letters by literary couples whose publication preceded theirs; at the risk of disappointing readers, they asserted their respectability not their sexuality.

In the deletion or recensions of references to certain bodily functions, consciously or otherwise a gender distinction is drawn between his body and hers, hers being significantly more personal. Xu Guangping's relative youth and lack of literary distinction also contribute to making her body more personal. Lu Xun can laugh off vulgarity, but the more vulnerable Xu Guangping needs his protection. Privacy allows or asserts power, and power confers privacy.[10]

Deletions and recensions about other aspects of their daily life are most likely to be due to their perceived limited interest to third-party readers, although reference to her use of a rickshaw and their disparaging remarks about servants are deleted for reasons of political correctness. Exchanging information on their living arrangements is an important way for Xu Guangping and Lu Xun to establish their intimacy in 1926; retention in part of the detail in *Letters between Two* also serves to underline the domesticity of their affection for each other, enhancing their respectability as a couple.

The many deletions and recensions about their families are attributable to three main reasons: to avoid disparaging remarks or revelation of personal detail about their family members causing hurt to the families or reflecting poorly on themselves; to protect their families from public curiosity; and to avoid boring third-party readers with complicated detail. Lu Xun's deletion of all but one reference to his younger brother is less a personal matter (all but one of the other references are equally innocuous) than sensitivity to their rupture. Lu Xun is similarly protective about students and colleagues who remain friends, but in regard to his enemies he is sometimes cautious (prudent suppression) and sometimes reckless (added invective).

Discretion in regard to their political beliefs, observations, and activities is not necessarily protection of personal space but protection from actual bodily harm for themselves and their associates: *Letters between Two* was edited at a time when one of their closest friends had recently been executed as a member of the Communist Party. Averting the attention of the Nationalist government must have been a factor in drastically reducing Xu Guangping's detailed analyses of political manoeuvring in Canton and in suppressing the identification of named individuals as anarchists or communists; Lu Xun, always more cautious, had less need for self-censorship in this regard. On the other hand, her suspicions about Communist activities in the student movement in Peking in the 1920s, references to her allegiance to the Nationalist Party, and her disparaging remarks about workers' rights in Canton, may have been deleted as inconsonant with their political allegiances in the 1930s.

They are less secretive about their intimate thoughts and emotions: the main areas of personal space are the language in which they express their mutual affection, the extent to which they miss each other when they are separated, their fluctuating moods (especially their depression and pessimism), and her opinions on his genius and on his shortcomings. In this regard, as also in the case of their political activities and opinions, revisions to Xu Guangping's letters may have had a somewhat different direction from Lu Xun's revisions to his own: it is acceptable for him to be irascible, for instance, but not for her. Otherwise, suppression of the differences between them in regard to emotional expression and political activism made them appear as evenly matched—except, of course, when he is acceptably shown as her superior in being male, older, her (former) teacher, and a famous literary figure.

Language and style may be regarded as an area of personal space both for a professional writer (as Lu Xun was at this time) whose livelihood was dependent on a high level of literacy and for the partner of a famous literary author. Even minor textual changes (such as correcting a wrong character) fall under the rubric of denying access to intimate information about the agent (for instance, that the agent was fallible in written expression). Lu Xun had his reputation as a famous writer to uphold, and Xu Guangping had to be seen as a worthy companion.

A wish for solitude or seclusion is not necessarily equivalent to a wish for personal space: visitors and social engagements also encroach on work time and may entail boredom. Lu Xun may have deleted or revised certain references to his unsociability (more rarely, to hers) in order to enhance his reputation as a friend and guide to students or in order to avoid embarrassing friends, but the addition to his final letter sends an unmistakable message to readers of *Letters between Two* that Lu Xun wants personal space for himself and Xu Guangping as a couple.

Additions

The additions, by contrast, reshape their identities for public display; a leading example is the transformation of Lu Xun's attitude towards gossip as more aggressive in *Letters between Two*. The additions concerning Lu Xun's political opinions and behaviour also make him appear more militant than in the letters. It is impossible to tell which is the 'real' Lu Xun: the grumbling caution he showed to Xu Guangping in the 1920s or the aggression on display to third-party readers in the 1930s. Another motive for the additions may be concern for the overall balance in his relationship with Xu Guangping. Since the substantial deletions make Xu Guangping appear much less politically informed and active as well as more prudent and controlled in her feelings, the blend of additions and deletions closes the gap between them in political and emotional maturity, so that they appear as a well-matched couple. The frequency of additions, their often considerable length, and their centrality in their story amount in places to transforming *Letters between Two* into a work of fiction.

Retentions

Finally, the retentions assert positive control. The gossip meant that other people were in control of their story; to take over their own story, they were obliged to publish it themselves. When we release information to friends, we retain some control over it; when we release the same information to strangers, however, we lose control.[11] Lu Xun's editing is an effort to control the release of information to strangers.

Apart from acknowledging their need for secrecy and seclusion and defending their private interests, Lu Xun and Xu Guangping do not discuss the mechanisms by which they establish and protect their personal space. In the context of their correspondence, there are three such mechanisms in plain view: first, writing and preserving their letters to each other; second, deciding to publish their letters; third, making decisions on rewriting their letters. Other mechanisms mentioned in the letters include keeping diaries and choosing to live off campus rather than on campus. Although the introduction of new material is far from common in the history of published letters, all of these mechanisms are covered in the first and third areas in Inness's definition of privacy: access to intimate information about the agent, and autonomy in the agent's decisions about intimate matters. We can, therefore, re-identify them as privacy mechanisms.

Functions

Lu Xun in his Preface to *Letters between Two* mentions only two reasons for making changes to the text: to avoid troubling friends and to avoid antagonizing enemies to the extent that they might sue him; readers were not to know that the changes were far more wide-ranging. There is no other direct evidence in the correspondence on the extent to which Lu Xun or Xu Guangping gave conscious attention to the functions of creating and establishing personal space, either in their letters or in their lives. The passages on gossip, rumour, secrecy, seclusion, and private interests indicate concern rather than an argued position.

The general function of privacy, according to Inness, is to assert control over and deny access to intimate information, whether by physical separation or seclusion, or by denial or deflection of information.[12] Its purpose is to protect our autonomy in creating and protecting our self-identity and our intimate relations with others. The difference in function between Lu Xun's personal space and Inness's definition of privacy is that as well as denying or deflecting intimate information, Lu Xun also releases intimate information and even introduces new information to attack his enemies. Even here, it could be argued that these attacks indirectly also serve to preserve his autonomy in his intimate relations with others. The purpose is identical: the personal space established by Lu Xun and Xu Guangping in writing, preserving, publishing, and editing the letters all protect the autonomy of the authors in creating and protecting their self-identity, their own intimate relations, and their intimate relations with their families and friends. In regard to function also, their personal space is equivalent to privacy.

Values

Measured by the quantity and importance of the changes between the original correspondence (OC) and *Letters between Two*, it is evident that Lu Xun and Xu Guangping placed a high value on their personal space. This evidence is supported by explicit references in the correspondence to rumour, gossip, secrecy, seclusion, and private interests. While the detail of the gossip about them is largely deleted in *Letters between Two*, condemnation of gossip is added, even though their life as a couple was by then accepted with little apparent opposition from family or associates. Intimate secrets are cherished and kept hidden (even the fact that they are hidden is deleted), while other kinds of secrets are repudiated. The privacy of letters and diaries is upheld, and intrusion by unauthorized persons is resented; seclusion free from interruption by random visits and social obligations is precious; time spent alone, or alone together, is longed for. Private or selfish interests are initially seen as less honourable than public service or the public interest, but as Lu Xun and Xu Guangping confide more intimately in each other, they reveal that their private lives individually and as a couple are deeply cherished. Above all, they hold by implication that letter-writers who choose to publish their correspondence may also choose to alter the texts at will, without apology or explanation. According to Inness's definition, all of this amounts to attributing a high value to privacy.

It is harder to judge whether Lu Xun and Xu Guangping regarded the value of privacy as instrumental or autonomous, that is, valued because it leads to desirable ends (such as room for personal or psychological growth), or desirable in itself as acknowledging personal autonomy in rational choice.[13] While their own privacy and that of their families, friends, and valued colleagues is guarded by Lu Xun as editor, the privacy of estranged friends or long-term enemies is afforded little if any protection: in their case, offensive remarks of a personal nature are added rather than deleted in *Letters between Two*. On the basis of the evidence provided above, it is likely that for Lu Xun and Xu Guangping, privacy was predominantly an instrumental value.

Conceptualization

The transformation of feelings and ideas into concepts is a matter for philosophers or historians of ideas. Although Lu Xun is often described as a thinker, and both he and Xu Guangping were given to extended reflections on the meaning of abstract concepts in literature, politics, and social life, neither of them ever chose to describe themselves as philosophers. Concepts of privacy as such did not attract their attention, nor did they formulate their own concepts of privacy in any systematic way. Nevertheless, the way in which personal space is constructed and protected in the correspondence is on the whole coherent and consistent, as are such views as they expressed in the correspondence. It is, therefore, more appropriate to refer in English to their 'sense of privacy' (a phrase which has no precise Chinese equivalent) than their 'concepts of privacy'.

A pattern of overall coherence in their personal space is evident from the analysis of the contents above. As Lu Xun shifts his editorial attention from topic to topic, the same kind of concern for personal space is evinced, whether with respect for themselves or for their families, whether about their sexual relations or aspects of their bodies, whether about their domestic habits, or about their intimate thoughts and feelings. In the original letters, they are particularly reticent about sexual matters, and there are many bodily functions they rarely or never discuss. The single topic on which Lu Xun is most sensitive is possibly his rupture with Zhou Zuoren. The areas in which the revisions are most common and substantive are their sexual relationship, their respective families, her expressions of emotion, and her political observations and activities. As editor, Lu Xun even imposes coherence by disguising the differences between the three phases of their relationship, their equivalents of courtship, engagement, and marriage.

Coherence in their expressed views is also evident, although here the change over time is more apparent both in the OC and in *Letters between Two*. Interest in each other's domestic arrangements, for example, is a more frequent topic in 1926 than in 1925 or 1929. Their views in regard to private interests also changed, as their need for the privacy in which they could freely be intimate increased, and as they became more willing to confide this need to each other; accordingly, their use of the word *si* changed from the disreputable sense of 'selfish' to correspond to the more positive sense of 'intimate'. This change was not articulated in the correspondence, but it was clearly one that they both understood.

Valuing our own privacy does not always rule out the pleasure we can obtain from intruding on the privacy of others, for example, by listening to gossip about other people's private lives. The only way in which this form of satisfaction to our curiosity can be rendered acceptable is when the subject of the gossip voluntarily raises the curtain or when he or she is dead.[14] The pleasure of reading old letters is attributable to this satisfaction of curiosity. Lu Xun is consistent in his reluctance both to pass on gossip and to read other peoples' old letters.

On the whole, the revisions to content are consistent, and some minor inconsistencies may be ascribed to indecision on borderline issues. Lu Xun is not too prudish to confess an interest in his female students but draws the line when it comes to his flirtation with Xu Guangping in class. In revealing that the possibility of sexual jealousy and possessiveness existed between them, however, Lu Xun seems here to acknowledge what elsewhere he conceals. In one of his letters from 1926 Lu Xun deletes an expression implying intimacy but adds another which is at least as intimate;[15] in one of her letters from 1929 he weakens an expression of intimacy and adds an unusually formal salutation,[16] although elsewhere her reference to fond memories [i.e. of him] in Peking is made even stronger.[17]

Lu Xun is also on occasion inconsistent in editing his own views, especially in regard to his life in Amoy. In some places he retains or even adds passages to indicate his dislike for the university, its chancellor, and his colleagues, but he also deletes or softens some of his more critical remarks.[18] The most obvious inconsistency is in regard to members of the Creation Society (see earlier). The revised account presented in *Letters between Two* by Lu Xun of his changing relationship with Guo Moruo and other members of the Creation Society is, nevertheless, historically accurate: this relationship was warmer, or at least not as hostile, in 1926 than in 1929.

Lu Xun is only occasionally inattentive about editorial consistency but is more inconsistent about changing colloquial expressions to more formal language and vice versa. Some changes may be attributed to his wish to present a more coherent style in individual letters, but many are difficult to justify. On the other hand, he also takes pains to conceal the extent of his editorial intervention, for example, in changing the 'this page' to 'two pages' to account for the greater length of the last letter in *Letters between Two*. In general, some of the inconsistencies are probably a matter of lapses in attention over the long period (a matter of several months) in which the editorial changes were carried out.[19] Apart from his *History of Chinese Fiction*, Lu Xun was not accustomed to writing or editing very long manuscripts.

Summary

On the whole, Lu Xun's treatment of personal space is coherent, consistent, and sensitive to changes in circumstances. Together with evidence from references in the correspondence, it amounts to an unarticulated, but nonetheless coherent and consistent sense of privacy. There is no evidence to show its theoretical underpinnings or whether it derives from Chinese or Western sources. A great deal can be traced to prevailing social and political factors, such as his relish in relating how he relieves himself in Amoy (which would not be out-of-place in his hometown in south-central China) and his caution in attributing anarchist or communist affiliations to others.

There is not enough evidence from references in the text to make a similar judgment on Xu Guangping's sense of privacy, except that it is not identical with Lu Xun's. Although in general she shares Lu Xun's views and was clearly influenced by them, there are significant differences in what she is willing to disclose to him or to third-party readers: she is much less inhibited about expressing her feelings, emotions, and political beliefs, and it was on her recommendation that the unedited correspondence was eventually released for publication. Xu Guangping is also less inhibited about mentioning aspects of her body such as picking her nose; in regard to urination, by contrast, she is notably more reticent than he is.

Some disparities in interpreting the evidence of the correspondence are due to problems of terminology. Wang Dehou claims that 'It is immediately apparent [from the revisions to the original correspondence] that they are not there to conceal any kind of private matter [*shenmo yinsi*], because there is not an iota of so-called private matters [*yinsi dongxi*] in the original correspondence'.[20] The term *yinsi* appears to have wholly negative connotations for Wang Dehou, since he emphasizes throughout that these are intimate love-letters. In his chapter on the origins and nature of the correspondence, Wang Dehou also asserts that there is no fundamental difference between the two versions in regard to the two writers' political, social, educational, moral, and philosophical views, in regard to their thoughts and feelings, or in regard to general tendency; the changes are chiefly to conceal matters [*neirong*] which they could not help but pour out in the private letters [*si xin*] but did not wish to make public.[21] Wang Dehou also asserts that the expressions of mutual love that have been deleted bear no relation to the 'nauseating' effusions that characterize the earlier *qingshu* publications, and that the greater number of deletions relate to the student movement and other political observations. He also states that the additions are not for the sake of making the two writers appear more in tune with the currents of the age or more committed to reform.[22] (Elsewhere he comments that Lu Xun's revisions in regard to the Chinese Communist Party take into account the political situation at the time of publication.[23]) Clearly there is room for continued debate over the contents and functions of the editorial process in *Letters between Two* and the place of privacy in Lu Xun and Xu Guangping's lives and thinking.

PART IV

Conclusion

The letters that should have been to you things sacred and secret beyond anything in the whole world!

Oscar Wilde, letter to Alfred Douglas,
on hearing of his intention to publish their correspondence

24

Revealing to Conceal: *Letters between Two* and the Original Correspondence

Although for decades *Letters between Two* and the original correspondence (OC) on which it is based were ignored, their significance is manifold. At the most fundamental level, the two together form an extraordinarily rich source of information about Lu Xun: his life, his views on literature and politics, his outlook on life, his sexuality, his domestic habits, his irritability, his heavy drinking and smoking, even his sensitivity to his short stature. It is not hard to understand the reason for their neglect at a time when his persona had become a symbol of loyalty to the communist cause, and thus an exemplar of right conduct: even the edited version of the correspondence reveals a man who decided to put his private interests above public duty by choosing to form an adulterous relationship with a former student.

No amount of romanticizing about Lu Xun can alter the facts about his life and views that in another deliberate move he chose to put before the public. In his own lifetime, these revelations only confirmed what was generally known, and although the book sold well, it was far from causing a sensation. It was only after his death that a prudish and politically narrow atmosphere began to make even edited information about his living arrangements, domestic habits, and unorthodox opinions much too controversial to be the subject of academic or popular scrutiny. Even today, some Chinese and Western studies of Lu Xun and modern Chinese history ignore the evidence from the correspondence. While some recent popularist accounts of Lu Xun's romance with Xu Guangping can be criticized for their sentimental avoidance of the whole picture, their use of the correspondence as a source is to be preferred to its repression.

Letters between Two and the original correspondence are also of unique importance in giving due attention to Xu Guangping, Lu Xun's partner for the last ten years of his life, and the woman for whom he defied the gossip-mongering of his enemies. Although disguised by editing, her knowledge and understanding of party politics at the time were in many respects superior to Lu Xun's, and she was always more of an activist. It was in her defence that Lu Xun 'came out of the trenches' to make his first public political protest at a national level, and it was at her repeated urging that he finally accepted the position at Zhongshan University. Although it is impossible to tell what direct influence she may have had on his thinking and writing in the late 1920s and 1930s, it is significant that he refused to allow her to take an outside job: she was needed as his personal assistant.

Letters between Two also provides copious information about Lu Xun's thinking on his writing and editorial work, although much of it is duplicated elsewhere and the original correspondence is not in this respect significantly more revelatory. Among the more important findings revealed or confirmed in *Letters between Two* are Lu Xun's continued self-identification as a fiction writer throughout 1926 (although he had not written original fiction for over a year), the ambiguous autobiographical elements in the short story 'Mourning the Dead', and the unambiguous autobiographical reference in the prose poems 'Hope' and 'Blighted Leaf'.

As a contribution to the history of modern Chinese letters, *Letters between Two* may have helped bring to an end the vogue for publishing love-letters, whether due to its emotional austerity, Lu Xun's own prestige as a public figure, or the sense of privacy that is affirmed throughout. (Many years later, however, it became an inspiration to other letter-writing couples.) The fundamental ambiguity between the twin public and private nature of letters, I believe, was behind Lu Xun and Xu Guangping's choice of letters as the text through which they could reveal and conceal their private lives.

The unstated theme throughout *Letters between Two* and the original correspondence is Lu Xun and Xu Guangping's search for privacy. As Lu Xun became ever more famous in the late 1920s and early 1930s, and as they both became 'an object in the public realm', the more they came to value their personal privacy. Their correspondence shows them seeking the privacy of a married couple, free from gossip and speculation about their relationship, free to spend time alone together without social condemnation. It also shows them in pursuit of their individual privacy: he did not discuss his wife or his estranged brother with her; she did not tell him about her early love affair. Writing and reading the letters reinforced the bond between them, creating their own world of intimacy; publication protected their intimacy.

Although the understanding of privacy has become more comprehensive in the last decades of the twentieth century, the philosophical, sociological, and legal literature on privacy in Western countries has been characterized as chaotic.[1] Privacy nevertheless demands attention because it is both an immensely powerful and a hotly contested interest. Disagreements cover considerable ground: many people accept the existence of a need for privacy but argue about its contents, functions, and values; others deny its universality and its independence as a moral interest.[2] Two questions arising from this study are whether there is a Chinese concept (or set of concepts) of privacy, and whether there is a concept (or set of concepts) of privacy that is uniquely Chinese.

The preceding chapters have shown that Lu Xun and Xu Guangping maintained a coherent and consistent sense of privacy. There is also evidence that their views were not identical, although Lu Xun's dominance as editor makes it difficult to tell to what extent Xu Guangping's ideas on privacy may have differed from his. Since both of them are indisputably Chinese, then the evidence regarding these two is sufficient to establish that at least two Chinese people writing in the 1920s and 1930s have two clear but distinct ideas on privacy.

Although Lu Xun cannot be considered a representative figure in modern Chinese literature, his status made his views influential. While many contemporary readers of *Letters between Two* were unaware of what kind of things Lu Xun left out in the letters, an acute reader would deduce that at least some personal information was missing, judging from clues such as the partial suppression of the letters around the time of Dragon Boat Day in Part I of *Letters between Two* and the use of initials in their terms of address in Part III. The retained or added remarks on gossip, rumour, solitude, and private interests made Lu Xun's views clear to all readers: he invested great value in guarding the privacy of himself, his family, and his close friends.

Even if it were plausible to maintain that Lu Xun was a representative writer of the 1920s and 1930s and not merely an influential one, it would still not be enough to claim that Lu Xun's sense of privacy was widely shared. Lu Xun's contemporaries have not left equally rich or robust documentation of their correspondence from which their concepts or sense of privacy can be evaluated, but enough textual and biographical evidence remains to indicate a wide range of diversity even in the limited sphere of writing and publishing love-letters from extramarital affairs, even although the diversity is not explicitly acknowledged or discussed by Chinese writers. When it is claimed that Chinese people have no sense of privacy, the statement can be reduced to the lesser claim that Chinese concepts of privacy differ from Western concepts. However, there is no evidence to suggest that Chinese concepts of privacy have any characteristics that are uniquely Chinese. Influenced by factors such as current politics, local customs, gender, age, and personal circumstances, the concepts of privacy held by Chinese literary figures in the Republican period are infinitely varied.

Zhang Longxi complains that some scholars have a 'willful tendency' to see only differences between cultures, and to do so at the expense of ignoring internal differences.[3] It is an indisputable duty of teachers and researchers to search out differences between cultures, to identify them, to explain them (in terms of the native tradition or otherwise), and to try to understand them. At the same time, it is also important for scholars to emphasize that in the end, commonality—the experiences and values that we share as humans—is more important than difference. Privacy is a human rights issue: deny a sense of privacy to a national culture, or claim that it is substantially different, and we deny the people of that culture basic rights of association and communication. To establish that educated people in China in the 1920s and 1930s valued their privacy, and moreover that they enjoyed a range of different ideas and opinions in regard to privacy, is one outcome of this study of Lu Xun and Xu Guangping's intimate lives.

As a collection of love-letters published by its authors, *Letters between Two* is not unique. Its special quality lies in the extent and nature of its editing, which give it the status of a semi-fictional work comparable to the semi-autobiographical epistolary fiction of its time. As one of the very few letter collections where the original letters can be read alongside the published version, it also allows readers a unique perspective on what Lu Xun regarded as most private in his life. Finally, the correspondence allows us an authentic glimpse into the changing face of social life in China: how one couple in the public eye coped with new thinking on love, sex, and marriage.

Notes

Chapter 1. Introduction

1. I have not seen reference to a culture where writing exists but where letters are not exchanged in some form, although in principle this is not inevitable.
2. George Steiner, 'Literature and Post-History' in Steiner, *Language and Silence, Essays 1958–1966*, Penguin, Harmondsworth, 1969, pp. 333–45, esp. pp. 335–6.
3. Just how widespread this belief has become is illustrated in a *New York Times* bestseller by Robert Daley, *Year of the Dragon*, Warner Books, New York, 1981. The fact that housing conditions in New York's Chinatown are extremely cramped is repeatedly attributed throughout the novel to an intrinsic lack of privacy awareness in the Chinese as a race.
4. See the distinction between 'emic' and 'etic' universals in Donald E. Brown, *Human Universals*, McGraw-Hill, New York, 1991, pp. 48–9. I am excluding from this discussion the associated meaning of 'private' as in 'private property' or 'private enterprise'. See also Bonnie S. McDougall and Anders Hansson (eds.), *Chinese Concepts of Privacy*, Brill, Leiden, 2002.
5. A useful introduction to the literature on privacy is Ferdinand David Schoeman, *The Philosophical Dimensions of Privacy: An Anthology*, Cambridge University Press, Cambridge, 1984. See also McDougall, 'Chinese Concepts of Privacy Workshop Briefing paper: concepts of privacy in English (draft)' at www.arts.ed.ac.uk/asianstudies/privacyproject (2001).
6. A more recent version of the same argument appears in Cecile M. Jagodzinski, *Privacy and Print: Reading and Writing in Seventeenth-Century England*, University Press of Virginia, Charlottesville, 1999.
7. See Brown, *Human Universals*, pp. 66–8.
8. Brown, *Human Universals*, p. 135; P. Brown & S. C. Levinson, *Politeness: some universals in language usage*, Cambridge University Press, New York, 1987. See also Chapter 10.
9. The most comprehensive statement on the long-acknowledged relationship between letters and privacy is in Samuel H. Hofstadter and George Horowitz, *The Right of Privacy*, Central Book Company, New York, 1964, pp. 155–60.
10. See also Julie C. Inness, *Privacy, Intimacy and Isolation*, Oxford University Press, New York, 1992, pp. 6, 9, 33, 63, 74, 78–81, and 83; Judith Jarvis Thomson, 'The Right to Privacy' and Ruth Davison, 'Privacy and the limits of law', both reprinted in Schoeman, *Philosophical Dimensions of Privacy*, pp. 272–89 and 346–402; see esp. pp. 275, 351. See also George Steiner, 'The Distribution of Discourse' in *George Steiner: A reader*, Penguin, Harmondsworth, 1984, p. 254.

11. *Lu Xun yanjiu shulu* was completed in December 1984 but was not published until 1987 for reasons that are not clear. The tables of contents in the books listed in the section on biographical studies do not mention Zhu An by name at all, and the tables of contents in the section on Lu Xun's writings do not feature LDS as a major work in its own right. The first periodical articles on Zhu An appear in 1983 and 1984, along with an article on Lu Xun's marriage and home life in 1983. The only book-length study on LDS is Wang Dehou's; there are a small number of journal articles on it in 1980–3.
12. See also Xu Guangping, *Xinwei de jinian* [In grateful commemoration], Renmin wenxue chubanshe, Beijing, 1951, pp. 17–20.
13. Zhou Zuoren's eldest son, Zhou Fengyi, also spent much of his adult life writing about his uncle; he died in 1997, having confided to Japanese scholars that what he had written was mostly false, and that he did not dare write truthfully.
14. Lin Zhihao, 'Shinian xieshou gong jianwei—Lu Xun he Xu Guangping' [Ten years of shared adversity hand-in-hand: Lu Xun and Xu Guangping], *Shiyue*, no. 77 (April 1991), pp. 182–6 and 182.
15. Ji Weizhou *et al.* (eds.), *Lu Xun yanjiu shulu*, pp. 725–8.
16. Chen Shuyu, *Xu Guangping yi sheng* [A life of Xu Guangping], Tianjin renmin chubanshe, Tianjin, 1981, p. 121.

Chapter 2. Xu Guangping 'in the Front Row': 1898–1925

1. LDSYJ, pp. 5–7; Letter 1, 11 March 1925.
2. From Xu Guangping's earliest account of her childhood, 'Wo de xiaoxue shidai' [My time at primary school], first published in 1939; see *Xu Guangping*, pp. 116–21; reprinted in XGPWJ, vol. 1, pp. 7–12.
3. According to reminiscences by Yu Lan, the actress who was cast as Xu Guangping in a film biography of Lu Xun in 1960, Xu Guangping told her that her paternal grandfather was the governor [*xunfu*] of Chekiang; Yu Lan, 'Xu Guangping de fengcai' [Xu Guangping's graciousness], *Xu Guangping*, pp. 43–50 and 44.
4. The movement to abolish footbinding started in the late Qing but did not have great effect until stronger measures were adopted after 1912; see Henrietta Harrison, *The Making of the Republican Citizen: Political Ceremonies and Symbols in China, 1911–1929*, Oxford University Press, Oxford, 2000, pp. 72–8 and 197–9.
5. LDSYJ, p. 163; Letter 100, 15 December 1926.
6. Xu Guangping's memoirs are not very clear about her extended family, and these details have been collected from several different sources, including 'Wo de douzheng shi' [My history of struggle], written in 1964; see *Xu Guangping*, pp. 109–15, esp. 109–10; reprinted in XGPWJ, vol. 1, pp. 92–9.
7. From an undated essay by Xu Guangping, 'Xiang raoluan, bu shi xuexi' [Like trouble, not study] in *Xu Guangping*, pp. 122–7 and 124.

8. Xu Guangping, 'Wo de xiaoxue shidai' p. 117 and 'Wo de douzheng shi', pp. 112–13; Yu Lan, 'Xu Guangping de fengcai', p. 46.
9. Xu Guangping gives at least three different versions of how she escaped footbinding. In the account she gave the actress Yu Lan in 1960, 'Xu Guangping de fengcai', p. 44, she does not mention her age. The next is her 1964 memoir, 'Wo de douzheng shi', p. 11; in this she is eight *sui*. The third is her undated memoir first published in 2000, 'Wo de tongnian' [My childhood] in *Xu Guangping jinian ji*, pp. 121–4, where she is six *sui*.
10. 'Wo de douzheng shi', p. 110.
11. Again, there are slightly different accounts in Yu Lan, 'Xu Guangping de fengcai', pp. 45–6; Xu Guangping, 'Wo de douzheng shi', p. 115, and 'Wo de tongnian', pp. 123–4.
12. Letter 7, 26 March 1925; see also 'Wo de douzheng shi', p. 114.
13. Letter 7, 26 March 1925.
14. Letter 23, 27 May 1925.
15. Yu Lan, 'Xu Guangping de fengcai', p. 46.
16. The mother in Guangping's story 'Bing tang hulu' [Candied haws], first published in 1946, appears to be based on Chang Ruilin; see *Xu Guangping jinian ji*, pp. 134–8.
17. LDSYJ, p. 120; Letter 78, 16 November 1926.
18. Reprinted in *Xu Guangping*, pp. 217–2 and XGPWJ, vol. 1, pp. 215–22. See also an undated and unpublished essay, probably written around 1945–6, 'Ji "wusi" shidai Tianjin de ji ge nüxing' [Recalling some women in Tientsin at the time of May Fourth] in *Xu Guangping*, pp. 210–12 and XGPWJ, vol. 1, pp. 209–12.
19. Letter 30, 17 June 1925; LBT, pp. 115–16.
20. Lee Chae-Jin, *Zhou Enlai: The Early Years*, Stanford University Press, Stanford, 1994, pp. 111–12, 125, and 135. For the anti-Japanese boycott in Tientsin, see pp. 141ff.
21. The college was founded in 1908 under the name Jingshi nüzi shifan xuetang; in 1912 its name was changed to Beijing nüzi shifan xuexiao; in 1919 it was renamed Guoli Beijing nüzi gaodeng shifan xuexiao; in 1924 it was again renamed Guoli Beijing nüzi shifan daxue; see Chen Shuyu, *Lu Xun zai Beijing* [Lu Xun in Beijing], Tianjin renmin chubanshe, Tianjin, 1978, p. 86. Hereinafter the college is referred to as Women's Normal College in the main text and WNC in the notes.
22. See Xu Guangping, 'Wo suo jing de Xu Shouchang xiansheng', first published in 1948 following Xu Shouchang's assassination; reprinted in Ma Tiji, comp., *Xu Guangping yi Lu Xun*, pp. 191–8 and XGPWJ, vol. 1, pp. 195–202.
23. See next chapter for references on Zhou Zuoren.
24. In Letter 23, 26 May 1925 (LBT, pp. 94–6), Xu Guangping mentions her illness and her attempted suicide but not Li Xiaohui, and the reference to her suicide attempt was deleted before publication in LDS. In January 1940, she wrote a fictionalized account of her illness and her cousin's death, which is classified as 'autobiography' in XGPWJ, vol. 1, pp. 19–22 and included in

the autobiographical section of *Xu Guangping*, pp. 128–31. In this account, 'Xin nian' [New Year], the protagonist is called Xia (Guangping's childhood name) and her cousin is called Hui (as in Li Xiaohui); her attempted suicide is not mentioned. At the end, the narrator comments that eighteen years on (i.e. since 1922), even the boy's family had probably forgotten the date, but not Xia, 'because it had broken a virgin's pure heart, which would never be restored'. This should not be taken as evidence that Xu Guangping was literally a virgin in 1922.

Teng huang [literally, rattan-yellow] is also known as *yu huang* [jade-yellow] and *yue huang* [moon-yellow], the resin of *Garcinia morella*. Described as sour and astringent in taste, it is toxic when taken internally but is used externally for carbuncles, skin infection, and gingivitis. It would have been easily available from pharmarcists. I am indebted to Bridie Andrews for this identification.

25. Letter 9, 6 April 1925; LBT, p. 48.
26. For speaking out in class, see LDSYJ, p. 6, Letter 1, 11 March 1925. Her article, 'Gongyuan he shaonian' [Parks and youth], was published in *Chenbao fukan* on 18 September 1923 under the pen-name Guizhen; reprinted in XGPWJ, vol. 1, pp. 223–6.
27. 'Yixi renshi de Lushan' [A dim recollection of Mount Lu], first published in the 16th anniversary issue of the WNC journal in 1924; reprinted in *Xu Guangping*, pp. 250–3 and XGPWJ, vol. 1, pp. 327–31.
28. LDSYJ, p. 20; Letter 13, 16 April 1925. Wang Dehou comments that lectures on 'physiology' are out of place in a course on literature and were probably about sex.
29. LDSYJ, p. 18; Letter 57, 14 October 1926 and Letter 58, 20 October 1926; LBT, pp. 199 and 204. See also Chapter 14.
30. Xu Guangping frequently alluded to the WNC affair in her memoirs; see, for example, *Xinwei de jinian*, pp. 33–49 (originally published 1940) and *Guanyu Lu Xun de shenghuo*, pp. 8–9 (originally published 1941); see also Chen Shuyu, *Lu Xun zai Beijing*, pp. 83–99.
31. Wang Shiqing, *Lu Xun: A Biography*, edited by Bonnie S. McDougall and Tang Bowen, Foreign Languages Press, Peking, 1984, p. 181; Fan Zhiting, *Lu Xun yu Xu Guangping*, p. 29.
32. For the large demonstrations accompanying Sun Yat-sen's funeral in 1925, see Henrietta Harrison, *The Making of the Republican Citizen*, pp. 337–44.
33. LDYYJ, pp. 36–7; Letter 7, 26 March 1925; Letter 24, 30 May 1925; Letter 30, 17 June 1925; LBT, pp. 36–40, 97–100, and 113–17. See also Chapter 16.

Chapter 3. Lu Xun's 'Life without Love': 1881–1925

1. Letter 2, 11 March 1925; LBT, p. 22.
2. For an account of Lu Xun's family origins and early life see Leo Ou-fan Lee, *Voices from the Iron House: A Study of Lu Xun*, Bloomington, Indiana University Press, 1987.

3. Lu Rui was born in 1857. She learned to read later in life and adapted to social change by unbinding her feet and cutting her hair short.
4. Lu Xun's grandfather, Zhou Fuqing (1837–1904), outlived Lu Xun's father, Zhou Fengyi (1860–96).
5. Lu Xun's younger brother was born in 1885; a sister was born in 1888 but died in infancy; his third brother was also born in 1888; another brother was born in 1893 and died in 1898. For Lu Xun's relationships with his brothers, see McDougall, 'Brotherly Love: Lu Xun, Zhou Zuoren and Zhou Jianren' in Christina Neder *et al.* (eds.), *China in seinen biographischen Dimensionen: Gedenkschrift für Helmut Martin*, Harrassowitz, Wiesbaden, 2001, pp. 259–76.
6. For an account of the late Qing programme to send Chinese students abroad, see Huang Fu-ch'ing, *Chinese Students in Japan in the late Ch'ing Period*, Centre for East Asian Cultural Studies, Tokyo, 1982 and Paula Harrell, *Sowing the Seeds of Change: Chinese Students, Japanese Teachers, 1895–1905*, Stanford University Press, Stanford, 1992.
7. For a description of the college see Huang, *Chinese Students in Japan*, pp. 103–5 and Harrell, *Sowing the Seeds of Change*, pp. 34–5 and 70.
8. Zhu An was born in 1879. Most of what we know about her comes from Yu Fang, *Wo jiyi zhong de Lu Xun xiansheng*, pp. 135–48; also cited in Sun Yu, *Lu Xun yu Zhou Zuoren* [Lu Xun and Zhou Zuoren], Hebei renmin chubanshe, Shijiazhuang, 1997, pp. 143–4, and LDSYJ, p. 265. Until the end of the 1980s, most mainland publications were notably reticent about Zhu An. The otherwise helpful compilation by Li Helin *et al.*, *Lu Xun shengping shiliao huibian* [Historical materials on Lu Xun's life], vol. 1, Renmin wenxue chubanshe, Tianjin, 1981, does not give her birthdate; *Lu Xun jianming cidian* [Simple Lu Xun dictionary], edited by Zhi Kejian, Gansu jiaoyu chubanshe, Lanzhou, 1990, mentions the marriage only briefly and Zhu An's name is not indexed. One of the first references to Lu Xun's wife in English is in Jonathan Spence's *The Gate of Heavenly Peace: The Chinese and Their Revolution, 1895–1980*, Penguin Books, Harmondsworth, 1982; the first systematic study of her life in English is Eva Hung's 'Reading Between the Lines: the Life of Zhu An (1878–1947)', in Neder (ed.) *China in seinen biographischen Dimensioneu*, pp. 245–58. I am grateful to Dr Hung for showing me an early version of this paper.
9. Wu Zuoqiao, *Lu Xun shuxin gouchen* [Delving for Lu Xun's letters], Dongbei shifan daxue chubanshe, Changchun, 1994, pp. 37–8.
10. Wu Zuoqiao, *Lu Xun shuxin gouchen*, pp. 41–2.
11. Huang, *Chinese Students in Japan*, pp. 145–6; Harrell, *Sowing the Seeds of Change*, pp. 102–6.
12. Although Lu Xun was very much influenced by Liang Qichao's ideas, Liang Qichao seems not to have noticed Lu Xun's early journalism. For a comparison of the two, see Wang Qiang, 'Lu Xun yu Liang Qichao' [Lu Xun and Liang Qichao], *Lu Xun yanjiu*, no. 14 (1989), pp. 259–75.
13. Niu Daifeng, *Lu Xun zhuan*, pp. 77–9. Some years later, Zhou Enlai also gave up the attempt and returned to China to enrol in the newly established Nankai

University. For the general difficulty of gaining university entrance see Huang, *Chinese Students in Japan*, p. 79.

14. Niu Daifeng, *Lu Xun zhuan*, pp. 88–9.
15. LDSYJ, p. 287. It is not clear when Lu Xun first contracted this disease.
16. Zhang Juxian and Zhang Tierong (eds.), *Zhou Zuoren nianpu*, pp. 56–7, and Appendix 2, pp. 942 and 946. Unless otherwise specified, references to Zuoren's life are from this source. Perry Link suggests that magazines at this period printed stories by men using feminine pseudonyms because women writers were so few; see Perry E. Link, *Mandarin Ducks and Butterflies: Popular Fiction in Early Twentieth-Century Chinese Cities*, University of California Press, Berkeley, 1981, p. 171.
17. Zhou Xiashou [Zhou Zuoren], *Lu Xun de gujia*, pp. 176 and 188, and *Lu Xun xiaoshuo li de renwu*, p. 161.
18. Zhou Xiashou, *Lu Xun de gujia*, pp. 179–80, 182–3, 193, and 199.
19. Guo Moruo married a nurse; other Chinese students married maids or waitresses. It was difficult for Chinese students to pursue affairs with young women of their own social class; see Huang, *Chinese Students in Japan*, p. 96, and Harrell, *Sowing the Seeds of Change*, pp. 84–5.
20. For brothel visits by Yu Dafu see 'Yi feng xin' [A Letter], originally published in *Dongfang zazhi*, no. 21 (25 January 1924), January 1924; reprinted in *Yu Dafu wen ji* [Yu Dafu's collected works], Sanlian shudian, Hong Kong, 1985, vol. 3, pp. 78–83; reprinted as *Zhi M jun F jun* [To M and F] in Luo Jiongguang (ed.) *Xiandai zuojia shuxin* [Letters by modern writers], Wenxin chubanshe, Zhengzhou, 1993, pp. 93–9 (M and F presumably stand for Guo Moruo and Cheng Fangu). Yu Dafu also mentions his attraction for brothels in an essay about his departure from Japan in 1922, 'Guihang' [Homeward voyage], originally published in *Chuangzao*, vol. 2, no. 2 (28 February 1924) under the title 'Zhongtu' [Midway journey]; reprinted in *Yu Dafu wen ji*, vol. 3, pp. 14–21. For dates, see Qin Xianci, 'Nianbiao' [Chronology] in *Yu Dafu*, edited by Zhou Yushan, Guangfu shuju, Taibei, 1987, pp. 71–80.
21. Hata Nobuko was born in 1888, the eldest of five children in a working-class Tokyo family. She has received an almost uniformly bad press in China, although as shown below she was initially on good terms with her elder brother-in-law. Xu Shouchang makes no mention of her in his memoirs of their life in Tokyo.
22. Song Jing, 'Min yuan qian de Lu Xun xiansheng' [Mr Lu Xun before 1911] in *Lu Xun huiyi lu (zhuanzhu)*, vol. 1, pp. 97–104; see p. 99.
23. Xie Dexi, *Lu Xun zai Shaoxing-fu zhongxuetang* [Lu Xun at the Shaoxing prefectural middle school], excerpted in Li Helin, *Lu Xun shengping shiliao huibian*, pp. 198–9.
24. See 'Lu Xun zai Shaoxing huodong jianbiao' [A brief chart of Lu Xun's activities in Shaoxing] in Li Helin, *Lu Xun shengping shiliao huibian*, p. 280.
25. This story is not included in the Foreign Languages Press translations but can be found under the title 'Remembrances of the Past' in Lyell's translations of

Lu Xun's fiction, *Diary of a Madman and Other Stories*, University of Hawaii Press, Honolulu, 1990, pp. 3–17.

26. Li Helin, *Lu Xun shengping shiliao huibian*, pp. 261–2. According to the account given by Lu Xun in 'Fan Ainong', he only submitted his resignation at the school after receiving the offer from Nanking; he does not mention his application to Shanghai.
27. Hata Yoshiko, born 1897, was Nobuko's youngest sister; the two other children had died young. Her brother returned to Japan in 1912, came back for a visit in 1914, and returned again to Tokyo in 1915.
28. For information on Zhou Jianren's marital affairs, see Yao Xipei, 'Wo suo tan Lu Xun jiazu fengbo—Badaowan fangchan "yiyue" yinchu de huati' [My comments on the storm in Lu Xun's family: topics arising from the 'Agreement' about the Badaowan property], *Lu Xun yanjiu yuekan*, no. 188 (December 1997). On the wedding and Lu Xun's absence, see p. 51.
29. The elder daughter died in 1929; the younger outlived him.
30. Zhou Zuoren, 'Guanyu Lu Xun' [About Lu Xun] in *Lu Xun zishu*, pp. 267–7, esp. p. 275.
31. Zhou Xiashou, *Lu Xun de guijia*, pp. 194, 168–70, 202, and 224–9.
32. Ibid.
33. Shu Wu, 'Xiongdi yiyi sishi nian—Lu Xun, Zhou Zuoren shihe yiqian de xiongdi guanxi' [Brothers in harmony for forty years: the brotherly relationship between Lu Xun and Zhou Zuoren before the rupture], *Lu Xun yanjiu niankan*, 1991–92 heben, pp. 647–87; see pp. 680–1.
34. For Lu Xun's own explanation of his pen-names see Xu Shouchang, *Wang you Lu Xun yinxiang ji* [Impressions of my late friend Lu Xun] in *Lu Xun huiyi lu (zhuanzhu)*, vol. 1, pp. 249–52.
35. Idem.
36. 'Sui gan lu (40)', first published in XQN in 1919; reprinted in LXQJ, vol. 1, 321–3; translated as 'Random Thoughts (40)' in LXSW, vol. 2, 34–6. See also LDSYJ, p. 295.
37. First published in XQN in 1919; see LXQJ, vol. 1, 129–43; translated as 'What is required of us as fathers today' in LXSW, vol. 2, 53–69.
38. See Sun Fuyuan, 'Wusi yundong zhong de Lu Xun xiansheng' [Mr Lu Xun in the May Fourth movement] in *Lu Xun huiyi lu (sanpian)*, vol. 1, pp. 74–6.
39. Chen Shuyu, *Lu Xun zai Beijing*, p. 143.
40. Mills notes his relative obscurity at this time compared with his younger brother; see 'Lu Xun: Literature and Revolution', p. 196. In 1920, for example, Zhou Zuoren joined the board of the Peking University student journal *Xin chao* [Renaissance] and became one of the co-founders of the Literary Association.
41. Shu Wu, 'Xiongdi yiyi sishi nian', pp. 682–3.
42. These included Xu Qinwen, Yu Fen, Rou Shi, and Feng Xuefeng; see Xu Qinwen, *Xuexi Lu Xun xiansheng*, p. 24. For further references to Xu Qinwen and Yu Fen, see below, pp. 24–5; for further references to Rou Shi and Feng Xuefeng, see below, pp. 60–1.

43. Jing Youlin, 'Lu Xun huiyi duanpian' [Fragmentary reminiscences of Lu Xun] in *Lu Xun huiyi lu (zhuanzhu)*, vol. 1, pp. 119–205; see p. 167.
44. See Xu Guangping, *Lu Xun huiyi lu*, pp. 51–2; Niu Daifeng, *Lu Xun zhuan*, pp. 224 and 243.
45. Zhou Jianren later claimed that the number of servants was an unnecessary extravagance on Nobuko's part; see Zhou Jianren, 'Lu Xun he Zhou Zuoren' [Lu Xun and Zhou Zuoren] in *Lu Xun huiyi lu (sanpian)*, vol. 1, p. 441; *Zhou Zuoren nianpu*, p. 239.
46. Xu Xiansu (1901–86) was the younger sister of Xu Qinwen (1897–1984); see Xu Xiansu, 'Huiyi Lu Xun xiansheng' [Reminiscences of Mr Lu Xun] in *Lu Xun huiyi lu (sanpian)*, vol. 1, pp. 309–25; Xu Qinwen, *Xuexi Lu Xun xiansheng*, pp. 1–3, 23–8; Wu Zuoqiao, *Lu Xun shuxin gouchen*, pp. 67–78, 105–7; Ma Tiji, *Lu Xun shenghuo zhong de nüxing* [The women in Lu Xun's life], Zhishi chubanshe, Beijing, 1996, pp. 110–21; Ma Tiji (ed.) *Wo keyi ai—Lu Xun de qinglian shijie* [I can love: Lu Xun's world of passion], Sichuan wenyi chubanshe, Chengdu, 1995, pp. 94–104.
47. See Yu Fang, *Wo jiyi zhong de Lu Xun xiansheng*, pp. 1–10; Xu Qinwen, *Xuexi Lu Xun xiansheng*, pp. 23–8; see also Chen Shuyu, *Lu Xun zai Beijing*, pp. 145–7. Yu Fang and her two sisters moved to Peking after their mother died; the house in Brick Pagoda Lane was owned by a friend of their father's.
48. See the exchange of letters between Zhou Zuoren and Hu Shi in Hu Shi *et al.*, *Hu Shi laiwang shuxin xuan* [Selected letters by and to Hu Shi], Zhonghua shuju, Hong Kong, 1983, pp. 131–3. Zhou Jianren does not acknowledge their help in his 1981 memoir 'Lu Xun yu Zhou Zuoren', in *Lu Xun huiyi lu (sanpian)*, vol. 1, pp. 440–50.
49. Shu Wu, 'Xiongdi yiyi sishi nian', p. 682.
50. LXQJ, vol. 14, p. 447. Yu Dafu's first contact with Zuoren was in November 1921, when he sent him a copy of his just-published collection *Chenlun* [Sinking]; Zuoren defended its artistic merits against those who attacked it on moral grounds. Yu Dafu wrote letters to Zuoren in October and November 1923, respectfully addressing him as 'Mr Zhongmi' and signing himself Yu Dafu; there are no letters to Lu Xun. For the letters, see *Yu Dafu wen ji*, vol. 9, pp. 332–4. See also Yu Dafu's 'Haishang tongxun' [Correspondence at sea], written in October 1923 on his way from Shanghai to Peking and first published in *Chuangzao zhoukan*, no. 24 (20 October 1923); reprinted in *Yu Dafu wen ji*, vol. 3, pp. 71–7; the unnamed addressees are Guo Moruo and Cheng Fangwu. Yu Dafu's first visit to Badaowan was in February 1923.
51. Lin Yutang (1895–1976) was at the time a professor of English at Peking University. For his up and down relationship with Lu Xun, see Chen Shuyu, ' "Xiangde" yu "shuli"—Lin Yutang yu Lu Xun de jiaowang shishi ji qi wenhua sikao'. ['Complementary' and 'estranged': the historical facts of Lin Yutang's association with Lu Xun, and reflections on culture], *Xin wenxue shiliao*, no. 67 (May 1995), pp. 125–37 and 94.

52. There are many accounts of the dispute: see the summaries in McDougall, 'Brotherly love' and Zhang Juxiang and Zhang Tierong, *Zhou Zuoren nianpu*, pp. 237–42.
53. Xu Xiansu, 'Huiyi Lu Xun xiansheng', p. 313; Zhou Jianren, 'Lu Xun yu Zhou Zuoren', in *Lu Xun huiyi lu (sanpian)*, vol. 1, p. 443.
54. See Yu Fang, *Wo jiyi zhong de Lu Xun xiansheng*, pp. 1–10; Xu Xiansu, 'Huiyi Lu Xun xiansheng', p. 313; Xu Qinwen, *Xuexi Lu Xun xiansheng*, pp. 23–8; Xu Qinwen, '*Lu Xun riji* zhong de wo' [Myself in Lu Xun's diary] in *Lu Xun huiyi lu (zhuanzhu)*, vol. 3, pp. 1226–333, esp. pp. 1236–45; see also Chen Shuyu, *Lu Xun zai Beijing*, pp. 145–7.
55. Yu Fang, pp. 139–40; also quoted by Sun Yu, *Lu Xun yu Zhou Zuoren*, pp. 159 and LDSYJ, p. 293.
56. For a description and map of the rooms and furniture used by Lu Xun and Zhu An see Yu Fang, 'Beijing Zhuanta hutong liushiyi hao' [No. 61, Brick Pagoda Lane, Peking], *Lu Xun yanjiu ziliao*, no. 9 (1982), pp. 183–94.
57. Ma Tiji, *Wo keyi ai*, pp. 46–9.
58. For the correspondence, see Zhou Zuoren, *Zhi Tang shuxin* [Zhi Tang's letters], Huaxia chubanshe, Beijing, 1995, pp. 250–8.
59. According to his 1938 memoir, Yu Dafu's first meeting with Shuren took place at Brick Pagoda Lane in the winter of 1923, but this is an error; see Yu Dafu, 'Huiyi Lu Xun' in *Huiyi Lu Xun ji qita* [Reminscences of Lu Xun, and others] edited by Zhou Li'an, Yuzhou feng chubanshe, Shanghai, 1940, pp. 1–30; see pp. 4–6. Yu Dafu wrote three tributes to Lu Xun: the first two, written in 1936 and 1937 respectively, were both very short; the third, 'Huiyi Lu Xun', was written in 1938 and published in two parts in 1938 and 1939. They are separately reprinted in *Lu Xun huiyi lu (sanpian)* according to the date of writing. According to Lu Xun's diary, Yu Dafu's visit was on 15 November; he came again in December. See also Niu Daifeng, *Lu Xun zhuan*, p. 204; Ma Tiji, *Wo keyi ai*, pp. 59–60; LDSYJ, p. 292.
60. Zhang Tingqian became a well-known writer under his pen-name Chuan Dao.
61. Yu Dafu and Sun Quan were married in 1920, and their first child, a son called Longer, was born in 1922.
62. See letter to Guo Moruo and Cheng Fangwu dated 7 March 1924; published in *Chuangzao zhoukan* no. 46 (28 March 1924) under the title 'Beiguo weiyin'; reprinted in Luo Jiongguang, *Xiandai zuojia shuxin ji*, pp. 100–5.
63. His lecture notes were mimeographed and later issued as *An Outline History of Fiction* (1921), which in turn became a two-part *Brief History of Chinese Fiction*, first published in 1923 and 1924.
64. LXSW, vol. 2, pp. 85–92.
65. Niu Daifeng, *Lu Xun zhuan*, p. 291.
66. There are many accounts of the layout and daily life at West Third Lane. See for instance Xu Qinwen, *Xuexi Lu Xun xiansheng*, pp. 29–33, 37–44.
67. Niu Daifeng, *Lu Xun zhuan*, p. 256.

68. Yu Fang, 'Diyi ci dao Lu Xun xiansheng de xin shi zuo ke' [The first time I visited Mr Lu Xun's new home], *Lu Xun yanjiu ziliao*, no. 9 (1982), pp. 195–200.
69. Niu Daifeng, *Lu Xun zhuan*, p. 245; Ma Tiji, *Lu Xun: wo keyi ai*, pp. 69–71.
70. Shu Wu, *Zhou Zuoren de shifei gongguo* [Zhou Zuoren's merits and faults], Renmin wenxue chubanshe, Beijing, 1993, pp. 339–42.
71. Chen Shuyu, *Lu Xun zai Beijing*, p. 90.
72. In 'Shuo huxu', LXQJ, vol. 1, pp. 174–80; 'My Moustache', LXSW, vol. 2, pp. 103–8.
73. See 'Wo he *Yu si* de shitong', LXQJ, vol. 1, pp. 164–75; 'The History of my Connection with Thread of Talk', LXSW, vol. 3, pp. 62–71; McDougall, *The Introduction of Western Literary Theories into China 1919–1925*, Center for East Asian Cultural Studies, Tokyo, 1971, p. 49; McDougall, 'The Impact of Western Literary Trends' in Merle Goldman (ed.) *Modern Chinese Literature in the May Fourth Era*, Harvard University Press, Cambridge, MA, 1977, pp. 37–62.
74. Not much is known about these young women, apart from Xu Xiansu. Lu Xun continued to entertain young women at his home in the spring of 1925: Xu Xiansu, who was presented with a copy of the newly printed *Symbols of Anguish* on 8 March, remained one of his most frequent visitors and correspondents. Lu Xun's first biographer, Cao Juren, believed that Lu Xun and Xu Xiansu were lovers: see his 'Wo yu Lu Xun' [I and Lu Xun] and 'Lu Xun yu wo' [Lu Xun and I] in *Lu Xun huiyi lu (sanpian)*, vol. 2, pp. 799–804 and 805–10, esp. pp. 801 and 808.
75. From 'Xiwang', first published in *Yusi* in 1925 and reprinted in *Yecao* [Weeds] in 1927; reprinted in LXQJ, vol. 2, pp. 177–9; 'Hope', LXSW, vol. 1, pp. 326–7.

Chapter 4. Courtship: March 1925–August 1926

1. Niu Daifeng, *Lu Xun zhuan*, p. 363.
2. Xu Guangping's earliest account of the Women's College Affair is in *Xinwei de jinian*, pp. 33–49, written in 1940. Coming so long after the event, it should be regarded as a valuable but not necessarily wholly reliable source. Lin Zhuofeng is also known as Lin Zhenpeng.
3. Letter 1, 11 March 1925; LBT, pp. 1–21.
4. Letter 2, 11 March 1925; LBT, pp. 22–5. According to Lu Xun's diary he received Xu Guangping's letter on 11 March and replied to it the following day, 12 March.
5. For further discussion on the terms of address used by Lu Xun and Xu Guangping and the appearance of their letters, see Chapter 10.
6. Founded in December 1924 by the students' Rose Society [Qiangwei she], it published 50 issues before its final special edition.
7. Wang Jiuling was promoted from Acting to full Minister of Education on 15 March, despite protests from the educational sector; the following day, the Police Commissioner provided him with an armed escort to assume his position.

8. For a brief sketch of his life and an introduction to his work, see Li Miaogen (ed.), *Zhang Shizhao wen xuan* [Zhang Shizhao's selected works], Yuandong chubanshe, Shanghai, 1996. After 1949, Zhang was appointed a member of the National Committee of the Chinese People's Political Consultative Conference and a member of the Political and Legal Commitee in the State Council headed by Zhou Enlai; also president of the Central Historical Museum in Beijing (see also following note).
9. See Lee Chae-Jin, *Zhou Enlai: The Early Years*, pp. 74, 161, 192 (n. 123) and 207 (n. 116). Lee points out that Zhou Enlai's family may have been distant relatives of Zhou Shuren's family, since both were originally from Shaoxing.
10. Letter 5, 20 March 1925; Letter 10, 8 April 1925; Letter 11, 10 April 1925; LBT, pp. 34, 52, 58.
11. Xu Guangping, *Xinwei de jinian*, pp. 33–5.
12. Letter 12, 14 April 1925; LBT, pp. 59–62.
13. LDSYJ, p. 255; Letter 13, 16 April 1925; LBT, pp. 63–5.
14. See Chapter 14.
15. Letter 14, 20 April 1925; LBT, pp. 66–7.
16. Letter 15, 22 April 1925; LBT, pp. 68–71.
17. For the circumstances of this publication, see Chen Shuyu, *Lu Xun zai Beijing*, pp. 37–40.
18. LXQJ, vol. 2, 195–7; translation in LXSW, vol. 1, 342–4. For a strictly non-biographical interpretation of 'Si huo' see Laura Wu, 'Paradox Lost in Retroactive Reading: Lu Xun's "Dead Fire"', *East Asia Forum* (University of Toronto Department of East Asian Studies), vol. 1 (October 1992), pp. 1–22.
19. Lee, *Voices from the Iron House*, p. 100.
20. LXQJ, vol. 2, p. 198; translation in LXSW, vol. 1, p. 345.
21. Lee, *Voices from the Iron House*, pp. 97–8.
22. For an attempt to correlate the prose poems in *Weeds* with Lu Xun's emotional state and involvement with Xu Guangping, see Liu Fuqin, *Lu Xun xin shi* [An intimate history of Lu Xun], Wenyi chubanshe, Shanghai, 1994, pp. 191–212.
23. Letter 16, 25 April 1925; LBT, pp. 72–6.
24. Letter 17, 28 April 1925; LBT, pp. 77–9.
25. Letter 18, 30 April 1925; LBT, pp. 80–3.
26. Letter 19, 3 May 1925; LBT, pp. 83–6.
27. A note in LDS between Letters 19 and 20 mentions a 'missing' letter from Lu Xun dated 8 May; however, Lu Xun does not record in his diary either writing or posting a letter to Xu Guangping on 8 or 9 May, and it might have been no more than a brief note. Xu Guangping acknowledges his 'letters of May 3 and May 8' in Letter 20, 9 May 1925; LBT, p. 88.
28. 'Huran xiangdao (7)', in LXQJ, vol. 3, pp. 60–1; translated as 'Sudden Notion No. 7' in LXSW, vol. 2, pp. 161–3.
29. Letter 21, 7 May 1925; LBT, p. 91.

30. Published in *Mangyuan*, No. 5. For Xu Guangping's pen-name, see Sun Fuyuan, 'Lu Xun xiansheng er san shi' [Two or three matters about Mr Lu Xun] in *Lu Xun huiyi lu (zhuanzhu)*, vol. 1, pp. 69–116; see p. 87.
31. Letter 22, 18 May 1925; LBT, pp. 92–3.
32. ' "Peng bi" zhi hou', in LXQJ, vol. 3, pp. 68–74; translated as 'After "knocking against the wall" ' in LXSW, vol. 2, pp. 171–7.
33. Letter 23, 27 May 1925; LBT, pp. 94–6.
34. *Xiandai pinglun*, vol. 1, no. 25; the issue was dated May 30 but was on sale the previous day.
35. Letter 24, 30 May 1925; LBT, pp. 97–100. The conventional belief that Chen Yuan singled out Lu Xun is probably mistaken. Lu Xun interpreted 'a certain locality' as Shaoxing, that is, referring to himself and Zuoren; see Sun Yu, *Lu Xun yu Zhou Zuoren*, pp. 220–3. His Letter 24 clearly refers to 'the others' or 'the other person', that is, the other person(s) from a certain department and a certain locality. See also Xu Guangping, *Lu Xun huiyi lu*, p. 12.
36. For more detail on the background of this term and its use by Lu Xun and then Xu Guangping, see Zhang Xiangtian, *Lu Xun riji shuxin shigao zhaji* [Notes on Lu Xun's diaries, letters, and poems], Sanlian chubanshe, Hong Kong, 1979, pp. 195–9.
37. 'Huran gandao (10)', in LXQJ, vol. 3, pp. 88–91; translation in LXSW, vol. 2, pp. 178–81; see also Pollard, 'Lu Xun's *Zawen*' in Leo Ou-fan Lee (ed.), *Lu Xun and His Legacy*, University of California Press, Berkeley, 1985, pp. 54–89; see p. 69. See also Letter 29.
38. LXQJ, vol. 3, pp. 75–80.
39. Letter 25, 1 June 1925; LBT, pp. 101–2. The remark about herself is deleted from LDS.
40. Letter 26, 2 June 1925; LBT, pp. 103–4.
41. Shen Jianshi, 'Wo suo renshi de Lu Xun xiansheng' [The Mr Lu Xun I knew] in *Lu Xun huiyi lu (sanpian)*, vol. 1, pp. 98–9.
42. Letter 27, 5 June 1925; LBT, pp. 105–8.
43. Letter 28, 12 June 1925; LBT, pp. 108–9.
44. Letter 29, 13 June 1925; LBT, pp. 109–13.
45. LXQJ, vol. 2, pp. 199–201; translated as 'The Good Hell That Was Lost' in LXSW, vol. 1, pp. 346–7.
46. LXQJ, vol. 2, pp. 202–3.
47. Lee, *Voices from the Iron House*, p. 109.
48. Letter 30, 17 June 1925; LBT, 113–17.
49. The reconstruction of these events is based on the OC; see LDSYJ, pp. 39–42.
50. This letter has been lost but its contents can be guessed at from Lu Xun's reply on 28 June 1925.
51. This part of the letter is omitted from LDS; see LDSYJ, pp. 40–2. The remainder appears in LDS as Letter 32, 28 June 1925; LBT, pp. 120–1.
52. This letter has also been lost but its contents can be guessed at from Lu Xun's reply on 29 June 1925.

53. Letter 33, 29 June 1925; LBT, pp. 121–3. The reference to having pressed down Xu Guangping's head is deleted from LDS; see LDSYJ, p. 42.
54. Omitted from LDS; see LDSYJ, pp. 43–5.
55. LDSYJ, p. 324. Wang believes they 'pledged their love' (*ding qing*) on Dragon Boat Day, not that they necessarily did or said anything special, but thereafter the letters were true love-letters; *ibid.*, p. 328. See also Li Yunjing, *Lu Xun de hunyin yu jiating*, pp. 78–83 and 84–91, and Ceng Zhizhong, *Sanrenxing*, pp. 138–52.
56. Letter 34, 9 July 1925; LBT, pp. 124–5.
57. LXQJ, vol. 2, pp. 204–6.
58. LXQJ, vol. 2, pp. 207–8; translation in LXSW, vol. 1, p. 348.
59. LXQJ, vol. 2, pp. 209–13; translation in LXSW, vol. 1, pp. 349–53.
60. The five letters are from Xu Guangping, dated 13 July 1925; from Lu Xun, dated 15 July 1925; from Xu Guangping, dated 15 July 1925; from Lu Xun, dated 16 July 1925; and from Xu Guangping, dated 17 July 1925; for the texts, see LDSYJ, pp. 45–57.
61. Letter 35, 29 or 30 July 1925; LBT, pp. 125–7.
62. In a letter to Wei Suyuan dated 29 December 1926, he wrote that she proof-read and copied manuscripts for him at this time, including part of *Fen*; LXQJ, vol. 11, p. 519. In 'Ma shang zhi ri ji' [A slapdash diary], he wrote that on 5 July, she copied out part of *Xiaoshuo jiu wen chao*; LXQJ, vol. 3, p. 33; see also *Lu Xun riji*, vol. 1, p. 514 and Chen Shuyu, *Xu Guangping yi sheng*, p. 32. As a rule Lu Xun avoided noting Xu Guangping's visits in his diary unless she was accompanied. See also Li Jiye, 'Jinian Xu Guangping tongzhi' [Commemorating comrade Xu Guangping] in *Xu Guangping*, pp. 4–5.
63. Xu Guangping, *Lu Xun huiyi lu*, pp. 3, 46–7.
64. Yu Dafu, 'Huiyi Lu Xun', pp. 13–14. Yu Dafu had resigned his position at Peking University in January 1925 for a teaching job in the arts faculty at the National Normal University in Wuchang. His wife and their first son remained in Peking. He left Wuchang in November 1925.
65. 'Liuyan he huanghua', in LXQJ, vol. 7, pp. 93–6.
66. 'Nüxiaozhang de nan-nü de meng', in LXQJ, vol. 7, pp. 290–9.
67. Fan Zhiting, *Lu Xun yu Xu Guangping*, p. 122.
68. Xu Guangping, *Lu Xun huiyi lu*, p. 10. Chinese scholars were for many years uncomfortable about this episode. There is no mention at all of Xu Guangping taking refuge in Lu Xun's home in Wang Shiqing's *Biography*, and even Wang Xiaoming, who discusses their relationship at length, fails to mention it (*Wufa zhimian de rensheng*, pp. 62–3 and 114–17). Lu Xun's diary makes no mention either of her temporary 'disappearance' or of her coming to stay in his house.
69. Li Yunjing, *Lu Xun de hunyin yu jiating*, pp. 92–7.
70. Xu Guangping recalled this scene in her Letter 47, 23 September 1926; LBT, p. 164.
71. Letter to Xu Qinwen, 30 September 1925, LXQJ, vol. 11, pp. 456–7.
72. Letter to Xu Qinwen, 29 September 1925, LXQJ, vol. 11, pp. 454–6.

73. LDSYJ, p. 318.
74. Chen Shuyu, 'Ai de kaige—Xu Guangping san pian yigao du hou' [Love's triumphal song: after reading three posthumous manuscripts by Xu Guangping], *Lu Xun yanjiu niankan*, 1990, pp. 613–17; see p. 614; the three manuscripts are published as an appendix, pp. 617–23. 'Tongxing-zhe' was originally published on 12 December in a supplement edited by Lu Xun for *Guomin xin bao* [The citizens' new journal]. The journal was an organ of the Nationalist Party in Peking, and Lu Xun edited supplements for it until it was closed down by the Peking government in early 1926.
75. XGPWJ, vol. 1, pp. 3–6; also reprinted as 'autobiography' in *Xu Guangping*, pp. 138–40.
76. Chen Shuyu, 'Ai de kaige', p. 615.
77. XGPWJ, vol. 1, 104–5; *Xu Guangping*, pp. 136–7.
78. 'Gudu-zhe', LXQJ, vol. 2, pp. 86–109; translated as 'The Misanthrope', LXSW, vol. 1, pp. 225–48; 'Shang shi', LXQJ, vol. 2, pp. 110–31; translated as 'Regret for the Past', LXSW, vol. 1, pp. 249–71. Wang Dehou believes that 'Mourning the Dead' sums up Lu Xun's attitudes to love, sex, and marriage up to 1925; LDSYJ, pp. 336–40. Zhou Zuoren, on the other hand, saw it as a disguised account of the rupture between himself and Lu Xun, like the story 'Dixiong' [Brothers], LXQJ, vol. 2, pp. 132–43; see his letter to Cao Juren in *Zhi Tang shuxin*, pp. 292–3.
79. Letter to Wei Suyuan, 29 December 1926, LXQJ, vol. 11, pp. 518–20.
80. Zhang Shizhao remained in Peking as Duan Qirui's secretary until the fall of the Duan government in April 1926, when he took refuge in the Japanese concession in Tientsin.
81. An account of Lu Xun's attacks on Chen Yuan, Zhang Shizhao, Gao Changhong, Xu Zhimo, Gu Jiegang and others can be found in Sun Yu (ed.), *Bei xiedu de Lu Xun* [The reviled Lu Xun], Qunyan chubanshe, Beijing, 1994, along with the texts attacking Lu Xun. See also Liang Shiqiu's comments in 'Lu Xun yu wo' in *Guanyu Lu Xun*, pp. 2–6.
82. 'Bing fei xianhua (3)', in LXQJ, vol. 3, pp. 148–56 (dated 22 November 1925); translated as 'Not Idle Chat (3)' in LXSW, vol. 2, pp. 205–11.
83. 'Guafu zhuyi' (23 November 1925); first published in *Funü zhoukan*, reprinted in LXQJ, vol. 1, pp. 262–9; translated as 'Guafuism', in LXSW, vol. 2, pp. 212–18.
84. Chuan Tang, 'Guanyu Nüshida shijian de yi shu shuxin' [A bundle of letters concerning the WCN affair], *Lu Xun yanjiu ziliao*, no. 4 (1990), pp. 338–44; Chen Shuyu, ' "Xiangde" yu "shuli" ', p. 127.
85. LXQJ, vol. 2, pp. 219–20; translated in LXSW, vol. 1, pp. 359–60. For the circumstances, see Xu Guangping, *Guanyu Lu Xun de shenghuo*, p. 9; Sun Fuyuan, 'Lu Xun xiansheng er san shi', pp. 86–9; Chen Shuyu, 'Ai de kaige', p. 615; Sun Yushi, 'Guanyu "La ye" ' [Concerning 'The blighted leaf'], *Lu Xun yanjiu yuekan*, no. 175 (November 1996), pp. 35–9. See also Lee, *Voices from the Iron House*, p. 215n.18.

86. 'Lun "Fei'e polai" yinggai huanxing', in LXQJ, vol. 1, pp. 270–81; translated as 'On Deferring Fair Play', in LXSW, vol. 2, pp. 228–37. For a summary of the debate, see Wang Shiqing, *Biography*, pp. 192–6.
87. There appears to be no documentary evidence to explain Lu Xun's animus against Hu Shi. Up until 1924 they had been on amicable terms, although Hu Shi had always been and continued to be closer to Zhou Zuoren. See Sun Yu, *Lu Xun yu Hu Shi: yingxiang ershi shiji Zhongguo wenhua de liang wei zhizhe* [Lu Xun and Hu Shi: two sages who have influenced 20th cent. Chinese culture], Liaoning renmin chubanshe, Shenyang, 2000.
88. Pollard, 'Lu Xun's *Zawen*', pp. 69–71; see also Wang Shiqing, *Biography*, pp. 196–200.
89. LXQJ, vol. 3, pp. 206–13; LXSW, vol. 2, pp. 241–5.
90. Xu Guangping, *Lu Xun huiyi lu*, p. 13. Lu Xun's diary does not record the demonstrations or even Xu Guangping's visit to his home that day. See also Xu Xiansu, 'Huiyi Lu Xun xiansheng', pp. 318–20.
91. His essays commemorating Liu Hezhen are typically cautious rather than revolutionary; see Eva Shan Chou, 'The Political Martyr in Lu Xun's Writings', *Asia Major*, 3rd series, vol. 12, pt. 2, pp. 139–62.
92. As for instance in 'Ke can yu ke xiao' in LXQJ, vol. 3, pp. 269–72; translated as 'A Tragi-comedy', in LXSW, vol. 2, pp. 264–6.
93. LXQJ, vol. 2, pp. 223–5; translation in LXSW, vol. 1, pp. 363–5.
94. Niu Daifeng, *Lu Xun zhuan*, p. 357.
95. 'Kong tan', in LXQJ, vol. 3, pp. 279–83; translated as 'Empty Talk', in LXSW, vol. 2, pp. 273–6.
96. The legal situation in regard to adulterous couples was complex, but whether under Qing law or the new Republican civil code of 1929–31, adultery was in principle punishable. See Kathryn Bernhardt, 'Women and the Law: Divorce in the Republican Period', in Kathryn Bernhardt and Philip C. C. Huang (eds.), *Civil Law in Qing and Republican China*, SMC Publishing, Taipei, 1994, pp. 187–214, esp. pp. 208–13. For the Qing code, see Xue Yunsheng, comp., *Du li chun yi* [Concentration on doubtful matters while pursuing the substatutes], Chengwen chubanshe, Taibei, 1970, vol. 5, p. 1079; translation in William C. Jones, *The Great Qing Code*, Clarendon Press, Oxford, 1994.
97. 'Yi Wei Suyuan jun', LXQJ, vol. 6, pp. 63–70; translated as 'In Memory of Wei Suyuan', in LXSW, vol. 4, pp. 65–70; dated 16 July 1934.
98. Xu Guangping, *Guanyu Lu Xun de shenghuo*, p. 10.
99. That is, she decided to return to Canton only after Lu Xun had accepted Lin's Amoy offer. See *Guanyu Lu Xun de shenghuo*, p. 10.
100. LDSYJ, p. 428.
101. LDSYJ, pp. 102–3.
102. LDSYJ, p. 131.
103. Xu Guangping, *Guanyu Lu Xun de shenghuo*, p. 10.
104. One of Lu Xun's Amoy students believed that it was Lu Xun's choice; see Zhuo Zhi, 'Lu Xun shi zhe yang zou de' [The way taken by Lu Xun] in *Lu Xun huiyi lu (sanpian)*, vol. 1, pp. 487–91.

105. LDSYJ, pp. 58–9.
106. The letters from 1926 are rarely explicit on these matters; see also Chapter 5 for further discussion.
107. 'Ji tanhua', in LXQJ, vol. 3, pp. 355–60; translated as 'Record of a Speech', LXSW, vol. 2, pp. 300–5.
108. Wei Suyuan promptly changed his name to Wei Shuyuan because the name Suyuan was so offensive. See Lu Xun's letter to him of 15 October 1926, LXQJ, vol. 11, pp. 487–8.
109. From Lu Xun's postscript to 'Record of a Speech'.

Chapter 5. Separation: September 1926–January 1927

1. Her father's younger brother.
2. LDSYJ, p. 58; Letter 37, 1–6 September 1926; LBT, pp. 134–40.
3. Letter 36, 4 September 1926; LBT, pp. 132–3.
4. Letter 38, 8 September 1926; LBT, pp. 140–1.
5. Letter 47, 23 September 1926; LBT, pp. 161–5.
6. LDSYJ, pp. 75–6; Letter 52, 7 October 1926; LBT, pp. 183–4.
7. Letter 51, 30 September and 4 October 1926; LBT, pp. 180–2.
8. LDSYJ, p. 60; Letter 38, 8 September 1926; LBT, pp. 140–1.
9. Letter 47, 23 September 1926; LBT, pp. 161–5.
10. Lim Boon Keng [Lin Wenqing] (1869–1957) spent his early life in the Malay Peninsula, which he wrote about in the semi-fictional *Tragedies of Eastern Life: An Introduction to the Probems of Social Psychology*, Commercial Press, Shanghai, 1927. For Lu Xun's views on him, see 'Hai shang tongxin', in LXQJ, vol. 3, pp. 398–403; translated as 'A Letter Written at Sea', in LXSW, vol. 2, pp. 323–7.
11. Tan Kha Kee [Chen Jiageng] (1847–1961), a Singaporean millionaire and philanthropist, founded the Jimei School in 1913 and Amoy University in 1921.
12. It seems that Lu Xun and Xu Guangping did not meet Wang Yunru (1900–1990) when they passed through Shanghai, but Jianren told Lu Xun about her: see Chapter 14.
13. LXQJ, vol. 2, pp. 339–431; partial English translation in LXSW, vol. 1, pp. 283–316. See also pp. 49 and 169. The title is thought to have been a deliberate variation on *Gu shi bian* (The study of ancient history), edited by Gu Jiegang *et al.*
14. LDSYJ, p. 152; Letter 93, 12 December 1926; LBT, pp. 296–300.
15. Letter 41, 12 September 1926; LBT, pp. 144–8.
16. Letter 42, 20 September 1926; Letter 60, 21 and 23 October 1926; LBT, pp. 149–52 and 208–13.
17. Letter 42, 20 September 1926; LBT, pp. 149–52.
18. Letter 46, 25 and 26 September 1926; LBT, pp. 157–61.
19. Letter 47, 23 September 1926; LBT, pp. 161–5.
20. LDSYJ, p. 70; Letter 48, 30 September 1926; LBT, pp. 166–70.
21. Letter 51, 4 October 1926; LBT, pp. 178–82.

22. Letter 52, 7 October 1926; LBT, pp. 183–4.
23. Yu Dafu had left Wuchang in November 1925, staying for a short while in Shanghai before returning to his old home in Fuyang. He returned to Shanghai in January 1926, and left again in March for Canton together with Guo Moruo. His second child, a daughter, was born in Peking the same month. His son fell ill in June and Yu Dafu went to Peking, arriving too late to see him before he died. He stayed in Peking for the funeral and returned to Canton in October, leaving Sun Quan pregnant with their third child.
24. Letter 53, 10 October 1926; LBT, pp. 184–8.
25. Letter 54, 12 and 15 October 1926; LBT, pp. 188–91.
26. Letter 56, 16 October 1926; LBT, pp. 195–8.
27. Letter 59, 18 October 1926; Letter 61, 21 and 22 Ocobter 1926; LBT, pp. 206–7 and 214–15.
28. Letter 58, 20 October 1926; LBT, pp. 202–6.
29. Letter 60, 21 and 23 October 1926; LBT, pp. 208–13.
30. Letter 58, 20 October 1926; Letter 60, 21 and 23 October 1926; LBT, pp. 202–6 and 208–13.
31. Letter 50, 4 October 1926; Letter 60, 21 and 23 October 1926; Letter 62, 28 October 1926; LBT, pp. 175–8, 208–13, and 218–21.
32. LXQJ, vol. 2, pp. 417–38; translation in LXSW, vol. 1, 296–316. The story was undated on first publication in *Mangyuan* in April 1927. On reprinting in *Gu shi xin bian* (1936), the date October 1926 was added. According to Lu Xun's diary, the final draft was completed in April 1927.
33. Letter 61, 21 and 22 October 1926; LBT, pp. 214–17.
34. Letter 63, 23 October 1926; LBT, pp. 221–2.
35. Letter 62, 28 October 1926; LBT, pp. 218–21.
36. Letter 64, 29 October 1926; LBT, pp. 223–4.
37. Letter 65, 27 October 1926; LBT, pp. 224–6.
38. Letter 66, 1 November 1926; LBT, pp. 226–8.
39. LDSYJ, p. 96; Letter 68, 3 and 4 November 1926; LBT, pp. 231–4.
40. Letter to Wei Suyuan, 17 November 1926, LXQJ, vol. 11, p. 496; see also his letter to Wei Suyuan, 21 November 1926, LXQJ, vol. 11, pp. 502–3.
41. Letter 69, 6–8 November 1926; LBT, pp. 235–9.
42. Letter 70, 4 November 1926; LBT, pp. 239–41.
43. Letter 71, 9 November 1926; LBT, pp. 241–3.
44. Letter 69, 6–8 November 1926; LBT, pp. 235–9.
45. LDSYJ, p. 103; Letter 72, 7 November 1926; LBT, pp. 243–5. In LBT the word 'comfort' is replaced by 'cheer up', which sounds less intimate. She had also been offered a job as an instructor at the Zhongshan University attached secondary school by Deng Yingchao.
46. Letter 62, 28 October 1926; LBT, pp. 218–21.
47. LDSYJ, p. 103; Letter 72, 7 November 1926: LBT, pp. 243–5.
48. Letter 74, 11 November 1926; LBT, pp. 249–51.
49. Letter 76, 13 November 1926; LBT, pp. 254–5.

50. Letter 77, 15 November 1926; LBT, pp. 256–8.
51. Letter 73, 15 November 1926; LBT, pp. 245–8.
52. Letter 75, 18 November 1926; LBT, pp. 251–4.
53. Letter 75, 18 November 1926; LBT, pp. 251–4.
54. Letter 78, 16 November 1926; LBT, pp. 259–61.
55. Letter 79, 20 November 1926; LBT, pp. 261–5.
56. Letter to Zhang Tingqian 21 November 1926, LXQJ, vol. 11, pp. 503–6. According to a note in LXQJ, Zhang's recollection was that he had heard from Zhou Zuoren that Lu Xun and Sun Fuyuan were planning to leave Amoy for Canton.
57. Letter 82, 21 and 22 November 1926; LBT, pp. 269–72.
58. LDSYJ, p. 125; Letter 81, 25 and 26 November 1926; LBT, pp. 265–8.
59. LDSYJ, pp. 125–6; Letter 81, 25 and 26 November 1926; LBT, pp. 265–8.
60. LDSYJ, p. 131; Letter 83, 28 November 1926; LBT, pp. 273–5.
61. LDSYJ, pp. 140–1; Letter 87, 30 November and 2 December 1926; LBT, pp. 283–6.
62. LDSYJ, p. 137; Letter 85, 2 December 1926; LBT, pp. 278–81. See also Chapter 12.
63. LDSYJ, p. 142; Letter 88, 6 December 1926; LBT, pp. 286–8.
64. Letter 92, 7 December 1926; LBT, pp. 293–6.
65. LDSYJ, p. 152; Letter 93, 12 December 1926; LBT, pp. 296–300. For their exchange on her 'order' see Chapter 14.
66. LDSYJ, p. 155; Letter 95, 14–16 December 1926; LBT, pp. 303–9.
67. Letter 94, 12 December 1926; LBT, pp. 300–3.
68. Letter 97, 19 December 1926; Letter 106, 27 December 1926; Letter 110, 5 January 1927; LBT, pp. 311–12, 324–7, and 332–4.
69. Letter 98, 23 December 1926; LBT, pp. 312–13.
70. Letter 98, 23 December 1926; Letter 99, 23 December 1926; LBT, pp. 312–14. Yu Dafu resigned from Zhongshan University at the end of November 1926 and travelled by boat to Shanghai after a fortnight spent mainly seeing friends and drinking heavily. See Yu Dafu, *Yu Dafu quan ji*, pp. 411–21.
71. Sun Peiqun was a graduate of Women's Normal College, a year or so junior to Xu Guangping; see also Chapter 21.
72. Letter 101, 24 December 1926; LBT, pp. 316–18.
73. Letter 102, 29 December 1926; LBT, pp. 318–19.
74. Letter 103, 23 December 1927; Letter 107, 30 December 1926; LBT, pp. 319–21 and 328–9.
75. Letter 104, 2 January 1927; Letter 105, 5 January 1927; Letter 109, 6 January 1927; Letter 110, 5 January 1927; Letter 112, 11 January 1927; LBT, pp. 321–4, 330–4, and 337–41. See also Chapter 21 on rumour.
76. Letter 104, 2 January 1927; LBT, pp. 321–2. In the first of Gu Jiegang's letters to Hu Shi about the situation in Amoy, written in February 1927 (i.e. after Lu Xun had left for Canton), he describes as intolerable the interference of the chancellor and others in the workings of the Institute, and acknowledges that

Lu Xun's resignation was a serious blow to the Institute's survival. In his letters of April and July the same year, he is much more critical of the rumours about him spread by Lu Xun and Zhang Tingqian: see *Hu Shi laiwang shuxin xuan*, pp. 424–2 and 440–2. Gu Jiegang nowhere mentions the rumours about Lu Xun's relationship with Xu Guangping.

77. Letter 105, 5 January 1927; LBT, pp. 323–4.
78. Letter 93, 12 December 1926; Letter 105, 5 January 1927; LBT, pp. 296–300 and 323–4.
79. Letter 112, 11 January 1927; LBT, pp. 337–41. For a full account see Chapter 14.
80. Letter 113, 17 January 1927; LBT, pp. 341–2.
81. Wang Dehou comments that on the question of love, Xu Guangping gave Lu Xun strength (LDSYJ, p. 304); Part II of LDS is about the persistence of love despite separation and other impediments (LDSYJ, pp. 257, 300–1, 341–52).
82. Wang Shiqing, *Biography*, pp. 216–17.

Chapter 6. Living Together: January 1927–June 1929

1. See 'Zai Zhonglou shang' in LXQJ, vol. 4, pp. 29–38; translated as 'In the Belfry', LXSW, vol. 2, pp. 367–76.
2. Xu Binru, 'Huiyi Lu Xun yijiuerqi nian zai Guangzhou de qingkuang' [Reminiscences of the circumstances of Lu Xun in Canton in 1927] in *Lu Xun huiyi lu (sanpian)*, vol. 1, pp. 501–10; see p. 506.
3. Letter to Xiao Jun, 16 July 1935, LXQJ, vol. 13, pp. 171–3.
4. See Zong Jinwen (ed.), *Lu Xun zai Guangdong* [Lu Xun in Canton], Beixin shuju, n.p., 1927 for both sides of the debate; see also Chen Shuyu, *Xu Guangping yi sheng*, pp. 41–2.
5. LXQJ, vol. 4, pp. 11–17; translation in LXSW, vol. 2, pp. 328–33; for an account of the visit, see Chen Shuyu, *Xu Guangping yi sheng*, pp. 42–3, Zong Jingwen (ed.), *Lu Xun zai Guangdong*, p. 66, and Niu Daifeng, *Lu Xun zhuan*, pp. 406–7.
6. Niu Daifeng, *Lu Xun zhuan*, pp. 409 and 412.
7. See Gu Jiegang's letter of 28 April 1927 to Hu Shi in *Hu Shi laiwang shuxin xuan*, vol. 1, pp. 430–2.
8. Chen Shuyu, *Xu Guangping yi sheng*, p. 43. According to Niu Daifeng, it was one of her elder brothers who managed the shop; see *Lu Xun zhuan*, pp. 414 and 421.
9. Mills, 'Lu Hsün', p. 81.
10. Xu Guangping, *Guanyu Lu Xun de shenghuo*, pp. 13–14.
11. Niu Daifeng, *Lu Xun zhuan*, p. 437.
12. Mills, 'Lu Hsün', p. 87.
13. Arif Dirlik, 'Narrativizing Revolution: The Guangzhou Uprising in Workers' Perspective', *Modern China*, vol. 23, no. 4 (October 1997), pp. 363–97.
14. 'Xiao zagan', in LXQJ, vol. 3, pp. 530–4; translated in part as 'Odd Fancies' in LXSW, vol. 2, pp. 356–8.

15. My translation.
16. *Lu Xun zai Shanghai*, plate 3; Ding Yanzhao, '*Yu Dafu riji* canpian zhong de Lu Xun' [Lu Xun in passages from *Yu Dafu's diary*], in *Lu Xun yanjiu yuekan*, no. 178 (February 1997), pp. 66–9; see p. 66. Some versions of this photograph have airbrushed out Sun Fuxi and Lin Yutang.
17. Yu Dafu, 'Huiyi Lu Xun', pp. 14–15.
18. It is not clear exactly what she saw. Entries for 26 January, for instance, described how he picked up a prostitute, stayed the night with her, and smoked opium with her the following day.
19. See Yu Dafu's letter to Wang Yingxia dated 23 April 1927.
20. Sun Quan outlived Yu Dafu by many years but never expressed her views on his desertion. She died in Fuyang in 1978, survived by three of their four children.
21. Ding Yanzhao, '*Yu Dafu riji* canpian zhong de Lu Xun', pp. 66–9.
22. For example, in *Lu Xun nianpu*, vol. 1, p. 364.
23. Hanchao Lu, *Beyond the Neon Lights: Everyday Shanghai in the Early Twentieth Century*, University of California Press, Berkeley, 1999, p. 122.
24. Fan Zhiting, *Lu Xun yu Xu Guangping*, p. 97.
25. Zhou Ye (b. 1926) and Zhou Jin (b. 1927), also known by her baby name Ah Pu. A third daughter was born during Lu Xun's lifetime.
26. See Wang Yunru, 'Huiyi Lu Xun zai Shanghai de pianduan' [Fragmentary reminiscences of Lu Xun in Shanghai] in *Lu Xun huiyi lu (sanpian)*, vol. 3, pp. 1399–406.
27. Xu Guangping, 'Lu Xun richang de shenghuo', pp. 9–10.
28. Yu Dafu, 'Huiyi Lu Xun', pp. 14–15; LDSYJ, p. 313. People in the know included Sun Fuyuan and Zhang Yiping. On their living together, see letter of 1 June 1929 (OC only).
29. Jing Youlin, 'Lu Xun huiyi duanpian', p. 170.
30. See Xu Guangping, *Guanyu Lu Xun de shenghuo*, p. 13–14.
31. LDSYJ, p. 364. The news seems to have been conveyed by a photograph of them together, possibly the group photograph mentioned above.
32. Yu Fang, *Wo jiyi zhong de Lu Xun xiansheng*, pp. 141–2; LDSYJ, p. 299.
33. Fan Zhiting, *Lu Xun yu Xu Guangping*, p. 71.
34. Chen Shuyu, *Xu Guangping yi sheng*, p. 50; Fan Zhiting, *Lu Xun yu Xu Guangping*, pp. 81, 96–8.
35. Yu Dafu, 'Huiyi Lu Xun', pp. 14–15.
36. Lin Yutang, 'Lu Xun', first published in English in 1928 and translated into Chinese in 1929; reprinted in *Lu Xun huiyi lu (sanpian)*, vol. 1, pp. 451–6; see also Chen Shuyu, ' "Xiangde" yu "shuli" ', pp. 126–7. The definition of a 'white elephant' is from the *Shorter Oxford English Dictionary* (1933). Dorothy Sayers in 1921 had worried that in the figure of Lord Peter Wimsey she had produced a 'White Elephant'; see Barbara Reynolds, *Dorothy L. Sayers: Her Life and Soul*, Hodder & Stoughton, London, 1993, p. 100.
37. For the first example in the correspondence, see LDSYJ, p. 190; Letter 114, 13 and 14 May 1929.

38. For the first example in the correspondence, see LDSYJ, p. 191; Letter 115, 15 and 16 May 1929.
39. Yu Dafu, 'Huiyi Lu Xun', p. 11.
40. Uchiyama Kanzô (1885–1959) came to Shanghai in 1913 and opened the Uchiyama Shoten [Neishan shudian] in Weisheng Alley off North Szechwan Road in 1917. Lu Xun and Xu Guangping paid their first visit to the bookshop on 5 October 1927, and met its proprietor a few days later; see Yamashita Tsuneo, 'Uchiyama Kanzô nianpu' [Uchiyama Kanzô chronology], p. 335. In 1929 the bookshop's main branch moved into North Szechwan Road, particularly convenient for Lu Xun in the 1930s. For photographs of Uchiyama Shoten see *Lu Xun zai Shanghai*, plates 76–80; for Uchiyama at home, see plates 98–101. See also Lu, *Beyond the Neon Lights*, p. 176.
41. Fan Zhiting reconstructs this conversation, p. 71.
42. Lu Xun did not record in his diary another instance of being drunk until April 1929. This need not be taken as conclusive evidence that he became more abstemious, but it is reasonable to assume that the first few months in Shanghai were an exceptional period for him.
43. LXQJ, vol. 14, p. 708.
44. Niu Daifeng, *Lu Xun zhuan*, p. 463.
45. According to Yu Dafu, Lu Xun was the more active partner right from the beginning; see 'Huiyi Lu Xun', p. 19.
46. Xu Qinwen, '*Lu Xun riji* zhong de wo', pp. 1316–27.
47. Fan Zhiting, *Lu Xun yu Xu Guangping*, pp. 74–5 and Niu Daifeng, *Lu Xun zhuan*, p. 483.
48. Yu Dafu, 'Huiyi Lu Xun', pp. 26–8.
49. For Lu Xun's antipathy to Shaoxing, see Yu Dafu, 'Huiyi Lu Xun', pp. 27–8. Xu Guangping in her later reminiscences tends to gloss over this. According to Zhang Gui, Lu Xun intended to visit Shaoxing several times after moving to Shanghai, but the only evidence cited is Lu Xun's mention in a letter to his mother in April 1934 that Xu Guangping wanted to go there; however, in the end they did not go. See Zhang Gui, 'Xu Guangping san fang Lu Xun guxiang' [Xu Guangping's three visits to Lu Xun's hometown] in *Xu Guangping*, pp. 68–73, p. 66.
50. For the friendship between Zhao Pingfu (1901–1931) and Lu Xun and Xu Guangping, see Fan Zhiting, *Lu Xun yu Xu Guangping*, pp. 131–4.
51. For their relationship with Feng Xuefeng, see Fan Zhiting, pp. 134–6.
52. See photograph of the inscribed copy of *Er yi ji*, 'For my wife [airen] Guangping', 26 November 1928; in Chen Shuyu, *Xu Guangping yi sheng*, front illustrations.
53. Lu Xun's letter to Ouyang Shan, 25 August 1936, LXQJ, vol. 13, pp. 410–12.
54. LDSYJ, p. 370. See also Lu Xun's letter to Li Bingzhong, 15 May 1931, LXQJ, vol. 12, pp. 43–4 and to Ouyang Shan (earlier).
55. Letter to Wei Suyuan, 22 March 1929, LXQJ, vol. 11, p. 660; see also Lin Zhihao, 'Shinian xieshou gong jianwei', p. 182.

56. Letter to Wei Suyuan, 22 March 1929, LXQJ, vol. 11, pp. 659–61.
57. Letter to Wei Suyuan, 7 April 1929, LXQJ, vol. 11, pp. 663–4.
58. Fan Zhiting, *Lu Xun yu Xu Guangping*, p. 124. Lu Xun's mother could read a little, but she found it difficult to write, and her letters to Lu Xun, about twice a month, were written at her dictation. From March 1930 to the summer of 1935, the scribe was ususally Yu Fang; before that it was usually Xu Xiansu or Song Zipei; see Yu Fang, *Wo jiyi zhong de Lu Xun xiansheng*, pp. 105–28. Song Zipei [Song Lin] had been Lu Xun's student in Shaoxing, and with his assistance became a librarian at Peiping Library; see Xu Xiansu, 'Huiyi Lu Xun xiansheng', pp. 322–3.
59. Published by the Chun Chang Press in Shanghai in 1929.
60. Letter 114, 13 and 14 May 1929; LBT, pp. 345–7.
61. Letter 116, 15 May 1929; LBT, pp. 349–50. He enclosed the letter with another to Jianren.
62. Ma Tiji, *Wo keyi ai*, pp. 98–100.
63. LDSYJ, pp. 372–3; Letter 117, 17 May 1929; LBT, pp. 350–2.
64. Lu Xun hinted at this difference again in a letter to Xiao Jun on 24 August 1935; see also Lin Zhihao, 'Shinian xieshou gong jianwei', p. 184.
65. Sun Yu, *Lu Xun yu Zhou Zuoren*, p. 144. Yu Fang reports a similar reaction when the family in Peiping received the news of the safe delivery; *Wo jiyi zhong de Lu Xun xiansheng*, p. 145.
66. Letter 116, 15 May 1929; LBT, pp. 349–50.
67. Letter 118, 19 and 21 May 1929; LBT, pp. 352–4.
68. Letter 133, 27 May 1929, LBT, pp. 376–8.
69. Letter 131, 24 May 1929; LBT, pp. 373–4.
70. Letter 133, 27 May 1929; LBT, pp. 376–8.
71. Letter 132, 29 and 30 May 1929; LBT, pp. 374–6.
72. Letter 118, 19 and 21 May 1929; Letter 121, 22 May 1929; LBT, pp. 352–4 and 357–8.
73. Letter 122, 23 May 1929; LBT, pp. 359–60.
74. Letter 126, 26 May 1929; LBT, pp. 365–7. Gu Jiegang, who had been at Zhongshan University since 1927, had been offered a job at Yenching University but declined; see his letter to Hu Shi dated 18 August 1929, in *Hu Shi laiwang shuxin xuan*, vol. 1, pp. 533–40.
75. Letter 135, 30 May and 1 June 1929.
76. For detail, see Chapters 12 and 20.
77. Letter 135, 30 May and 1 June, 1929.
78. Letter 134, 28 May 1929.

Chapter 7. Birth and Death: 1929–68

1. Niu Dafeng gives the date as September 28 without further explanation; *Lu Xun zhuan*, p. 511.
2. Fan Zhiting, *Lu Xun yu Xu Guangping*, p. 108.

3. Chen Shuyu, *Xu Guangping yi sheng*, p. 54; Fan Zhiting, *Lu Xun yu Xu Guangping*, p. 108.
4. Lu Xun's letter to Xiao Hong and Xiao Jun, dated 6 December 1934; reprinted in Luo Jiongguang, *Xiandai zuojia shuxin*, pp. 17–20.
5. Chen Shuyu, ' "Xiangde" yu "shuli" ', pp. 126–7. For Lu Xun's pet name see Chapter 6.
6. See Lu Xun's diary entries for 31 October 1929 and 9 January 1930; Zhou Haiying, 'Chonghui Shanghai yi tongnian' [Reminiscences of childhood on re-visiting Shanghai] in *Lu Xun huiyi lu (sanpian)*, vol. 3, pp. 1237–72.
7. Fan Zhiting, *Lu Xun yu Xu Guangping*, pp. 81–2.
8. Chen Shuyu, *Xu Guangping yi sheng*, pp. 52–3; Fan Zhiting, *Lu Xun yu Xu Guangping*, p. 83.
9. Fan Zhiting, *Lu Xun yu Xu Guangping*, pp. 90–1.
10. Chen Shuyu, *Xu Guangping yi sheng*, p. 54; Fan Zhiting, pp. 86–7.
11. See Lu Xun's 1934 letter to Xiao Hong and Xiao Jun, reprinted in Luo Jiongguang, *Xiandai zuojia shuxin*, pp. 17–20, and Mei Zhi, 'Nanwang de xiaorong—huainian Xu Guangping xiansheng' [An unforgettable smile: cherishing the memory of Ms Xu Guangping] in *Xu Guangping*, pp. 34–42, p. 36.
12. Chen Shuyu, *Xu Guangping yi sheng*, pp. 56–7; Fan Zhiting, *Lu Xun yu Xu Guangping*, pp. 94–5.
13. Fan Zhiting, p. 85.
14. See Yu Dafu, 'Huiyi Lu Xun', pp. 16–17; Fan Zhiting, *Lu Xun yu Xu Guangping*, pp. 85–6. Yu Dafu and Lu Xun shared a taste for Shaoxing wine; Lu Xun gave him a bottle of aged Shaoxing wine in June 1928 and a bottle of Yue wine in February 1930; it is not recorded if Yu Dafu ever made presents of wine or liquor to Lu Xun, but at a dinner given by Yu Dafu for Japanese visitors in April 1928, Lu Xun took home an unfinished bottle.
15. Chen Shuyu, ' "Xiangde" yu "shuli" ', pp. 127–8; Yu Dafu, 'Huiyi Lu Xun', pp. 22–3.
16. LDSYJ, pp. 370–1; see also Lee, *Voices from the Iron House*, p. 181.
17. Fan Zhiting, *Lu Xun yu Xu Guangping*, pp. 91–2.
18. LDSYJ, pp. 374–5.
19. See 'Wanju' in LXQJ, vol. 5, pp. 496–7; translated as 'Toys' in LXSW, vol. 4, pp. 52–3; and 'Cong haizi de zhaoxiang shuoqi', in LXQJ, vol. 6, pp. 80–3; translated as 'Thoughts on a Child's Photographs', in LXSW, vol. 4, pp. 81–4; numerous diary entries in the 1930s; LDSYJ, pp. 375–6; Lee, *Voices from the Iron House*, p. 181.
20. *Lu Xun zai Shanghai*, plate 9.
21. Yu Dafu, 'Huiyi Lu Xun', pp. 19–20.
22. Chen Shuyu, *Xu Guangping yi sheng*, pp. 52–3.
23. It has been suggested that going into hiding at this point and later may have been more gesture than need.

24. Fan Zhiting, *Lu Xun yu Xu Guangping*, p. 98. See *Lu Xun zai Shanghai*, plates 11 and 12, for this apartment.
25. This is as recorded in Lu Xun's diary; see also Wang Shiqing, *Biography*, pp. 251–2. A dramatized account is given by Agnes Smedley, who arranged the party, in *Battle Hymn of China*, Knopf, New York, 1943, pp. 77–86; Smedley says that about a hundred people attended. See *Lu Xun zai Shanghai*, plate 13, for his birthday photograph with Guangping and Haiying, and plates 38–9 for the birthday party.
26. Chen Shuyu, *Xu Guangping yi sheng*, p. 55; Fan Zhiting, *Lu Xun yu Xu Guangping*, p. 114; LDSYJ, p. 310; *Lu Xun zai Shanghai*, plates 40–1.
27. Xu Xiansu, 'Huiyi Lu Xun xiansheng', pp. 322–3.
28. For a picture of the two families together, see *Lu Xun zai Shanghai*, plate 42; note that Lu Xun and Xu Guangping are wearing Chinese-style clothing, while Feng is wearing a Western jacket and tie (it is not clear what Feng's wife is wearing).
29. Yu Dafu's renewed contact with Sun Quan in 1930 had caused Wang Yingxia great anxiety, and Yu Dafu admitted in a letter to Zhou Zuoren in July 1931 that he found it difficult being married. See his letter to Zhou Zuoren dated 6 July 1931, *Yu Dafu shuxin ji*, pp. 114–15.
30. Fan Zhiting, *Lu Xun yu Xu Guangping*, p. 111.
31. Ibid., pp. 126–7.
32. Chen Shuyu, *Xu Guangping yi sheng*, pp. 55–6; Fan Zhiting, *Lu Xun yu Xu Guangping*, pp. 116–17. See also Lu, *Beyond the Neon Lights*, p. 122.
33. *Lu Xun zai Shanghai*, plate 43.
34. *Lu Xun zai Shanghai*, plate 44.
35. Fan Zhiting, *Lu Xun yu Xu Guangping*, p. 117.
36. Sun Yu, *Lu Xun yu Zhou Zuoren*, p. 213.
37. Ibid., pp. 209–10.
38. This correspondence came too late for inclusion in LDS. Lu Xun's 1929 letters to Xu Guangping are not included in LXQJ but are in *Lu Xun zhi Xu Guangping shujian*; both sides of the correspondence are in LDSYJ, pp. 225–44 and LXZPQB, pp. 635–50.
39. Lin Zhihao, 'Shinian xieshou gong jianwei', p. 184.
40. It is noticeable that except for Shen Jianshi and Ma Yuzao, these Peking friends are all much younger than Lu Xun. His friends of his own age, as Niu Daifeng points out, were dead, in prison, or estranged (Niu Daifeng, *Lu Xun zhuan*, p. 598.)
41. *Lu Xun zai Shanghai*, plates 14–17.
42. Fan Zhiting, *Lu Xun yu Xu Guangping*, pp. 99–103; *Lu Xun zai Shanghai*, plates 18–29.
43. Fan Zhiting claims that it was quieter than his previous apartment, but Lu Xun complained of the noise from neighbours; see 'Ajin' in LXQJ, vol. 6, pp. 198–203; translated as 'Ah Chin', in LXSW, vol. 4, pp. 156–60, written in

December 1934. Fan also points out that the building was designed and built by Chinese.

44. *Lu Xun zai Shanghai*, plate 28.
45. Xiao Hong, 'Huiyi Lu Xun xiansheng' [Reminiscences of Mr Lu Xun] in *Lu Xun huiyi lu (sanpian)*, vol. 2, pp. 706–40; see pp. 714, 724 *et passim*.
46. Xu Guangping, 'Yi Xiao Hong' [Remembering Xiao Hong] in *Xu Guangping*, pp. 213–16.
47. Yu Dafu had three sons and one daughter by Wang Yingxia, but he took a dislike to the daughter and arranged to have her fostered; she died less than two years later. Yu Dafu, who once compiled a biography of Rousseau, was aware that Rousseau had all five of his children brought up in orphanages.
48. Chen Shuyu, '"Xiangde" yu "shuli"', pp. 127–8.
49. See Jon Eugene von Kowallis, *The Lyrical Lu Xun: A Study of His Classical-Style Verse*, University of Hawai'i Press, Honolulu, 1996, pp. 298–306.
50. In his letter of 6 December 1934 to Xiao Hong and Xiao Jun, Lu Xun claims to have given up drinking except when entertaining friends (LXQJ, vol. 12, pp. 584–7; see p. 584). Xiao Hong also confirms that at this time he did not drink much; Xiao Hong, 'Huiyi Lu Xun xiansheng', p. 718.
51. Chen Shuyu, '"Xiangde" yu "shuli"', p. 129; see also Wu Zuoqiao, *Lu Xun shuxin gouchen*, pp. 193–5.
52. See Fan Zhiting, *Lu Xun yu Xu Guangping*, pp. 136–42; Lee, *Voices from the Iron House*, pp. 176–83.
53. Lee, *Voices from the Iron House*, p. 178. The contrast between photographs of Lu Xun taken in 1930 and 1933 with those in 1936 is striking: see plates 30–2 and 58 in *Lu Xun zai Shanghai*.
54. Mei Zhi, 'Nanwang de xiaorong', *Xu Guangping*, p. 35. Despite Mei Zhi's fawning tone, Xu Guangping and Lu Xun appear as thoughtless and condescending on this occasion. It is difficult to tell whether the actual circumstances were as damaging as they appear.
55. Mei Zhi, 'Nanwang de xiao rong', *Xu Guangping*, pp. 36–7.
56. Ibid., p. 36; Xu Fancheng, 'Xing hua jiu ying—dui Lu Xun xiansheng de yi xie huiyi' [Old reflections of stars and flowers: a few reminiscences of Mr Lu Xun] in *Lu Xun huiyi lu (sanpian)*, vol. 3, pp. 1308–34; see p. 1327.
57. Masuda Wataru, 'Lu Xun de yinxiang' [An impression of Lu Xun] in *Lu Xun huiyi lu (zhuanzhu)*, vol. 3, pp. 1335–463; see pp. 1374–5.
58. For a reproduction of the inscription see Chen Shuyu, *Xu Guangping yi sheng*; see also Fan Zhiting, *Lu Xun yu Xu Guangping*, p. 110; for translation and commentary, see Kowallis, *The Lyrical Lu Xun*, pp. 326–30.
59. Wu Sihong, 'Guanyu Lu Xun xiansheng de pianduan huiyi' [Fragmentary reminiscences concerning Mr Lu Xun] in *Lu Xun huiyi lu (sanpian)*, vol. 3, pp. 1407–15; see p. 1412.
60. Chen Shuyu, *Xu Guangping yi sheng*, p. 141; Fan Zhiting, *Lu Xun yu Xu Guangping*, pp. 127–8.

61. This debate has attracted endless commentary. See for instance Fan Zhiting, *Lu Xun yu Xu Guangping*, pp. 175–82; Lee, *Voices from the Iron House*, pp. 182–6; David Holm, 'Lu Xun in the Period 1936–1949: The Making of a Chinese Gorki' in Lee (ed.), *Lu Xun and His Legacy*, pp. 153–79. For the letter to Xu Maoyong (drafted by Feng Xuefeng; copied out by Xu Guangping with alterations in Lu Xun's hand) see Ba Jin, 'Xuefeng—In Memorium' in *Random Thoughts*, Joint Publications, Hong Kong, 1984, pp. 177–85.
62. Fan Zhiting, *Lu Xun yu Xu Guangping*, p. 184.
63. Yu Dafu, 'Huiyi Lu Xun', p. 30.
64. LXQJ, vol. 6, pp. 608–13; LXSW, vol. 4, pp. 291–6; see also LDSYJ, pp. 377–9.
65. The letter has not been preserved, and there is no record of it in Lu Xun's diary, although he records receiving a letter from his mother on October 1. See Sun Yu, *Lu Xun yu Zhou Zuoren*, p. 209.
66. Fan Zhiting, *Lu Xun yu Xu Guangping*, pp. 187–9.
67. According to Yu Dafu, writing in 1938, Lu Xun once told him that his life in Peking in the 1920s was a performance: performing at the Ministry, performing as a teacher ('Huiyi Lu Xun', p. 9).
68. See especially Howard Goldblatt, 'Lu Xun and Patterns of Literary Sponsorship' in Lee (ed.), *Lu Xun and his Legacy*, pp. 199–215.
69. Lucian W. Pye, *The Spirit of Chinese Politics: A Psychological Study of the Authority Crisis in Political Development*, MIT Press, Cambridge, MA, 1968, p. 156.
70. Xiao Hong, 'Huiyi Lu Xun xiansheng' in *Lu Xun huiyi lu (sanpian)*, vol. 2, pp. 706–40; see p. 712; Zhou Haiying, 'Chonghui Shanghai yi tongnian' in *Lu Xun huiyi lu*, vol. 2, pp. 1237–72; see p. 1241.
71. Zhou Zuoren was contacted by the press the same day and gave an interview which is quoted in Sun Yu, *Lu Xun yu Zhou Zuoren*, pp. 209–10.
72. Fan Zhiting, *Lu Xun yu Xu Guangping*, p. 199.
73. *Lu Xun zai Shanghai*, plates 125–7.
74. Yu Dafu had moved from Hangchow to Foochow earlier in 1936. Yu Dafu, 'Huiyi Lu Xun', pp. 1–2.
75. Fan Zhiting, *Lu Xun yu Xu Guangping*, pp. 193–5; *Lu Xun zai Shanghai*, plates 129–33.
76. Fan Zhiting, *Lu Xun yu Xu Guangping*, pp. 204–5.
77. Lin Zhihao, 'Shinian xieshou gong jianwei', p. 182.
78. Chen Shuyu, *Xu Guangping yi sheng*, p. 141; Fan Zhiting, *Lu Xun yu Xu Guangping*, pp. 206–8.
79. Yao Yipei, 'Suo tan Lu Xun jiazu fengbo', p. 46.
80. Ibid.
81. Xu Guangping, 'Muqin' [Mother] in XGPWJ, vol. 3, pp. 4–8; first published in March 1937.
82. Zhou Haiying, 'Yi fen Badaowan fangchan de "yiyue"' [An 'Agreement' about the Baodaowan property], *Lu Xun yanjiu yuekan*, no. 188 (December 1997), p. 43; Yao Yipei, 'Suo tan Lu Xun jiazu fengbo', pp. 45–6.

83. Chen Shuyu, *Xu Guangping yi sheng*, p. 73.
84. See also Holm, 'Lu Xun in the Period 1936–1949', pp. 157–60 and Poshek Fu, *Passivity, Resistance, and Collaboration: Intellectual Choices in Occupied Shanghai, 1937–1945*, Stanford University Press, Stanford, 1993, p. 61.
85. Fan Zhiting, *Lu Xun yu Xu Guangping*, pp. 227–8. Fan claims that she only accepted royalties of one dollar from the 1938 *Lu Xun quan ji*; elsewhere, it is claimed that the publication helped her resume her payments to Peking.
86. Yao Yipei, 'Suo tan Lu Xun jiazu fengbo', p. 53; LDSYJ, pp. 305–6; Chen Shuyu, *Xu Guangping yi sheng*, pp. 142–4.
87. Yu Dafu had gone to Singapore in 1938 to work as a newspaper editor. In a letter to Xu Guangping in February 1939, he suggested that she send him essays and reminiscences of Lu Xun; *Yu Dafu shuxin ji*, pp. 183–4. See also Chen Shuyu, *Xu Guangping yi sheng*, pp. 138–9. This was their last contact before Yu Dafu died in 1945. He had separated from Wang Yingxia in 1940; she subsequently married in 1942 and had two more children. He had a brief affair with a younger woman in Singapore, and after fleeing to Sumatra he formed another liaison with a young Chinese woman by whom he had two more children. Fan Zhiting does not mention Singapore but claims that the Communist Party wanted Guangping to join them at their base in northern Kiangsu; *Lu Xun yu Xu Guangping*, p. 230.
88. Jing Song, *Zaonan qianhou* [Before and after facing adversity], first published 1947; reprinted in XGPWJ, vol. 1, pp. 23–91.
89. Eva Hung, 'Reading Between the Lines'.
90. See Yu Fang, pp. 145–8; Fan Zhiting, *Lu Xun yu Xu Guangping*, pp. 23–31.
91. Chen Shuyu, *Xu Guangping yi sheng*, p. 140.
92. See also Fu, *Passivity, Resistance, and Collaboration*, p. 201.
93. Ernst Wolff, *Chou Tso-jen*, Twayne Publishers, New York, 1971, pp. 9–10.
94. Sun Yu, *Lu Xun yu Zhou Zuoren*. This declaration was made in 1966.
95. Fan Zhiting, *Lu Xun yu Xu Guangping*, p. 209.
96. There is a photograph of Xu Guangping and Mao Dun standing by the grave in 1947 in *Lu Xun zai Shanghai*, plate 134, but nothing for 1946.
97. Chen Shuyu, *Xu Guangping yi sheng*, pp. 106–7.
98. Lin Zhihao, 'Shinian xieshou gong jianwei', p. 185.
99. LDSYJ, p. 309; Chen Shuyu, *Xu Guangping yi sheng*, p. 148.
100. LDSYJ, p. 265.
101. Eva Hung, 'Reading Between the Lines'.
102. LDSYJ, pp. 265–6.
103. Wolff, *Chou Tso-jen*, pp. 10–11.
104. Chen Shuyu, *Xu Guangping yi sheng*, pp. 118–19.
105. Fan Zhiting, *Lu Xun yu Xu Guangping*, p. 233.
106. See note on sources in the Introduction, p. 7.
107. See *Lu Xun zai Shanghai*, plates 135–9.
108. Chen Baichen, 'Yi xiang wei wancheng de jinian' [An incomplete commemoration], *Lu Xun yanjiu*, May 1981; reprinted in *Chen Baichen lun ju*, Zhongguo

xiju chubanshe, Peking 1987. See also Paul Clark, *Chinese Cinema: Culture and Politics since 1949*, Cambridge University Press, Cambridge, 1987, p. 84; the note cites announcements in *Dazhong dianying*, 7: 20 (July 1961) and *Wenyi bao*, 3: 29–31 (March 1961).

109. Yu Lan, 'Xu Guangping de fengcai', *Xu Guangping*, pp. 43–50; see above, Chapter 2, pp. 14 and note 9.
110. Chen Shuyu, *Xu Guangping yi sheng*, p. 122.
111. The English translation was published by the Foreign Languages Press in Peking under the title *Commemorating Lu Hsun—Our Forerunner in the Cultural Revolution* in 1967.
112. Wolff, *Chou Tso-jen*, p. 12; see also note on sources in the Introduction, p. 6.
113. Zuoren left a large family behind. Nobuko died in 1962; Yoshiko in 1964. Jianren survived all the brothers, living until 1984; Yunru died in 1990.
114. Wolff, *Chou Tso-jen*, pp. 4 and 11. The diary is still held in the Museum but access to it is restricted. It was published in 1996.

Chapter 8. Traditional Chinese and Western Letters

1. For a more detailed examination of this subject, see McDougall, 'Revealing to Conceal: Love-letters and Privacy in Republican China' in *Concealing to Reveal* [conference volume], Center for Chinese Studies, Taipei, forthcoming.
2. See the list of functions in Stanley K. Stowers, *Letter Writing in Greco-Roman Antiquity*, Westminster Press, Philadelphia, 1986, pp. 15–16.
3. The distinction is clearly stated by Qian Liqun, *Zoujin dangdai de Lu Xun* [Approaching the Lu Xun of our age], Beijing daxue chubanshe, Beijing, 1999, p. 213.
4. From the Introduction by Nigel Nicolson to Virginia Woolf, *A Reflection of the Other Person: The Letters of Virginia Woolf, Vol. IV: 1929–1931*, Chatto & Windus, London, 1978, p. xix. Although Woolf mentions having completed a 'theory of letterwriting' in 1931 none is expounded; instead, we are left with her own voluminous letters and reviews of letter collections; see p. 274.
5. What Burton Watson calls 'pronouncements' by the Duke of Zhou addressed to the people of Yin or to King Cheng appear to be close to letters; see Burton Watson, *Early Chinese Literature*, Columbia University Press, New York, 1962, p. 26.
6. *Hanyu da cidian*, vol. 5, pp. 713–14.
7. For the early history of Chinese letters and its terminology, see Huang Baozhen (ed.), *Gudai wenren shuxin jinghua* [Prime selection of letters by literati of the past], Renmin wenxue chubanshe, Beijing, 1992, pp. 1–5 and Endymion Wilkinson, *Chinese History: A Manual*, Harvard University Asia Center, Cambridge, MA, 1998, pp. 437–8.
8. See Ch'en Shou-yi, *Chinese Literature: A Historical Introduction*, Ronald Press Company, New York, 1961, pp. 214–16. For a detailed study of personal letters in early China, see David Pattinson, 'Privacy and Letter Writing in Han and

Six Dynasties China' in McDougall and Hansson (eds.) *Chinese Concepts of Privacy*, pp. 97–118.

9. Zhou Yiliang [and] Zhao Heping, *Tang Wudai shuyi yanjiu* [Research on letter-writing manuals of the Tang and Five Dynasties], Zhongguo shehui kexue chubanshe, Beijing, 1996, preface, p. 1. Over a hundred manuals compiled over three hundred years from the reign of Empress Wu were discovered among the Dunhuang manuscripts. See also Patricia Ebrey, 'T'ang Guides to Verbal Etiquette', *Harvard Journal of Asiatic Studies*, vol. 45, no. 2 (1985), pp. 581–613.
10. Wilkinson, *Chinese History*, pp. 115–17; *Hanyu da cidian*, vol. 1, p. 1415.
11. Liu Hsieh [Liu Xie], *The Literary Mind and the Carving of Dragons: A Study of Thought and Pattern in Chinese Literature*, translated and annotated by Vincent Yu-chung Shih, Chinese University Press, Hong Kong, 1987, pp. 144–54.
12. For a useful annotated selection of the letters in *Wenxuan*, see Huang Baozhen's anthology, *Gudai wenren shuxin jinghua*.
13. The original line is 'Jia shu di wan jin': David Hawkes translates as 'A letter from home would be worth a fortune'; David Hawkes, *A Little Primer of Du Fu*, Clarendon Press, Oxford, 1967, pp. 45–8.
14. *Hanyu da cidian*, vol. 5, p. 714 and vol. 1, p. 1415; Huang Baozhen, *Gudai wenren shuxin jinghua*, p. 4.
15. Note by Stephen Owen, *Renditions*, nos 41 and 42 (Spring and Autumn 1994), special issue on classical letters, p. 51. Examples of letters by Han Yu and Liu Zongyuan are also included in Wang Li (ed.), *Gudai Hanyu* [Ancient Chinese], Zhonghua shuju, Beijing, 1963.
16. For letter-writing by women in China see Ellen Widmer, 'The Epistolary World of Female Talent in Seventeenth-Century China', *Late Imperial China*, vol. 10, no. 2 (1989), pp. 1–43. See also Patricia Buckley Ebrey, *The Inner Quarters: Marriage and the Lives of Chinese Women in the Sung Period*, University of California Press, Berkeley, 1993, pp. 158, 201.
17. Chu Chia-hua [Zhu Jiahua], *China's Postal and Other Communications Services*, Kegan Paul, London, 1937, p. 17; Cheng Ying-wan, *Postal Communication in China and its Modernization 1860–1896*, Harvard East Asian Monographs, Cambridge, MA, 1970, pp. 8–9.
18. Timothy Brook, 'Communications and commerce' in *Cambridge History of China*, vol. 8, Cambridge University Press, Cambridge, 1998, pp. 579–707, esp. pp. 594–5.
19. Chu Chia-hua, *China's Postal and Other Communications Services*, p. 17; Cheng Ying-wan, *Postal Communication in China*, p. 3.
20. David Pattinson, 'Zhou Lianggong and *Chidu xinchao*: Genre and Political Marginalisation in the Ming-Qing Transition', *East Asian History*, no. 20 (December 2000), pp. 61–82; see p. 62; see also Widmer, 'The Epistolary World of Female Talent', p. 4.
21. Patrick Hanan, *The Invention of Li Yu*, Harvard University Press, Cambridge, MA, 1988, pp. 185–6; Andrew H. Plaks, *The Four Masterworks of the Ming Novel*, Princeton University Press, Princeton, 1987, pp. 34–5. The advantage

of marginality is the subject of David Pattinson's 'Zhou Lianggong and *Chidu xinchao*'.

22. See 'Personal Letters in Seventeenth-Century Epistolary Guides', translated by Kathryn Lowry, in Susan Mann and Yu-Yin Cheng (eds.), *Under Confucian Eyes: Writings on Gender in Chinese History*, University of California Press, Berkeley, 2001, pp. 155–67, and Kathryn Lowry, 'The Space of Reading: Seventeenth-century *qingshu*, Melancholy, and the Innermost Thoughts as Public Performance', unpublished paper presented at the conference 'Concealing to Reveal: the "Private" and "Sentiment" in Chinese History and Culture', Taipei, August 2001; cited with permission.
23. See A. Leo Oppenheim (ed.), *Letters from Mesopotamia: Official, Business, and Private Letters on Clay Tablets from Two Millennia*, University of Chicago Press, Chicago, 1967.
24. *Oxford English Dictionary*, Clarendon Press, Oxford, 2nd edn. 1989, vol. 5, pp. 338–9. See also Stowers, *Letter Writing in Greco-Roman Antiquity*, pp. 17–20.
25. *Oxford English Dictionary*, vol. 8, pp. 852–3.
26. Stowers, *Letter Writing in Greco-Roman Antiquity*, p. 186.
27. Quoted in Linda S. Kauffamn, *Discourses of Desire: Gender, Genre, and Epistolary Fictions*, Cornell University Press, Ithaca, 1986, p. 17, from Jacques Derrida, *La Carte postale: de Socrates à Freud et au-delà*, Flammarion, Paris, 1980.
28. George Saintsbury (ed.), *A Letter Book: Selected with an Introduction on the History and Art of Letter-Writing*, Bell, London, 1922, pp. 83–90. Kauffman, *Discourses of Desire*, and Mary A. Favret, *Romantic Correspondence: Women, politics and the fiction of letters*, Cambridge University Press, Cambridge, 1993, are extended treatments with feminist perspectives.
29. See *Ovid in Six Volumes*, Loeb Classical Library, Harvard University Press, Cambridge, MA, 1977, translated by Grant Showerman, pp. 1–311. For a general discussion see Howard Jacobson, *Ovid's Heroides*, Princeton University Press, New Jersey, 1974; for its place in epistolary literature, see Kauffman, *Discourses of Desire*, pp. 17–18 and 30–61.
30. The recipient of the tablet could erase or leave the original message while adding a reply to be returned; both recipient and sender could transcribe the contents onto parchment: see Constant J. Mews, *The Lost Love Letters of Heloise and Abelard: Perceptions of Dialogue in Twelfth-century France*, Macmillan, London, 1999, pp. 47–8. In this way, both parties could maintain a permanent two-sided record, much as it is now possible to do by email.
31. Among the many literary uses of Abelard–Heloise letters is George Moore's *Éloïse and Abélard*, first published in a limited edition in 1921 and openly published in 1925. Its rambling and sentimental narrative does not attract contemporary readers, but the bibliography in Mews (see above) is testament to the enduring interest in the twelfth-century lovers.

32. Cecile M. Jagodzinski traces the publication of private letters to the seventeenth-century in *Privacy and Print: Reading and Writing in Seventeenth-Century England*, University Press of Virginia, Charlottesville, 1999, pp. 74–93. See also Ruth Perry, *Women, Letters, and the Novel*, AMS Press, New York, 1980; Lawrence Stone, *The Family, Sex and Marriage in England, 1500–1800*, Weidenfeld and Nicolson, London, 1977, p. 222; Favret, *Romantic Correspondence*, pp. 12–33; Saintsbury, *A Letter Book*, pp. 21–45; Jürgen Habermas, *The Structural Transformation of the Public Sphere: An Enquiry into a Category of Bourgeois Society*, MIT Press, Cambridge, MA, 1989, pp. 48–9.
33. Jane Austen, *Northanger Abbey and Persuasion*, Oxford University Press, Oxford, 1969, p. 203.
34. Favret, *Romantic Correspondence*, p. 22.
35. One of the few examples of the epistolary detective novel is *The Documents in the Case* by Dorothy L. Sayers and Robert Eustace [pseud. of Eustace Barton], first published by Ernest Benn, London, 1930. Sayers's friend and biographer, Barbara Reynolds, admits that 'The book is engaging and ingenious . . ., but little more . . . The epistolary form in which she chose to tell the story does not help . . . The letters which unfold the plot are amusing and, for the most part, slight in style and characterization, while the impact of the whole is weakened by the continual switching of view-points'; see Reynolds, *Dorothy L. Sayers*, pp. 221–2. Sayers also called the book 'a failure' in her correspondence with her co-author, although she does not seem to understand why the novel failed to live up to the 'brilliant plot'; see Sayers, *The Letters of Dorothy L. Sayers, 1899–1936: The Making of a Detective Novelist*, edited by Barbara Reynolds, Hodder and Stoughton, London, 1995, pp. 287–8, 304–5.
36. This is not to say that epistolary novels are no longer written, but it is significant that in her study of twentieth-century epistolary texts, Kauffmann chooses two 'novelized' theoretical texts alongside five novels which do not take the letter form as their main structural device; of the strictly epistolary novels that she lists in her Prologue, none has made a significant impact. See Linda S. Kauffman, *Special Delivery: Epistolary Modes in Modern Fiction*, University of Chicago Press, Chicago, 1992, esp. p. xxv.
37. Frank Kermode and Anita Kermode (eds.), *The Oxford Book of Letters*, Oxford, Oxford University Press, 1995, p. xx.
38. *Selected Letters of Charles Dickens*, edited and arranged by David Paroissien, Macmillan, London, 1985, p. xi.
39. See Emile Zola, *The Dreyfus Affair: 'J'accuse' and Other Writings*, Yale University Press, New Haven, 1996, pp. 43–53, and Eric Cahm, *The Dreyfus Affair in French Society and Politics*, Longman, London, 1994, pp. 63–7.
40. Jerome Loving, *Walt Whitman: The Song of Himself*, University of California Press, Berkeley, 1999, pp. 18 and 107.
41. For a brief discussion of the uninvited letter see Saintsbury, *A Letter Book*, pp. 88–9.

42. The 13-year-old Dorothy Sayers already saw herself as a famous writer; writing to her cousin in 1906, she adds the postscript: 'You must keep this letter for the signature will be valuable . . . We shall see in the *Strand* or some other mag, thus: "Fig. 19 is a very interesting and unusual specimen taken from a most valuable autograph letter now in the possession of Miss Ivy Shrimpton."' Quoted in Reynolds, *Dorothy L. Sayers*, p. 24.
43. First edited by Robert Wiedemann Barrett Browning as *The Letters of Elizabeth Barrett Browning* in 1897 and then as *The Letters of Robert Browning and Elizabeth Barrett Browning* in 1899. See Daniel Karlin (ed.), *Robert Browning and Elizabeth Barrett: The Courtship Correspondence 1845–1846, A Selection*, Clarendon Press, Oxford, 1989.
44. Ellen Terry and [George] Bernard Shaw, *Ellen Terry and Bernard Shaw: A Correspondence*, edited by Christopher St. John, Constable, London, 1931; for the term 'intimate' see pp. xii and xlii. See also Woolf, *A Reflection of the Other Person*, p. 376.
45. Leo Tolstoy, *Tolstoi's Love Letters, with a Study on the Autobiographical Elements in Tolstoi's Work*, by Paul Biryukov, Hogarth Press, Richmond, 1923.
46. Oscar Wilde, *Selected Letters*, edited by Rupert Hart-Davis, Oxford University Press, Oxford, 1979. The early love-letters are on pp. 107 and 111; the full version of the letter to Douglas published in part as *De Profundis* is on pp. 152–240; Wilde's comments on the early letters are on p. 169, and his protest at the publication of the prison letters is on pp. 182–4. Douglas claimed to have destroyed 150 letters from Wilde, but enough survive to trace the alternation between love and hatred in Wilde's emotions towards Douglas.
47. For a more recent but briefer summary, see Peter Gay, *The Naked Heart: The bourgeois experience Victoria to Freud*, HarperCollins, London, 1995, pp. 311–29.
48. Saintsbury, *A Letter Book*, pp. 3–5.
49. Ibid., pp. 21–45.
50. Ibid., p. 19.
51. Ibid., p. 1.
52. Ibid., p. 24. In the absence of newspapers, for example, de Sévigné's letters to her daughter in the provinces bring her the news of the capital, and to that end they are not necessarily private; see Madame de Sévigné, *Selected Letters*, translated with an introduction by Leonard Tancock, Penguin Books, London, 1982, p. 14.
53. Although not as scholarly, M. Lincoln Schuster's 1940 anthology, *A Treasury of the World's Great Letters*, Simon and Schuster, New York, 1940, ranges more widely in time and geography, and is of particular interest in including both sides of selected love-letters. Anthologies and manuals of love-letters include Walter S. Keating, *How to Write Love Letters*, Stravon, USA, 1943, rev. ed. 1953; Robin Hamilton and Nicolas Soames, *Intimate Letters*, Marginalia Press, London, 1994; Antonia Fraser, *Love Letters: An Anthology*, Weidenfeld and

Nicholson, London, 1976; Ara John Movsesian, *Pearls of Love: How to Write Love Letters and Love Poems*, Electric Press, Fresno, 1983.

54. Kermode and Kermode, *The Oxford Book of Letters*, p. xvi.
55. Philip Horne (ed.), *Henry James: A Life in Letters*, Allen Lane, London, 1999, p. xvii; Woolf, *The Question of Things Happening: The Letters of Virginia Woolf, Vol. II: 1912–1922*, Hogarth Press, London, 1976, p. 522. Only about 12–15,000 of Henry James's letters are thought to survive, but Horne estimates he may have written some 40,000 (idem).
56. de Sévigné, *Selected Letters*, p. 310.
57. Henry James, *Literary Criticism: Essays on Literature; American Writers; English Writers*, Library of America, New York, 1984, p. 211.
58. George Steiner, 'The Distribution of Discourse', p. 254. The requirement that personal and social letters should be hand-written, not typed, had disappeared by the 1970s. For Virginia Woolf's dislike of typed letters, see *A Reflection of the Other Person*, pp. 6, 55, 90–1, 157, 177, 257, and 277.
59. For examples of love-letters by obscure or anonymous writers, see Fraser's *Love Letters* and Hamilton and Soames's *Intimate Letters: Correspondence of the heart*; see also the comment by Aldous Huxley quoted by Fraser in *Love Letters*, p. xx. Obscure letter-writers are specifically included in *The Oxford Book of Australian Letters*, edited by Brenda Niall and John Tompson, Oxford University Press, London, 1998. Most published collections of letters fall into the category of unintended for third-party readers. According to Patricia Mayer Spack, 'In reading other people's published letters, we seek reassurance not only about the stability of a continuous self but about the possibility of intimacy, of fruitful human exchange between members of the same sex as well as between men and women . . . Despite the objectification involved in reading letters, the text, by offering vicarious participation in a harmless simulacrum of gossip, provides comfort: as gossip does.' Spack, *Gossip*, Knopf, New York, 1985, pp. 77–8.
60. See Chapter 10, p. 94.

Chapter 9. Modern Chinese Letters and Epistolary Fiction

1. Although some early anthologists routinely lopped opening and closing salutations from letters (see Huang Baozhen, *Gudai wenren shuxin jinghua*, pp. 5–7), manuals supply evidence of epistolary conventions. For late Qing conventions, see Yuan Baoshan, comp., *Zeng guang xie xin bi du* [Expanded essential reader for letter-writing], Huiwentang shuju, Shanghai, 1911. Some conventions remain in place for conservative letter-writers decades later: see Dian Wen K. Chinn, *Practical Chinese Letter Writing*, Chinese Materials Center, San Francisco, 1980; Kaidi Zhan, *The Strategies of Politeness in the Chinese Language*, Center for Chinese Studies, Institute of East Asian Studies, University of California, Berkeley, 1992; and Cai Diqiu (ed.), *Shiyong xiexin bu qiu ren* [Practical letter-writing unaided], Wenguo shuju, Tainan, 1994.

2. The English terminology for these forms is not standard; the terms given here were in common use in the early twentieth-century. See note 3.
3. From the letters in Saintsbury's *A Book of Letters* and Kermode and Kermode, *The Oxford Book of Letters*, the date and place of composition were commonly placed at the head of the letter by seventeenth- and early eighteenth-century writers, but by the end of the eighteenth-century the foot became more common again. In early twentieth-century manuals, the address of the sender appears sometimes at the head of the letter and sometimes at the foot, depending on circumstance. See for example *Everybody's Letter-writer* (Foulsham, London, n.d.; bequeathed by Chiang Monglin [Jiang Menglin] to the National Central Library, Taipei, in 1961, and probably dating from the 1920s), and Mary Owens Crowther, *The Book of Letter*s: *What Letters to Write for Every Purpose, Business and Social*, Garden City Publishing, New York, 1922. There is a vast gap between the complexity and social anxiety of these books and more recent works such as Tim Hodlin and Sue Hodlin, *Writing Letters in English: a Practical Guide*, Oxford University Press, Oxford, 1979.
4. Wu Ansun, *Seqing chidu* [Love-letters], Zhiqun shuju, Shanghai, 1915, as described by Raoul David Findeisen, 'From Literature to Love: Glory and Decline of the Love-letter Genre' in Michel Hockx (ed.) *The Literary Field of Twentieth-Century China*, Curzon Press, Richmond, 1999, pp. 79–112, p. 84.
5. The reprint does not provide the date of publication; see *Zhongguo jindai xiaoshuo shiliao huibian* [Historical materials on modern Chinese fiction], vol. 9, Guangwen shuju, Taipei, 1980, cited in 'Theatricality and Early Republican Subjectivity: Zhou Shoujuan's Pillow Talk "In the Nine-flower Curtain"', unpublished paper by Chen Jianhua presented at a conference on 'The Modern Chinese Literary Essay: Defining the Chinese Self in the 20th Century', Achern, 2000; cited with permission.
6. Published first in 1912 in the magazine where Xu Zhenya worked as editor and in book form in 1914. See Link, *Mandarin Ducks and Butterflies*, pp. 49–51.
7. That is, on the mainland; it remained as a standard term for letters as a genre in Taiwan.
8. For the letter see original appearance in XQN; see also Luo Jiongguang, *Xiandai zuojia shuxin*, pp. 151–4. The letter was itself the result of a voluminous correspondence with fellow-students in the US on the topic of literary reform.
9. Ding Xilin, 'Yi zhi mafeng' [A wasp] in *Xilin dumu ju ji* [Xilin's one-act plays], Wenhua shenghuo chubanshe, Shanghai, 1947, pp. 1–69, esp. pp. 3–5.
10. Reprinted in *Yu Dafu wen ji*, vol. 9, pp. 326–7. (A note says that the text is from *Hu Shi laiwang shuxin xuan* (1980) but it does not appear in the Hong Kong edition.) Yu Dafu's original name was Yu Wen, hence Youwen; 'James' might have been bestowed at one of the missionary schools Yu Dafu attended in Jiaqing and Hangchow. At that stage the two were unacquainted, but Yu Dafu was full of praise for Hu Shi and his friends' 'renaissance in literature and the arts' and likened him to Thomas Carlyle. In 1921 Yu Dafu criticized

a translation by one of Hu Shi's friends and was criticized in turn by Hu Shi, after which the relationship between the two cooled.

11. Ba Jin's novels and short stories aroused particular warmth among his readers. One of them, Chen Yunzhen, wrote to him in 1933 and the two finally met in Shanghai in 1936. He was 29; she was 20, and had recently been expelled from school. According to his later reminiscences, they lived as friends in Guilin for three years and then married in Guiyang in 1944. See 'In Loving Memory of Xiao Shan' in Ba Jin, *Random Thoughts*, pp. 43–4. Xiao Shan was Chen Yunzhen's pen-name.
12. Guo Moruo, Tian Han, and Zong Baihua, *Sanye ji* [Trefoil], Yadong tushuguan, Shanghai, 1920. For translated excerpts from these letters see McDougall, *The Introduction of Western Literary Theories*, pp. 125–33.
13. For a recent edition of these ever-popular letters, see Bing Xin, *Ji xiao duzhe* [To young readers], Hebei jiaoyu chubanshe, Shijiazhuang, 1995. For early epistolary fiction by Bing Xin, see Wendy Larson, 'Female Subjectivity and Gender Relations: The Early Stories of Lu Yin and Bing Xin' in Liu Kang and Xiaobing Tang (eds.), *Politics, Ideology, and Literary Discourse in Modern China: Theoretical Interventions and Cultural Critique*, Duke University Press, Durham, NC, 1993, pp. 132–3, and Larson, *Women and Writing in Modern China*, Stanford University Press, Stanford, 1998, pp. 126–7.
14. Amy D. Dooling and Kristina M. Torgeson, *Writing Women in Modern China: An anthology of women's literature from the early twentieth century*, Columbia University Press, New York, 1998, pp. 101–3, 115–17, 135–8, 157–9, and 197–9.
15. For a detailed examination of epistolary fiction by Huang Luyin, Shi Pingmei, Feng Yuanjun, and Guo Moruo, see McDougall, 'Revealing to Conceal: Love-letters and Privacy'.
16. The story appeared in the literary magazine *Luoto* [Camel], edited by Zhang Dinghuang, Xu Zuzheng, and Zhou Zuoren; it was founded in June 1926 and issued at irregular intervals by Beixin Press.
17. Yu Dafu, 'Du "Lansheng di de riji"', in *Yu Dafu wen ji*, vol. 5, pp. 244–6.
18. Originally published in *Yusi*, no. 101 (1926), pp. 1–11; reprinted in *Yu si (ying yin ben)* [Thread of Talk (photolithographic edition)], Shanghai wenyi chubanshe, Shanghai, 1982, vol. 2, pp. 341–51.
19. Letter 71, 9 November 1926; Letter 78, 16 November 1926.
20. The transition from epistolary fiction to published authentic letters is described in McDougall, 'Revealing to Conceal: Love-letters and Privacy'. For a detailed analysis of the letter collections see Findeisen, 'From Literature to Love'.
21. For a summary of Zhou Zuoren's published letters, see the editor's 'Qianyan' [Preface] , in *Zhi tang shuxin* (1995), pp. 1–3.
22. Zhou Zuoren collected letters written by scholars from the Shaoxing region and wrote three short articles on the charm of old letters. See David E. Pollard, *A Chinese Look at Literature: The Literary Values of Chou Tso-jen in Relation to the Tradition*, Hurst, London, 1973, p. 53.

23. *Zhou Zuoren shu xin* [Zhou Zuoren's letters], Qing guang shuju, Shanghai, 1933.
24. Zhou Zuoren, 'Xu xin' [Prefatory letter] in *Zhou Zuoren shuxin*, pp. 1–6; reprinted in Luo Jiongguang, *Xiandai zuojia shuxin*, pp. 46–8.
25. Zhou Zuoren, 'Xu xin', pp. 1–2; see also Findeisen, p. 85.
26. Michel Hockx, 'Playing the Field: Aspects of Chinese Literary Life in the 1920s', in Michel Hockx (ed.), *The Literary Field of Twentieth-Century China*, pp. 61–78, esp. p. 67. Note also the negative connotations of *si* in the same preface, *si yu yi shen*, making fun of Lu Xun; see Shu Wu, *Zhou Zuoren de shifei gonguo*, p. 340.
27. Zhou Zuoren, 'Xu xin', pp. 4–5; see also Findeisen, p. 85.
28. See Chapter 3.
29. Zhou Zuoren, 'Riji yu chidu' [Diaries and correspondence] in *Yu tian de shu* [A book for rainy days], Shiyong shudian, Hong Kong, n.d., pp. 11–16.
30. See also Pollard, *A Chinese Look at Literature*, p. 53.
31. 'Bi hu du shu' [On reading behind closed doors], *Zhitang wen ji*, pp. 29–33; partly ridiculing the leftist slogan *du shu bu wang qiu guo*. According to Zhou Zuoren, reading the twenty-four dynastic histories is particularly good, but unofficial histories are even better.

Chapter 10. The Making of *Letters between Two*

1. For a brief history of the publication of Lu Xun's letters, see Yi Jin's introduction to Wu Zuoqiao, *Lu Xun shuxin gouchen*, pp. 1–12 and Wu's own introduction, pp. 1–2. Some letters to Xu Guangping were not recorded in Lu Xun's diary, but there seem to have been no other instances of unrecorded letters; it is reasonable to assume that special cases aside, Lu Xun was consistent in his practice, and that the number of unrecorded letters would have been small.
2. LBT, p. 9, and Jing Song [Xu Guangping], 'Lu Xun de richang shenghuo' in Jing Song et al., *Lu Xun de chuangzuo fangfa ji qita* [Lu Xun's creative methods, and other articles], Dushu chubanshe, Chongqing, 1942, pp. 1–13; see esp. pp. 8–9.
3. For the ubiquity of brush-written letters see the anthology *Xiandai mingren shuxin shouji* [Letters by famous men of the present age in their own calligraphy], Zhonghua shuju, Beijing, 1992.
4. LDSYJ, pp. 205, 213, and 217; Letter 124, 20 May 1929; Letter 129, 29 May 1929; Letter 132, 29 and 30 May 1929 all refer to mail for Xu Guangping from Lu Xun in Peking addressed to Zhou Jianren at the Commercial Press; all of these references are deleted in LDS.
5. Letter 31, 19 June 1925; LBT, p. 118.
6. LXQJ, vol. 6, pp. 414–16. Lu Xun's preface was written in 1935; the anthology was published in 1936 by Shenghuo shudian in Shanghai. See also LDSYJ, p. 251; Qian Liqun, *Zoujin dangdai de Lu Xun*, pp. 211–12.

7. *Lu Xun shujian*, Sanxian shushi, Shanghai, 1937. A revised and expanded edition was published under the same name as a supplement to the 1946 *Lu Xun quan ji*, with 855 letters and three fragments.
8. The 1958 *Lu Xun quan ji* included two volumes of letters, altogether 334. In the 1976 *Lu Xun shuxin ji* there are 1381 letters. The 1981 *Lu Xun quan ji* has 1333 letters plus 112 letters to foreigners; it excludes the letters in *Ji wai ji shi yi* and *Liang di shu*. The letters in the 1981 *Lu Xun quan ji* are numbered by date, for example, a letter dated 8 October 1904 is numbered 041008, followed where necessary by an additional number in the order recorded in Lu Xun's diary. In letters before 1911, dates have been converted to the solar calendar; dates not given in the letter itself are given in brackets. Corrections, missing characters, and added punctuation are all indicated, and there are extensive notes.
9. Xu Xiansu, 'Huiyi Lu Xun xiansheng', p. 324; Wu Zuoqiao, *Lu Xun shuxin gouchen*, pp. 106–7. Eva Hung suggests that Zhu An felt awkward about being their keeper and may have destroyed them; see Hung, 'Reading Between the Lines'.
10. Xu Guangping's letter to Chang Ruilin about how she fell in love with Lu Xun is printed in LDSYJ, pp. 191–3, and a selection of her letters written after Lu Xun's death is printed in XGPWJ, vol. 3.
11. Xu Guangping compares her use of a fountain pen with his use of a brush in Letter 3, 15 March 1925; LBT, p. 28.
12. There is no mention in his lists of purchased books of famous Western epistolary novels, but this is not to say that he had not read any. In 1928 he purchased Goethe's *Briefe und Tagebücher* in two volumes, and in 1930 Rilke's *Briefe* and *Briefe an Gorki*: not evidence of an overwhelming interest. In a letter to Chao Jingshen written in the late 1920s, Zhu Xiang mentions having just read Chekhov's *Letters*, but since he was abroad at the time it is not clear if this book was available in China; see *Zhu Xiang shu ji* [Zhu Xiang's collected letters], Rensheng yu wenxue she, Tianjin, 1936; facsimile reprint, Shanghai shudian, Shanghai, 1983, p. 87. Zhou Zuoren quotes a passage from Natsume Sôseki's diary in which Sôseki discusses Chekhov's *Letters*; see Zhou Zuoren, 'Riji yu chidu'. Zuoren's essay was written in 1925, Sôseki's diary entry in 1909, and Chekhov's letter in 1890.
13. LBT, p. 9.
14. As noted by Findeisen, couples whose courtship has resulted in marriage (or, as in this case, cohabitation) find it easier to compile their love-letters (p. 94).
15. LDSYJ, pp. 250–1.
16. See letters from Xu Guangping dated November 16 and 24, 1932, LDSYJ, pp. 230 and 241.
17. LDSYJ, pp. 252–3. For other evidence on Lu Xun's attitude towards Zhang Yiping and his collection see Chapter 18, pp. 169–70.
18. Although the expression *liang di shu* may now be permanently associated with Lu Xun on the Chinese mainland, the same is not true of Taiwan. In *Taiwan wenxue liang di shu* [Letters between two in Taiwan literature], a collection of

letters between two men, Zhong Zhaozheng and Dong Fangbai, published in Taipei in 1993, there is no reference at all to the correspondence between Lu Xun and Xu Guangping. Zhong (b. 1952), a literary editor born and resident in Taiwan, chose the title; his younger correspondent Dong Fangbai (pseudonym of Lin Wende), a novelist, was born in Taipei and now lives in Canada. I am indebted to Tsai Li-na for bringing this book to my attention.

19. Yuan Paoshan, *Zengguang xi xin bi du*, section 1. Writing to Wang Yingxia, Yu Dafu laments that they are *fenkai liang di* [separated in two different places]; see *Yu Dafu shuxin ji*, p. 87 (letter dated 11 May 1927). Hu Shi uses a similar expression when letters between him and Zhou Zuoren cross: *liang di xiang si* [thinking of each other from two different places]; see *Hu Shi laiwang shuxin xuan*, vol. 1, p. 274 (letter dated 12 November 1924).
20. See LDSZS: YS. SG and LDSYJ, p. 250; Wang Dehou believes that Lu Xun wanted to keep the manuscript as a memento.
21. Chang Hui, 'Huiyi Lu Xun xiansheng' [Reminiscences of Mr Lu Xun] in *Lu Xun huiyi lu (sanpian)*, vol. 1, pp. 420–33, esp. p. 429.
22. Zhou Haiying, 'Wo dui *Liang di shu* banquan de lijie' [My understanding of the copyright to *Letters between two*], *Lu Xun yanjiu yuekan*, no. 181 (May 1997), p. 33.
23. See the statement by the editor of *Lu Xun yanjiu yuekan*, no. 184 (August 1997), p. 67 that Zhou Haiying's letter had aroused a large number of letters and articles, of which three were published in that issue (pp. 67–70) and one in no. 182 (June 1997), p. 43.
24. Wang Dehou, 'Bu lijie' [I don't understand], *Lu Xun yanjiu yuekan*, no. 184 (August 1997), pp. 69–70.
25. This is particularly noticeable in Part II of *Letters between Two*: her letter of September 17 follows his of September 20; her letter of September 18 follows his of September 22; her letter of September 23 follows his of September 25 and 26; and so on.
26. Wang Shiqing, 'Zhenzhi de aiqing, wusi de fengxian' in *Xu Guangping*, pp. 26–33.
27. Prefatory note by Zhou Haiying to LDSZH: YX. SG , vol. 1.
28. Writing in 1921, Saintsbury discussed briefly the preparation of letters for publication, including publication by the author. On one point he was certain: 'Nothing must be put in—that is clear'. Saintsbury, *A Letter Book*, p. 59.
29. An example from Lu Xun's contemporaries is the unacknowledged revision by Yu Pingbo of his correspondence with Gu Jiegang on the interpretation of *Hong lou meng*: see Louise Edwards, 'New Hongxue and the "Birth of the Author": Yu Pingbo's "On Qin Keqing's Death" ', forthcoming.
30. LDSYJ, p. 35; Letter 29, 13 June 1925; LBT, p. 113.
31. LDSYJ, p. 39; Letter 31, 19 June 1925; LBT, p. 118.
32. LDSYJ, p. 224; Letter 135, 30 May and 1 June 1929; LBT, p. 383.
33. LDSYJ, p. 134; Letter 85, 2 December 1926; LBT, pp. 280.
34. Letter 114, 13 and 14 May 1929; LBT, p. 346.

35. LDSYJ, pp. 88–9; Letter 61, 21 and 22 October 1926; Letter 62, 28 October 1926; LBT, pp. 216 and 218.
36. LBT, p. 10.
37. Ibid., p. 11.
38. Ibid., p. 11.
39. Ibid., p. 12.
40. See for instance Saintsbury, pp. 95–7.
41. A famous example of a patently insincere letter (a joke? an insult?) is Anthony Trollope's 1861 letter to Dorothea Sankey (Kermode and Kermode, *The Oxford Book of Letters*, pp. 365–6).
42. Woolf, *The Question of Things Happening*, pp. xxiv, 409.
43. See Yu Dafu's diary entries for 25 and 26 January 1927, 11–12 days after his first meeting with Wang Yingxia, cited in Sang Fengkang, *Yu Dafu: sheng fei rongyi si fei gan* [Yu Dafu: living is not easy, death is not sweet], Sichuan wenyi chubanshe, Chengdu, 1995, p. 177; his first letter to Wang Yingxia is dated 28 January (*Yu Dafu shuxin ji*, pp. 30–1).
44. Undated letter, *Yu Dafu shuxin ji*, pp. 41–5. Diary entries place the date of composition as 4 March 1927. Reprinted in Luo Jiongguang, *Xiandai zuojia shuxin ji*, pp. 112–17, where it is dated 9 February (probably confusing the solar and lunar calendars), and Liu Yanwen [and] Ai Yi, *Xiandai zuojia shuxin jizhen* [A collection of letters by modern writers], Hanyu da cidian chubanshe, Shanghai, 1999, pp. 223–37.
45. LBT, p. 11.
46. Ibid., p. 12.
47. In the end Gu Jiegang did not go to court. His anger had been triggered by provocative remarks by one of Lu Xun's supporters along with a letter by Lu Xun published on Gu Jiegang's arrival in Canton from Amoy shortly after Lu Xun had left Canton for Shanghai. See Laurence A. Schneider, *Ku Chieh-kang and China's New History: Nationalism and the Quest for Alternative Traditions*, University of California Press, Berkeley, 1971, pp. 101–3.
48. See diary entries for 18 and 19 April, 3, 15, and 27 May, and 4 September in 1933; the last entry about LDS is in June 1934.
49. LDSYJ, p. 262. Writing in 1981, Wang Dehou noted that for many years Lu Xun's involvements in love were a taboo subject on the mainland and that even at the beginning of the 1980s, some people prohibited talk of Lu Xun's love and marriage; LDSYJ, p. 248. This was not of course the case at the time.
50. LDSYJ, p. 261.
51. See Lu Xun's letter to Xiao Jun and Xiao Hong dated 6 December 1934, LXQJ, XII, 584–7; reprinted in Luo Jiongguang, *Xiandai zuojia shuxin*, pp. 17–20; also cited in Wang Dehou, LDSYJ, p. 258.
52. H. H. Asquith (1852–1928) fell in love with Venetia Stanley, the childhood friend of his elder daughter and twenty-five years younger than himself. His love-letters were first published in 1933, under the title *H. H. A.: Letters of the Earl of Oxford and Asquith to a Friend, First Series 1915–1922*, Geoffrey Bles,

London. Desmond MacCarthy's introduction is very discreet, not revealing the name of the addressee, and includes a brief discussion on privacy. See also *H. H. Asquith: Letters to Venetia*, edited by M. Park and E. Park, Oxford University Press, Oxford, 1982, 1985; excerpted in Kermode and Kermode, *The Oxford Book of Letters*, pp. 475–7.

53. One of the most scandalous publications in Taipei in recent years was the correspondence between Liang Shiqiu and the singer Han Jingqing, who was about thirty years younger. The couple met in 1974, not long after the death of Liang's first wife; their marriage lasted thirteen years and appears to have been happy, despite opposition from his friends and former students. After Liang's death, his editor suggested publishing their love-letters, referring to Lu Xun's [sic] *Liang di shu* as a model. Liang had previously sanctioned publication and Han gave her permission, and the book appeared in 1992 under the title *Liang Shiqiu, Han Jingqing qingshu xuan* [Selected love-letters between Liang Shiqiu and Han Jingqing], Zhengzhong shuju, Taibei, 1992. Liang's friends were shocked and embarrassed by the passion shown by the elderly scholar, and, as if to restore his reputation, a few years later Yu Guangzhong and other friends jointly compiled a collection of Liang Shiqiu's letters under the ultra-respectable title, *Yashe chidu—Liang Shiqiu shuzha zhenji* [Yashe's correspondence: facsimile letters by Liang Shiqiu], Jiuge chubanshe, Taibei, 1995.
54. I am grateful to Hsiung Ping-chen for pointing out this distinction.
55. Tang Tao, 'Ying yi ben *Liang di shu* xu' [Preface to the English translation of *Letters between two*], in *Tang Tao shu hua* [Tang Tao's book talk], Beijing chubanshe, 1996, pp. 228–33. Although very interesting in itself, this short article was not suitable for its original purpose and was not used when the English translation was eventually published.
56. Article in *Da wan bao*, 13 September 1933, quoted in LDSYJ, p. 261.
57. LDSYJ, p. 269.
58. To represent the voice of the wife in a triangular relationship, Fraser includes in *Love Letters* a letter from Ida John (1873–1906), the wife of Augustus John, to her husband's mistress, Dorothy McNeill (pp. 87–8; cited from Michael Holyrood, *Augustus John*, Heinemann, London, 1974).

Chapter 11. Frequency, Appearance, and Terms of Address

1. See Editor's Preface, p. 11, in *The Letters of Lydia Lopokova and John Maynard Keynes*, edited by Polly Hill and Richard Keynes. An improbable but happy couple (Virginia Woolf called their affair 'a fatal, and irreparable mistake'; *A Change of Perspective*, p. 33), she was a young ballet dancer who came to England with Diaghilev in 1918, and he was an economist, senior government advisor, and Cambridge academic. A selection of letters written during their courtship, from December 1918 to June 1925, was published in 1989.

2. Virginia Woolf, *A Change of Perspective: The Letters of Virginia Woolf, Vol. III: 1923–1928*, Hogarth Press, London, 1977, p. 471.
3. *Yu Dafu shuxin ji*, p. 68.
4. Ibid., p. 84.
5. See the Table of Letters in LBT, pp. 385–93.
6. LDSYJ, p. 8; Letter 3, 15 March 1925. Wang Dehou believes that she was too deeply affected by it to reply immediately.
7. Judging from the times noted at the close of her two-part letters and other internal evidence, Xu Guangping's Letter 55 (10 October 1926) took over an hour to write; part of her Letter 61 (21 October 1929) took about forty minutes. Lu Xun does not give the times of starting and finishing letters, but since they are often as long as hers, he must also have spent an hour or more over the longer ones. Generally speaking, the original letters are longer than the published ones.
8. The comments below on the appearance of the letters are based on the facsimile versions in LDSZS: YX. SG, vol. 1.
9. This practice is sometimes referred to in the letters, for example, Lu Xun's Letter 29 (13 June 1925); LBT, p. 112.
10. LDSYJ, p. 79.
11. See Mary Soames (ed.), *Speaking for Themselves: The Personal Letters of Winston and Clementine Churchill*, Black Swan, London, 1999, pp. 37, 38, 248, 257, 277, 311 *et passim*.
12. Chinn notes *xiong* as a common polite form among male friends; Zhan does not mention either *xiong* or *jun*. A fictional but presumably reliable source for terms of address and salutation between males of different generations in the mid-1920s is Xu Zuzheng's epistolary short story mentioned above: a teacher, Luo Lansheng, addresses his former student by his personal name plus *jun*; the student addresses him as 'Wo jing ai de Lansheng xiansheng' [Respected Mr Lansheng]; a friend the same age or older addresses him as 'Lansheng ren xiong xiansheng da jian' [For the perusal of my dear elder brother Mr Lansheng].
13. Chen Hengzhe and Ling Shuhua, who both knew Hu Shi very well, address him as Shizhi and sign themselves Hengzhe and Linghua in their letters from the 1920s and 1930s; see *Hu Shi laiwang shuxin xuan*, vol. 1, pp. 153, 155, and 212, and vol. 2, pp. 88–9, 147–8, and 162–3. The letter from one woman to another in Huang Luyin's first (1921) epistolary short story, 'Yi feng xin', is addressed in an artificial Western fashion to 'Wo qin'ai de lao you Yixi' [My dear friend Yixi] with no salutation apart from 'Zai tan' [until next time], but in her next epistolary story (1923), the young women address each other more conventionally by their personal names with *jun*, *wu you* or *xiansheng* or alone. See [Huang] Luyin, *Rensheng xiaoshuo* [Life stories], Shanghai wenyi chubanshe, Shanghai, 1994, pp. 11, 18, 75, 83, 86–7, 104–5, 107, 113, and 118.
14. The conventional 'Dear' in the address of English letters appears to date from the 18th century. Writing to friends in 1820, Keats addresses them with the formula 'My dear [surname]'; writing to Fanny Brawne, he addresses her as

'My dearest Girl'; see Kermode and Kermode, *The Oxford Book of Letters*, pp. 234–8.

15. *Yu Dafu shuxin ji*, p. 3.
16. *Liu Mei qing si—xin, shi he zagan* ('Writings from the Heart: Lo Chia-luen in the United States (1920–1923)') by Luo Jialun, *Tianwai jikan* ('Outer Sky Journal'), No. 9 (January 1999); edited and introduced by their daughter Jiu-Fong Lo Chang [Luo Jiufang], shortly after her mother's death. Zhang Weizhen's letters to Luo Jialun were not preserved. I am most grateful to Luo Jiurong for presenting me with this material.
17. Zhu Xiang, *Zhu Xiang shu ji*, pp. 1–10.
18. The use of closing salutations with 'your' in English letters dates back to the 16th century.
19. Neither Zhan nor Chinn give examples of *zuo3 you4* or *zuo4you4*. According to Huang Baozhen, *zuoyou* is used between people of the same social class (p. 5); Cai gives *zuo3you4* as an address between equals and *zuo4you4* as an address in the educational field (Appendix, pp. 22–3). Zhang Shizhao writing in 1915 and Chen Duxiu writing in 1916 used *zuo3you4* for Hu Shi (see *Hu Shi laiwang shuxin xuan*, vol. 1, pp. 1, 3–5), but as used in 1917 by Lu Xun and later jokingly by Xu Guangping in 1925, it was becoming reserved for people of an older generation and/or superior position.
20. See Qian Liqun, *Zoujin dangdai de Lu Xun*, pp. 211–14, on a letter written by Lu Xun to his mother in 1933.
21. LDSYJ, p. 10.
22. LDSYJ, p. 27; Letter 18, 30 April 1926; LBT, p. 80.
23. Dorothy Ko, *Teachers of the Inner Chamber: Women and Culture in Seventeenth-Century China*, Stanford University Press, Stanford, 1994, p. 278.
24. Hamilton and Soames, *Intimate Letters*, pp. 62–6.
25. The use of roman initials for names of people and places in a Chinese text was probably adopted from Russian fiction and quickly became widespread in the early days of the new literature movement. To use initials in a letter signature was an obvious further step. In English letters it seems to have become a common practice since the 18th century.
26. In the OC the address sometimes appears as 'Xun *shi*' (e.g. 12 and 17 September) and the signature as '*ni de* H. M.' (e.g. 9 and 17 September), '*ni de hai ma*' (18 September) or simply 'H. M.' (28 September); Lu Xun changed all the signatures to 'YOUR H. M.'
27. In his draft translation of *Letters between Two*, William Lyell nicely rendered 'MY DEAR TEACHER' as 'Cher Maître'. The expression 'Cher Maître' appears in Edith Wharton's letters to Henry James (Kermode and Kermode, *The Oxford Book of Letters*, pp. 437–9).
28. See Woolf, *The Question of Things Happening*, p. 41 for the use of third-person reference for oneself to give the effect of intimacy.
29. Letter 92, 7 December 1926; LBT, p. 296.
30. See above Chapter 6, p. 59 for the explanation of Lu Xun's pet name.

31. LDSYJ, p. 194; LXZPQB, p. 611.
32. LDSYJ, p. 205; LXZPQB, p. 616.
33. For more detail on the changes, see Chapter 14, pp. 148–9.
34. LDSYJ, p. 223.
35. Ibid., p. 194.
36. LDSYJ, p. 223; Letter 117, 17 May 1929; LBT, p. 351.
37. LDSYJ, pp. 196, 198; Letter 116, 15 May 1929; Letter 117, 17 May 1929; LBT, pp. 350–1.
38. Kermode and Kermode, *The Oxford Book of Letters*, pp. 146–50.
39. Woolf, *The Question of Things Happening*, pp. 21, 32–5, 192–3, and 388. Woolf used her childhood pet name, Ape or Apes, when she was writing to her sister, Vanessa Bell, and towser, weevil, insect, squirrel, mole etc. for herself in writing to Vanessa and to her lover Vita Sackville-West (but usually in the body of letter, not in the address or signature).
40. Simone de Beauvoir's *Beloved Chicago Man: Letters to Nelson Algren 1947–64* (Victor Gollancz, London, 1988) was published two years after her death by the author's daughter. De Beauvoir (1908–1986) and Algren (1909–1981) began an affair in 1947 that continued for many years although the lovers rarely met. The publication of her book, *Force of Circumstance*, in the United States in 1965 led to a final break between them. According to her daughter's Preface, de Beauvoir's letters to Algren were sold after his death; she agreed to their publication but the project was not achieved during her lifetime. Her daughter retains possession of Algren's letters to de Beauvoir but notes without explanation that the publication of both sides of the correspondence was not possible.
41. Saintsbury, *A Letter Book*, p. 158.
42. Ibid., p. 155.
43. LDSYJ, p. 214.
44. Ibid., p. 223.
45. For use as address to a husband, see Yuan Baoshan, *Zengguang xie xin bi du*, section 1.
46. LDSYJ, pp. 225 and 227 *et passim*.

Chapter 12. Defining Identities, Testing Roles

1. LTB, p. 11.
2. For example, Xu Guangping's reference to the possibility of publishing extracts from his first letter to her indicates rereading (Letter 31, 19 June 1925); Lu Xun repeats his remarks about the oversupply of fiction to *Mangyuan* in several letters (see later).
3. Marcus Tullius Cicero, *Selected Letters*, Penguin Books, Harmondsworth [1982], pp. 28 and 48.
4. Mews, *The Lost Love Letters of Heloise and Abelard*, p. 110.
5. Saintsbury, *A Letter Book*, p. 156.
6. De Sévingé, *Selected Letters*, pp. 93, 118, and 120.

7. Ludwig von Beethoven, *The Letters of Beethoven*, vol. 1, edited by Emily Anderson, Macmillan, London, 1961, pp. 373–6. The identity of the addressee is still unknown.
8. Quoted in Fraser, *Love Letters*, p. xvii.
9. Fraser, *Love Letters*, pp. 187–90.
10. Terry and Shaw, *Ellen Terry and Bernard Shaw*, p. xiv.
11. *Yu Dafu shuxin ji*, p. 57.
12. LBT, Letter 1, 11 March 1925, pp. 19–21.
13. LDSYJ, pp. 5–7 and 8–9.
14. Letter 5, 20 March 1925; LBT, p. 34.
15. Letter 6, 23 March 1925; LBT, p. 36.
16. LDSYJ, p. 14; Letter 11, 10 April 1925; LBT, pp. 53–4. Wang Dehou notes that the full text of the opening paragraph of this letter is more intimate than *Liang di shu*.
17. Letter 12, 14 April 1925; LBT, p. 62.
18. LDSYJ, pp. 33–4; Letter 25, 1 June 1925; LBT, p. 101.
19. Letter 26, 2 June 1925; LBT, p. 103.
20. Kenneth Ellis, *The Post Office in the Eighteenth Century: A Study in Administrative History*, Oxford University Press, London, 1958, pp. 60–77 and pp. 138–42.
21. Letter 49, 28 September 1926; Letter 50, 4 October 1926; LBT, p. 171.
22. Letter 51, 30 September and 4 October 1926; LBT, p. 180.
23. Letter 55, 10 October 1926; LBT, p. 193.
24. Letter 53, 10 October 1926; LBT, p. 188.
25. Letter 54, 12 and 15 October 1926; LBT, p. 189.
26. Letter 58, 20 October 1926; LBT, p. 202.
27. Letter 59, 18 October 1926; LBT, p. 206.
28. Letters 36, 4 September 1926; Letter 41, 12 and 14 September 1926; Letter 46, 25 September 1926; LBT, pp. 133, 145, 157.
29. Letter 45, 8 September 1926; LBT, p. 156.
30. Letter 61, the first part, dated 21 October 1926; LBT, p. 214.
31. Letter 61, the second part, dated 22 October 1926; LBT, p. 215.
32. LDSYJ, p. 89.
33. Letter 60, 23 October 1926; LBT, p. 213.
34. Letter 62, 28 October 1926; LBT, p. 218.
35. Letter 65, 27 October 1926; LBT, p. 224.
36. Letter 64, 29 October 1926; LBT, p. 223.
37. Letter 76, 13 November 1926; LBT, p. 254.
38. LDSYJ, pp. 111–12.
39. Letter 94, 12 December 1926; LBT, p. 300.
40. Letter 86, 3 December 1926; LBT, p. 281.
41. Letter 92, 7 December 1926; LBT, p. 293.
42. LDSYJ, p. 152; Letter 93, 12 December 1926; LBT, p. 300.
43. Letter 100, 15 December 1926; LBT, p. 316.

44. Letters 98 and 99, both 23 December 1926; LBT, pp. 312–13, 313–14.
45. Letter 101, 24 December 1926; LBT, p. 316.
46. Letter 114, 13 and 14 May 1929; LBT, p. 345.
47. Letter 119, 17 May 1929; LBT, p. 354.
48. Letter 120, 17 May 1929; LBT, p. 120.
49. Letter 124, 20 May 1929; LBT, p. 363.
50. Letter 116, 15 May 1929; Letter 121, 22 May 1929; Letter 126, 26 May 1929 and so on.
51. Letter 126, 26 May 1926 and Letter 129, 29 May 1929; LBT, pp. 365 and 370. For the translation of Sun Yat-sen's coffin to Nanking, and the problems caused by the continued warfare along the Peking–Shanghai line, see Harrison, *The Making of the Republican Citizen*, pp. 214–16.
52. LDSYJ, p. 217; Letter 132, first part, 29 May 1929; LBT, p. 375.
53. LDSYJ, p. 217; Letter 132, second part, 30 May 1929; LBT, p. 375.
54. LDSYJ, pp. 221–4; Letter 135, 30 May and 1 June 1929; LTB, p. 383.
55. Findeisen describes this as expressing a need for the 'authentication of emotions'; see 'From Literature to Love', pp. 99–102.
56. Mews, *The Lost Love Letters of Heloise and Abelard*, p. 17.
57. Woolf, *A Question of Things Happening*, pp. 36 and 40–1; *A Change of Perspective*, pp. 30–1.
58. For an account of this correspondence see Kauffmann, *Discourses of Desire*, pp. 160–70.
59. The letters between Hannah Arendt and Martin Heidegger have only recently come to light. Hannah Arendt (1906–75) and Martin Heidegger (1889–1976) met in 1924 when she was a young student and he was her teacher, married with two sons, and about to become one of the major philosophers of the 20th century. The correspondence was initiated by him and led to an affair: their letters from this phase lasted from 1925 to 1930. They also corresponded, at Arendt's initiative, when they formed a new kind of relationship after the war, between 1950 and 1975. See Hannah Arendt and Martin Heidegger, *Briefe 1925–1975*, edited by Ursula Ludz, Klostermann, Frankfurt, 1998; see also *Hannah Arendt, Martin Heidegger* by Elzbieta Ettinger, Yale University Press, New Haven, 1995. George Steiner, reviewing *Briefe 1925–1975* for the *Times Literary Supplement* (29 January 1999: 3–4) compares them with Abelard and Heloise.
60. There is a wealth of material on this bond. See for instance Michel Hockx, 'Playing the Field', pp. 64–5 and Findeisen, 'From Literature to Love', pp. 99–100.
61. See for instance in the story 'Seeing off L. on a journey south' by Xu Zuzheng, referred to in Chapter 9 above.
62. LDSYJ, p. 255.
63. Ibid., p. 330.
64. See below.
65. LDSYJ, p. 137; Letter 85, 2 December 1926; LBT, p. 279.

66. Letter 85, 2 December 1926, LBT, p. 279. Compare Asquith's instructions on Greek and his written test for 'Hilda' in Asquith, *H. H. A.*, pp. 153, 163, and 171.
67. Letter 114, 13 and 14 May 1929; LBT, p. 345.
68. LDSYJ, p. 259.
69. Letter 12, 14 April 1926; LTB, p. 59.
70. LDSYJ, p. 18; Letter 13, 16 April 1926; LTB, p. 63.
71. Findeisen, 'From Literature to Love', p. 87. Fraser's *Love Letters* includes a section on separation.
72. Kermode and Kermode, *Oxford Book of Letters*, p. 237.
73. Ibid., p. 240.
74. Mary Wordsworth duly preserved the letters, but after her death they were separated from the other family papers and sold as scrap to a stamp dealer. See *The Love Letters of William and Mary Wordsworth*, edited by Beth Darlington, Cornell University Press, Ithaca, 1981, pp. 7, 60, and 183.
75. Written at the end of March 1922. The letters from Franz Kafka (1883–1924) to Milena Jezenská (1896–1944) were first published in 1952; her letters to him have been lost. The correspondence took place between April and November, 1920, during which period they met only twice. Their first contact came after Jezenská translated one of Kafka's short stories, although Kafka was still virtually unknown. The affair was kept secret since Jezenská was then married. Kafka's letters were entrusted by her to a friend of both parties, Willy Hass, whose heavily edited version was published after her death in a concentration camp. A revised edition with all but four omissions restored was published in 1986. For the English translation see Franz Kakfa, *Letters to Milena*, translated with an Introduction by Philip Boehm, Schocker Books, New York, 1990.
76. Kermode and Kermode, *The Oxford Book of Letters*, pp. 487–8.
77. LDSYJ, p. 119; Letter 78, 16 November 1926; LBT, p. 259.
78. LDSYJ, p. 123; Letter 79, 20 November 1926; LBT, p. 263.
79. LDSYJ, p. 124; Letter 79, 20 November 1926; LBT, p. 264.
80. Letter 1, 11 March 1925; LBT, p. 19.
81. Letter 2, 11 March 1925; LBT, p. 22.
82. Letter 2, 11 March 1925; LBT, p. 22.
83. Letter 3, 15 March 1925; LBT, p. 26.
84. Letter 4, 18 March 1925; LBT, pp. 26–7.
85. Xu Guangping first discusses the College protest in detail in Letter 7, 26 March 1926; LBT, pp. 36–40.
86. LDSYJ, p. 102; Letter 72, 7 November 1926; LBT, p. 245.
87. For example, in Letter 99, 23 December 1926; LBT, p. 314.
88. Letter 132, 29 and 30 May 1929; LBT, p. 376.
89. Letter 121, 21 May 1929; Letter 126, 25 and 26 May 1929; LBT, pp. 357 and 366. There is no indication whether a formal offer was made to Lu Xun from Yenching University.

90. Letter 122, 23 May 1926; LBT, p. 359. On this occasion it was a suggestion by students in the Chinese department. In the same letter Lu Xun states that several places have offered him a rice bowl.
91. Letter 118, 21 May 1929; Letter 135, May 30 and June 1, 1929; LBT, pp. 353 and 382.
92. Letter 121, 22 May 1929; LBT, p. 357.
93. Findeisen, 'From Literature to Love', pp. 102–4.
94. See *The Letters of Charlotte Bronte*, vol. 2, 1848–1851, Clarendon Press, Oxford, 2000.
95. Letter 17, 28 April 1925; LBT, p. 79.
96. Letter 19, 3 May 1925; LBT, p. 85.
97. Letter 33, 29 June 1925; LBT, p. 123.
98. Letter 34, 9 July 1925; LBT, p. 124.
99. Letter 17, 28 April 1925; LBT, p. 78.
100. Letter 22, 18 May 1925; LBT, pp. 92–3.
101. Letter 20, 9 May 1925; LTB, p. 89.
102. Letter 23, 27 May 1925; LBT, p. 96.
103. Letter 24, 30 May 1925; LBT, p. 100.
104. Letter 32, 28 June 1925; LBT, pp. 120–1.
105. Letter 7, 26 March 1926; LBT, p. 38.
106. Letter 8, 31 March 1926; LBT, p. 41.
107. Letter 8, 31 March 1926; LBT, p. 43.
108. Letter 9, 6 April 1925; LBT, p. 46.
109. LDSYJ, p. 13; Letter 9, 6 April 1925; LBT, pp. 49–50.
110. Letter 10, 8 April 1925; LBT, pp. 52–3.
111. LDSYJ, p. 17; Letter 11, 10 April 1925; LBT, pp. 56–8.
112. Letter 12, 14 April 1925; LBT, pp. 61–2.
113. Letter 15, 22 April 1925; LBT, p. 70.
114. Letter 8, 31 March 1925; LBT, p. 43.
115. Letter 16, 25 April 1925; LBT, p. 73.
116. Letter 15, 22 April 1925; LBT, p. 68.
117. Letter 17, 28 April 1925; LBT, p. 77.
118. Letter 21, 17 May 1925; Letter 22, 18 May 1925; LBT, pp. 91, 92.
119. Letter 28, 12 June 1925; LBT, pp. 108–9.
120. Letter 29, 13 June 1925; LBT, pp. 111–12. It was published in *Mangyuan*, no. 9 (19 June 1925) under the pen-name Jing Song.
121. Letter 33, 29 June 1925; LBT, p. 123.
122. Letter 34, 9 July 1925; LBT, p. 124.
123. Letter 35, 29 [or 30] July 1925; LBT, p. 126.
124. LDSYJ, p. 59.
125. LDSYJ, pp. 59–60; Letter 37, 1–6 September 1926; LBT, p. 137.
126. Letter 71, 9 November 1926; Letter 78, 16 November 1926; LBT, p. 241.
127. Letter 94, 12 December 1926; LBT, p. 302.

128. Letter 42, 20 September 1926; Letter 49, 28 September 1926; LBT, pp. 152, 173–4.
129. Letter 60, 21 and 23 October 1926; LBT, p. 210.
130. Letter 78, 16 November 1926; LBT, p. 260.
131. LDSYJ, p. 167.
132. Letter 60, 21 and 23 October 1926; LBT, p. 213.
133. Letter 105, 5 January 1927; LBT, p. 323.
134. Letter 54, 12 and 15 October 1926; LBT, p. 189.
135. Letter 73, 15 November 1926; LBT, p. 246.
136. LDSYJ, pp. 34–5; Letter 27, 5 June 1925; LTB, pp. 105–6.
137. Letter 29, 13 June 1926; LBT, p. 110.
138. Letter 29, 13 June 1926; LBT, p. 111.
139. Letter 30, 17 June 1925; LBT, p. 115.
140. Letter 34, 9 July 1925; LBT, p. 125. Zhang Shizhao resigned in December.
141. For example, in Letter 135, 30 May and 1 June 1929; LBT, p. 382.
142. Letter 17, 28 April 1925; LBT, p. 78. Her response came in Letter 20, 5 May 1925.
143. Letter 11, 10 April 1925; Letter 12, 14 April 1925; Letter 13, 16 April 1925; Letter 18, 30 April 1925; Letter 19, 3 May 1925; LBT, pp. 55, 59, 64, 82, and 86.
144. Letter 7, 26 March 1925; LBT, p. 39.
145. Letter 7, 26 March 1925; LBT, p. 37.
146. Letter 8, 31 March 1925; LBT, p. 41.
147. Letter 9, 6 April 1925; LBT, p. 47. The deletion of personal names is not noted in LDSYJ; see LXZPQB, p. 408.
148. Letter 16, 25 April 1925; LBT, p. 76.
149. Letter 47, 23 September 1926; LBT, p. 163.
150. For the full text, which cites He Xiangning's influence, see LDSYJ, p. 68.
151. Letter 94, 12 December 1926; LBT, pp. 302–3.
152. Letter 95, 14, 15 and 16 November 1926; LBT, p. 307.
153. Letter 1, 11 March 1925; LBT, p. 21.
154. Letter 2, 11 March 1925; LBT, p. 24.
155. Letter 2, 11 March 1925; LBT, pp. 24–5.
156. First published in *Yusi* 17 (9 March 1925); reprinted in *Ye cao*; see LSQJ, vol. 2, pp. 188–94; LXSW, vol. 1, pp. 336–41.
157. LDSYJ, pp. 8–9; Letter 3, 15 March 1925; LBT, pp. 27–8.
158. Letter 3, 15 March 1925; LBT, p. 28.
159. Letter 4, 18 March 1925; LBT, pp. 30–1.
160. Letter 23, 27 May 1925; LBT, pp. 94–6.
161. Letter 24, 30 May 1925; LTB, pp. 98–100.

Chapter 13. Mapping Personal Space

1. LDSYJ, pp. 3–4.

2. One of the few theorists to emphasize differences in thinking on privacy within a given society is T. M. Scanlon in *What We Owe to Each Other*, Harvard University Press, Cambridge, MA, 1999, pp. 338–42.
3. See McDougall, 'Privacy in Contemporary China: A Survey of Student Opinion, June 2000', *China Information*, vol. 15, no. 2 (2001), pp. 140–52.
4. Charles Taylor, 'Understanding and Ethnocentricity', first published in 1981 and reprinted in his *Philosophy and the Human Sciences: Philosophical Papers 2*, Cambridge University Press, Cambridge, 1985, pp. 116–33, esp. p. 125.
5. Ibid., pp. 125–6.
6. Ibid., p. 129.
7. Gary Saul Emerson and Caryl Morson, *Mikhail Bakhtin: Creation of a Prosaics*, Stanford University Press, Stanford, 1990, pp. 54–5; see also p. 289 for context and more detail.
8. Zhang Longxi, *Mighty Opposites: From Dichotomies to Differences in the Comparative Study of China*, Stanford University Press, Stanford, 1998, p. 112.
9. *Oxford English Dictionary*, vol. 12, pp. 515–19.
10. The 1890 declaration by Warren and Brandeis on rights to privacy under US law is frequently taken as a turning point in the development of modern concepts of privacy. On the normative function of 'privacy' and its distinction from the adjective 'private', see Inness, *Privacy, Intimacy, and Isolation*, p. 13. Jagodzinski traces the shift in meaning from the negative sense of 'not holding public office' to a 'more netural, even positive and humanizing' sense in 17th-century. Britain; see *Privacy and Print*, p. 24 *et passim*.
11. The terminology for privacy states in Chinese and European languages are discussed in the introduction and by several contributors in McDougall and Hansson (eds.), *Chinese Concepts of Privacy*.
12. Examples of *si* in modern Chinese will be given below; for a recent example of Western assumptions about Chinese assumptions on undesirable privacy, see the boxed aside in Elizabeth Scurfield, *Teach Yourself Chinese*, Hodder & Stoughton, London, 1991, p. 98.
13. I am most grateful to Professor McMullen for allowing me to see an early draft of his paper on public and private domains in the Tang dynasty on the combinations of *si* with other words.
14. David H. Flaherty (ed.), *Privacy and Data Protection: An International Bibliography*, Mansell Publishing, London, 1984, p. 5. Swedish has a close equivalent for private ('privat') but not for privacy. The Finnish words related to privacy, such as 'yksitisasia' [private or intimate affairs], 'yksityinen' [private as opposed to public] and 'yksityisyydensuoja' [private data protection] are derived from the word 'yksi' meaning 'one' or 'single'. I am most grateful to Anders Hansson and Juha Tähkämaa for this information. On the Russian vocabulary for public and private realms, see Marc Garcelon, 'The Shadow of the Leviathan: Public and Private in Communist and Post-Communist Society' and Oleg Kharkhordin, 'Reveal and Dissimulate: A Genealogy of Private Life in Soviet Russia', both in Jeff Weintraub and Krishnan Kumar (eds.), *Public and*

Private in Thought and Practice: Perspectives on a Grand Dichotomy, University of Chicago Press, Chicago, 1997, pp. 303–2, esp. pp. 304–5, 318, and 325 and pp. 333–63, esp. 342–5 and 358.

15. Steven Pinker, *The Language Instinct: The New Science of Language and Mind*, Penguin Books, Harmondsworth, 1994, p. 82. Pinker's argument, which runs directly counter to the Sapir–Whorf hypothesis on language and culture, is sustained by recent work on human universals, mentioned above in the Introduction, note 8.
16. Taylor, 'Understanding and Ethnocentricity', p. 131.
17. The term 'personal space' is used here with a much broader meaning than indicated in Erving Goffman's definition in *Relations in Public: Microstudies of the Public Order*, Basic Books, New York, 1971, pp. 29–30; it is closer to his larger category of 'territories of the self'.

Chapter 14. Sex and Sexual Relationships

1. Hannah Arendt, *The Human Condition*, University of Chicago Press, Chicago, 1958, p. 51.
2. LDSYJ, pp. 18, 24, and 36.
3. Letter 13, 16 April 1925; Letter 16, 25 April 1925; Letter 30, 17 June 1925; LBT, pp. 63, 74, and 113.
4. LDSYJ, p. 20.
5. LDSYJ, p. 36; Letter 30, 17 June 1925; LBT, p. 114.
6. LDSYJ, pp. 40–2; LBT, p. 120.
7. Letter 32, 28 June 1925; LTB, p. 120.
8. LDSYJ, p. 42; Letter 33, 29 June 1925; LTB, pp. 121–3.
9. LDSYJ, pp. 43–5; LBT, p. 123.
10. LDSYJ, pp. 45–57; LBT, p. 125.
11. LDSYJ, p. 59.
12. LDSYJ, pp. 63–4.
13. Letter 48, 28 and 30 September 1926; LBT, p. 170.
14. Letter 57, 14 October 1926; LBT, p. 199.
15. LDSYJ, p. 81.
16. Letter 58, 20 October 1926; LBT, p. 204.
17. LDSYJ, pp. 45, 50, 52, and 54.
18. Letter 15, 22 April 1925; LBT, p. 70.
19. Letter 16, 25 April 1925; LBT, p. 76.
20. Letters 17, 18, 19, and 20, from 28 April to 5 May, 1925.
21. LDSYJ, p. 69.
22. Ibid., p. 70.
23. Ibid., p. 80.
24. Ibid., p. 71.
25. Ibid., p. 72.
26. Ibid., p. 94. Wang Dehou gives no explanation for this term of address.

27. For Xu Guangping's prose poems, see above, p. 40. Another possible source is the epistolary short story by Feng Yuanjun, 'Lin xiansheng de xin' [Mr Liu's letters] (1925); see Chapter 8, p. 91, note 15.
28. LDSYJ, p. 199.
29. Ibid., p. 18.
30. Ibid., p. 95.
31. Ibid., p. 97.
32. Ibid., p. 108.
33. Ibid., p. 109.
34. Ibid., p. 140.
35. Ibid., p. 137.
36. LDSYJ, p. 42; Letter 33, 29 June 1925; LBT, p. 122.
37. Letter 34, 9 July 1925; LBT, p. 124.
38. Letter 49, 28 September 1926; LBT, p. 171.
39. Letter 50, 4 October 1926; LBT, p. 175.
40. LDSYJ, p. 106.
41. Ibid., p. 179.
42. Ibid., p. 145.
43. Ibid., p. 149.
44. See the letter from Jane Carlyle (1801–66) to Edinburgh on 21 October 1859, in Saintsbury, *A Letter Book*, pp. 251–2.
45. Luo Jialun, *Liu Mei qing si*, pp. 24, 25, and 28–9.
46. Zhu Xiang, *Zhu Xiang shu ji*, p. 12.
47. LDSYJ, p. 111.
48. Ibid., p. 150.
49. Letter 37, 1–6 September, 1926; LBT, p. 135.
50. LDSYJ, p. 60. Wang Dehou comments that many passages of this kind are omitted.
51. Ibid., p. 75.
52. Ibid., p. 78.
53. LDSYJ, p. 96; Letter 68, 3 and 4 November 1926; LBT, p. 233.
54. LDSYJ, p. 100; Letter 70, 4 November 1926; LBT, p. 240.
55. LDSYJ, pp. 126–9. According to Wang Dehou, these deletions are the most significant in the whole correspondence in regard to their affair.
56. Ibid., p. 125.
57. LDSYJ, p. 131; Letter 83, 28 November 1926; LBT, p. 274.
58. Letter 85, 2 December 1926; LBT, p. 278.
59. LDSYJ, p. 141.
60. Letter 87, 30 November and 2 December 1926; LBT, pp. 285–6.
61. LDSYJ, p. 145.
62. Ibid., p. 173.
63. LDSYJ, pp. 150 and 152; Letter 93, 12 December 1926; LBT, p. 300. Wang Dehou comments about the latter remark that it is saturated with feeling.

64. LDSYJ, p. 184; Letter 111, 7 January 1929; LBT, p. 336. Wang Dehou comments that this is one of the rare occasions when Xu Guangping or Lu Xun uses the kind of language that is commonly found in love-letters.
65. LDSYJ, pp. 185–9; Letter 112, 11 January 1927; LBT, pp. 337–41.
66. LDSYJ, p. 197.
67. LDSYJ, p. 203; Letter 122, 23 May 1929; LBT, p. 360.
68. LDSYJ, p. 212; Letter 128, 27 May 1929; LBT, p. 369.
69. LDSYJ, p. 213; Letter 128, 27 May 1929; LBT, p. 369.
70. LDSYJ, pp. 205–7; Letter 124, 20 May 1929; LBT, p. 363.
71. LSDYJ, p. 215; Letter 130, 23 May 1929; LBT, p. 373. Wang Dehou comments that the salutation is strangely formal, and that the weakened expression in the earlier phrase is significant.
72. LDSYJ, p. 216; Letter 131, 24 May 1929; LBT, p. 373.
73. LDSYJ, p. 190; Letter 114, 13 and 14 May 1929; LBT, pp. 345–6.
74. LDSYJ, p. 194. Wang Dehou believes that a lover's joke is contained in this exchange.
75. LXZPQB, pp. 611, 616, 625, 627, and 631–4; Letter 116, 15 May 1929; Letter 124, 20 May 1929; Letter 125, 25 May 1929; Letter 129, 29 May 1929; Letter 132, 29 and 30 May 1929; Letter 135, 30 May and 1 June 1929.
76. LDSYJ, p. 210.
77. Ibid., p. 213. The term 'little lotus pod' turns up in Letters 128, 130, 132, and 135.
78. LDSYJ, pp. 197, 209, and 212.
79. Ibid., pp. 191–3.
80. Ibid., p. 199. According to Wang Dehou, this passage may be the most important deletion in the whole correspondence.
81. Ibid., p. 199.
82. Ibid., p. 218.
83. Ibid., pp. 221–4. Wang Dehou notes that this is one of the letters in which there are most changes, especially in the form of additions.
84. Ibid., pp. 196 and 199.
85. The OC has 'beautiful and lively': this is changed to 'plump and lively' in *Letters between Two*. Wang Dehou comments that the change was made to show emphasize Lu Xun's concern with local health problems; it may also have been to avoid the impression that Lu Xun liked looking at beautiful women.
86. LDSYJ, p. 31.
87. Letter 23, 27 May 1925; LBT, pp. 95–6.
88. LDSYJ, p. 31; Letter 24, 30 May 1925; LBT, p. 99.
89. LDSYJ, p. 120.
90. Virginia Woolf, *The Question of Things Happening*, p. 598, letter to Gerald Brenan.

Chapter 15. Bodies, Bodily Functions and Activities, and Hygiene

1. Arendt, *The Human Condition*, p. 72.
2. Carl D. Schneider, *Shame, Exposure, and Privacy*, Norton, New York, 1992.
3. Schneider, *Shame, Exposure, and Privacy*, pp. 46–8.
4. Ibid., p. 49.
5. Ibid., p. 50.
6. Ibid., pp. 51–4.
7. Letter 30, 17 June 1925; LBT, p. 114.
8. For example, in Letter 51, 30 September and 4 October 1926; Letter 89, 11 December 1926; Letter 93, 12 December 1926; LBT, pp. 182, 289, and 299.
9. LDSYJ, pp. 91 and 113.
10. Ibid., p. 73.
11. Ibid., pp. 191, 193, 201, and 208.
12. Letter 116, 15 May 1929; Letter 120, 17 May 1929; Letter 124, 20 May 1929; Letter 125, 25 May 1929; Letter 126, 26 May 1929; Letter 127, 21 May 1929; Letter 128, 27 May 1929; Letter 129, 29 May 1929; Letter 130, 22 and 23 May 1929.
13. LDSYJ, p. 206.
14. Letter 126, 26 May 1929; LBT, p. 366.
15. Letter 41, 12 and 14 September 1926; LBT, p. 146. Diary entries for 1928 and 1929 show that Lu Xun took a bath [*yu*] in June each year.
16. LDSYJ, p. 214. Wang Dehou does not record the deletion from Letter 108, 30 December 1926.
17. Diary entries for 1928 and 1929 show that Lu Xun had his feet washed eleven times and eight times respectively.
18. LDSYJ, p. 201.
19. Letter 49, 28 September 1926; LBT, p. 173.
20. Letter 48, 28 and 30 September 1926; LBT, p. 167.
21. LDSYJ, p. 112.
22. Writing around the same time, Virginia Woolf is relatively candid about both to close friends: see, for example, *A Reflection of the Other Person*, pp. 44, 183, 214, 252, 334, and 372.
23. Virginia Woolf, *The Question of Things Happening*, pp. 124–5, 275, 284, and 318; p. 360; *A Change of Perspective*, pp. 236, 251, 348, and 430.
24. David Schroeder, *Mozart in Revolt: Strategies of Resistance, Mischief and Deception*, Yale University Press, New Haven, 1999, pp. 127–40.
25. Virginia Woolf, *The Question of Things Happening*, pp. 146, 210, 234, 267, etc.
26. *Yu Dafu shuxin ji*, p. 63.
27. Letter 48, 28 and 30 September 1926; LBT, p. 169.
28. Letter 62, 28 October 1926; LBT, p. 221.
29. LDSYJ, p. 90.
30. LDSYJ, p. 201; Letter 119, 17 May 1929; LBT, p. 354.

31. For an account of nightstools in Shanghai in the 1930s, see Lu, *Beyond the Neon Lights*, pp. 189–98.
32. The first mention is in Letter 46, 25 and 26 September 1926; subsequent mentions are too numerous to list.
33. See 'Guanyu Lu Xun de shenghuo yu chuangzuo', written in 1956, in *Xu Guangping jinian ji*, pp. 205–33, p. 206.
34. Letter 55, 10 October 1926; LBT, p. 194.
35. Letter 56, 16 October 1926; LBT, p. 197.
36. Letter 41, 12 and 14 September 1926; LBT, p. 147.
37. Letter 42, 20 September 1926; LBT, p. 152.
38. Letter 46, 25 and 26 September 1926; LBT, p. 160.
39. LDSYJ, pp. 81–2; Letter 50, 4 October 1926; Letter 55, 10 October 1926; LBT, pp. 176 and 194.
40. For example, Letter 92, 7 December 1926; LBT, pp. 294–5.
41. LDSYJ, p. 58; Letter 37, 1–6 September 1926; LBT, p. 134.
42. LDSYJ, p. 59.
43. Ibid., pp. 60–1.
44. For example, Letter 120, 17 May 1929; Letter 121, 22 May 1929; Letter 129, 29 May 1929.
45. Letter 41, 12 and 14 September 1926; LBT, p. 146.
46. Letter 42, 20 September 1926; LBT, p. 151.
47. Letter 57, 14 October 1926; LBT, p. 199.
48. Letter 76, 13 November 1926; LBT, p. 255.
49. Letter 43, 17 September 1926; LBT, p. 153.
50. Letter 57, 14 October 1926; Letter 62, 28 October 1926; Letter 66, 1 November 1926; Letter 67, 30 October 1926; Letter 68, 3 and 4 November 1926; Letter 92, 7 December 1926; Letter 118, 19 and 21 May 1929; Letter 121, 22 May 1929.
51. LDSYJ, p. 89.
52. Letter 99, 23 December 1926; LBT, p. 314.
53. Letter 44, 22 September, 1926; Letter 46, 25 and 26 September 1926; Letter 48, 28 and 30 September 1926; Letter 68, 3 and 4 November 1926. An old bottle of Sanatogen is preserved in the Lu Xun Museum at Amoy University.
54. Letter 44, 22 September 1926; LBT, p. 154.
55. Letter 44, 22 September 1926; Letter 121, 22 May 1929; LBT, pp. 154 and 358.
56. LDSYJ, p. 202; Letter 132, 29 and 30 May 1929; LBT, p. 375.
57. LDSYJ, pp. 193 and 216.
58. For example, Letter 115, 15 and 16 May 1929; LBT, pp. 347–8.
59. Letter 121, 22 May 1929; Letter 122, 23 May 1929; LBT, pp. 358–9.
60. Letter 42, 20 September 1926; LBT, p. 149.
61. Letter 89, 11 December 1926. LBT, p. 289.
62. LDSYJ, p. 159.
63. Ibid., p. 173.
64. Letter 115, 15 and 16 May 1929; LBT, pp. 347–8.

65. LDSYJ, p. 201; Letter 120, 17 May 1929; LBT, p. 356.
66. LDSYJ, p. 210; Letter 127, 21 May 1929.
67. Letter 13, 16 April 1925.
68. LDSYJ, p. 69.
69. Letter 51, 30 September and 4 October 1926; LBT, p. 179.
70. Letter 54, 12 and 14 October 1926; LBT, p. 189.
71. Letter 86, 3 December 1926; LBT, p. 282.
72. LDSYJ, p. 138.
73. Letter 93, 12 December 1926; Letter 94, 12 December 1926; LBT, pp. 295 and 297.
74. Letter 25, 1 June 1925; LBT, p. 102.
75. LDSYJ, p. 33.
76. Letter 29, 13 June 1925; LBT, pp. 109 and 111.
77. Letter 30, 17 June 1925; LBT, p. 117.
78. Letter 32, 28 June 1925; LBT, p. 122.
79. Letter 33, 29 June 1925; LBT, p. 122.
80. Letter 41, 12 and 14 September 1926; Letter 54, 12 and 15 October 1926; Letter 62, 28 October 1926; LBT, pp. 148, 189, and 221.
81. Letter 45, 18 September 1926; LBT, p. 157.
82. LDSYJ, p. 69.
83. Chuan Dao [Zhang Tingqian], 'Lu Xun xiansheng shenghuo suoji' [Fragments from Mr Lu Xun's life] in *Lu Xun huiyi lu (sanpian)*, vol. 1, pp. 326–9.
84. Letter 129, 29 May 1929; LBT, pp. 370–1.
85. LDSYJ, p. 224; Letter 135, 30 May and 1 June 1926; LBT, p. 382.

Chapter 16. Domestic Life and Habits

1. Letter 25, 1 June 1925; LBT, p. 102.
2. LDSYJ, p. 34; Letter 26, 2 June 1925; LBT, p. 104.
3. LDSYJ, p. 18; Letter 13, 16 April 1925; LBT, p. 63.
4. LDSYJ, p. 61.
5. Ibid., pp. 67 and 71–2.
6. LDSYJ, p. 66; Letter 46, 25 and 26 September 1926; LBT, p. 158.
7. LDSYJ, p. 71.
8. Letter 67, 30 October 1926; LBT, p. 230. Wang Dehou is incorrect in claiming that this passage is deleted; LDSYJ, p. 95.
9. Letter 103, 23 December 1926; LBT, p. 320.
10. Letter 104, 2 January 1927; LBT, p. 322. Among his luggage on leaving Amoy was a bag containing the spirit stove, his teapot, and other utensils; in that respect his addition corrects the record. See Chuan Dao [Zhang Tingqian], 'He Lu Xun xiansheng zai Xiamen xiangchu de rizi li' [Shared times with Mr Lu Xun in Amoy] in *Lu Xun huiyi lu (sanpian)*, vol. 1, pp. 474–86; see esp. p. 486.
11. LDSYJ, p. 170.

12. Letter 41, 12 and 14 September 1926; Letter 54, 12 and 15 October 1926; Letter 60, 21 and 23 October 1926; Letter 68, 3 and 4 November 1926; Letter 69, 6–8 November 1926; Letter 99, 23 December 1926.
13. Letter 119, 17 May 1929; Letter 123, 19 May 1929; LBT, pp. 354 and 362.
14. LDSYJ, pp. 66, 147, 151, and 158.
15. Woolf, *The Question of Things Happening*, p. 169.
16. LDSYJ, p. 25.
17. Letter 27, 5 June 1925; LBT, p. 106.
18. Letter 8, 31 March 1925; Letter 9, 6 April 1925; Letter 92, 7 December 1926; Letter 117, 17 May 1929; Letter 122, 23 May 1929; LBT, pp. 43, 49, 294, 351, and 360.
19. LDSYJ, p. 69; Letter 47, 23 September 1926; LBT, p. 163.
20. Letter 97, 19 December 1926; Letter 120, 17 May 1929; Letter 123, 18 and 19 May 1929; Letter 127, 21 May 1929; Letter 130, 22 and 23 May 1929; LBT, pp. 312, 356, 362, 368, and 372.
21. Letter 74, 11 November 1926; LBT, p. 251.
22. Letter 37, 1–6 September 1926; Letter 76, 13 November 1926; Letter 92, 7 December 1926; Letter 120, 17 May 1929; Letter 123, 18 and 19 May 1929; Letter 130, 22 and 23 May 1929.
23. Letter 122, 23 May 1929; Letter 129, 29 May 1929; LBT, pp. 359 and 370.
24. Letter 135, 30 May and 1 June 1929; LBT, p. 383.
25. Letter 118, 19 and 21 May, 1929; LBT, p. 352.
26. Letter 85, 2 December 1929; LBT, p. 280.
27. LDSYJ, pp. 75–6, 207–8, and 214–15; Letter 52, 7 October 1926; Letter 125, 25 May 1929; Letter 130, 22 and 23 May 1929.

Chapter 17. Family Matters

1. Letter 7, 26 March 1925; LBT, p. 39.
2. Letter 23, 27 May 1925; LBT, p. 95.
3. LDSYJ, p. 58.
4. Ibid., p. 102.
5. Ibid., p. 103.
6. LDSYJ, p. 135; Letter 84, 27 November 1926; LBT, p. 277.
7. Letter 47, 23 September 1926; LBT, p. 164.
8. LDSYJ, pp. 76, 86, 103, 129, and 178.
9. A remark that she might stay in Canton because she has many connections there is deleted; LDSYJ, p. 130.
10. Ibid., p. 73.
11. Ibid., p. 167.
12. LDSYJ, p. 60; Letter 38, 8 September 1926; LBT, p. 141.
13. LDSYJ, p. 182.
14. Letter 51, 30 September and 4 October 1926. Wang Dehou does not note this deletion.

15. LDSYJ, p. 89; Letter 62, 28 October 1926; LBT, p. 219.
16. Letter 73, 15 November 1926; LBT, p. 245.
17. LDSYJ, p. 26.
18. Ibid., p. 38.
19. Letter 47, 23 September 1926; Letter 52, 7 October 1926: LBT, pp. 165 and 184.
20. LDSYJ, p. 114.
21. Ibid., pp. 126–9.
22. Letter 55, 10 October 1926; LBT, p. 194
23. LDSYJ, p. 63.
24. Ibid., p. 64.
25. Ibid., p. 71.
26. LDSYJ, pp. 88–9; Letter 61, 21 and 22 October 1926; LBT, p. 216.
27. LDSYJ, p. 89; Letter 62, 28 October 1926; LBT, p. 218.
28. Wang Dehou, p. 89. More reasonably, *San xiansheng* in her Letter 111 (7 January 1927) is changed to Mr Keshi (LDSYJ, p. 184).
29. LDSYJ, p. 94.
30. Ibid., p. 188.
31. Ibid., p. 104.
32. LDSYJ, p. 188; Letter 112, 11 January 1927; LBT, p. 340.
33. LDSYJ, p. 72; Letter 50, 4 October 1926; LBT, p. 177.
34. LDSYJ, p. 118; Letter 112, 11 January 1927; LBT, p. 340.
35. LDSYJ, p. 195.
36. LDSYJ, p. 195; Letter 116, 15 May 1929; LBT, p. 350.
37. LDSYJ, p. 196; Letter 117, 17 May 1929; LBT, p. 351.
38. LDSYJ, pp. 196–7.
39. Letter 115, 15 and 16 May 1929; LBT, p. 348.
40. Letter 133, 27 May 1929; LBT, p. 377.
41. Letter 117, 17 May 1929; LBT, p. 351.
42. LDSYJ, pp. 198, 200, 203–4, 207, 212–13, and 215.
43. Letter 134, 28 May 1929; LBT, p. 379.
44. LDSYJ, pp. 205 and 219.
45. LDSYJ, pp. 191, 193, and 205; Letter 114, 13 and 14 May 1919; Letter 115, 15 and 16 May 1929; Letter 123, 18 and 19 May 1929.
46. LDSYJ, p. 202.
47. Letter 115, 15 and 16 May 1929; LBT, p. 347.
48. Letter 123, 18 and 19 May 1929; LBT, p. 361.
49. LDSYJ, p. 217.
50. Ibid., p. 211.
51. LXYJ, p. 212.
52. LDSYJ, pp. 218–19.
53. LDSYJ, pp. 220–1; Letter 134, 28 May 1929; LBT, pp. 378–9.

Chapter 18. Friends and Enemies

1. LDSYJ, p. 7; Letter 2, 11 March 1925; LBT, p. 24.
2. LDSYJ, p. 28; Letter 19, 3 May 1925; LBT, p. 84.
3. LDSYJ, p. 30; Letter 22, 18 May 1925; LBT, p. 92.
4. LDSYJ, pp. 25–6, 28, and 39.
5. LDSYJ, p. 36; Letter 29, 13 June 1925; LBT, p. 112.
6. LDSYJ, pp. 63, 84–5, 93–4, 168, 174–5, and 177; Letter 41, 12 and 14 September 1926; Letter 60, 21 and 23 October 1926; Letter 65, 27 October 1926; Letter 67, 30 October 1926; Letter 103, 23 December 1926; Letter 106, 27 December 1926; Letter 107, 30 December 1926.
7. Letter 67, 30 October 1926; LBT, p. 229.
8. LDSYJ, p. 85; Letter 48, 28 and 30 September 1926; LBT, p. 169.
9. LDSYJ, p. 76.
10. There are too many instances to cite in full; see for example LDSYJ, pp. 109–11; Letter 75, 18 November 1926; LTB, p. 254.
11. LDSYJ, p. 155; Letter 95, 14–16 December 1926; LBT, p. 304.
12. LDSYJ, pp. 70, 79, 82, and 90.
13. Letter 47, 23 September 1926; LBT, 164.
14. Letter 135, 30 May and 1 June 192; LBT, p. 380.
15. Letter 112, 11 January 1927; LDSYJ, p. 188.
16. LDSYJ, p. 178.
17. Ibid., p. 68.
18. Ibid., p. 75.
19. Ibid., pp. 83 and 85.
20. Ibid., p. 155.
21. Ibid., p. 187.
22. LDSYJ, p. 118; Letter 77, 15 November 1927; LBT, p. 258.
23. Letter 49, 28 September 1926; Letter 55, 10 October 1926: LTB, pp. 171–2 and 193–4.
24. LDSYJ, pp. 198, 222, and 299.
25. Ibid., p. 200.
26. Ibid., pp. 191–3 and 218.
27. Ibid., pp. 199 and 219.
28. Ibid., p. 201.
29. Ibid., p. 23.
30. LDSYJ, p. 26; Letter 17, 28 April 1925; LBT, p. 78.
31. LDSYJ, p. 35; Letter 29, 13 June 1925; LBT, p. 112.
32. LDSYJ, p. 39.
33. Gao Changhong, 'Yi dian huiyi—guanyu Lu Xun he wo' [A recollection: concerning Lu Xun and me], in *Lu Xun huiyi lu* (*sanpian*), vol. 1, pp. 178–97; see p. 193.
34. LDSYJ, pp. 85–6; Letter 60, 21 and 23 October 1926; LBT, p. 213.

35. LDSYJ, p. 89; Letter 62, 28 October 1928; LBT, p. 219. Lu Xun might have had Li Yu'an in mind here rather than Gao Changhong; see below.
36. LDSYJ, p. 95; Letter 67, 30 October 1926; LBT, p. 230.
37. LDSYJ, p. 97.
38. LDSYJ, p. 101; Letter 71, 9 November 1926; LBT, p. 242.
39. Letter 54, 12 and 15 October 1926; LBT, p. 190.
40. Letter 61, 22 October 1926; LBT, p. 217.
41. Letter 69, 6 and 7 November 1926; LBT, pp. 235–6.
42. Letter 70, 4 November 1926; LBT, p. 240.
43. LDSYJ, p. 101; Letter 71, 9 November 1926; LBT, p. 241.
44. LDSYJ, pp. 116, 121, 144, and 160; Letter 77, 15 November 1926; Letter 78, 16 November 1926; Letter 90, 6 December 1926; Letter 97, 19 December 1926. There is a difference in interpretation of Xu Guangping's Letter 97 between the version printed in the Hunan collection and that by Wang Dehou; Wang's makes better sense.
45. Letter 83, 28 November 1926; LBT, p. 275.
46. Letter 101, 24 December 1926; LBT, p. 317.
47. LDSYJ, pp. 104–5; Letter 73, 15 November 1926; LBT, p. 246.
48. LDSYJ, pp. 122–3; Letter 79, 20 November 1926; LBT, pp. 262–3.
49. LDSYJ, p. 129. Further reflections about Gao Changhong are also deleted from her Letter 84, 27 November 1926.
50. Letter 79, 20 November 1929; LBT, p. 263. See also Lu Xun's letter to Wei Suyuan, 20 November 1926. The announcement also appeared in *Yusi*, *Xin funü* and *Beixin*, and was reprinted in *Fringed Literature*, II.
51. Letter to Wei Suyuan, LXQJ, p. 11.
52. Letter 85, 2 December 1926; LBT, p. 281.
53. In the edition of *Letters between Two* in LXQJ, Lu Xun's Letter 112 (11 January 1927) gives November 1926 as the date when he first heard about the poem, but in the original letter no date is mentioned (LDSYJ, p. 187). In the edition of *Letters between Two* in LXZPQB, a note explains that 'November' is an error for 'December' (p. 329). Lu Xun frequently exchanged letters with Wei Suyuan at this time. For example, Wei wrote to Lu Xun on 23 and 28 November; Lu Xun received these letters on 30 November and 4 December, and wrote back on 5 December. In this letter Lu Xun refers to Gao Changhong's attack on him in *Kuangpiao zhoukan*, No. 5; there is no mention of Gao's poem. He received another letter from Wei Suyuan on 8 December, to which he replied the same day; there is no mention of Gao Changhong in this letter either. His next letter from Wei Suyuan arrived on 13 December, which it seems he did not answer until 29 December, the day on which he actually read the poem for the first time. It, therefore, seems likely that Lu Xun first heard about the poem on 13 December. Fang Xiangdong's account, in *Lu Xun yu ta 'ma' guo de ren* [Lu Xun and the people he 'cursed'], Shanghai shudian chubanshe, Shanghai, 2000, pp. 137–49, contains several errors of this kind.

54. The issue in which the poem appeared is dated 21 November, but dates of publication are not necessarily the actual date of issue.
55. Letter 95, 14–16 December 1926; LBT, pp. 304–5, 307–8.
56. LDSYJ, p. 163.
57. LXQJ, vol. 11, pp. 357–70; translation in LXSW, vol. 1, pp. 283–95. It is not clear when 'Ben yue' was written, but it was probably some time between 13 and 29 December. It was posted to *Mangyuan* on 4 January. Gao Changhong was shocked by Lu Xun's attack on him but did not on this account suspend his literary activities. Gao Changhong spent the war years in Yenan as a teacher and writer but died in obscurity in the mid-1950s, regarded as crazy for such habits as reciting poems by Goethe and Byron in their original language. See 'Gao Changhong wannian shifou feng le?' [Did Gao Changhong go mad at the end of his life?], *Lu Xun yanjiu yuekan*, No. 175 (November 1996), p. 39.
58. It seems unlikely that this is the letter Lu Xun wrote to Zhang Tingqian on on 21 November (see earlier). Zhang sent a reply on 26 November, which Lu Xun received on 30 November. Lu Xun wrote again on 30 November, still not mentioning rumours or Gao Changhong. Zhang wrote back on 1 December and again on 15 December; Lu Xun received these letters on 8 and 22 December, but does not record sending any other letters to Zhang before his arrival on 24 December.
59. Letter 112, 11 January 1926; LBT, pp. 338–40.
60. Huang Jian's return from Peking to Amoy is reported in Letter 95, 14–16 December 1926; LBT, p. 306.
61. Zhang Tingqian's arrival in Amoy is reported in Letter 101, 24 December 1926; LBT, p. 317.
62. Letter to Wei Suyuan, 22 March 1929, LXQJ, vol. 11, pp. 659–61; Chuan Dao [Zhang Tingqian], 'He Lu Xun xiansheng zai Xiamen xiangchu de rizi li'.
63. Recalling the circumstances in 1957, Zhang Tingqian claimed that Lu Xun's reason for leaving Amoy was because of the backward atmosphere there; he denied that it was due to the so-called Hu Shi faction, and asserted that the rumour about 'the moon' was intended to divert attention from the problems (pp. 484–5). Zhang would have read LDS but not the OC.
64. Letter to Wei Suyuan, 29 December 1926, LXQJ, vol. 11, pp. 519–21.
65. Letter 102, 29 December 1926; LBT, p. 319.
66. LDSYJ, p. 166.
67. Ibid., pp. 168–9.
68. LDSYJ, p. 172; Letter 105, 5 January 1927; LBT, p. 323. The mention of *Kuangpiao zhoukan* is an addition.
69. LDSYJ, pp. 185–9; Letter 112, 11 January 1927; LBT, p. 338–40.
70. LDSYJ, pp. 64 and 67.
71. LDSYJ, p. 70; Letter 48, 30 September 1926; LBT, p. 169
72. LDSYJ, p. 159; Letter 96, 20 December 1926; LBT, p. 310.
73. LDSYJ, p. 97.
74. LDSYJ, pp. 208–9; Letter 126, 26 May 1929; LBT, p. 365.

Chapter 19. Political Opinions, Observations, and Activities

1. LDSYJ, p. 8; Letter 3, 15 March 1925; LBT, p. 27.
2. LDSYJ, p. 10; Letter 5, 20 March 1925; LBT, p. 33.
3. LDSYJ, pp. 15, 21, and 24.
4. Ibid., p. 21.
5. Ibid., pp. 31–2.
6. Ibid., pp. 32–3.
7. LDSYJ, pp. 36–8; Letter 30, 17 June 1925; LBT, p. 116.
8. LDSYJ, p. 34.
9. LDSYJ, p. 36.
10. LDSYJ, p. 29; Letter 19, 3 May 1925; LBT, p. 85.
11. LDSYJ, p. 30; Letter 22, 18 May 1925; LBT, p. 92.
12. LDSYJ, p. 34; Letter 26, 2 June 1925; LBT, p. 103.
13. LDSYJ, p. 34; Letter 26, 2 June 1925; LBT, p. 103. For the reference to 'departments' and 'localities', see Chapter 4.
14. LDSYJ, pp. 81–2 and 96.
15. Ibid., p. 97.
16. Ibid., p. 80.
17. LDSYJ, p. 83; Letter 60, 21 and 23 October 1926; LBT, p. 208.
18. LDSYJ, p. 84.
19. Ibid., p. 94.
20. LDSYJ, p. 96; Letter 68, 3 and 4 November 1926; LBT, pp. 231–2.
21. LDSYJ, p. 149; Letter 93, 12 December 1926; LBT, p. 296.
22. LDSYJ, p. 84; Letter 60, 21 and 23 November 1926; LBT, p. 209.
23. LDSYJ, pp. 151 and 156; Letter 93, 12 December 1926; Letter 95, 14–16 December 1926; LBT, pp. 297 and 306.
24. LDSYJ, p. 150; Letter 93, 12 December 1926; LTB, p. 297; see also similar deletions in Letters 96, 101–2, and 104.
25. LDSYJ, p. 170.
26. LDSYJ, p. 165; Letter 102, 29 December 1929; LTB, pp. 318–19.
27. Individual instances are too numerous to cite in full; examples can be found in her Letters 67, 72, 74, 76–7, 82, 84, 87, 90–1, 103, and 106.
28. Individual instances are too numerous to cite in full; examples can be found in her Letters 61, 63, 65, 74, 91, and 110.
29. Individual instances are too numerous to cite in full; examples can be found in her Letters 37, 51, 55, 82, 92, 94, and 106.
30. LDSYJ, pp. 111–13. There is a brief reference to Chen Yanxin's invitation to her to go to Panyu in the second half (all deleted) of Letter 76, 13 November 1926. The full account of her visit is in a letter dated 14 November 1926 that is not included in *Letters between Two*.
31. LDSYJ, p. 60. It is, nevertheless, the case that Wang Dehou is not as thorough in noting revisions to her letters as to Lu Xun's, for example, in Letter 74 and Letter 77.

32. LDSYJ, pp. 58–60, 68–70.
33. LDSYJ, pp. 61, 64, 68, 99, 118–19; Letter 39, 12 September 1926; Letter 43, 17 September 1926; Letter 47, 23 September 1926; Letter 70, 4 November 1926; Letter 78, 16 November 1926.
34. LDSYJ, pp. 98–100 and 101–2; Letter 70, 4 November 1926; Letter 71, 9 November 1926; Letter 72, 7 November 1926; Letter 74, 11 November 1926. A passage to this effect in Letter 74 is not picked up by Wang Dehou.
35. LDSYJ, p. 107; Letter 74, 11 November 1926; LBT, p. 249.
36. LDSYJ, p. 115; Letter 77, 15 November 1926; LBT, p. 256.
37. LDSYJ, pp. 60, 71, 87, 117, 133–4, 162, 172–5; Letter 38, 8 September 1926; Letter 49, 28 September 1926; Letter 61, 21 and 22 October 1926; Letter 77, 15 November 1926; Letter 84, 27 November 1926; Letter 100, 15 December 1926; Letter 106, 27 December 1926.
38. LDSYJ, p. 140.
39. Ibid., p. 106.
40. Ibid., pp. 93, 115, and 149.
41. Ibid., p. 111.
42. Ibid., pp. 95 and 116.
43. Ibid., p. 162.
44. Ibid., pp. 162 and 166.
45. Ibid., p. 149.
46. Ibid., pp. 119, 217, and 222.
47. LDSYJ, pp. 217 and 222; Letter 132, 29 and 30 May 1929; Letter 135, 30 May and 1 June 1929; LBT, pp. 376 and 382.
48. LDSYJ, p. 202; Letter 121, 22 May 1929; LBT, p. 357.
49. LDSYJ, p. 83; Letter 59, 18 October 1926; LBT, p. 206.
50. LDSYJ, p. 182; Letter 110, 5 January 1927; LBT, p. 333.
51. LDSYJ, p. 124; Letter 79, 20 November 1926; LTB, p. 264.
52. LDSYJ, p. 202.
53. LDSYJ, p. 224; Letter 135, 30 May and 1 June 1929; LBT, pp. 382–3.

Chapter 20. Thoughts and Emotions

1. LDSYJ, p. 6.
2. Ibid., p. 8.
3. Ibid., p. 12.
4. LDSYJ, p. 65, Letter 43, 17 September 1926; LBT, p. 153; LDSYJ, p. 65.
5. LDSYJ, p. 103; Letter 72, 7 November 1926; LBT, p. 245.
6. Letter to Leonid Andreev, 10–16 March 1912, cited in Maksim Gorky, *Selected Letters*, translated and edited by Andrew Barratt and Barry P. Scherr, Clarendon Press, Oxford, 1997, p. 16.
7. LDSYJ, p. 29.
8. Ibid., p. 30.
9. LDSYJ, p. 30; Letter 21, 17 May 1925; LBT, p. 91.

10. LDSYJ, pp. 31–2.
11. Letter 66, 1 November 1926; LBT, p. 228.
12. LDSYJ, p. 107.
13. Letter 73, 15 November 1926; LBT, p. 247.
14. LDSYJ, pp. 104–5; Letter 73, 15 November 1926; LBT, p. 248.
15. In the original manuscript for *Letters between Two* Lu Xun writes that he has followed the third path for two years; Wang Dehou thinks that this could have been a slip of the pen in making the fair copy.
16. LDSYJ, pp. 126–31.
17. Wang Dehou, p. 126; but many people in Lu Xun's circle were aware of his dislike for his wife.
18. LDSYJ, p. 109.
19. Letter 75, 18 November 1926; LBT, p. 254.
20. LDSYJ, p. 120; Letter 78, 16 November 1926; LBT, p. 260.
21. LDSYJ, p. 123; Letter 79, 20 November 1926; LBT, p. 263.
22. Letter 121, 22 May 1929; LBT, p. 357.
23. LDSYJ, pp. 203–4.
24. LDSYJ, p. 20. Wang Dehou comments that Lu Xun regarded her praise as excessive, and was always uneasy about being called a genius; in his Letter 38, reporting a comment from a third party, he deletes in *Letters between Two* a remark that he 'doesn't look like a famous scholar'.
25. LDSYJ, p. 36.
26. Letter 50, 4 October 1926; LBT, p. 176.
27. LDSYJ, p. 179; Letter 55, 10 October 1926; LBT, p. 194.
28. Letter 57, 14 October 1926; LBT, p. 201.
29. Letter 62, 28 October 1926; LBT, p. 220.
30. LDSYJ, p. 103; Letter 72, 7 November 1926; LBT, p. 245.
31. LDSYJ, p. 103.
32. LDSYJ, p. 117; Letter 77, 15 November 1926; LBT, p. 258.
33. LDSYJ, p. 114.
34. LDSYJ, p. 143; Letter 90, 6 December 1926; LBT, p. 290.
35. LDSYJ, p. 145; Letter 91, 7 December 1926; LBT, p. 292.
36. Letter 85, 2 December 1926; LBT, p. 279.
37. LDSYJ, pp. 222–3; Letter 135, 30 May and 1 June 1929; LBT, p. 381.
38. A confession of laziness, for example, is retained in his Letter 99, 23 December 1926; LBT, p. 314.
39. LDSYJ, p. 18.
40. Letter 42, 20 September 1926; Letter 60, 21 and 23 October 1926; Letter 75, 18 November 1926; Letter 93, 12 December 1926; Letter 95, 14–16 December 1926; additions in Letter 95 make it even more irascible.
41. LDSYJ, p. 180; Letter 109, 6 January 1927; LBT, pp. 331–2.
42. Letter 122, 23 May 1929; LBT, p. 360.
43. Letter 135, 30 May and 1 June 1929; LBT, p. 382.
44. For example, LDSYJ, p. 73.

45. Ibid., p. 116.
46. See Appendix II, LBT, pp. 394–6.
47. Letter 11, 10 April 1925; LBT, p. 58.
48. Bai Juyi (*Renditions*, 41–2, pp. 51–4) claims to be 'scribbling at random', as also Queen Elizabeth I (Kermode and Kermode, *Oxford Book of Letters*, p. 12).
49. LXZPQB, p. 432; Letter 20, 9 May 1925. This change is not noted in LDSYJ.
50. LSDYJ, p. 201; Letter 119, 17 May 1929.
51. LDSYJ, p. 125; Letter 80, 17 November 1926.
52. LDSYJ, pp. 147–8; Letter 92, 7 December 1926.
53. LDSYJ, p. 220; Letter 134, 28 May 1929.
54. LDSYJ, pp. 9–10; Letter 4, 18 March 1925.
55. LXZPQB, p. 431; Letter 19, 3 May 1925. These changes are not noted in LDSYJ.
56. LDSYJ, p. 64; Letter 42, 20 September 1926.
57. LDSYJ, p. 158; Letter 96, 20 December 1926.
58. LDSYJ, p. 179; Letter 109, 6 January 1927.
59. LDSYJ, p. 180; Letter 109, 6 January 1927.
60. LDSYJ, p. 181; Letter 109, 6 January 1927.
61. LDSYJ, p. 223; Letter 135, 30 May and 1 June 1929.
62. LDSYJ, p. 224; Letter 135, 30 May and 1 June 1929.

Chapter 21. Rumour and Gossip

1. When Hans-Joachim Neubauer's *The Rumour: A Cultural History* (1999) was reviewed by two literary magazines in Britain, the response was lukewarm. Frank Cioffi in *The London Review of Books* (22 June 2000, pp. 20–1) was dismissive, recommending the reader to go back to the 1947 textbook, *The Psychology of Rumor* by Gordon W. Allport and Leo Postman, while John Sutherland in *The Times Literary Supplement* (7 July 2000, p. 36) largely ignored it in favour of his own thoughts on the subject. Among the many works on the subject of rumour and gossip since 1947, two in particular relate gossip to literature (including letters): Patricia Meyer Spack, *Gossip*, and Jan B. Gordon, *Gossip and Subversion in Nineteenth-Century British Fiction: Echo's Economies*, Macmillan, Basingstoke, 1996.
2. This definition is based on Allport and Postman; Tamotsu Shibutani reduces the emphasis on falsehood in his *Improvised News: A Sociological Study of Rumor*, Bobbs-Merrill, Indianapolis, 1996, p. 17.
3. Shibutani, *Improvised News*, pp. 41–2. Feminist critics have maintained on the hand that men gossip as frequently as women but their exchanges are otherwise described, while on the other hand gossip is viewed negatively because of its association with women. See, for example, Spack, *Gossip*, pp. 35 and 38 *et passim*, and Melanie Tebbutt, *Women's Talk? A Social History of 'Gossip' in Working-class Neighbourhoods, 1880–1960*, Scolar Press, Aldershot, 1995, pp. 1–2.

4. *Yu Dafu shuxin ji*, pp. 38 and 71–73.
5. Ibid., pp. 76 and 78.
6. Sissela Bok, *Secrets: On the Ethics of Concealment and Revelation*, Oxford University Press, Oxford, 1984, pp. 89–129. Examples given by Shibutani are rumours occurring in the wake of John F. Kennedy's assassination in 1963 and those spread among Japanese residents in the US in 1941.
7. LXQJ, vol. 6, pp. 331–4; 'Gossip is a Fearful Thing', LXSW, vol. 4, pp. 193–7.
8. Ferdinand David Schoeman, *Privacy and Social Freedom*, Cambridge University Press, Cambridge, 1992, Chapter 8. See also Tebbutt, *Women's Talk?* pp. 4–6.
9. Summarized from Spack, *Gossip*, p. 34.
10. Virginia Woolf not only gossiped in letters to her sister and friends but often expressed a mania for gossip: see *The Question of Things Happening*, pp. 41–43, 104, 143, 146, 200–2, and 209–12. Her editor comments that her rumour-mongering rarely caused distress (pp. 179–80). For gossipy letters from Dora Carrington and Aldous Huxley, see Kermode and Kermode, *The Oxford Book of Letters*, pp. 482–8, 493–5.
11. Kermode and Kermode, *The Oxford Book of Letters*, p. 90; see also Saintsbury, *A Letter Book*, pp. 31–7.
12. See the letter by Ma Yuan (14 BC to AD 49) to his nephews, preserved in his biography in the *Hou Han shu* [History of the Later Han dynasty], translated in *Renditions*, 41–2 (Spring and Autumn 1994), pp. 4–6.
13. LDSJY, p. 17; Letter 12, 14 April 1925; LBT, p. 59. Wang Dehou also provides extracts from other letters by Lu Xun condemning gossip (LDSYJ, pp. 17–18).
14. Letter 24, 30 May 1925; LBT, p. 98.
15. LDSYJ, p. 63; Letter 41, 12 and 14 September 1926; LBT, p. 147.
16. Letter 47, 23 September 1926; LBT, p. 165.
17. LDSYJ, p. 70; Letter 48, 29 and 30 September 1926; LBT, p. 169.
18. For further detail on Sun Fuyuan see Chapters 5 and 18.
19. For further detail on Gao Changhong see Chapters 5 and 18.
20. Letter 62, 28 October 1926, Letter 83, 28 November 1926, and Letter 112, 11 January 1927; LBT, pp. 219, 275, and 338–40.
21. Letter 104, 2 January 1927; LBT, p. 322.
22. Letter 110, 5 January 1927; LBT, p. 334. Some of Xu Guangping's remarks on the gossip about them in Letter 111, 7 January 1927, is deleted in *Letters between Two*; see LDSYJ, p. 184.
23. LDSYJ, p. 189; Letter 112, 11 January 1927; LBT, p. 341.
24. Letter 117, 17 May 1929; Letter 132, 29 and 30 May 1929; LBT, pp. 351 and 376.
25. LDSYJ, p. 209; Letter 126, 25 and 26 May 1929; LBT, p. 366.
26. LDSYJ, p. 216.
27. Ibid., p. 212.
28. Ibid., p. 209.

Chapter 22. Secrecy, Seclusion, and Private/Selfish Interests

1. *The Sociology of Georg Simmel*, translated, edited, and with an introduction by Kurt H. Wolff, Free Press, New York, 1950; see Part Four: The Secret and the Secret Society, pp. 307–76.
2. Ibid., p. 330.
3. Ibid., p. 331.
4. Ibid., p. 332.
5. Ibid., pp. 333–4.
6. Erving Goffman, *The Presentation of Self in Everyday Life*, Allen Lane, Penguin Press, London, 1969, pp. 123–4.
7. Inness, *Privacy, Intimacy, and Isolation*, pp. 60–1.
8. Carol Warren and Barbara Laslett, 'Privacy and Secrecy: A Conceptual Comparison', (1997); reprinted in *Secrecy: A Cross-Cultural Perspective*, Stanton K. Tefft (ed.), Human Sciences Press, New York, 1980, pp. 25–34.
9. Ibid., p. 25.
10. Ibid., p. 30.
11. Ibid., p. 32.
12. Stanton K. Tefft, 'Secrecy, Disclosure and Social Theory', in *Secrecy: A Cross-Cultural Perspective*, pp. 35–74.
13. Ibid., p. 63.
14. Ibid., p. 67.
15. Ibid., p. 32.
16. For Bok's distinction between secrecy and privacy, see pp. 10–14; for privacy as a legal right, see pp. 90 and 141.
17. LDSYJ, p. 255; Letter 13, 16 April 1925; LTB, p. 63.
18. LDSYJ, p. 209; Letter 126, 25 and 26 May 1929; LBT, p. 366.
19. Letter 31, 19 June 1925; LBT, p. 118.
20. LDSYJ, p. 34; Letter 25, 1 June 1925; LBT, p. 101.
21. Letter 26, 2 June 1925; LBT, p. 103.
22. Letter 64, 209 October 1926; LBT, p. 223.
23. LDSYJ, p. 201; Letter 120, 17 May 1929; LBT, pp. 355–6.
24. Letter 66, 1 November 1926; LBT, p. 226.
25. LDSYJ, p. 106.
26. Letter 110, 5 January 1927; LBT, p. 333.
27. Letter 116, 15 May 1929; Letter 118, 19 and 21 May 1929; LBT, pp. 350 and 353.
28. Letter 120, 17 May 1929; LBT, p. 355.
29. LDSYJ, p. 189; Letter 113, 17 January 1927; LBT, p. 342.
30. Fernand G. Renier, *Dutch Dictionary: Dutch–English, English–Dutch*, Routledge, London, 1989.
31. See Eva Shan Chou, 'Tu Fu's "General Ho" Poems: Social Obligations and Poetic Response', *Harvard Journal of Asiatic Studies*, vol. 60, no. 1 (June 2000), pp. 165–204, esp. pp. 199–201.

32. Letter 85, 2 December 1926; Letter 86, 3 December 1926; LBT, pp. 280 and 282.
33. Letter 93, 12 December 1926; LBT, p. 298.
34. LDSYJ, p. 151.
35. Ibid., p. 151.
36. LDSYJ, p. 165; Letter 102, 29 December 1926; LBT, p. 318.
37. LDSYJ, p. 180; Letter 109, 6 January 1927; LBT, p. 332.
38. Letter 51, 30 September and 4 October 1926; LBT, p. 180.
39. LDSYJ, p. 178; Letter 107, 30 December 1926.
40. Letter 121, 22 May 1929; LBT, p. 358.
41. Letter 122, 23 May 1929; LBT, p. 360.
42. Letter 134, 28 May 1929; LBT, p. 379.
43. LDSYJ, p. 220.
44. LDSYJ, p. 224; Letter 135, 30 May and 1 June, 1929; LBT, p. 383.
45. For Rousseau's views on privacy, see Margaret Ogrodnick, *Instinct and Intimacy: Political Philosophy and Autobiography in Rousseau*, University of Toronto Press, Toronto, 1999, Chapter 7, 'Public and Private Realms', pp. 162–93; for his interest in solitude and nature, see pp. 165–6.
46. See Inness, *Privacy, Intimacy, and Isolation*, p. 13 for a distinction between 'privacy', the state she discusses, and 'private', which she declines to include in her discussion; unfortunately, the distinction is left vague, but I take it to refer to such uses as 'private interests', where 'private' is equivalent to 'selfish'.
47. An example of *si* meaning 'personal' is in Yu Dafu's essay title, 'Yiwen si jian' [A personal view on literature and the arts]; see *Yu Dafu wen ji*, vol. 5, pp. 117–19.
48. Charlotte Furth, 'Culture and Politics in Modern Chinese Conservatism' in *The Limits of Change: Essays on Conservative Alternatives in Republican China*, Harvard University Press, Cambridge, MA, 1976, pp. 22–53; see p. 27. Passing references in the correspondence can be found in Letter 9, 6 April 1925; Letter 19, 3 May 1925; LBT, pp. 46 and 84.
49. Letter 27, 5 June 1925, LBT, p. 106.
50. LDSYJ, p. 34; Letter 27, 5 June 1925, LBT, p. 106.
51. Letter 57, 14 October 1926; LBT, p. 199.
52. Letter 58, 20 October 1926; LBT, p. 204.
53. Letter 58, 20 October 1926; LBT, p. 202.
54. LDSYJ, p. 92; Letter 64, 29 October 1926; LBT, p. 223.
55. LDSYJ, p. 159; Letter 97, 19 December 1926.
56. Letter 105, 5 January 1927; LBT, p. 324.
57. LDSYJ, pp. 191–3.

Chapter 23. Personal Space as Privacy

1. For an introductory survey of recent research on privacy in English, see McDougall, 'Chinese Concepts of Privacy Workshop Briefing paper: concepts

of privacy in English (draft)' at www.ed.ac.uk/asianstudies/privacy project (2001).

2. Alan F. Westin, *Privacy and Freedom*, Bodley Head, London, 1967, pp. 31–2.
3. Ibid., pp. 32–9.
4. Schoeman, *Privacy and Social Freedom*, p. 13–14.
5. Adapted from Inness, *Privacy, Intimacy, and Isolation*, p. 56.
6. Ibid., 74–94.
7. Goffman, *The Presentation of Self in Everyday Life*, pp. 111–12, 114, 123–4, and 149–54.
8. June Noble and William Noble, *The Private Me*, Delacorte Press, New York, 1980, pp. 13–14.
9. Goffman, *The Presentation of Self in Everyday Life*, 119–20.
10. Noble and Noble, *The Private Me*, pp. 15–17.
11. Inness, *Privacy, Intimacy, and Isolation*, p. 52.
12. Adapted from Inness, *Privacy, Intimacy, and Isolation*, pp. 138–9.
13. Inness, *Privacy, Intimacy, and Isolation*, pp. 7–8, 95–115. Inness proposes a third option, that 'privacy is valuable because it acknowledges our respect for persons as autonomous beings with the capacity to love, care and like—in other words, persons with the potential to freely develop close relationships'. (p. 95) While this argument is persuasive it is not yet commonly adopted.
14. For Virginia Woolf's fondness for reading old letters, see *A Change of Perspective*, p. 69.
15. LDSYJ, pp. 150 and 152; Letter 93, 12 December 1926; see also above, p. 147.
16. LSDYJ, p. 215; Letter 130, 23 May 1929. Wang Dehou comments that the salutation is strangely formal, and that the weakened expression in the earlier phrase is significant.
17. LDSYJ, p. 216; Letter 131, 24 May 1929.
18. LDSYJ, p. 84; Letter 60, 21 and 23 November 1926; LDSYJ, p. 150; Letter 93; see also similar deletions in Letters 96, 101, 102, and 104; LDSYJ, p. 170; Letter 104; see also Letter 81; LDSYJ, p. 165; Letter 102, 29 December 1929.
19. For example, he retains in one of his letters a reference to a remark of hers in an earlier letter that he deleted: see LDSYJ, p. 150; Letter 93, 12 December 1926.
20. LDSYJ, p. 1.
21. Ibid., p. 258.
22. Ibid., pp. 263–4.
23. LDSYJ, p. 162; Letter 100, 15 December 1926.

Chapter 24. Revealing to Conceal: *Letters between Two* and the Original Correspondence

1. Adapted from the Introduction to her book by Inness, *Privacy, Intimacy, and Isolation*, p. 3.
2. Ibid., p. 4.
3. Zhang Longxi, *Mighty Opposites*, p. 113.

References

Allport, Gordon W. and Leo Postman, *The Psychology of Rumor*, Henry Holt, New York, 1947.

Altman, Janet Gurkin, *Epistolarity: Approaches to a Form*, Ohio State University Press, Columbia, 1982.

Arendt, Hannah and Martin Heidegger, *Briefe 1925 bis 1975 und andere Zeugnisse*, ed. Ursula Ludz, Klostermann, Frankfurt, 1998.

Arendt, Hannah, *The Human Condition*, University of Chicago Press, Chicago, 1958.

Ariès, Philippe and Georges Duby, eds, *A History of Private Life*, vol. 1, Harvard University Press, Cambridge, Mass., 1987.

Asquith, H. H., *H. H. A.: Letters of the Earl of Oxford and Asquith to a Friend, First Series 1915–1922*, ed. Desmond MacCarthy, Geoffrey Bles, London, 1933.

Austen, Jane, *Northanger Abbey and Persuasion*, Oxford University Press, Oxford, 1969.

Ba Jin, *Random Thoughts*, Joint Publications, Hong Kong, 1984.

Bakewell, Michael and Melissa Bakewell, *Augusta Leigh: Byron's Half-sister*, Chatto and Windus, London, 2000.

Baum, Richard, *Burying Mao: Chinese Politics in the Age of Deng Xiaoping*, Princeton University Press, Princeton, 1994.

Beethoven, Ludwig von, *The Letters of Beethoven*, ed. Emily Anderson, Macmillan, London, 1961.

Behn, Aphra, *Love Letters between a Nobleman and His Sister*, Virago Press, London, 1987.

Bernhardt, Kathryn, 'Women and the Law: Divorce in the Republican Period' in *Civil Law in Qing and Republican China*, ed. Kathryn Bernhardt and Philip C. C. Huang, SMC Publishing, Taibei, 1994, pp. 187–214.

Bing Xin, *Ji xiao duzhe* [To young readers], Hebei jiaoyu chubanshe, Shijiazhuang, 1955.

Birch, Cyril, ed., *Anthology of Chinese Literature*, Penguin Books, Harmondsworth, 1965.

Bok, Sissela, *Secrets: On the Ethics of Concealment and Revelation*, Oxford University Press, Oxford, 1984.

Bourdieu, Pierre, *The Field of Cultural Production: Essays on Art and Literature*, ed. Randal Johnson, Polity Press, Oxford, 1993.

Bradbury, Malcolm, *The History Man*, Arrow Books, London, 1977.

Brontë, Charlotte, *The Letters of Charlotte Brontë*, vols 1 & 2, ed. Margaret Smith, Clarendon Press, Oxford, 1995 & 2000.

Brook, Timothy, 'Communications and commerce' in *Cambridge History of China*, vol. 8, ed. Denis Twitchett and Frederick W. Mote, Cambridge University Press, Cambridge, 1998, pp. 579–707.

Brown, Donald E., *Human Universals*, McGraw-Hill, New York, 1991.

Cahm, Eric, *The Dreyfus Affair in French Society and Politics*, Longman, London, 1994.

Cai Diqiu, ed., *Shiyong xie xin bu qiu ren* [Practical letter-writing unaided], Wenguo shuju, Tainan, 1998.

Cao Juren, 'Wo yu Lu Xun' [I and Lu Xun] and 'Lu Xun yu wo' [Lu Xun and I] in *Lu Xun huiyi lu (sanpian)*, vol. 2, pp. 799–804 and 805–10.

Cao Juren, ed., *Sanshi niandai zuojia shuxin* [Letters by 1930s writers], Chuangken chubanshe, Hong Kong, 1988.

Cao Zhaolan, ed., *Lidai nüzi qingshu xuan* [Selected love-letters by women from history], Baichuan shuju, Taibei, 1988.

Carson, James, 'Narrative Cross-Dressing and the Critique of Authorship in the Novels of Richardson' in Goldsmith, *Writing the Female Voice*, pp. 95–113.

Ceng Minzhi, *Lu Xun zai Guangzhou de rizi* [Lu Xun's time in Canton], Guangdong renmin chubanshe, Guangzhou, 1956.

Ceng Zhizhong, *Sanren xing: Lu Xun yu Xu Guangping, Zhu An* [A love triangle: Lu Xun with Xu Guangping and Zhu An], Zhongguo qingnian chubanshe, Beijing, 1990.

Chang Hui, 'Huiyi Lu Xun xiansheng' [Reminiscences of Mr Lu Xun] in *Lu Xun huiyi lu (sanpian)*, vol. 1, pp. 420–33.

Chao, Buwei Yang, *Autobiography of a Chinese Woman*, Greenwood Press, Westport, 1947.

Chartier, Roger, Alain Boureau and Cécile Dauphin, *Correspondence: Models of Letter-Writing from the Middle Ages to the Nineteenth Century*, Polity Press, Cambridge, 1997.

Chen Baichen, 'Yi xiang wei wancheng de jinian' [An incomplete commemoration], *Lu Xun yanjiu*, May 1981; reprinted in *Chen Baichen lun ju* [Chen Baichen on the theatre], ed. Dong Jian, Zhongguo xiju chubanshe, Beijing, 1987, pp. 315–19.

Ch'en Shou-yi, *Chinese Literature: A Historical Introduction*, Ronald Press Company, New York, 1961.

Chen Shuyu, ' "Xi shou gong jianwei": jinian Lu Xun de qinmi zhanyou Xu Guangping tongzhi' [Facing hardship hand-in-hand: commemorating Lu Xun's intimate comrade-in-arms, comrade Xu Guangping] in Ma Tiji, comp., *Xu Guangping yi Lu Xun*, pp. 724–56.

Chen Shuyu, ' "Xiangde" yu "shuli"—Lin Yutang yu Lu Xun de jiaowang shishi ji qi wenhua sikao' ['Complementary' and 'estranged': the historical facts of Lin Yutang's association with Lu Xun, and reflections on culture], *Xin wenxue shiliao*, no. 67 (May 1995), pp. 125–36, 94.

Chen Shuyu, 'Ai de kaige—Xu Guangping san bian yigao du hou' [Love's triumphal song: after reading three posthumous manuscripts by Xu Guangping], *Lu Xun yanjiu niankan*, 1990, pp. 613–23.

Chen Shuyu, 'Lu Xun yu Hu Shi' [Lu Xun and Hu Shi], *Lu Xun yanjiu niankan*, 1991–1992 heben, pp. 95–115.

Chen Shuyu, *Lu Xun de fengyue xiantan* [Lu Xun's remarks on romance], Hunan wenyi chubanshe, Changsha, 1994.

Chen Shuyu, *Lu Xun yu Nüshida xuesheng yundong* [Lu Xun and the student movement at WNC], Beijing renmin chubanshe, Beijing, 1978.

Chen Shuyu, *Lu Xun zai Beijing* [Lu Xun in Peking], Tianjin renmin chubanshe, Tianjin, 1978.

Chen Shuyu, *Xu Guangping yi sheng* [A life of Xu Guangping], Tianjin renmin chubanshe, Tianjin, 1981.

Cheng, Ying-wan, *Postal Communication in China and its Modernization 1860–1896*, Harvard East Asian Monographs, Cambridge, Mass., 1970.

Chidu huibian [An anthology of letters], Guangwen shuju, Taibei, n.d.

Chinn, Dian Wen K., *Practical Chinese Letter Writing*, Chinese Materials Center, San Francisco, 1980.

Chou, Chih-p'ing, comp., *A Collection of Hu Shi's English Writings*, Yuanliu chubanshe, Taibei, 1995.
Chou, Chih-p'ing, *Yüan Hung-tao and the Kung-an School*, Cambridge University Press, Cambridge, 1988.
Chou, Eva Shan, 'The Political Martyr in Lu Xun's Writings', *Asia Major*, 3rd series, vol. 12, pt 2, pp. 139–62.
Chow, William C. S., 'Chou Tso-jen and the New Village Movement', *Chinese Studies*, vol. 10, no. 1 (June 1992), pp. 105–34.
Chow, William Cheong-loong, 'Chou Tso-jen: A serene radical in the new culture movement', Universisty of Wisconsin-Madison PhD dissertation, 1990.
Chu Chia-hua [Zhu Jiahua], *China's Postal and Other Communications Services*, Kegan Paul, London, 1937.
Chuan Dao [Zhang Tingqian], 'He Lu Xun xiansheng zai Xiamen xiangchu de rizi li' [Shared times with Mr Lu Xun in Amoy] in *Lu Xun huiyi lu (sanpian)*, vol. 1, pp. 474–86.
Chuan Dao [Zhang Tingqian], 'Lu Xun xiansheng shenghuo suoji' [Fragments from Mr Lu Xun's life] in *Lu Xun huiyi lu (sanpian)*, vol. 1, pp. 326–29.
Chuan Tang, 'Guanyu Nüshida shijian de yi shu shuxin' [A bundle of letters concerning the WCN affair], *Lu Xun yanjiu ziliao*, no. 4 (1990), pp. 338–44.
Chung, Eva Yuen-wah, *Study of the shu (letters) of the Han Dynasty (206 B.C.–A.D. 220)*, UMI Dissertation Services, Ann Arbor, 1994.
Chuzo Ichiko, 'Political and institutional reform, 1901–11' in*Cambridge History of China*, vol. 11, ed. John K. Fairbank and Kwang-ching Liu, Cambridge University Press, Cambridge, 1980, pp. 375–415.
Cicero, Marcus Tullius, *Letters to His Friends*, Loeb Classical Library, Harvard University Press, Cambridge, Mass., 1927.
Cicero, Marcus Tullius, *Letters to Atticus*, ed. D. R. Shackleton Bailey, Loeb Classical Library, Harvard University Press, Cambridge, Mass., 1999.
Cicero, Marcus Tullius, *Selected Letters*, trans. D. R. Shackleton Bailey, Penguin Books, Harmondsworth, [1982].
Clark, Paul, *Chinese Cinema: Culture and Politics since 1949*, Cambridge University Press, Cambridge, 1987.
Cochran, Sherman, ed., *Inventing Nanjing Road: Commercial Culture in Shanghai, 1900–1945*, Cornell University Press, Ithaca, 1999.
Commemorating Lu Hsun—Our Forerunner in the Cultural Revolution, Foreign Languages Press, Beijing, 1967.
Co-operative Working Women, *Life as We Have Known It*, ed. Margaret Llewelyn Davies, Virago, London, 1977.
Crocker, Lester G., *Jean-Jacques Rousseau: The Prophetic Voice (1758–1778)*, Macmillan, New York, 1973.
Crowther, Mary Owens, *The Book of Letters: What Letters to Write for Every Purpose, Business and Social. The Ettiquette of Correspondence*, Garden City Publishing, New York, 1922.
Day, Katherine J., 'Perspectives on Privacy: a Sociological Analysis', PhD dissertation, University of Edinburgh, 1985.
de Beauvoir, Simone, *Beloved Chicago Man: Letters to Nelson Algren 1947–64*, comp. Sylvie Le Bon de Beauvoir, Victor Gollancz, London, 1988.
de Lavergne, Gabriel, *Vicomte de Guilleragues*, *The Love Letters of a Portuguese Nun*, trans. Guido Waldman, Harvill, London, 1996.

de Sévigné, *Madame*, *Selected Letters*, trans. Leonard Tancock, Penguin Books, Harmondsworth, 1982.

Dickens, Charles, *Selected Letters of Charles Dickens*, ed. David Paroissien, Macmillan, London, 1985.

Ding Xilin, *Xilin dumuju ji* [Xilin's one-act plays], Wenhua shenghuo chubanshe, Shanghai, 1947.

Ding Yanzhao, '*Yu Dafu riji* can pian zhong de Lu Xun' [Lu Xun in passages from *Yu Dafu's diary*], *Lu Xun yanjiu yuekan*, no. 178 (February 1997), pp. 66–69.

Dirlik, Arif, 'Narrativizing Revolution: The Guangzhou Uprising in Workers' Perspective', *Modern China*, vol. 23, no. 4 (October 1997), pp. 363–97.

Dooling, Amy D. and Kristina M. Torgeson, *Writing Women in Modern China: An anthology of women's literature from the early twentieth century*, Columbia University Press, New York, 1998.

Ebrey, Patricia Buckley, *The Inner Quarters: Marriage and the Lives of Chinese Women in the Sung Period*, University of California Press, Berkeley, 1993.

Ebrey, Patricia, 'T'ang Guides to Verbal Etiquette', *Harvard Journal of Asiatic Studies*, vol. 45, no. 2 (1985), pp. 581–613.

Edwards, Louise, 'New Hongxue and the "Birth of the Author": Yu Pingbo's "On Qin Keqing's Death" ', forthcoming.

Egan, Ronald C., *Words, Image, and Deed in the Life of Su Shi*, Harvard University Press, Cambridge, Mass., 1994.

Egerton, George, *A Leaf from the Yellow Book: the correspondence of George Egerton*, ed. Terence de Vere White, Richards Press, London, 1958.

Elias, Norbert, *On Civilization, Power, and Knowledge*, ed. Stephen Mennell and Johan Goudsblom, University of Chicago Press, Chicago, 1998.

Elias, Norbert, *The Civilizing Process, The History of Manners and State Formation and Civilization*, Blackwell, Oxford, 1994.

Ellis, Kenneth, *The Post Office in the Eighteenth Century: A Study in Administrative History*, Oxford University Press, London, 1958.

Emerson, Gary Saul and Caryl Morson, *Mikhail Bakhtin: Creation of a Prosaics*, Stanford University Press, Stanford, 1990.

Ettinger, Elzbieta, *Hannah Arendt, Martin Heidegger*, Yale University Press, New Haven, 1995.

Etzioni, Amitai, *The Limits of Privacy*, Basic Books, New York, 1999.

Everybody's Letter-writer, by A Society Lady, with a specially-written section on Love, Courtship, and Marriage, Foulsham, London, n.d.

Fan Zhiting, *Lu Xun yu Xu Guangping*, Henan renmin chubanshe, Shijiazhuang, 1986.

Fang Xiangdong, *Lu Xun yu ta 'ma' guo de ren* [Lu Xun and the people he 'cursed'], Shanghai shudian chubanshe, Shanghai, 1996.

Fang Xiangdong, *Lu Xun: zui shou wumie de ren* [Lu Xun: the most reviled man], Shanghai shudian chubanshe, Shanghai, 2000.

Favret, Mary A., *Romantic Correspondence: Women, politics and the fiction of letters*, Cambridge University Press, Cambridge, 1993.

Feng Xuefeng, *Huiyi Lu Xun* [Reminiscences of Lu Xun], Renmin chubanshe, Beijing, 1952.

Feuerwerker, Albert, 'The foreign presence in China' in *Cambridge History of China*, vol. 12, ed. John K. Fairbank, Cambridge University Press, Cambridge, 1983, pp. 128–208.

Findeisen, Raoul David, 'From Literature to Love: Glory and decline of the love-letter genre' in Hockx, *The Literary Field of Twentieth-Century China*, pp. 79–112.
Flaherty, David H., ed., *Privacy and Data Protection: An International Bibliography*, Mansell Publishing, London, 1984.
Flaherty, David H., *Protecting Privacy in Surveillance Societies: the Federal Republic of Germany, Sweden, France, Canada, & the United States*, University of North Carolina Press, Chapel Hill, 1989.
Flaherty, David H., *Protecting Privacy in Two-Way Electronic Services*, Knowledge Industry Publications, White Plains, 1985.
Fodor, Jerry A., *Concepts: Where Cognitive Science Went Wrong*, Clarendon Press, Oxford, 1998.
Fraser, Antonia, ed., *Love Letters: An Anthology*, Weidenfeld and Nicolson, London, 1976.
Fu, Poshek, *Passivity, Resistance, and Collaboration: Intellectual Choices in Occupied Shanghai, 1937–1945*, Stanford University Press, Stanford, 1993.
Fujii Shôzô, 'Ta shi Niuyue Dada pai: Hu Shi de lianren E. Kulifuduo.Weiliansi de yi sheng' [She was a New York dadaist: a biography of Hu Shi's lover E. Clifford Williams], trans. Wang Huimin, *Lu Xun yanjiu yuekan*, no. 182 (June 1997), pp. 50–57.
Fujii Shôzô, *Lu Xun bijiao yanjiu* [Comparative studies of Lu Xun], trans. Chen Fukang, Waiyu jiaoyu chubanshe, Shanghai, 1997.
Furth, Charlotte, ed., *The Limits of Change: Essays on Conservative Alternatives in Republican China*, Harvard University Press, Cambridge, Mass., 1976.
Gao Changhong, 'Yi dian huiyi: guanyu Lu Xun he wo' [A recollection: concerning Lu Xun and me], *Lu Xun huiyi lu (sanpian)*, vol. 1, pp. 178–97.
'Gao Changhong wannian shi fou feng le' [Did Gao Changhong go mad at the end of his life?], *Lu Xun yanjiu yuekan*, no. 175 (November 1996), p. 39.
Gao Daoyi, '*Liang di shu* chuquan zhi wo jian' [My view on the copyright of *Letters between two*], *Lu Xun yanjiu yuekan*, no. 182 (June 1997), p. 43.
Gay, Peter, *The Naked Heart: The bourgeois experience Victoria to Freud*, HarperCollins, London, 1996.
Gillis, Christina Marsden, *The Paradox of Privacy: Epistolary Form in 'Clarissa'*, University Presses of Florida, Gainesville, 1984.
Goethe, Johann Wolfgang von, *Letters from Goethe*, trans. M. von Herzfeld and C. Melvil Sym, Edinburgh University Press, Edinburgh, 1957.
Goethe, Johann Wolfgang von, *The Sorrows of Young Werther*, trans. Michael Hulse, Penguin Books, Harmondsworth, 1989.
Goffman, Erving, *Relations in Public: Microstudies of the Public Order*, Basic Books, New York, 1971.
Goffman, Erving, *The Presentation of Self in Everyday Life*, Allen Lane, Penguin Press, London, 1969.
Goldsmith, Elizabeth C., 'Authority, Authenticity, and the Publication of Letters by Women' in Goldsmith, *Writing the Female Voice*, pp. 46–59.
Goldsmith, Elizabeth C., ed., *Writing the Female Voice: Essays on Epistolary Literature*, Northeastern University Press, Boston, 1989.
Gordon, Jan B., *Gossip and Subversion in Nineteenth-Century British Fiction: Echo's Economies*, Macmillan, Basingstoke, 1996.
Gorky, Maksim, *Selected Letters*, trans. & ed. Andrew Barratt and Barry P. Scherr, Clarendon Press, Oxford, 1997.

Grundy, Isobel, *Lady Mary Wortley Montagu*, Oxford University Press, Oxford, 1999.

Gu, Edward X., 'Cultural Intellectuals and the Politics of the Cultural Public Space in Communist China (1979–1989): A Case Study of Three Intellectual Groups', *Journal of Asian Studies*, vol. 38, no. 2 (May 1999), pp. 389–431.

Guo Moruo, *Moruo wen ji* [Moruo's selected works], Renmin wenxue chubanshe, Beijing, 1957.

Guo Moruo, Tian Han [and] Zong Baihua, *Sanye ji* [Trefoil], Yadong tushuguan, Shanghai, 1920.

Habermas, Jürgen, *The Structural Transformation of the Public Sphere: An Inquiry into a Category of Bourgeois Society*, trans. Thomas Burger, MIT Press, Cambridge, Mass., 1989.

Habermas, Jürgen, *The Theory of Communicative Action, vol. 2: Lifeworld and System: A Critique of Functionalist Reason*, Polity Press, Cambridge, 1987.

Hall, David L. and Roger T. Ames, *Thinking Through Confucius*, State University of New York Press, Albany, 1987.

Hamilton, Robin and Nicolas Soames, eds, *Intimate Letters*, Marginalia Press, London, 1994.

Hanan, Patrick, *The Chinese Vernacular Story*, Harvard University Press, Cambridge, Mass. 1981.

Hanan, Patrick, *The Invention of Li Yu*, Harvard University Press, Cambridge, Mass., 1988.

Harrell, Paula, *Sowing the Seeds of Change: Chinese Students, Japanese Teachers, 1895–1905*, Stanford University Press, Stanford, 1992.

Harrison, Henrietta, *The Making of the Republican Citizen: Political Ceremonies and Symbols in China, 1911–1929*, Oxford University Press, Oxford, 2000.

Hart, Francis R., *Lockhart as Romantic Biographer*, Edinburgh University Press, Edinburgh, 1971.

Hartley, L. P., *The Go-Between*, Hamish Hamilton, London, 1953.

Hawkes, David, *A Little Primer of Du Fu*, Clarendon Press, Oxford, 1967.

Hockx, Michel, 'Playing the Field: Aspects of Chinese Literary Life in the 1920s' in Hockx, *The Literary Field of Twentieth-Century China*, pp. 61–78.

Hockx, Michel, ed., *The Literary Field of Twentieth-Century China*, Curzon Press, Richmond, 1999.

Hodlin, Tim and Sue Hodlin, *Writing letters in English; a practical guide*, Oxford University Press, Oxford, 1979.

Hoffman, Lance J., ed., *Computers and Privacy in the Next Decade*, Academic Press, New York, 1980.

Hofstadter, Samuel H. and George Horowitz, *The Right of Privacy*, Central Book Company, New York, 1964.

Horne, Philip, ed., *Henry James: A Life in Letters*, Allen Lane, London, 1999.

Hsiao Ch'ien [Xiao Qian], *Traveller without a Map*, Stanford University Press, Stanford, 1993.

Hsiung Ping-chen [Xiong Bingzhen], 'The Domestic, the Personal, and the Intimate: "Privacy" and Father-Daughter Bonds in Late Imperial China', unpublished conference paper.

Hu Shi *et al.*, *Hu Shi laiwang shuxin xuan* [Selected letters by and to Hu Shi], Zhonghua shuju, Hong Kong, 1983.

Hu Shi, 'Hu Shi zaoqi de shuxin he shiwen' [Early letters, poems and prose by Hu Shi], comp. Shen Ji, *Jindai shi ziliao*, no. 65 (May 1987), pp. 71–78.

Hu Shi, *Hu Shi jiashu* [Hu Shi's family letters], ed. Lu Fachun, Anhui renmin chubanshe, Hefei, 1996.

Hu Shi, *Sishi zishu* [My life at forty], Jindai Zhongguo shiliao congkan xubian, Wenhai chubanshe, Taibei, 1983, vol. 952, pp. 1–175.

Huang Baozhen, ed., *Gudai wenren shuxin jinghua* [Prime selection of letters by literati of the past], Renmin wenxue chubanshe, Beijing, 1992.

Huang Fu-ch'ing, *Chinese Students in Japan in the Late Ch'ing Period*, Centre for East Asian Cultural Studies, Tokyo, 1982.

Huang, Philip C. C., *Civil Justice in China: Representation and Practice in the Qing*, Stanford University Press, Stanford, 1996.

Hung, Eva, 'Reading Between the Lines: The Life of Zhu An (1878–1947)', in *China in seinen biographische Dimensionen, Gedenkschrift für Helmut Martin*, ed. Christina Neder *et al.*, Harrassowitz, Wiesbaden, 2001, pp. 245–58.

Hymes, Robert P. and Conrad Schirokauer, eds, *Ordering the World: Approaches to State and Society in Sung Dynasty China,* University of California Press, Berkeley, 1993.

Inness, Julie C., *Privacy, Intimacy, and Isolation*, Oxford University Press, New York, 1992.

Jacobson, Howard, *Ovid's Heroides*, Princeton University Press, New Jersey, 1974.

Jagodzinski, Cecile M., *Privacy and Print: Reading and Writing in Seventeenth-Century England*, University Press of Virginia, Charlottesville, 1999.

James, Henry, *Literary Criticism: Essays on Literature; American Writers; English Writers*, Library of America, New York, 1984.

Jensen, Katherine A., 'Male Models of Feminine Epistolarity; or, How to Write Like a Woman in Seventeenth-Century France' in Goldsmith, *Writing the Female Voice*, pp. 25–45.

Ji Weizhou *et al.*, *Lu Xun yanjiu shulu* [A bibliography of Lu Xun studies], Shumu wenxian chubanshe, Beijing, 1987.

Jing Song [Xu Guangping] *et al.*, *Lu Xun de chuangzuo fangfa ji qita* [Lu Xun's creative methods, and other articles], Dushu chubanshe, Chongqing, 1939, 3rd ed., 1942.

Jing Song [Xu Guangping], 'Min yuan qian de Lu Xun xiansheng' [Mr Lu Xun before 1911] in *Lu Xun huiyi lu (zhuanzhu)*, vol. 1, pp. 97–104 and in *Xu Guangping wen ji*, vol. 2, pp. 442–46.

Jing Song [Xu Guangping], *Zaonan qianhou* [Before and after adversity], Shanghai chuban gongsi, Shanghai, 1947, rev. ed. 1951.

Jing Youlin, 'Lu Xun huiyi duanpian' [Fragmentary reminiscences of Lu Xun] in *Lu Xun huiyi lu (zhuanzhu)*, vol. 1, pp. 119–205.

Jones, William C., trans., *The Great Qing Code*, Clarendon Press, Oxford, 1994.

Kakfa, Franz, *Letters to Milena*, trans. Philip Boehm, Schocker Books, New York, 1990.

Karlin, Danield, ed., *Robert Browning and Elizabeth Barrett: The courtship correspondence 1845–1846, A selection*, Clarendon Press, Oxford, 1989.

Kauffman, Linda S., *Discourses of Desire: Gender, Genre, and Epistolary Fictions*, Cornell University Press, Ithaca, 1986.

Kauffman, Linda S., *Special Delivery: Epistolary modes in modern fiction*, University of Chicago Press, Chicago, 1992.

Kawase Ryôji, 'Rôjin to Kô Chôkô' [Lu Xun and Gao Changhong], *Nishô-gakusha Daigaku Daigakuin-kiyô*, 1992, pp. 447–78.

Keating, Walter S., *How to Write Love Letters*, Stravon, 1943, rev. ed. 1953.

Kenyon, Olga, *800 Years of Women's Letters*, Allan Sutton, Stroud, 1992.

Kermode, Frank and Anita Kermode, eds, *The Oxford Book of Letters*, Oxford, Oxford University Press, 1995.

Kinkley, Jeffrey, *The Odyssey of Shen Congwen*, Stanford, Stanford University Press, 1987.

Kishi Yôko, 'Imatsu sôju: Rojin naki ato no Shu An to Kyo kôhei' [Mutual help in adversity: Zhu An and Xu Guangping after Lu Xun's death], *Chûgoku Bungaku Kenkyû*, vol. 17 (1991), pp. 46–62.

Ko, Dorothy, *Teachers of the Inner Chambers: Women and Culture in Seventeenth-Century China*, Stanford University Press, Stanford, 1994.

Kowallis, Jon Eugene von, *The Lyrical Lu Xun, A Study of His Classical-Style Verse*, University of Hawai'i Press, Honolulu, 1996.

Kuo, Ting-yee, 'Self-Strengthening: the pursuit of Western technology' in *Cambridge History of China*, vol. 10, ed. Denis Twitchett and Frederick W. Mote, Cambridge University Press, Cambridge, 1978, pp. 491–542.

Laclos, Choderlos de, *Les Liaisons dangereuse,* trans. Richard Aldington, Folio Society, London, 1962.

Larson, Wendy, 'Female Subjectivity and Gender Relations: The Early Stories of Lu Yin and Bing Xin' in *Politics, Ideology, and Literary Discourse in Modern China: Theoretical Interventions and Cultural Critique*, ed. Liu Kang and Xiaobing Tang, Duke University Press, Durham, N.C., 1993, pp. 124–43.

Larson, Wendy, *Women and Writing in Modern China*, Stanford University Press, Stanford, 1998.

Lee, Chae-Jin, *Zhou Enlai: The Early Years*, Stanford University Press, Stanford, 1994.

Lee, Leo Ou-fan, ed., *Lu Xun and His Legacy*, University of California Press, Berkeley, 1985.

Lee, Leo Ou-fan, *Voices from the Iron House: A Study of Lu Xun*, Indiana University Press, Bloomington, 1987.

Lewis, Mark Edward, *Writing and Authority in Early China*, State University of New York Press, Albany, 1999.

Li Helin *et al.*, eds, *Lu Xun shengping shiliao huibian* [Historical materials on Lu Xun's life], Renmin wenxue chubanshe, Tianjin, 1981.

Li Wenbing, 'Li Wenbing zhi Zhou Haiying xin—tan *Liang di shu* shi hezuo zuopin haishi bianji zuopin' [A letter from Li Wenbing to Zhou Haiying: on whether *Letters between two* is a jointly-authored or an edited work], *Lu Xun yanjiu yuekan*, no. 184 (August 1997), pp. 67–8.

Li Yu, *A Tower for the Summer Heat*, trans. Patrick Hanan, Columbia University Press, New York, 1999.

Li Yunjing, *Lu Xun de hunyin yu jiating* [Lu Xun's marriage and family], Shiyue wenyi chubanshe, Beijing, 1990.

Liang Ch'i-ch'ao and Hu Shih, *Two Self-Portraits: Liang Ch'i-ch'ao and Hu Shih*, ed. Li Yuning, Outer Sky Press, New York, 1992.

Liang Shiqiu [and] Han Jingqing, *Liang Shiqiu, Han Jingqing qingshu xuan* [Selected love-letters between Liang Shiqiu and Han Jingqing], comp. Huang Yonglie, Zhengzhong shuju, Taibei, 1992.

Liang Shiqiu, *Yashe chidu: Liang Shiqiu shuzha zhenji* [Yashe's correspondence: facsimile letters by Liang Shiqiu], comp. Yu Guangzhong *et al.*, Jiuge chubanshe, Taibei, 1995.

Liang, James C.P., Lloyd Haft and Gertie Mulder, *Business and Correspondence Chinese: An Introduction*, Foris Publications, Dordrecht, 1983.

Lim Boon Keng [Lin Wenqing], *Tragedies of Eastern Life: An Introduction to the Problems of Social Psychology*, Commercial Press, Shanghai, 1927.

Lin Dongsheng [and] Zhuang Biguang, *Ai. qingshu* [Love and love-letters], Wen jing she, Taibei, 1994.

Lin Yutang, 'Lu Xun' in *Lu Xun huiyi lu (sanpian)*, vol. 1, pp. 451–56.

Lin Zhihao, 'Shinian xieshou gong jianwei—Lu Xun he Xu Guangping' [Ten years of shared adversity hand-in-hand: Lu Xun and Xu Guangping], *Shiyue*, no. 77 (April 1991), pp. 182–86.

Ling Shan, 'Bisheng nanwang de Xu Guangping xiansheng' [The unforgettable Ms Xu Guangping] in *Xu Guangping*, pp. 51–63.

Link, E. Perry, *Mandarin Ducks and Butterflies: Popular Fiction in Early Twentieth-Century Chinese Cities*, University of California Press, Berkeley, 1981.

Lipsi, Justi, *Principles of Letter-writing: A Bilingual Text of Justi Lipsi, Epistolica Institutio*, ed. R. V. Young and M. Thomas Hester, Southern Illinois University Press, Carbondale, 1996.

Liu Fuqin, ed., *Lu Xun xin shi* [An intimate history of Lu Xun], Guangxi jiaoyu chubanshe, Shanghai, 1994.

Liu Hsieh [Liu Xie], *The Literary Mind and the Carving of Dragons: A Study of Thought and Pattern in Chinese Literature*, trans. Vincent Yu-chung Shih, Chinese University Press, Hong Kong, 1987.

Liu Xuyuan, *Jiedu Zhou Zuoren* [An interpretative reading of Zhou Zuoren], Wenyi chubanshe, Shanghai, 1994.

Liu Yanwen [and] Ai Yi, eds, *Xiandai zuojia shuxin ji* [A collection of letters by modern writers], Hanyu da cidian chubanshe, Shanghai, 1999.

Liu Zhen, comp. [and] Fang Zushen, ed., *Dangdai mingren shuzha* [Letters by famous men of our age], Zhengzhong shuju, Taibei, 1999.

Liu, Kwang-Ching, 'Education for Its Own Sake: Notes on Tseng Kuo-fan's *Family Letters*' in *Education and Society in Late Imperial China, 1600–1900*, ed. Benjamin A. Elman and Alexander Woodside, University of California Press, Berkeley, 1994, pp. 76–108.

Lo Chia-luen [Luo Jialun], *Liu Mei qing si—xin, shi he zagan* [Writings from the heart: Lo Jialun in the United States] ed. Jiu-Fong Lo Chang [Luo Jiufang], special issue of *Tianwai jikan* ['Outer Sky Journal'], no. 9 (January 1999).

Lopokova, Lydia and John Maynard Keynes, *The Letters of Lydia Lopokova and John Maynard Keynes*, ed. Polly Hill and Richard Keynes, Deutsch, London, 1989.

Loving, Jerome, *Walt Whitman: The Song of Himself*, University of California Press, Berkeley, 1999.

Lowry, Kathryn, 'The Space of Reading: Seventeenth-century *qingshu*, melancholy, and the innermost thoughts as public performance', unpublished paper presented at the conference 'Concealing to Reveal: the "Private" and "Sentiment" in Chinese History and Culture', Taibei, August 2001.

Lu Hanxiu, ed., *Gongkai de qingshu* [Open love-letters], Maitian chuban gongsi, Taibei, 1994.

Lu Jun, ed., *Jing shi hai su cai nüqing—Luyin de bu liao yuan* [The shockingly unconventional passions of a female genius: Luyin's unending fate], Sichuan wenyi chubanshe, Chengdu, 1995.

Lu Lusha, ed., *Qingshu daquan: Zui juyou moli de chuanda fangfa* [Love-letters compendium: the most seductive way of communication], Zonghe chubanshe, Tainan, n.d. [1999].

Lu Xinyuan, comp., *Wan Qing wushi mingjia shuzha* [Letters by fifty famous men of the late Qing], first published 1893, reprinted Guangwen shuju, Taibei, 1968.

Lu Xun [and] Jing Song, *Liang di shu* [Letters between two], Lu Xun zuopin quan bian, ed. Wang Dehou, Qian Liqun and Zhou Zhenfu, Zhejiang wenyi chubanshe, Hangzhou, 1998.

Lu Xun [and] Jing Song, *Liang di shu quan bian* [Letters between two: complete edition], Zhejiang wenyi chubanshe, Hangzhou, 1998.

Lu Xun [and] Jing Song, *Liang di shu: Lu Xun yu Jing Song de tongxin* [Letters between two: Lu Xun's correspondence with Jing Song], Beixin shuju, Shanghai, 1st edition, April 1933, 5th ed., 1937.

Lu Xun [and] Jing Song, *Liang di shu: Lu Xun yu Jing Song de tongxin* [Letters between two: Lu Xun's correspondence with Jing Song], Lu Xun quan ji chubanshe, n.p., 1941, 3rd ed., 1949.

Lu Xun [and] Jing Song, *Lu Xun Jing Song tongxin ji: 'Liang di shu' de yuanxin* [The correspondence between Lu Xun and Jing Song: the original letters in *Letters between two*], Hunan renmin chubanshe, Changsha, 1984.

Lu Xun [and] Xu Guangping, '*Liang di shu' zhenshu: yuanxin. shougao* [Facsimile of *Letters between two*: the original letters; the manuscript], Guji chubanshe, Shanghai, 1996.

Lu Xun and Xu Guangping, *Letters between Two*, trans. Bonnie S. McDougall, Foreign Languages Press, Beijing, 2000.

Lu Xun huiyi lu (sanpian) [Reminiscences of Lu Xun (articles)], ed. Beijing Lu Xun bowuguan *et al.*, Beijing chubanshe, Beijing, 1991.

Lu Xun huiyi lu (zhuanzhu) [Reminiscences of Lu Xun (monographs)], ed. Beijing Lu Xun bowuguan *et al.*, Beijing chubanshe, Beijing, 1991.

Lu Xun nianpu [Lu Xun chronology], ed. Fudan daxue *et al.*, Anhui renmin chubanshe, Hefei, 1979.

Lu Xun riji [Lu Xun's diary], Renmin chubanshe, Beijing, 1976.

Lu Xun tupian ji [Lu Xun photograph album], Renmin meishu chubanshe, Beijing, 1957.

Lu Xun yanjiu [Lu Xun studies], various publishers, 1980–89.

Lu Xun yanjiu jikan [Collected papers in Lu Xun studies], Shanghai wenyi chubanshe, Shanghai, 1979-.

Lu Xun yanjiu luncong [Collected articles in Lu Xun studies], ed. Shehui kexue zhanxian bianji bu, Renmin wenxue chubanshe, Changchun, 1980.

Lu Xun yanjiu niankan [Lu Xun studies annual], Zhongguo heping chubanshe, Beijing, 1979-.

Lu Xun yanjiu yuekan [Lu Xun studies monthly], Beijing Lu Xun bowuguan, Beijing, 1980-.

Lu Xun yanjiu ziliao [Lu Xun studies materials], ed. Beijing Lu Xun bowuguan, Tianjin renmin chubanshe, Tianjin, 1979-.

Lu Xun yanjiu ziliao [Lu Xun studies materials], Shanghai shifan daxue Zhongwen xi Lu Xun zhuzuo zhushi zu, Shanghai, 1978.

Lu Xun zai Shanghai [Lu Xun in Shanghai], ed. Shanghai Lu Xun jinianguan, Jiaoyu chubanshe, Shanghai, 1981.

Lu Xun zai Xiamen [Lu Xun in Amoy], ed. Xiamen daxue Zhongwenxi, Fujian renmin chubanshe, Fuzhou, rev. ed. 1978.

Lu Xun zishu [Lu Xun in his own words], Zuoqun jilu, Dongbi shushi, Shanghai, 1936.

Lu Xun, *Diary of a Madman and Other Stories*, trans. William A. Lyell, University of Hawaii Press, Honolulu, 1990.

Lu Xun, *Lu Xun quan ji* [Lu Xun's complete works], Renmin wenxue chubanshe, Beijing, 1981.

Lu Xun, *Lu Xun zhi Xu Guangping shujian* [Lu Xun's letters to Xu Guangping], Hebei renmin chubanshe, Shijiazhuang, 1979.

Lu Xun: 1881–1936, ed. Beijing Lu Xun bowuguan, Wenwu chubanshe, Beijing, 1977.

Lu, Hanchao, *Beyond the Neon Lights: Everyday Shanghai in the Early Twentieth Century*, University of California Press, Berkeley, 1999.

Luyin [Huang Luyin] and [Li] Weijian, *Yun Ou qingshu ji* [Love-letters between Cloud and Seagull], Shenzhou guoguang she, Shanghai, 1933.

Luyin [Huang Luyin], *Rensheng xiaoshuo* [Life stories], Shanghai wenyi chubanshe, Shanghai, 1994.

Luo Jiongguang, ed., *Xiandai zuojia shuxin* [Letters by modern writers], Wenxin chubanshe, Zhengzhou, 1993.

Ma Tiji, comp., *Xu Guangping yi Lu Xun* [Xu Guangping reminisces about Lu Xun], Hunan renmin chubanshe, Changsha, 1979.

Ma Tiji, ed., *Wo keyi ai—Lu Xun de qinglian shijie* [I can love: Lu Xun's world of passion], Sichuan wenyi chubanshe, Chengdu, 1995.

Ma Tiji, *Lu Xun shenghuo zhong de nüxing* [The women in Lu Xun's life], Zhishi chubanshe, Beijing, 1996.

Magnusson, Lynne, *Shakespeare and Social Dialogue: Dramatic Language and Elizabethan Letters*, Cambridge University Press, Cambridge, 1999.

Malvezzi, Piero and Giovanni Pirelli, eds, *Letze Briefe zum Tode Verurteilter aus dem europäischen Widerstand*, Deutscher Taschenbuch Verlag, München, 1962.

Mann, Susan and Yu-Yin Cheng, eds, *Under Confucian Eyes: Writings on Gender in Chinese History*, University of California Press, Berkeley, 2001.

Mann, Susan, *Precious Records: Women in China's Long Eighteenth Century*, Stanford University Press, Stanford, 1997.

Mao Yanwen, *Wangshi* [Past events], Yongyu yinshuachang, Taibei, 1990.

Maruo Jôki, *'Ren' yu 'gui' de jiuge—Lu Xun xiaoshuo lunxi* [A dispute between 'man' and 'demon': an analysis of Lu Xun's fiction], trans. Qin Gong, Renmin wenxue chubanshe, Beijing, 1995.

Masuda Wataru, 'Lu Xun de yinxiang' [An impression of Lu Xun], *Lu Xun huiyi lu (zhuanzhu)*, vol. 3, pp. 1335–463.

McDougall, Bonnie S., *The Introduction of Western Literary Theories into China 1919–1925*, Centre for East Asian Cultural Studies, Tokyo, 1971.

McDougall, Bonnie S., 'The Impact of Western Literary Trends' in *Modern Chinese Literature in the May Fourth Era*, ed. Merle Goldman, Harvard University Press, Cambridge, Mass, 1977, pp. 37–62.

McDougall, Bonnie S., 'Privacy in contemporary China: A survey of student opinion, June 2000', *China Information*, vol. 15, no. 2 (2001), pp. 140–52.

McDougall, Bonnie S., 'Brotherly Love: Lu Xun, Zhou Zuoren and Zhou Jianren', in *China in seinen biographische Dimensionen, Gedenkschrift für Helmut Martin*, ed. Christina Neder *et al.*, Harrassowitz, Wiesbaden, 2001, pp. 259–78.

McDougall, Bonnie S., 'Author/Audience Complicity in Modern Chinese Fiction' in McDougall, *Fictional Authors, Imaginary Audiences*, Chinese University Press, Hong Kong, 2002.

McDougall, Bonnie S., 'Revealing to Conceal: Love-letters and Privacy in Republican China' in *Concealing to Reveal* [conference volume], Center for Chinese Studies, Taibei, forthcoming (2003).
McDougall, Bonnie S. and Anders Hansson, eds, *Chinese Concepts of Privacy*, Brill, Leiden, 2002.
McLean, Deckle, *Privacy and its Invasion*, Praeger, Westport, 1995.
Mei Zhi, 'Nanwang de xiaorong—huainian Xu Guangping xiansheng' [An unforgettable smile: cherishing the memory of Ms Xu Guangping] in *Xu Guangping*, pp. 34–42.
Mews, Constant J., *The Lost Love Letters of Heloise and Abelard: Perceptions of dialogue in twelfth-century France*, St. Martin's Press, New York, 1999.
Mills, Harriet Cornelia, 'Lu Hsün: 1927–1936: The Years on the Left' PhD thesis, Columbia University, 1963; University Microfilms, Ann Arbor, Michigan.
Mizoguchi Yûzo, 'Chûgoku ni okeru kô/shi gainen no tenkai' [The development of the concepts of *gong* and *si* in China], *Shisô*, no. 669 (March 1980), pp. 19–38.
Mizoguchi Yûzo, 'Chûgoku no "kô/shi" ' ['*Gong/si*' in China], *Bungaku*, no. 56 (September 1988), pp. 88–102 & no. 57 (October 1988), pp. 73–84.
Moore, Barrington, *Jr*, *Privacy: Studies in Social and Cultural History*, Sharpe, Armonk, 1984.
Moore, George, *Héloïse and Abélard*, Heinemann, London, 1925.
Morson, Gary Saul and Caryl Emerson, *Mikhail Bakhtin: Creation of a Prosaics*, Stanford University Press, Stanford, 1990.
Movsesian, Ara John, *Pearls of Love: How to Write Love Letters and Love Poems*, Electric Press, Fresno, CA., 1983.
Naquin, Susan and Evelyn S. Rawski, *Chinese Society in the Eighteenth Century*, Yale University Press, New Haven, 1987.
Ni Moyan [and] Chen Jiuying, *Lu Xun yu Xu Guangping* [Lu Xun and Xu Guangping], Shanghai shudian, Shanghai, 2001.
Niall, Brenda and John Tompson, eds, *The Oxford Book of Australian Letters*, Oxford University Press, London, 1998.
Niu Daifeng, *Lu Xun zhuan* [A biography of Lu Xun], Zhongguo wenlian chubanshe, Beijing, 1998.
Noble, June & William, *The Private Me*, Delacorte Press, New York, 1980.
Norback, Craig T., *The Computer Invasion*, Van Nostrand Reinhold, New York, 1981.
Ogrodnick, Margaret, *Instinct and Intimacy: Political Philosophy and Autobiography in Rousseau*, University of Toronto Press, Toronto, 1999.
Oppenheim, A. Leo, ed., *Letters from Mesopotamia: Official, Business, and Private Letters on Clay Tablets from Two Millenia*, University of Chicago Press, Chicago, 1967.
Ovid in Six Volumes, trans. Grant Showerman, Loeb Classical Library, Harvard University Press, Cambridge, Mass., 1977.
Owen, Stephen, ed., *An Anthology of Chinese Literature*, Norton, New York, 1996.
Owen, Stephen, *Remembrances: The Experience of the Past in Classical Chinese Literature*, Harvard University Press, Cambridge Mass, 1986.
Ozaki Bunshô, 'Shô Teiken to iu hito, kare to Shû shi kyôdai no kankei' [Zhang Tingqian on the relationship between the two Zhou brothers], *Meiji daigaku kyôyô ronshû*, no. 193 (March 1986), pp. 30–67.
Ozawa Masamoto, *Uchiyama Kanzô den* [A biography of Uchiyama Kanzô], Banchô shobô, Tokyo, 1972.

Pateman, Carole, *The Sexual Contract*, Polity Press, Cambridge, 1988.

Pattinson, David, 'Zhou Lianggong and *chidu xinchao*: Genre and Political Marginalisation in the Ming-Qing Transition', *East Asian History*, no. 20 (December 2000), pp. 61–82.

Peng Hsiao-yen, *Antithesis Overcome: Shen Congwen's Avant-Gardism and Primitivism*, Institute of Chinese Literature and Philosophy, Academia Sinica, Taibei, 1994.

Perry, Ruth, *Women, Letters, and the Novel*, AMS Press, New York, 1980.

Pictorial Biography of Lu Xun 1881–1936, A, People's Fine Arts Publishing House, Beijing, [1980].

Pinker, Steven, *The Language Instinct: The New Science of Language and Mind*, Penguin Books, Harmondsworth, 1994.

Plaks, Andrew H., 'Towards a Critical Theory of Chinese Narrative' in Plaks, *Chinese Narrative: Critical and Theoretical Essays*, Princeton University Press, Princeton, 1977, pp. 309–52.

Plaks, Andrew H., *The Four Masterworks of the Ming Novel*, Princeton University Press, Princeton, 1987.

Pollard, David E., *A Chinese Look at Literature: The Literary Values of Chou Tso-jen in Relation to the Tradition*, Hurst, London, 1973.

Pollard, David E., 'The Life of Lu Xun as told in China', in *China in seinen biographische Dimensionen, Gedenkschrift für Helmut Martin*, ed. Christina Neder *et al.*, Harrassowitz, Wiesbaden, 2001, pp. 239–44.

Polly, Gregory Paul, 'Private and public letters: epistolary negotiations in the early republic', PhD dissertation, Harvard University, 1997 .

Pye, Lucian W., *The Spirit of Chinese Politics: A Psychological Study of the Authority Crisis in Political Development*, MIT Press, Cambridge, Mass., 1968.

Qian Chaochen, 'Yu *Liang di shu* youguan de ji jian shishi' [A few historical facts about *Letters between two*], *Zhongguo xiandai wenxue yanjiu congkan*, no. 2 (1981), pp. 336–43.

Qian Liqun, *Zoujin dangdai de Lu Xun* [Approaching the Lu Xun of our age], Beijing daxue chubanshe, Beijing, 1999.

Qiao Feng [Zhou Jianren], 'Lüe jiang guanyu Lu Xun de shiqing' [A few words on matters concerning Lu Xun], *Lu Xun huiyi lu (zhuanshu)*, vol. 2, pp. 737–80.

Radice, Betty, ed., *The Letters of Abelard and Heloise*, Penguin Books, Harmondsworth, 1974.

Ralegh, Walter, *The Letters of Sir Walter Ralegh*, ed. Agnes Latham and Joyce Youings, University of Exeter Press, Exeter, 1999.

Renditions, A Chinese-English Translation Magazine, nos 41 & 42 (Spring and Autumn 1994): special issue on letters ed. David E. Pollard and Eva Hung.

Reynolds, Barabara, *Dorothy L. Sayers: Her Life and Soul*, Hodder and Stoughton, London, 1993.

Richardson, Samuel, *Clarissa, or, The History of a Young Lady*, Viking, Harmondsworth, 1985.

Rosenthal, Margaret F., 'A Courtesan's Voice: Epistolary Self-Portraits in Veronica Franco's *Terza Rime*' in Goldsmith, *Writing the Female Voice*, pp. 3–24.

Saintsbury, George, ed., *A Letter Book; Selected with an Introduction on the History and Art of Letter-Writing*, Bell, London, 1922.

Sang Fengkang, *Yu Dafu: sheng fei rongyi si fei gan* [Yu Dafu: living is not easy, death is not sweet], Sichuan wenyi chubanshe, Chengdu, 1995.

Sayers, Dorothy L. and Robert Eustace [pseud. of Eustace Barton], *The Documents in the Case*, Ernest Benn, London, 1930.

Sayers, Dorothy L., *The Letters of Dorothy L. Sayers, 1899–1936: The Making of a Detective Novelist*, ed. Barbara Reynolds, Hodder and Stoughton, London, 1995.

Scanlon, T. M., *What We Owe to Each Other*, Harvard University Press, Cambridge, Mass., 1998.

Schneider, Carl D., *Shame, Exposure, and Privacy*, Norton, New York, 1977; rev. ed. 1992.

Schneider, Laurence A., *Ku Chieh-kang and China's New History: Nationalism amd the Quest for Alternative Traditions*, University of California Press, Berkeley, 1971.

Schoeman, Ferdinand David, ed., *Philosophical Dimensions of Privacy: An Anthology*, Cambridge University Press, Cambridge, 1984.

Schoeman, Ferdinand David, *Privacy and Social Freedom*, Cambridge University Press, Cambridge, 1992.

Schroeder, David, *Mozart in Revolt: Strategies of Resistance, Mischief and Deception*, Yale University Press, New Haven, 1999.

Schultz, W. R., 'Lu Hsün: The Creative years', PhD dissertation, University of Washington, 1955; University Microfilms, Ann Arbor, Michigan.

Schuster, M. Lincoln, ed., *A Treasury of the World's Great Letters*, Simon and Schuster, New York, 1940.

Scott, Gini Graham, *Mind Your Own Business: The Battle for Personal Privacy*, Insight Books, Plenum Press, New York, 1995.

Scurfield, Elizabeth, *Teach Yourself Chinese*, Hodder and Stoughton, London 1991.

Shen Congwen and Zhang Zhaohe, *Shen Congwen jia shu: 1930–1966 Congwen, Zhaohe shuxin xuan* [Shen Congwen's family letters, 1930–1966; selected letters between Congwen and Zhaohe], Taiwan shangwu yinshuguan, Taibei, 1998.

Shen Congwen, *Fei you cundi* [Letters never mailed], Wenli chubanshe, Hong Kong, 1960.

Shen Jianshi, 'Wo suo renshi de Lu Xun xiansheng' [The Mr Lu Xun I knew] in *Lu Xun huiyi lu (sanpian)*, vol. 1, pp. 98–9.

Shibutani, Tamotsu, *Improvised News: A Sociological Study of Rumour*, Bobbs-Merrill, Indianapolis, 1996.

Shu Wu, 'Xiongdi yiyi sishi nian—Lu Xun, Zhou Zuoren shihe yiqian de xiongdi guanxi' [Brothers in harmony for forty years: the brotherly relationship between Lu Xun and Zhou Zuoren before the rupture], *Lu Xun yanjiu niankan*, 1991–1992 heben, pp. 647–87. Reprinted as 'Lu Xun, Zhou Zuoren shihe yiqian de xiongdi guanxi' in Shu Wu, *Zhou Zuoren de shifei gongguo*, pp. 291–367.

Shu Wu, *Zhou Zuoren de shifei gongguo* [Zhou Zuoren's merits and faults], Renmin wenxue chubanshe, Beijing, 1993.

Simmel, Georg, *The Sociology of Georg Simmel*, trans. Kurt H. Wolff, Free Press Paperback, New York, 1950.

Sizer, Richard and Philip Newman, *The Data Protection Act: A practical guide*, Gower, Aldershot, 1984.

Smedley, Agnes, *Battle Hymn of China*, Knopf, New York, 1943.

Smith, H. Jeff, *Managing Privacy: Information Technology and Corporate America*, University of North Carolina Press, Chapel Hill, 1994.

Soames, Mary, ed., *Speaking for Themselves: The Personal Letters of Winston and Clementine Churchill*, Black Swan, London, 1999.

Song Yiqiao, *Xu Zhimo zhuan* [A biography of Xu Zhimo], Wenguo shuju, Tainan, 1999.

Spack, Patricia Meyer, *Gossip*, Knopf, New York, 1985.

Spence, Jonathan, *The Gate of Heavenly Peace: The Chinese and Their Revolution, 1895–1980*, Penguin Books, Harmondsworth, 1982.

Staples, William G., *The Culture of Surveillance: Discipline and Social Control in the United States*, St. Martin's Press, New York, 1997.

Steiner, George, 'The Distribution of Discourse' in *George Steiner: A Reader*, Penguin Books, Harmondsworth, 1984.

Steiner, George, *Language and Silence, Essays 1958–1966*, Penguin Books, Harmondsworth, 1969.

Steiner, George, *No Passion Spent: Essays 1978–1996*, Faber and Faber, London, 1996.

Stone, Lawrence, *The Family, Sex and Marriage in England, 1500–1800*, Weidenfeld and Nicolson, London, 1977.

Stowers, Stanley K., *Letter Writing in Greco-Roman Antiquity*, Westminster Press, Philadelphia, 1986.

Su Xuelin, *Wo lun Lu Xun* [My thoughts on Lu Xun], Zhuanji wenxue congshu zhi jiu si, Zhuanji wenxue chubanshe, Taibei, 1979.

Sun Fuyuan, 'Lu Xun xiansheng er san shi' [Two or three matters about Mr Lu Xun] in *Lu Xun huiyi lu (zhuanzhu)*, vol. 1, pp. 69–116.

Sun Fuyuan, 'Wusi yundong zhong de Lu Xun xiansheng' [Mr Lu Xun in the May Fourth movement] in *Lu Xun huiyi lu (sanpian)*, vol. 1, pp. 74–6.

Sun Ying, *Lu Xun zai jiaoyubu* [Lu Xun in the Ministry of Education], Tianjin renmin chubanshe, Tianjin, 1979.

Sun Yu, ed., *Bei xiedu de Lu Xun* [The reviled Lu Xun], Qunyan chubanshe, Beijing, 1994.

Sun Yu, *Lu Xun yu Hu Shi: yingxiang ershi shiji Zhongguo wenhua de liang wei zhizhe* [Lu Xun and Hu Shi: two sages who have influenced 20th century Chinese culture], Liaoning renmin chubanshe, Shenyang, 2000.

Sun Yu, *Lu Xun yu Zhou Zuoren* [Lu Xun and Zhou Zuoren], Hebei renmin chubanshe, Shijiazhuang, 1997.

Sun Yushi, 'Guanyu "La ye"' [Concerning 'The blighted leaf'], *Lu Xun yanjiu yuekan*, no. 175 (November 1996), pp. 35–9.

Tang Tao, *Tang Tao jin zuo* [Recent work by Tang Tao], Sichuan renmin chubanshe, Chengdu, 1982.

Tang Tao, *Tang Tao shu hua* [Tang Tao's book talk], Beijing chubanshe, Beijing, 1996.

Tanner, Tony, *Jane Austen*, Macmillan, London, 1986.

Taylor, Charles, *Philosophy and the Human Sciences: Philosophical Papers 2*, Cambridge University Press, Cambridge, 1985.

Tebbutt, Melanie, *Women's Talk? A Social History of 'Gossip' in Working-class Neighbourhoods, 1880–1960*, Scolar Press, Aldershot, 1995.

Tefft, Stanton K., ed., *Secrecy: A Cross-Cultural Perspective*, Human Sciences Press, New York, 1980.

Terry, Ellen and [George] Bernard Shaw, *Ellen Terry and Bernard Shaw: A Correspondence*, ed. Christopher St. John, Constable, London, 1931.

Tillman, Hoyt Cleveland, *Ch'en Liang on Public Interest and the Law*, University of Hawai'i Press, Honolulu, 1994.

Todd, Janet, *Mary Wollstonecraft: A Revolutionary Life*, Weidenfeld & Nicolson, London, 2000.

Todd, Janet, *The Secret Life of Aphra Behn*, Andre Deutsch, London, 1996.

Tolstoy, Leo, *Tolstoi's Love Letters, with a Study on the Autobiographical Elements in Tolstoi's Work*, ed. Paul Biryukov, Hogarth Press, Richmond, 1923.

Uchiyama Kanzô, *Rôjin no omoide* [Recollections of Lu Xun], Shakai shisôsha, Tokyo, 1979.

Wakeman, Frederic *Jr*, and Richard Louis Edmonds, eds, *Reappraising Republican China*, Oxford University Press, Oxford, 2000.

Wang Dehou, 'Bu lijie' [I don't understand], *Lu Xun yanjiu yuekan*, no. 184 (August 1997), pp. 69–70.

Wang Dehou, *'Liang di shu' yanjiu* [Research on *Letters between two*], Tianjin renmin chubanshe, Tianjin, 2nd ed., 1995.

Wang Dehou, *Lu Xun xin jie* [An interpretation of Lu Xun's mentality], Shuzhai wencong, Zhejiang wenyi chubanshe, Hangzhou, 1996.

Wang Jingshan, 'Wang Jingshan zhi Haiying xin' [A letter from Wang Jingshan to Haiying], *Lu Xun yanjiu yuekan*, no. 184 (August 1997), p. 70.

Wang Jingshan, *Lu Xun shuxin kaoshi* [Research on Lu Xun's letters], Yishu chubanshe, Beijing, 1982.

Wang Li, ed., *Gudai Hanyu* [Ancient Chinese], Zhonghua shuju, Beijing, 1963.

Wang Qiang, 'Lu Xun yu Liang Qichao' [Lu Xun and Liang Qichao], *Lu Xun yanjiu*, no. 14 (1989), pp. 259–75.

Wang Shiqing, 'Zhenzhi de aiqing, wusi de fengxian—jinian Xu Guangping xiansheng' [Steadfast love, selfless offering: in commemoration of Ms Xu Guangping] in *Xu Guangping*, pp. 26–33.

Wang Shiqing, *Lu Xun zhuan* [A biography of Lu Xun], Zhongguo qingnian chubanshe, Beijing, 1959.

Wang Shiqing, *Lu Xun: A Biography*, trans. Bonnie S. McDougall and Tang Bowen, Foreign Languages Press, Beijing, 1984.

Wang Xiaoming, *Wufa zhimian de rensheng: Lu Xun zhuan* [Life that cannot be faced directly: a biography of Lu Xun], Shanghai wenyi chubanshe, Shanghai, 1993.

Wang Yunru, 'Huiyi Lu Xun zai Shanghai de pianduan' [Fragmentary reminiscences of Lu Xun in Shanghai] in *Lu Xun huiyi lu (sanpian)*, vol. 3, pp. 1399–406.

Wang, Shaoguang, 'The politics of private time: changing leisure patterns in urban China' in *Urban Spaces in Contemporary China: the potential for autonomy and community in post-Mao China*, ed. Deborah S. Davis *et al.*, Woodrow Wilson Center Press, New York, 1995, pp. 149–72.

Watson, Burton, *Early Chinese Literature*, Columbia University Press, New York, 1962.

Weintraub, Jeff and Krishan Kumar, eds, *Public and Private in Thought and Practice: Perspectives on a Grand Dichotomy*, University of Chicago Press, Chicago, 1997.

Westin, Alan F., *Privacy and Freedom*, Bodley Head, London, 1967.

Westin, Alan F., *The Dimensions of Privacy: A National Opinion Research Survey of Attitudes Towards Privacy*, Garland, New York, 1981.

Widmer, Ellen, 'The Epistolary World of Female Talent in Seventeenth Century China', *Late Imperial China*, vol. 10, no. 2 (1989), pp. 1–43.

Wilde, Oscar, *Selected Letters*, edited by Rupert Hart-Davis, Oxford University Press, Oxford, 1979.

Wilkinson, Endymion, *Chinese History: A Manual*, Harvard University Asia Center, Cambridge, Mass., 1998.

Williams, Raymond, *Keywords: A vocabulary of culture and society*, Fontana Press, London, 1988.

Wolff, Ernst, *Chou Tso-jen*, Twayne Publishers, New York, 1971.

Wollstonecraft, Mary, *Letters Written During a Short Residence in Sweden, Norway, and Denmark*, ed. Carol H. Poston, University of Nebraska Press, Lincoln, 1976.

Woolf, Virginia, *A Change of Perspective: The Letters of Virginia Woolf, vol. III: 1923–1928*, ed. Nigel Nicolson, Hogarth Press, London, 1977.

Woolf, Virginia, *A Reflection of the Other Person: The Letters of Virginia Woolf, vol. IV: 1929–1931*, ed. Nigel Nicolson, Chatto & Windus, London, 1978.

Woolf, Virginia, *The Question of Things Happening: The Letters of Virginia Woolf, vol. II: 1912–1922*, ed. Nigel Nicolson, Hogarth Press, London, 1976.

Woolf, Virginia, *The Sickle Side of the Moon: The Letters of Virginia Woolf, vol. V: 1932–1935*, ed. Nigel Nicolson, Chatto & Windus, London, 1979.

Wordsworth, William and Mary Wordsworth, *The Love Letters of William and Mary Wordsworth*, ed. Beth Darlington, Cornell University Press, Ithaca, 1981.

Wortley Montague, *Lady* Mary, *Letters*, ed. David Campbell, David Campbell Publishers, London, 1992.

Wu Sihong, 'Guanyu Lu Xun xiansheng de pianduan huiyi' [Fragmentary reminiscences concerning Mr Lu Xun] in *Lu Xun huiyi lu (sanpian)*, vol. 3, pp. 1407–15.

Wu Zuoqiao, *Lu Xun shuxin gouchen* [Delving for Lu Xun's letters], Dongbei shifan daxue chubanshe, Changchun, 1994.

Xiandai mingren shuxin shouji [Letters by famous men of the present age in their own calligraphy], Zhonghua shuju, Beijing, 1992.

Xiao Hong, 'Huiyi Lu Xun xiansheng' [Reminiscences of Mr Lu Xun] in *Lu Xun huiyi lu (sanpian)*, vol. 2, pp. 706–40.

Xu Binru, 'Huiyi Lu Xun yijiuerqi nian zai Guangzhou de qingkuang' [Reminiscences of the circumstances of Lu Xun in Canton in 1927] in *Lu Xun huiyi lu (sanpian)*, vol. 1, pp. 501–10.

Xu Fancheng, 'Xing hua jiu ying—dui Lu Xun xiansheng de yi xie huiyi' [Old reflections of stars and flowers: a few reminiscences of Mr Lu Xun] in *Lu Xun huiyi lu (sanpian)*, vol. 3, pp. 1308–34.

Xu Guangping jinian ji [Xu Guangping commemorative volume], ed. Shanghai Lu Xun jinianguan, Baijia chubanshe, Shanghai, 2000.

Xu Guangping wen ji [Xu Guangping's collected works], ed. [Zhou] Haiying, Jiangsu wenyi chubanshe, Huaiyang, 1998.

Xu Guangping, ed. Zhongguo minzhu cujin hui zhongyang xuanchuanbu and Beijing Lu Xun bowuguan, Kaiming chubanshe, Beijing, 1995.

Xu Guangping, *Lu Xun huiyi lu* [Reminiscences of Lu Xun], Zuojia chubanshe, Beijing, 1961.

Xu Guangping, *Xinwei de jinian* [In grateful commemoration], Renmin wenxue chubanshe, Beijing, 1951.

Xu Qinwen, '*Lu Xun riji* zhong de wo' [Myself in Lu Xun's diary] in *Lu Xun huiyi lu (zhuanzhu)*, vol. 3, pp. 1226–333.

Xu Qinwen, *Xuexi Lu Xun xiansheng* [Studying Mr Lu Xun], Shanghai wenyi chubanshe, Shanghai, 1959.

Xu Shouchang, *Wang you Lu Xun yinxiang ji* [Impressions of my late friend Lu Xun] in *Lu Xun huiyi lu (zhuanzhu)*, vol. 1, pp. 249–52.

Xu Shouchang, *Wo suo renshi de Lu Xun* [The Lu Xun I knew], Renmin wenxue chubanshe, Beijing, 1952.

Xu Xiansu, 'Huiyi Lu Xun xiansheng' [Reminiscences of Mr Lu Xun] in *Lu Xun huiyi lu (sanpian)*, vol. 1, pp. 309–25.
Xu Zhimo [and] Lu Xiaoman, *Xu Zhimo v.s. Lu Xiaoman* [Xu Zhimo versus Lu Xiaoman], ed. Chen Xinyuan, Yeqiang chubanshe, Taibei, 2000.
Xu Zhimo, *Xu Zhimo quan ji* [Xu Zhimo's complete works], Shangwu yinshuguan, Hong Kong, 1983.
Xu Zhimo, *Xu Zhimo quan ji* [Xu Zhimo's complete works], Wangjia chubanshe, Tainan, 1994.
Xu Zhimo, *Xu Zhimo quan ji bubian* [Xu Zhimo's complete works: supplement], Shangwu yinshuguan, Hong Kong, 1993.
Xue Yunsheng, *Du li cun yi* [Concentration on doubtful matters while pursuing the substatutes], Chengwen chubanshe, Taibei, 1970, vol. 5, p. 1079.
Yamashita Tsuneo, 'Neishan Wanzao nianpu' [Uchiyama Kanzô chronology], trans. Zhao Xiaoyan, *Lu Xun yanjiu ziliao*, no. 9 (1982), pp. 321–52.
Yao Xipei, 'Wo suo tan Lu Xun jiazu fengbo—Badaowan fangchan "yiyue" yinchu de huati' [My comments on the storm in Lu Xun's family: topics arising from the 'agreement' about the Badaowan property], *Lu Xun yanjiu yuekan*, no. 188 (December 1997), pp. 45–55.
Ye Yuchuan, ed., *Xiongdi wenhao* [Fraternal cultural heroes], Sichuan renmin chubanshe, Chengdu, 1997.
Yip, Terry Siu-han, 'The Reception of *Werther* and the Rise of the Epistolary Novel in China', *Tamkam Review*, vol. 12, nos 1–4 (Autumn 1991–Summer 1992), pp. 287–304 .
Yu Dafu [and] Wang Yingxia, *Yu Dafu yu Wang Yingxia* [Yu Dafu and Wang Yingxia], Huashan wenyi chubanshe, Shijiazhuang, 1993.
Yu Dafu, 'Huiyi Lu Xun' [Reminiscences of Lu Xun] in *Huiyi Lu Xun* [Reminiscences of Lu Xun], ed. Zhou Li'an, Yuzhou feng chubanshe, Shanghai, 1940, pp. 1–30.
Yu Dafu, ed. Zhou Yushan, Daxing dangdai shijie xiaoshuojia duben, no. 43, Guangfu shuju, Taibei, 1987.
Yu Dafu, *Yu Dafu quan ji* [Yu Dafu's complete works], Dafu shuju, Tainan, 1992.
Yu Dafu, *Yu Dafu shuxin ji* [Yu Dafu's collected letters], Daxing chubanshe, Tainan, 1989.
Yu Dafu, *Yu Dafu wen ji* [Yu Dafu's collected works], Sanlian shudian, Hong Kong, 1985.
Yu Fang, 'Beijing Zhuanta hutong liushiyi hao' [No. 61, Brick Pagoda Lane, Peking], *Lu Xun yanjiu ziliao*, no. 9 (1982), pp. 183–94.
Yu Fang, 'Diyi ci dao Lu Xun xiansheng de xin shi zuo ke' [The first time I visited Mr Lu Xun's new home], *Lu Xun yanjiu ziliao*, no. 9 (1982), pp. 195–200.
Yu Fang, *Wo jiyi zhong de Lu Xun xiansheng* [The Mr Lu Xun of my memories], Zhejiang renmin chubanshe, Hangzhou, 1981; reprinted in *Lu Xun huiyi lu (zhuanzhu)*, vol. 3, pp. 1465–587.
Yu Lan, 'Xu Guangping de fengcai' [Xu Guangping's graciousness] in *Xu Guangping*, pp. 43–50.
Yu si (ying yin ben) [Thread of talk (photolithographic edition)], Shanghai wenyi chubanshe, Shanghai, 1982.
Yuan Baoshan, comp., *Zeng guang xie xin bi du* [Expanded essential reader for letter-writing], Huiwentang shuju, Shanghai, 1913.
Zhan, Kaidi, *The Strategies of Politeness in the Chinese Language,* Center for Chinese Studies, Institute of East Asian Studies, University of California, Berkeley, 1992.
Zhang Enhe, *Lu Xun Xu Guangping*, Mingren qingjie congshu, Zhongguo qingnian chubanshe, Beijing, 1995.

Zhang Gui, 'Xu Guangping san fang Lu Xun guxiang' [Xu Guangping's three visits to Lu Xun's hometown] in *Xu Guangping*, pp. 68–73.

Zhang Jing, *Lu Xun zai Guangzhou* [Lu Xun in Canton], Guangdong renmin chubanshe, Guangzhou, 1977.

Zhang Juxiang [and] Zhang Tierong, eds, *Zhou Zuoren nianpu* [Zhou Zuoren chronology], Tianjin renmin chubanshe, Tianjin, 2000.

Zhang Juxiang [and] Zhang Tierong, eds, *Zhou Zuoren yanjiu ziliao* [Zhou Zuoren research materials], Tianjin renmin chubanshe, Tianjin, 1986.

Zhang Longxi, *Mighty Opposites: From Dichotomies to Differences in the Comparative Study of China*, Stanford University Press, Stanford, 1998.

Zhang Shizhao, *Zhang Shizhao wen xuan* [Zhang Shizhao's selected works], ed. Li Miaogen, Yuandong chubanshe, Shanghai, 1996.

Zhang Xiangtian, *Lu Xun riji shuxin shigao zhaji* [Notes on Lu Xun's diaries, letters and poems], Sanlian chubanshe, Hong Kong, 1979.

Zhang Xianliang, *Grass Soup*, trans. Martha Avery, Secker & Warburg, London, 1994.

Zhi Kejian, ed., *Jianming Lu Xun cidian* [Simple Lu Xun dictionary], Gansu jiaoyu chubanshe, Lanzhou, 1990.

Zhong Zhaozheng [and] Dong Fangbai, *Taiwan wenxue liang di shu* [Letters between two in Taiwan literature], ed. Zhang Liangze, Qianwei chubanshe, Taibei, 1993.

Zhou Haiying, 'Chonghui Shanghai yi tongnian' [Reminiscences of childhood on re-visiting Shanghai] in *Lu Xun huiyi lu (sanpian)*, vol. 3, pp. 1237–72.

Zhou Haiying, 'Wo dui *Liang di shu* chuquan de lijie' [My understanding of the copyright to *Letters between two*], *Lu Xun yanjiu yuekan*, no. 181 (May 1997), p. 33.

Zhou Haiying, 'Yi fen Badaowan fangchan de "yiyue" ' [An 'agreement' about the property Badaowan], *Lu Xun yanjiu yuekan*, no. 188 (December 1997), pp. 43–4.

Zhou Jianren *et al.*, *Wo xin zhong de Lu Xun* [The Lu Xun in my heart], Hunan renmin chubanshe, Changsha, 1979.

Zhou Jianren, 'Lu Xun yu Zhou Zuoren' [Lu Xun and Zhou Zuoren] in *Lu Xun huiyi lu (sanpian)*, vol. 1, pp. 440–50.

Zhou Jianren, *An Age Gone By: Lu Xun's Age in Decline*, New World Press, Beijing, 1988.

Zhou Jianren, *Lu Xun gujia de bailuo* [The decline of Lu Xun's old family], Hunan renmin chubanshe, Changsha, 1984.

Zhou Qifu, 'Lu Xun yu Hu Shi' [Lu Xun and Hu Shi], *Lu Xun yanjiu niankan*, 1990, pp. 290–50.

Zhou Qiming [Zhou Zuoren], 'Lu Xun de qingnian shidai' in *Lu Xun huiyi lu (zhuanzhu)*, vol. 2, pp. 783–893.

Zhou Xiashou [Zhou Zuoren], *Lu Xun de gujia* [Lu Xun's old home], Wenhua shenguo chubanshe, Shanghai, 1953.

Zhou Xiashou [Zhou Zuoren], *Lu Xun xiaoshuo li de renwu* [The characters in Lu Xun's fiction], Shanghai chubanshe, Shanghai, 1954.

Zhou Yiliang [and] Zhao Heping, *Tang Wudai shuyi yanjiu* [Research on letter-writing manuals of the Tang and Five Dynasties], Zhongguo shehui kexue chubanshe, Beijing, 1996.

Zhou Zhiping, *Hu Shi conglun* [Collected articles on Hu Shi], Sanmin shuju, Taibei, 1992.

Zhou Zhiping, *Hu Shi yu Weiliansi: shenqing wushi nian* [Hu Shi and Williams: deep feelings for fifty years], Lianjing chuban shiye gongsi, Taibei, 1998.

Zhou Zuoren, 'Bi hu du shu lun' [On reading behind closed doors] in *Zhi Tang wen ji* [Zhi Tang's collected works], pp. 29–33, Shanghai shudian, Shanghai, 1981.

Zhou Zuoren, 'Riji yu chidu' [Diaries and letters] in *Yu tian de shu* [A book for rainy days], Shiyong shudian, Hong Kong, n.d., pp. 11–16.

Zhou Zuoren, *Zhi Tang shuxin* [Zhi Tang's letters], ed. Huang Kaifa, Huaxia chubanshe, Beijing, 1995.

Zhou Zuoren, *Zhi Tang shuxin ji* [Zhi Tang's collected letters], ed. Li Jiru, Nantian shuye gongsi, Hong Kong, 1971.

Zhou Zuoren, *Zhou Zuoren shuxin* [Zhou Zuoren's letters], Qing guang shudian, 2nd ed., 1935.

Zhou Zuoren, *Zhou Zuoren zaoqi sanwen xuan* [Zhou Zuoren's selected early prose], Shanghai wenyi chubanshe, Shanghai, 1984.

Zhu Jinghua [and] Ma Shouzhong, eds, *Lidai shuxin xuan* [Selected letters from history], Zhongguo qingnian chubanshe, Beijing, 1989.

Zhu Xiang, *Zhu Xiang shu ji* [Zhu Xiang's collected letters], ed. Luo Niansheng, Rensheng yu wenxue she, Tianjin, 1936; facsimile reprint by Shanghai shudian, Shanghai, 1983.

Zhuo Zhi, 'Lu Xun shi zhe yang zou de' [The way taken by Lu Xun] in *Lu Xun huiyi lu (sanpian)*, vol. 1, pp. 487–91.

Zola, Émile, *The Dreyfus Affair: 'J'accuse' and Other Writings*, Yale University Press, New Haven, 1996.

Zong Jinwen, ed., *Lu Xun zai Guangdong* [Lu Xun in Canton], Beixin shuju, n.p., 1927.

Index

The manufacturer's authorised representative in the EU for product safety is Oxford University Press España S.A. of el Parque Empresarial San Fernando de Henares, Avenida de Castilla, 2 – 28830 Madrid (www.oup.es/en or product.safety@oup.com). OUP España S.A. also acts as importer into Spain of products made by the manufacturer.

www.ingramcontent.com/pod-product-compliance
Lightning Source LLC
Chambersburg PA
CBHW071302180926
51613CB00001B/108
9780199256792